DATE DUE			

LEADING A
CHURCH SCHOOL

LEADING A
CHURCH SCHOOL

by
RALPH D. HEIM

Professor of Christian Education
Gettysburg Seminary

FORTRESS PRESS • PHILADELPHIA

CONTENTS

Page

PREFACE ix

PART ONE
FOUNDATIONS IN HISTORY AND THEORY

CHAPTER I

KNOWING THE CHURCH SCHOOL OF YESTERDAY AND TODAY . . . 2
The Problem. History of the Church School. Present Status of the
Church School. Promise.

CHAPTER II

UNDERSTANDING WHAT CHRISTIAN EDUCATION IS 23
Terminology: Problem and Solution. What is Education? What is
Christian Education?

CHAPTER III

HAVING OBJECTIVES 43
The Need for Objectives. The Functions. Types. Determination.
Statements of Objectives. Objectives in a Local Church School.
Criteria for Objectives.

PART TWO
ORGANIZATION AND ADMINISTRATION
OF PUPILS AND STAFF

CHAPTER IV

UNDERTAKING THE TASK 58
Being a Leader. General Leadership Activities. Organizing, Administering, and Supervising. Correct General Principles. Taking Hold
to Improve. Meeting Personal Standards.

Page

CHAPTER V

DEVELOPING THE EDUCATIONAL ORGANIZATION   75

Standards. Integrating the Educational Organization. Unifying the
Educational Organization.

CHAPTER VI

ADMINISTERING THE STAFF   93

Allotting Duties: Job Analyses. Selecting Staff Members. Providing
Staff Members. Control Within Leader Relationships.

CHAPTER VII

DEVELOPING THE LEADERSHIP 116

Needs. Means. Motivation for Development. A Standard.

CHAPTER VIII

ADMINISTERING PUPILS 130

Grouping. Securing Regular Attendance. Securing Punctuality.
Having "Discipline." Fostering Other Favorable Responses.

PART THREE

SUPERVISION OF THE PROGRAM AND TEACHING IN IT

CHAPTER IX

PROVIDING A PUPIL PROGRAM 146

The New Curriculum. Basic Theory. The Place of the Bible. The
Place of Theology. Curricular Activities. Providing a Total Church
School Program. Materials. Time Schedules.

CHAPTER X

GUIDING PUPIL ACTIVITIES (I) 166

Learning. Teaching. Team Teaching. Learning-Teaching as Group
Activity. Directing Study and Instruction.

CHAPTER XI

GUIDING PUPIL ACTIVITIES (II) 186

Directing Worship. Directing Fellowship. Directing Service.

CHAPTER XII

CONDUCTING OTHER GROUP SESSIONS AND DIRECTING UNITS . . . 208

Other Group Sessions. Units in the Program. From the Old to the
New. Adaptation to Size and Location.

Page

PART FOUR
GENERAL MANAGEMENT: SELECTED ITEMS

CHAPTER XIII
PROVIDING PHYSICAL FACILITIES 230
Purpose. Major Considerations. Demands of Current Trends. Basic Needs. Buildings. Furnishings and Supplies. Rendering Present Resources More Effective. Securing New Equipment.

CHAPTER XIV
FINANCING THE SCHOOL 246
Principles. Purpose. Motivation. Systems. Budgeting. Securing Funds. Expending Funds. The Treasurer.

CHAPTER XV
GATHERING AND USING DATA: EVALUATING 258
Evaluation. Securing Data (researching, surveying, record-keeping, measuring). Utilizing Data.

CHAPTER XVI
MAINTAINING WIDER RELATIONSHIPS 274
With the Congregation. The Home. The Public School. Denominational Agencies. Interdenominational and Interfaith Agencies. Other Community Agencies. Education for World Churchmanship.

CHAPTER XVII
PROMOTING THE SCHOOL 287
Why? Public Relations in General. Giving Publicity. Securing Increased Enrollment.

PART FIVE
EXPANDING THE SCHOOL'S MINISTRY

CHAPTER XVIII
ENLARGING THE PROGRAM (I) 300
More Time: On Sundays. At Home. Within General Education.

CHAPTER XIX
ENLARGING THE PROGRAM (II) 318
Vacation Church Schools. Weekday Church School Work. Youth and Adult Groups. Confirmation, Communicants', Membership or Pastor's Classes.

CHAPTER XX
ENLARGING THE PROGRAM (III) 334
Camps, Conferences and Retreats. Mass Agencies. Unusual Ministries.

INDEX 351

LIST OF DIAGRAMS

Diagram		Page
I	Contrasting Emphases of Major Educational Types . .	34
II	Educational Agencies Separated and Divided	76
III	Educational Agencies Partially Integrated and Unified .	76
IV	Further Integration and Unification of Educational Agencies	78
V	An Integrated and Unified Church School	88
VI	Operation of a Unitary Financial System	252

PREFACE

Leading A Church School has been written for any church school leader who wishes to make a thorough study of his task. It is meant chiefly as a textbook for college, seminary, university, or training school students; it can also be a manual for denominational or interdenominational staff personnel. Yet it is almost equally intended as a resource for advanced workers in local church schools: pastors, directors, superintendents—teachers, too.

For all these leaders the book aims to lift the level of their effectiveness by doing two things: being a guide for intelligent understanding of their work and providing a ready compendium of helps for their major activities. It is designed for study, then for frequent reference.

Comprehensiveness has been a fundamental standard. So *Leading A Church School* surveys the scope of Christian education, weekday and Sunday, in the local church school and beyond. On that broad front it not only sets forth ideals and shows directions but also strives to answer questions, give clues, offer suggestions, and open vistas. To be further comprehensive, both theory and practice are seen in historical perspective and set within the present churchwide and world-wide scene; the author even essays a timorous look into the future.

There had been a previous work of similar nature, the author's *Leading A Sunday Church School,* published in 1950. The thrust of the original work did not need to be changed; the principles it enunciated remain valid. But many things have happened in the intervening period. In some instances the visions of a half generation ago have become actualities; there have been new and unexpected developments. Christian education has expanded after the manner of an explosion and is changing still in a way almost revolutionary.

So this volume is more than a revision. It has been rewritten in almost every paragraph and updated in almost every chapter—as notable examples in history, objectives, and curriculum. It has, above all, been augmented; for instances, there are new materials on leadership in general and on group process. Most significantly it now covers the whole church school field, not only the Sunday church school.

The work began with a one page outline in 1927. It has grown principally by the stimulating interchange in college, seminary, and university classes, yet leaders of church schools have contributed generously in many ways. At one time a hundred pastors wrote letters in response to inquiries about selected problems; some are reported in the book. Many church schools have been observed in action; students have annually discussed their field experiences. Mimeographed editions and the former book have been evaluated by uncounted scores of students. There have been profitable discussions with other professionals in related fields as well as Christian education. Naturally the conclusions of personal experience and exhaustive reading have been included; travel with lecturing on all the continents has provided a global view.

Manifestly it is impossible to offer detailed acknowledgment and render due thanks in any precise or personal fashion. One can only say that deepest gratitude is expressed herewith to each helper.

The meanings of two words should be mentioned at this earliest opportunity. "Leader" is used with several connotations. Usually it refers to an executive charged with major or minor responsibilities in management. In many chapters though, especially IX through XII, leader may mean a teacher or even a pupil who is helping with some learning enterprise. "Activity" or "activities," used so frequently, are always to be taken as referring to *any* item of human behavior, not only to that which is chiefly muscular.

The book is dedicated to the companion of all the years of its development, my wife, Leona.

PART ONE

FOUNDATIONS IN HISTORY
AND THEORY

CHAPTER I

KNOWING THE CHURCH SCHOOL OF YESTERDAY AND TODAY

A church school will be defined soon as a congregation at work educating itself. To accomplish this task churches organize agencies for learning and teaching. The Sunday church school is the primary organizational form. However, there are numerous allies, the vacation church school and various other groups for children, youth, or adults. The leadership of all these agencies—the entire church school, with its relationships beyond local church walls—is to be considered in these pages.

THE PROBLEM

In 1780 Robert Raikes gathered the first pupils for his educational experiment that became our present Sunday church school. This event was a watershed in the history of Christian education. Before 1780 such educational work in the churches had been sporadic and not so broadly conceived, consciously practiced, or formally organized. Since Robert Raikes, hundreds of millions of devoted men and women have labored in behalf of the Sunday agency and its allies. It is estimated that every fiftieth person one meets in America today is one of these.

What are the activities of a church school worker, either pastor, director of Christian education, superintendent, teacher, or other leader; also how can he be most effective in them? This is our concern.

As we proceed to answer that question the emphasis will be on the work of an executive, a leader of teachers rather than a teaching leader. Yet much of the substance will pertain directly to a teacher's responsibilities; other material, by providing broad understanding of the entire work of the school, will shape a fitness for teaching.

A church school leader, whatever his particular task, may sometimes wish for a brief list of specific directives for next Sunday morning or Wednesday evening. Yet something else can be more helpful: to possess the background of understanding against which his task becomes meaningful. Then he is able to choose or devise and evaluate for himself the effective procedures for his immediate need.

For that kind of orientation leaders need a degree of general knowledge about the whole field of educational work in the church, including its history and fundamental theory. This Part One aims to meet that need. Its first chapter answers the question, "How did the church school, especially the Sunday church school agency, come to be and what is its present status?" A second chapter presents the major theories of Christian education with an emphasis on the type that has been gaining world-wide acceptance through several decades. Chapter III recognizes the priority of purpose in church school work and deals with the principal issues concerning objectives.

HISTORY OF THE CHURCH SCHOOL

Modern Christian education is the end product of an agelong development. All mankind is and doubtless always has been religious. Thus religious education, in a broad sense of the term, is as old as human life and institutions—older than preaching or sacred music, even the Bible itself, older than anything but the most elementary theology and worship.

Pre-Christian and Non-Christian Relations

While our special concern here is the Protestant church school in America, there will be value in seeing briefly its relation to pre-Christian, non-Christian, and non-Protestant practices everywhere. Also worthwhile is a quick glance at the Christian development which preceded the church school of today.

The term "primitive" is applicable to the religion of uncultured peoples whether they are of ancient times or modern. At present its adherents number a few million, distributed broadly over the earth. Surprisingly, certain characteristics of primitive religious education are similar to those of present-day Christian education. As instances, it has a practical purpose and an immediacy of aim which relate to persons; also learning is largely by participating in life instead of merely verbalizing about it.

Egyptians, Assyrians, Babylonians, Greeks, and Romans had more or less elaborate systems of religious education. Presently existing though ancient non-Christian religions have their programs: Hindus, Jains, Buddhists, and Sikhs in South Asia; Confucianists, Taoists, and Shintoists in East Asia; Zoroastrians and Mohammedans in West Asia. Several of these, reanimated, are proceeding along lines which in some cases parallel Christian ways. For example, Japanese Buddhists conduct kindergartens that resemble Christian ones.

Christian education's direct forerunner is Jewish education; it is rooted in the Hebrew history and literature. No doubt a considerable amount of experience in the worship of God and of direct teaching about his nature and his will for the lives of his people took place in the tents of the patriarchs. More formal work for Jewish education began as early as Moses. This continued through the reigns of kings who fostered educational programs and the ministries of prophets who were essentially teachers of the people. Priests, rabbis, scribes and sages, too, were teachers. A new era began with the return of Ezra. Synagogues were established and people assembled in them for instruction as well as worship. Later, wherever a synagogue was founded a school was set up, usually for young boys. The report of Paul's experience under his teacher Gamaliel in Jerusalem (Acts 22:3) indicates that higher education had been established there.

In harmony with that long history of the faith, Judaism has a strong educational program today. Different branches of it have varied educational philosophies and practices but in general they are committed to public schools for general education. So, like Protestants, they provide supplementary religious education on Sundays and weekdays. About 80 percent of the Jews in the United States attend these sessions during their school years. Sunday schools may meet from one and a half to two hours; weekday schools are conducted after public school hours, as many as three days a week for as long as two hours. A high degree of leadership competence is expected; there are relatively few volunteer teachers. The home has continued from earliest times to be a basic seat of Jewish education.

A study of all such forms of religious education in their earlier historical development reveals interesting characteristics for contrast or comparison with Christian practice today. Because the aims of all education were religious there was no sharp distinction between "religious" and "secular" education. Sacred scriptures were the major element in the curricular subject matter with memorization as a chief method. The students were usually boys. Much of the program was informal; formal efforts were centered about the home and the temple so that the teachers were chiefly parents and priests. All the faiths, when virile, have had programs of education which were in one way or another closely associated with daily living.

Christian Education before the Sunday Church School

The Christian religion was inaugurated by means of teaching; from that beginning it has won adherents and fostered the spiritual growth of its members by educational methods.

CHRIST AS TEACHER

Christian practice throughout history, when at its best, has been in harmony with the spirit and manner of Christ. Not overlooking anything else he was, he was a pre-eminent teacher. Whatever else he did, he used teaching as a chief means to accomplish what he had come into the world to do. It is appropriate that our current work reflects his ways.

Jesus taught in the closest relationship to vital issues of people in their daily lives. He always had an aim and it was definite. His approach was to begin with a questing person where he was in his spiritual experience and strive to lead him where he could better be.

The Master's practice in his teaching ministry was twofold: work with groups, large or small, and with individuals, especially his chosen twelve. In both types of work he proceeded chiefly in an informal, conversational manner, not so often trying to instruct people by a continuous discourse. He would teach whenever the opportunity arose—in a temple court, a synagogue, a private home, along the public highway, by the seaside, or from a boat. Even with the twelve, his teaching was typically occasional although there were instances when he took them aside for special instruction in the work they were to do. Just associating with him must have been full of lessons.

Among Christ's specific methods, counseling and discussion were favorites. We marvel at his artistic and effective use of storytelling. He frequently asked a searching question that probed to the heart of a problem. He found visual aids in nature. He used also what more recently has been called the project, laboratory, workshop, or learning-by-doing way when, for example, he sent out the twelve to have field experience for their later work.

BEFORE THE REFORMATION

The continuing ministry of Jesus in Christian education was carried forward first by the apostles and later by leaders scripturally designated as "teachers." Peter and Paul were essentially educators responding to the great commission: "Go . . . teaching . . . ." Peter's sermon (Acts 2:14-36) is apostolic teaching about Jesus. Paul's journeys were pre-eminently teaching expeditions after the manner of a present-day missionary evangelist who meets individuals alone or in casual groups. It is not difficult to see that Paul's epistles were intended primarily as teaching material for the growth of members in the young churches. The church fathers followed the apostolic pattern.

The first formal effort of the church to instruct its membership is known as the catechumenate (c. A.D. 100-400). It provided systematic instruction in Christian doctrine to prepare members for admission into the church. Usually the students were adult converts or young people approaching maturity. The period of instruction, largely sermonic exhortation, lasted three or four years; then it culminated in baptism and admittance to the sacrament of the altar. As higher education became necessary, particularly for the clergy, catechetical schools—forerunners of modern Christian colleges—were established beginning about A.D. 200 in Alexandria.

We see that the early church did not undertake an extensive program of education for children; they grew in the faith-life through the informal influence of the home. Their elders, too, lived and learned chiefly in the relationships of the Christian community.

For the remaining centuries before the Reformation, the church's chief educational work was done in several types of agency such as monastic, conventual, bishops', cathedral, or parish schools. These were established at institutional centers, mainly to perpetuate the clergy or orders. While children of a neighborhood might attend, attention was concentrated on those who came to live at the institution and enter lifetime church vocations. Work in the monasteries was particularly important for the preservation of manuscripts. Long before the Reformation, several universities had been established; it is said that Bologna, usually recognized as the first, had as many as five thousand students enrolled by the year 1200.

The picture of education during the Middle Ages is gloomy, yet all the centuries preceding the Renaissance produced great educators whose writings strike familiar notes and whose practices have been important tributaries of the ongoing stream. Such progressive and ardent men as Alcuin (735-804), Charlemagne (742-814), Gerson (c. 1363-c. 1429) and their associated workers had not failed to prepare the way for the Renaissance. In the Renaissance itself, the name of Erasmus (1467-1536) is memorable for influences that still pertain. Meantime, printing had been invented. Then the concurrent movements, Renaissance and Reformation, changed the whole realm of education, including Christian education.

THE REFORMATION

As we consider the Reformation's contributions we must not forget that Luther's fellow reformers including Calvin, Knox, and Zwingli, also his assistants such as Melanchthon, were significant figures for education. Yet, despite that fact and the further one that most educational views and practices had more ancient origins it is scarcely an exaggeration to say that modern, Christian, religious education—public education too—began with Martin Luther. He was an educator by profession, beginning as an instructor at the University of Wittenberg in the autumn of 1508 and continuing until his death in 1546. Naturally a pedagogical interest permeated all his writing and speaking to the degree that there are few phases of education to which he did not contribute.

The theological principles Luther enunciated, "by grace alone" and "by faith alone," also Christian vocation and the spiritual priesthood of all believers, gave to our church school work an orientation in both form and content. In such writings as the *Sermon on the Duty of Sending Children to School, Letter to the Mayors and Aldermen,* and *Address to the Christian Nobility,* he supported our life-oriented goal: a Christian man fitted to perform all the activities of life in a Christian way.

Because Luther observed and appreciated child life he paved the way for further study of the child's religious nature and for a rational, interesting, and joyous method of Christian education in harmony with the child's own concerns. He saw the need for adapting and grading lessons to the nature, experience, and concerns of pupils. He favored rational methods of instruction rather than mere memorization. He saw the values of pictures, storytelling, dramatization, discussion, and play in education. He advocated the use of extrabiblical materials along with the biblical. There is more. Luther recognized very clearly the place of the home in any complete program of Christian education. His translation of the Bible into the common language of the German people gave impetus toward our modern translations. His Small Catechism, along with other men's catechisms, are among Protestantism's chief heritages by way of manuals for religious instruction. His productions as the first Protestant hymnist are only a little less important.

Unfortunately, the impetus Luther gave education lay largely dormant through roughly two and a half centuries. Yet men like Comenius (1592-1670) and Pestalozzi (1746-1827) kept the precious flame burning until the nineteenth century brought a new enlightenment.

EARLY AMERICA

The first Christian educators in America were the monks who accompanied early explorers. From that day to this, Roman Catholic education has been prominent on the American scene. Catholics have more than two hundred colleges and universities, besides many seminaries, nearly three thousand secondary schools and more than ten thousand elementary schools. There are Sunday schools in some Catholic churches.

Protestant Christian education began with colonization along the

Atlantic seaboard where three types of schooling developed. In the South, children of the well-to-do were tutored at their homes or sent to private schools like the Latin schools of England; poor boys were bound out to artisans as apprentices. In middle colonies, such as New York and Pennsylvania, parochial schools flourished. The New England colonies developed their educational endeavor along lines which resulted in the present free public school system.

While there was no uniformity as to the type of school attended by American colonial youth religion was an outstanding feature of the curriculum in all of them. Until the approach of Revolutionary times, the Bible and the catechism were the chief materials used and the content of other texts, such as Hornbook and New England Primer, was largely religious. Meantime, religion not only dominated elementary and secondary education but also motivated higher education. The earliest colleges or universities founded—Harvard (1636), William and Mary (1693), and Yale (1701)—had the education of ministers as a chief purpose.

As the Revolution neared, education began to be secularized. Study of grammar, history, geography, and arithmetic gradually displaced the emphasis on religion. New textbooks were introduced in which the religious element was abridged. This trend resulted in a sense of need that favored the acceptance and growth of the Sunday school movement when it reached America.

Beginnings of the Sunday Church School

There had been Sunday schooling earlier, but the modern Sunday church school movement was inaugurated by Robert Raikes, a publisher in Gloucester, England, during July of 1780. He was an aristocrat with a Christian spirit that expressed itself in deep concern for the poor and criminal in the city.

Historians give a grim report on social conditions in England when the Sunday school arose. Rural masses—about two-thirds of the entire population—were coarsely clothed, poorly housed and fed, also illiterate. In the industrial towns such as Gloucester where Raikes lived, the conditions were even more lamentable. One result was a prevalence of vice and crime which even drastic laws with severe penalties could not suppress.

Robert Raikes sympathized with the victims of the social system. He concerned himself especially with the plight of prisoners in Gloucester jails. Those were the days before prison reform in England or anywhere else. Hardened criminals mingled with prisoners for debt, starving and destitute, in filth and risk of contagion. Raikes went personally to help those he could reach with gifts of food, clothing, money, and other ministrations of mercy.

Yet this philanthropist realized that something more fundamental than charitable contributions was needed. Ignorance, he concluded, was the root cause of the deplorable situation. If he could educate the young, especially of the poor, he might remedy the social disorder. Very few were going to school, for there was no system of popular education in England. Also, child labor was not forbidden; most of the children worked in Gloucester's pin factories. After spending their weekdays in long hours of labor, they were turned loose to carouse on Sunday.

Raikes had pondered his dream of teaching the children for a long time before he conceived the possibility of using Sunday for this purpose. When he was walking home from a service at the cathedral one day, it is said, the word "try" suddenly came to his mind so forcibly that he felt it was a divine command.

Acting at once, he engaged a Mrs. Meredith who resided in Sooty Alley, where the chimney sweeps lived, as a teacher. The first school met in her kitchen. But she was unable to handle the boys, even with the aid of Mr. Raikes and his cane; so that first venture failed. As the teacher of his second school Raikes secured a Mrs. Critchley who had managed an inn near the county jail. She was equal to the task and so was the first successful teacher of the first permanent Sunday school in Robert Raikes' experiment.

Mr. Raikes paid Mrs. Critchley's salary and supplemented her work, but his first task was to secure pupils. When possible, he enlisted the co-operation of parents. More often he went where the boys were playing and urged them to come, even bribed them with gifts. He appealed particularly to those he had helped while in jail. In the school itself, Mr. Raikes would tell stories from the Bible and try to impress moral precepts upon his charges. For especially fine work he was ready to give combs, pennies, and New Testaments as rewards.

In those earliest schools, the program stressed learning to read, learning to say the Church of England catechism, and attending church services. Children came soon after ten in the morning, stayed until twelve, then went home until one. On their return they would read a lesson and be conducted to a service in the cathedral which Gloucester children still can attend. Afterward they repeated the catechism till half-past five. When dismissed, they were to go home quietly and by no means play in the streets.

Soon the basic plans and methods were altered. Paid teachers were supplanted by volunteers. The general education aspect became less emphatic. More Bible study and the memorization and singing of Dr.

Watts' hymns were included. The age of the pupils was limited from about six to twelve or fourteen. Girls were admitted as well as boys. The pupils were grouped by grades. By 1787 Raikes described his procedure as follows:

> The hour of assembly on Sunday mornings prescribed in our rules is eight o'clock.... Twenty is the number allotted to each teacher, the sexes kept separate. The twenty are divided into four classes; the children who show any superiority in attainment are placed as leaders of these small classes, and are employed in teaching the others their letters, or in hearing them read in a low whisper.... Their attending the service of the church once a day has to me seemed sufficient.[1]

"Bobby Wildgoose's" experiment of "botanizing in human nature," as he called it, was carried on quietly for three years. By that time, the first school had expanded to perhaps a hundred pupils and others had been established. The effect had proved so beneficent that Raikes began to publicize the plan through his *Gloucester Journal*.

The time was ripe. Public-spirited people everywhere were ready to try any plan that promised to meet the need. An interest in Sunday schools swept over England despite any opposition by church or state. Before Raikes died in 1811 educational, social, and political leaders came from far and wide to study the movement and it was rapidly adopted in all the British Isles, in America, and elsewhere.

American Developments

Attempts at Sunday schooling in America are reported from the middle sixteen hundreds in Massachusetts, Connecticut, and elsewhere. Schools on the new English model were introduced in 1785 when William Elliott in Accomack County, Virginia, organized a school in his own home "for the purpose of teaching his own children how to read the Bible." The church itself was slow to promote the Sunday school and in some cases opposed it. Yet, by the 1830's, denominations had accepted it as their chief teaching agency and were lending their influence to its spread.

Early Sunday schools were promoted by organizations of socially minded lay people. The first of them originated in Philadelphia, 1790, and was known as the First Day or Sunday School Society. A merger of similar societies, soon established in all leading cities, formed the American Sunday School Union in 1824 and led to the most romantic Christian educational development in the United States. In 1830 it was

---

[1]Ernest H. Hayes, *Raikes the Pioneer* (London: The National Sunday School Union, 1930), p. 70.

resolved: "That the union, in reliance upon divine aid, will within two years establish a Sunday school in every destitute place where it is practicable throughout the valley of the Mississippi." During the next two years seventy-eight "dollar-a-day" missionaries organized 2,857 schools. The Union has continued its missionary work to the present time (see Chapter XVI). Significant other promotional agencies that have served and still serve similar purposes will be mentioned in Chapter XVI.

These groups have also provided program helps. Catechisms had held first place among the materials of instruction in the American Sunday school during the quarter-century 1790-1815. After 1850 the Bible became the central resource although extrabiblical materials have been included since the beginning of this century. During many of those early years the memorization of the Book was the chief method in vogue. Prodigious numbers of verses were committed to memory, as many as a thousand in a single quarter by children ten or twelve years of age.

In those instances pupils were allowed to make a more or less random selection of the materials. Some "rhyme and reason" was introduced in "selected" lessons. Prepared in 1825, "Selected Scripture Lessons" of the American Sunday School Union attained the widest usage. When question-and-answer method began to supplant rote memorization, "question books" were developed. From 1840 to 1870, a "Babel Period" in Sunday school curriculum followed in which there were many personal, community, and denominational efforts to provide basic helps.

It was in 1872 that a National Sunday School Convention in Indianapolis adopted the International Uniform Lesson plan. These lessons, improved in 1918 and again revised for the period beginning 1945, continue to be in use. The next historic step was a struggle for "graded lessons." There had been grading of instruction, even when the catechism was the chief material, but there was no adequate provision until the International Sunday School Association promoted closely graded lessons in 1908 and group graded work in 1922. By that time the denominations were working at the task and now are largely responsible for all curriculum materials.

Allies of the Sunday Church School

It became apparent early that the Sunday church school unaided cannot provide adequately for the religious development of the Christians of the land. Earnest leaders and groups, therefore, have devised and promoted additional agencies which serve as allies. Two of the most prominent introductions of recent times share their title with the Sunday church school, namely, vacation church school and weekday church school. The former developed according to three types, more or less simultaneously; the one which became most prevalent, sometimes called "Boville," originated in New York City in 1901. The typical weekday school is the "released time" type fostered by ministers and the superintendent of public schools in Gary, Indiana, beginning in 1914. Numerous other agencies have developed and will be mentioned in Chapters XVIII and XX. Outstanding examples appear in a brief chronology that follows. It includes a variety of other historical developments that shape modern programs and methods in Christian education.

A SHORT CHRONOLOGY OF RELIGIOUS EDUCATION

(certain dates are approximate)

550 B.C.	Early synagogue schools
27–30 A.D.	JESUS THE MASTER TEACHER
30–100	Pentecost and apostolic teaching and writing
400	Canonization of New Testament; the Bible completed
1200 (circa)	Rise of universities
1450	Invention of printing
1517	The Lutheran Reformation
1529	Luther's smaller catechism and others; also hymns
1611	The King James version
1620–1750	Colonial school curriculum primarily religious
1636	Harvard University
1694	Germantown Christian day school
1750	Beginning of secularization of public schools
1780	Robert Raikes and inauguration of the Sunday school
1785	First Sunday school in America (Raikes type)
1790	American Methodists recognize the Sunday school
1800–1900	The Bible century in American Christian education
1804	British and Foreign Bible Society
1805–1820	Period of scripture memorization
1824	American Sunday School Union
1830	Beginnings of denominational curricular publication
1832	First National Sunday School Convention and Association
1839	First leadership education text, *The Teacher Taught*
1872	International uniform lessons authorized
1877	"Talking machine" (Edison, U.S.A.)
1881	Young people's society (Christian Endeavor)
1893	Motion picture machine (Edison, U.S.A.)
1900–date	Era of extrabiblical with biblical materials
1901	"The Daily Vacation Bible School" (Boville type)
1902	Radio broadcasting (Stubblefield, U.S.A.)
1902	Missionary education movement inaugurated
1903	First denominational leadership education
1903	Religious Education Association

1907	Beginning of present World Council of Christian Education
1908	International "closely graded" lessons authorized
1911	Chair of Religious Education, Boston University
1914	The weekday church school (Gary type, released time)
1915	The camp movement developed
1922	International Council of Religious Education
1923	16 mm. motion pictures
1928	Sound motion pictures
1934	Television (Zworykin, U.S.A.)
1937	Bible translated into 1,000th language (Sakata of the Belgian Congo)
1939	White House Conference on Children
1943	Christian Family Week becomes national observance
1946	RSV New Testament; 1952, Old Testament
1948	First Assembly of World Council of Churches, Amsterdam
1950	First World Institute on Christian Education, Toronto
1950	National Council of Churches of Christ in the U.S.A. (with its Division of Christian Education)
1963	The Abington case (Supreme Court decision)

The "Modern Movement" in Christian Education

An unusual upsurge of effort in Christian education which began early in this century can be called the modern movement. There had been forerunners in the eighteen hundreds: scientific study of the Bible, the child study movement, recognition of the social character of the educational process. On such foundations the modern movement established itself. The Sunday church school prospered; one by one the other new agencies arose. Approximately coincident, too, departments of religious education in colleges, seminaries, and universities developed. By 1925, several thousands of students were taking courses and numerous texts were written for their use. There were important advances in leadership development on other levels, also. While this work fostered the whole movement, it made particularly significant contributions toward the current forms of theory and practice.

Like all new movements, this one met opposition, faced handicaps, and possessed weaknesses; it has had impressive results. As a prime instance, major denominations have revised and are revising their curricular series more or less in harmony with principles that grew out of the movement. Many of the Christian education departments in higher institutions remain and minister to students who will be avocational if not vocational workers in the church; other leadership education effort goes on, hopefully upward. The books produced earlier are perennially superseded, but have similar emphases. A spirit of scientific study and research, initiated then, continues to refine programs and procedures. Congregational agencies established then are still serving. The basic approach to education that has been steadily winning its way around the world was fostered by the movement.

An enterprise responsible for such results possesses values that cannot soon be overcome. This one, tested and refined or purged in part, has been proved in part. It can be expected that "the modern movement" will mark the second half of the century as well as its first with a continuing increase of effectiveness.

PRESENT STATUS OF THE CHURCH SCHOOL

We see that the church has been busy at its learning-teaching process throughout its history. Never before, though, has there been such educational fervor and ferment everywhere.

International Concern and Transition

Christian education is increasingly a concern of the nations. Its international character has been recognized particularly since the first World Sunday School Convention at London in 1889. Other conventions have followed at intervals. More recently world institutes have been held: 1950 in Toronto; 1958 in Nishinomiya; 1962 in Belfast; 1967 in Nairobi, Kenya. These brought together two hundred or more selected leaders who explored, more intensively than can be done in large conventions, some of the basic aspects and problems of the field. In publications as well as such meetings we sense the universal interest in Christian education. At the same time we learn that while there is diversity in the international outlook and practice, there is more agreement than difference. The church is, among other things, a United Nations of Christian Educators.

Persons acquainted with Christian education anywhere know it is in a remarkable state of transition everywhere. That denominations and regional groups in unprecedented numbers are revising their curricular theories, materials, and programs is only one indication. Four major influences have been reshaping the mold: Bible, psychology, sociology, and theology. A fifth could be added, public education, but we must be content to say only that it permeates almost every phase of our work. The same influences were busy a generation ago but now, it may be said, we have somewhat changed and are changing biblical, phychological, sociological, and theological outlooks. While the final effect of all these influences remains for the future to unfold, the present situation offers an exciting prospect everywhere.

Nature and Place of Educational Work in the Church as School

What is the church in which educational leaders are serving and what is its general character as a school?

THE CHURCH

No one book, perhaps no library, could provide a complete description of the church with all its ramifications and implications. Further, several polarities are involved. This is to say that the church is in orbit between numerous poles so that any observer, at a given time and in a particular circumstance, sees it nearer to certain poles than others. Yet the church is always this and that: organism and institution; locality and universality; democracy and authority; the gathered and the scattered people of God; the working and the worshiping community; a dynamic and a static body. As the inner meaning of the church has been restudied in recent times the thrust has been toward what can be called dynamic organism. The usual concept has been more nearly a static institutionalism and, unless carefully reconsidered, this could make of the church a fallow field instead of a productive one. Through what we do in Christian education the church dare not become a ghetto for the faithful just as it must not hope to be a rootless fruitbearer. Rightly, inward nurture and outward service, with an emphasis on the latter, seems to be the dominating stress in thoughtful circles.

More terms have been used to describe the church than can possibly be cited. We confess our belief in it as "the communion of saints." It has been called "the assembly of saints in which the gospel is taught purely and the sacraments are administered rightly."[2] A somewhat recent term for Christianity, fitting also for the church, is "life-of-God-and-man-together-in-love." Not unnaturally, the church has been called "community" and "mission."

One of the most common theological definitions of the church is "body of Christ." Christ is conceived as the head of the body, a benevolent authority who cares for the body's welfare, co-ordinates its efforts, suffers with it, and by the Holy Spirit renders it effective. We members of the body may be viewed as cells having our own lives nourished and rendered available for service by and to one another. Each cell has a function including, but also beyond, the continuance of its own life. The function of each alone, as well as in the total body, is, shall we say, the purpose of God in the world. This will illuminate a further definition. Occasionally in recent years, and there are intimations in earlier

[2]"The Augsburg Confession," art. VII, in *The Book of Concord*, ed. Theodore G. Tappert (Philadelphia: Fortress Press, 1959), p. 32.

Christian history, the church has been described as "the continuing ministry of Jesus Christ." This concept recognizes it as a historic fellowship, reaching back to Christ himself with his first disciples-apostles to whom he committed the work he had been doing. Scriptural support for the concept is ample. There is a rich background in the Old Testament, such as the suffering servant doctrine. New Testament references include Mark 3:14; Matthew 28:19,20; Mark 10:45; and John 20:21b.

Joining together the ancient and widely accepted theological description with this concept that seems to be quite consonant with both ancient and modern thought, it seems proper to think of the church as "the continuously ministering body of Christ."

THE SCHOOL

When that body is educating, what is it doing? Broadly, the church educates whenever it ministers by learning-teaching process.

In a local church there is little or nothing that can be done without some form of learning and teaching. Consequently the educational work of the church is a comprehensive incessant task which permeates the whole ecclesiastical effort. Yet it is necessary to say for practical reasons that the church accomplishes its total purpose in six ways of which education is a fundamental one. These six works of the church are, alphabetically: education, evangelism, fellowship, social ministry, stewardship, and worship.

While the church ceases to be itself when any one of those works is neglected or eliminated, it is easily possible to recognize the fundamental service of education indirectly as well as directly. Evangelism requires education for the evangelist and he evangelizes largely by educational means. Fellowship takes place most fully in the educational agencies of church work and rests upon backgrounds of teaching which unite the group and facilitate fellowship activity. The social ministry of the church is supported by education of the workers. Stewardship awaits teaching to guide and promote it. Education in worship is essential to its finest expression. By those indirect values as well as its direct nurturing and energizing, education ministers indispensably to the maturing spiritual life and service of its people. If ever the question is asked, "Why Christian education?" one answer is in this interdependent functioning of it.

But the Sunday church school arose outside the institutional orbit; so did other agencies. For this reason church school agencies have sometimes been looked upon as auxiliaries if not optional ones. More widely now, though, education is conceived as a function of the entire church in all its activities. In this view, Christian education is, then, the requisite work of the church in educating itself, the Sunday church school and similar agencies being the congregation operating for educational purposes.

This has given us the definition: *a church school is a congregation at work educating itself.* A few congregations possess, and others have been moving toward one unified educational organization and program integrated as a part of the total congregational structure and program—one church school in which the conscious educational work of the congregation is done in various groups and sessions. Such a school is described in Chapter V.

Characteristics of Current Church School Work

Clearly, Christian education—the learning-teaching process as one of its ways of working—has a secure and growing place in the church. As for the church at large, we may think of workers engaged, publications used, money spent, or organizational machinery involved. Similarly, we may think of local congregations in terms of workers, money, or organization. In any case the overwhelming significance of the church school is apparent and growing. What are the trends in it?

Let it first be repeated that a strong, new spirit is stirring. The modern movement reached a peak about 1930 and seemed to lose force during the following decade but in the late 1940's it had a renascence. In this revived movement certain trends of theory and practice have had a long history, others developed earlier in the modern movement, still others are products of the more recent revival. A few have been selected for special consideration to introduce the chapters that follow while they describe educational work in the church on its more advanced if not customary levels.

EXTENDING REACH AND SCOPE

Christian educators assume that all normal persons are open to growth in Christian living by educational means at all stages of life and in every situation. That fact poses a twofold responsibility for the church. First, her workers are to view the whole world of men, women, youth, and children as their constituency. Second, as long as there is one who is not living the Christian life at his highest possible level, the task is unfinished.

The church is increasingly aware of the need to extend the *reach* of its educational program. Enrollments are far from satisfactory. Until about 1945 the Sunday church school had been losing numbers for a decade; just now it seems to be gaining about a million pupils a year in the United States. Until recently the membership of the weekday church schools on released time was increasing; vacation church schools and youth and adult groups are growing still, so are camps and other external agencies. Yet all the allies are reaching less than half as many people as the Sunday church school, and its membership includes only about a fifth of the population in the United States. Similar facts appear in a study of the *scope* of the Christian educational program. Protestant Christians on the average have not more than an hour a week in formal Christian education. Thus, just as a goal for the reach of the educational program might be a doubling of numbers, the objective with regard to scope might reasonably be two hours instead of one.

The church shows determination to act in these matters. Major denominations are renewing their efforts at enlistment, and the search for more time is expressing itself vigorously in such patterns as the widespread endeavor for weekday Christian education of many types.

FOCUSING ON PERSONS IN GROUPS

Current Christian education puts its emphasis on the life of persons in both private and social relationships where living God and man meet each other. Not, as of old, on the maintenance and dissemination of the end products of past religious experience, the emphasis is on current life, the actual present activities of growing persons as those activities undergo interpretation, analysis, appraisal, control, and consequent change. Regarding central purposes, it appears that there has been a permanent shift away from transmission of biblical information and theological concepts, the continuation of cultic techniques, and the prolongation of institutions. Yet those have become subordinate only in the sense of contributory while the focus is on persons maturing within a Christian way of living, all the possible resources serving to that end.

Twentieth-century Christian education has a keen consciousness of the social implications of the Christian life. We are concerned about the whole individual, not only his inner self but also all his socially significant dimensions. We seek to develop Christians who, among other things, are devoted to the social good and capable of working at the improvement of social conditions. While Christ came to redeem individuals, the individual and society develop reciprocally. Recently, too, we have emphasized the necessary role of the church as the Christian educational matrix.

BEING INCLUSIVE

Current Christian education is comprehensive in outlook and practice. Once it may have connoted no more than Sunday church school classes. Now it includes all the agencies to be mentioned in Chapters XVIII through XX. Furthermore, it is not a series of agencies alone but chiefly a means used throughout, as we have seen, the entire range of church work. Moreover, Christian education is not for study and instruction alone, but also for worship, fellowship, and service. Nor is it Bible study alone, for it uses materials from many sources, particularly current experience. It is not only for children but for all persons from earliest to eldest years. Further, it deals with all fundamentals—God, man, immortality, moral responsibility, sin, freedom, the highest good, and salvation as well as any lesser things.

Finally, Christian education is for all phases of life. It involves the whole person in all his relationships, individual and social. It includes past, present, and future. It is for every aspect of personality—knowledge and judgment, feeling and appreciation, character and conduct. Yet it is not for isolated experience only, but for an integrated totality of Christian experience.

USING DEVELOPMENTAL EDUCATION WITH CREATIVE EMPHASIS

There is no widely accepted word to name the particular theory and related procedure which have been elaborated within twentieth-century Christian education. Various persons speak of new, modern, scientific, pupil-centered, life-centered, experience-centered, creative, or activity education. None of those quite meets the requirements. We shall discuss the need later (especially in Chap. II) and adopt "developmental education" that employs techniques creatively.

"Developmental education" suggests growth, change, development all along the line. Present day Christian education views its work in precisely that way. Its task is cumulative pupil experience in Christian living for satisfying personal growth and an ongoing social order. Thus "developmental" is used here for the type of education that characterizes the modern movement at its present stage.

"Creative," properly understood, describes the special characteristic of the techniques now in the ascendancy. Briefly, it means that the learner works within a learning situation which is developed as far as possible by himself for a purpose which is his own. He meets the learning situation in a way which he develops for himself, albeit with whatever guidance and resources are necessary. The result achieved is creative, too, in the sense of something novel to the degree which may be fitting for all interests concerned.

These concepts will receive full attention especially in Chapter II and later.

EMPHASIZING CHRISTIAN SPECIFICS

Among other recent trends in Christian education is an increased appreciation of Bible, church, theology, and worship. A majority of Christian educators always upheld their importance. However, it is alleged that some of those who early favored a "life-centered" approach may have tended to equate culture and religion. Developments, particularly in the last decades, have served to correct any of the more superficial and romantic views. Now it is unquestionably recognized that Christian personality finds essential aids to growth in scripture and devotional literature, also that historic faith, institutions and concepts can be brought into functioning relations with current religious experience. Indeed, the great resources out of past experience, while not used for their own sakes, are essential for the activating and directing of Christian living. However, there must be watchfulness lest this emphasis go too far.

DEPENDING ON SCIENTIFIC METHOD AND NORMAL PROCEDURE

Christian educators rely on several supporting sciences, including general education, psychology, and sociology. In general, they assume that whatever truth educational research may disclose about the ways in which human beings learn anywhere will guide procedure in this area. They proceed as if pupils are dependent for learning in the field of religion on the same psychological equipment employed in any other field; also that whatever is true about the psychology of childhood, adolescence, and adulthood anywhere will apply here. Lately, too, they are employing the findings of sociology, for example what we know about group dynamics.

SERVING UNDER THE SPIRIT

This is not to say that the proponents of Christian education view it humanistically as a man-made process alone, a boot-strap for lifting oneself into God's kingdom. They believe that the Holy Spirit works in an orderly manner and that devoted students of life working from either the religious or from the so-called secular angle have discovered, just as consecrated workers have observed and earnest pupils have come to know, the Spirit's ways in some degree. There is regeneration, salvation, sanctification, renewal. The Holy Spirit accomplishes all, but he does it as leaders and learners, and he, come into appropriate relationships of the type we call educational. Thus man in his lostness is met by God's graciousness in educational settings. His Holy Spirit then renders the teacher's faithful efforts fruitful.

The above catalogue does not exhaust the list of current characteristics of church school work. At least as many others could be mentioned: the unit concept in curriculum, the functional way of using the Bible, the ecumenical ideal, the employment of audile and visual materials and equipment, developments in children's and youth work, a new emphasis on adult work, efforts at the promotion of Christian family life.

The Sunday Church School in the Present Program

Within all Protestantism, the Sunday church school agency is central in the educational work whose current characteristics have been described. This work now engages more leaders and learners than any other. Reliable statistics will likely never be available but, speaking in round numbers, there must be more than six million workers and sixty million pupils in the world's six hundreds of thousands of Protestant Sunday church schools. A large percentage of these are in the United States, the others distributed over all the continents and many of the isles. This means there is something like one Sunday church school member for each fifty persons in the world's population. But this agency for Christian education not only reaches the largest number of persons, it also represents the most highly developed form with the longest background of experience. It has the most carefully worked out curricular materials. It is the most universally understood and fully recognized Christian educational endeavor.

Yet, when the church evaluates its Sunday church school, various weaknesses appear and are rather highly publicized. A major one was never more devastatingly described than in 1839 when Frederick Adolphus Packard wrote *The Teacher Taught*. His words are still too relevant:

> It is to be feared that of a large proportion of our Sunday school children it may be justly said that they are bewildered with verbal mysteries, where there is no refreshment of truth for the eye, and are wearied with wandering from shadow to shadow, where there is all the fatigue of continual progress, without the advance of a single step in real knowledge.[3]

Even so, church school leaders cannot permit this agency to lose its place for any lesser program. Such values as these need to be conserved:

It is a principal setting for commitment to Christ and growth in it.
It is the major agency for fostering work with the Bible.
It serves as an important recruiting ground for the church.
It provides a period of corporate worship and gives many persons their first experiences in Christian service.
It makes Christian social fellowship available.
It has international recognition.
It develops leadership for the whole church.
It is the major ally of homes for moral and religious development.
It provides the major portion of Christian literature used by the people.
It has an impressive record of guiding and stimulating Christian conduct.

Unquestionably the typical Sunday church school must be gradually altered and expanded; possibly it will be replaced sometime for more effective educational results. Yet what has been done in Christian education during the nineteenth and twentieth centuries, it has had a share in

[3]Frederick Adolphus Packard, *The Teacher Taught* (Philadelphia: American Sunday School Union, 1839), p. 16.

doing. Also, for what is yet to be done it will likely be indispensable for a considerable time to come.

PROMISE

But the Sunday church school is only one phase of the total church school. What can be said for the future of the whole complex?

Its weaknesses have been rather elaborately discussed by Alva I. Cox in his recent *Christian Education in the Church Today.*[4] He mentions these "signs of failure": "fewer persons"; "drop-outs"; "innocuous . . . irrelevant"; "yesterday's methods"; "too little time and money"; "unauthentic materials"; "looking at the past"; "lack of relevance." Happily, Dr. Cox's chapter ends with a few paragraphs on "some signs of promise." There is, indeed, promise in the trends that have just been described and more that is hopeful will appear in subsequent chapters. Weaknesses are being redressed.

The situation is formidable. We struggle against odds: expansion of populations; rivalry of ideologies; overflow of technology; urbanization of society; increase of leisure; extension of knowledge; changing family life; rise of new nations; automation of processes; mobility of persons. All of these developments clamor for the church to adapt herself, but with basic fidelity. She will, and in that evolution find new forms of Christian education although there is no reason to expect overnight changes of great magnitude.

Dr. Paul Vieth once wrote of our attempt to do with a fifty horsepower machine "a work which requires many hundreds of horsepower."[5] This was the fairest of all appraisals. Since he wrote, however, the church school movement has been advancing at an accelerating pace. We can describe in succeeding chapters an improved machine; we can also discern in the church an increase of power for its operation. There is ample reason to believe that decades ahead will continue to see the beneficent results of church school work within even new crises the modern world will face as a result of its epoch-making strides.

[4](Nashville: Graded Press, 1965), Chap. 10.

[5]Paul H. Vieth, *The Church and Christian Education* (St. Louis: Bethany Press, 1947), p. 294.

CHAPTER II

UNDERSTANDING WHAT CHRISTIAN EDUCATION IS

"What is Christian education, anyhow?" That is properly a major question of church school workers as they lay foundations for a wise outlook on their tasks and better performance in them.

The nature of Christian education is changing constantly. Throughout this century the understanding of religion itself has been under clarification by study of its racial origin, its social function and the inner experience of it. The broad field of education has been undergoing similar study with important results in philosophy and procedure. Christian education responds to both these formative influences as it proceeds with its own reconstruction and reappears with altered features. Indeed, in view of the transitional situation in which we live, we have to be thinking about emerging Christian education. Yet, where are we at present?

TERMINOLOGY: PROBLEM AND SOLUTION

Convenience demands general terms to name the current educational forms. Yet none have been universally accepted. This lack is easily explained. Education has been shaped by many philosophies: existentialism, experimentalism, idealism, pragmatism, realism, and others. Theories of education have been called, as instances: essentialism, neo-Thomism, perennialism, progressivism, reconstructionism, regressionism. We find, however, that educational practice is not based on any one philosophic system and the procedures come from a variety of sources. J. M. Hughes has well said that we have an "intermingling of ideas"[1] and Van Cleve Morris rightly acknowledges that most of us are "the kind of person we call an eclectic."[2]

[1]James M. Hughes, *Education in America* (New York: Harper and Row, 1965).
[2]Van Cleve Morris, *Philosophy and the American School* (Boston: Houghton Mifflin Company, 1961).

Yet the need for terminology remains. So we are using "traditional" and "developmental" to describe the two types we meet in church schools. The terms may not be entirely satisfactory to anyone; objections are easily raised. Yet if it be true that a definition "merely states how a word is used" we may justify the usage by ample definition. Besides, we shall see that there are more substantial supports for the terminology.

Briefly now, the type of education called traditional is the one that, too simply stated, is concerned chiefly with subject matter. Because "developmental" is the more novel term, also because it names the currently favored type of Christian education, it will receive the ampler definition in subsequent pages. Just to begin, it is the type whose name, as we have said, "suggests growth, change, development all along the line." It is an "eclectic" form that fits not too far from the center of the philosophic Pentagon. As an "intermingling of ideas," it is sensitive to sociological findings, especially to growth within group processes. It also uses relevant insights from any school of psychology but, particularly, seems reasonably congruent with Havighurst's concept of "developmental tasks." All together, as a learner-oriented view, it is close to a basic meaning of education as personality development. So the name is developmental.

It will be described fully within definitions of education, religion, religious education, and Christian education where it will be compared and contrasted with the traditional counterpart. Two expressions will be appearing frequently there: "activity" and "abundant life."

Activity usually suggests only physical behavior—muscular movement; indeed, it is sometimes used with that meaning in current educational literature. In these pages, though, activity refers not only to overt acts but also to the inward thoughts, feelings, and purposes that accompany them. Defining in that larger way, the life of an individual or group is viewed here as a system of activities that occur in our several relationships—to God, one another, self, and objects.

"Abundant life" stems from words of Jesus, John 10:10, "I came that they may have life and have it abundantly" (RSV). As used here it is by no means merely an economic value; rather it is meant to be consonant with the ultimates of Christian meaning. Hence the abundant life of self and others, seemingly a fulfilling of the purpose of God in Christ, is regarded as a proper goal and standard of human activities, and so a purpose and measure for educational endeavor.

WHAT IS EDUCATION?

It has been urged that everyone should attempt to define education. The literature suggests that almost everyone has tried.

Typical Definitions

Following are a few efforts by representative thinkers through two millenniums:

> The true aim of education is the attainment of happiness through perfect virtue. —ARISTOTLE
> We define education as a sound training from childhood in the path of virtue. —CLEMENT
> We thus reach a definition of education. It is that reconstruction or reorganization of experience which adds to the meaning of experience, and which increases ability to direct the course of subsequent experience.
> —DEWEY
> Education means the natural, progressive, and systematic development of all the powers. —PESTALOZZI
> Education is preparation for life. —SPENCER
> Education means the universal distribution of extant knowledge.
> —WARD

A church body expressed its view in this comprehensive paragraph:

> Education deals with persons, and it is concerned with their growth and development according to their nature and the laws of their being. It seeks the progressive change of the person toward the goal conceived as defining the good person and the good society—a process which never ends as long as life lasts. It is concerned with the transmission of the cherished elements in the heritage of the educating group, not merely for the sake of transmission, but so that the heritage may be appropriated and utilized in meeting life's needs. Education is a process by which a community seeks to open its life to all the individuals within it, so far as it is good, and also to evaluate and improve it. This includes sharing the ideals by which the community lives, the values it holds dearest, the behavior which constitutes its mores. Good education seeks to develop individuals who are creative in contributing to the culture and in meeting the emerging problems which every generation must face. In all this, education is mindful of the progressively developing capacities of growing persons, and seeks to deal with them at each stage of growth in ways that are appropriate to that stage of development.[3]

An Activity Definition

One more definition of education, in activity terms, will be attempted. It aims to comprehend the essence of the subject, however conceived. A definition more fully descriptive of the developmental outlook and practice in general and specifically in Christian education will appear later. *Education is the process of accomplishing some change in someone's*

[3]*Parish Education* (Philadelphia: The Board of Parish Education, The United Lutheran Church in America, n.d.), p. 2.

system of activities. Change may involve (1) the development of a new activity; (2) the elimination of an old activity; (3) the intensification of an old activity; or (4) the diminution of an old activity. *More formally, education is a planned process in which a leader fosters change in a learner's activities to the end of an enlarging abundance of life.* From the learner's point of view, it is a learning process through which he achieves such a change in his activities as will result in more abundant living; from the leader's point of view, it is a teaching process in which he assists the learner with his learning process. In practice the roles are sometimes reversed; at its best it is a co-operative process.

Senses of Definitions

An analysis of those and other definitions of education reveals a wide variation in their senses. As a basic and troublesome but inescapable differentiation, we may think at one time of education as something that happens to the learner—within him; at another time it is something being done for him—from outside the learner. The former is the fundamental and more desirable meaning but the term often denotes the means that the learner and his leaders are using, not infrequently the schools. Definitions differ in numerous other ways. One must always tarry to realize the stance of a writer or speaker.

The most significant differences in meanings of education arise at the point of the pupil's or teacher's way of looking at the educative process and his general way of going about it. Here we meet those two major types: traditional education that emphasizes *transmissive preparation for life* and developmental education that is concerned chiefly with *creative experience in living.*

There have long been, still are, and probably will continue to be, those two. Both traditional and developmental education have had long histories. Neither is anything new and neither is the work of any one proponent. It is possible to trace them back to Greece and beyond. Thereafter they appear and reappear; sometimes one is in the ascendancy and then the other. They are implied in the Bible, both Old and New Testaments. Kendig Cully's *Basic Writings in Christian Education*[4] shows that they have been known throughout the history of Christianity. The traditional type has been quite common in church schools; recent events have increased its prominence somewhat in public school work. Even so, education in our daily lives, outside the schools, is usually conducted on a developmental basis and this outlook moves steadily

---

[4]Kendig Brubaker Cully, *Basic Writings in Christian Education* (Philadelphia: The Westminster Press, 1960).

forward in educational philosophy as well as practice in schools both public and religious.

Traditional Education:
Emphasizing Transmissive Preparation for Life

When we call education traditional we do not mean that it is old; we refer to a backward looking characteristic. This conservative tendency is most apparent in its aim. Certain achievements of the race must be preserved: knowledges, practices, institutions, and aesthetic, moral, or spiritual values. Those "traditions" are to be sustained by oncoming generations. So the social purpose of this education is to have people possess and preserve the racial heritages. As its goal for the pupil himself, it aims at his competence in adulthood, especially because of what he has received from the past.

This twofold purpose of traditional education—social preservation and personal preparation—is to be achieved by transmission of the heritages. The content is mostly organized subject matter, the techniques are chiefly memoriter and the control may be largely authoritarian. Pupils are to store up items of knowledge as if in a psychic refrigerator where they may go at will to get the mental eggs preserved there. More recently, too, there was added the concept that you can do with attitudes and skills what it had been thought you could do with ideas. If pupils are but trained in certain ways as children, they will act accordingly when they grow up. That training is meant to provide, at one and the same time, for the maintenance of society and the mature well being of the individual.

Something of that traditional view probably dominates the educational thinking of the masses today. It has elements of truth. No one would wish the great heritages to be lost. A transmissive element and a preparatory aspect can never be omitted properly from any educational program. There must be some mastery of fact or there are no materials with which to build intelligent judgments and perform requisite functions. We need certain emotional and executive habits, established by long and frequent exercise, in order to carry us along in our daily walk.

Yet, while more people may hold this view, a majority of educators do not consider it an adequate philosophy. For one important reason, the heritages must be reconstructed to some degree in each age, radically in such an era of change as ours. As for learners themselves, this education does not fit the needs of dynamic personalities growing individually within a changing society. They want satisfaction and achievement that are real and they want them now as well as in the future. Being concerned primarily about their moving present, the past has value largely as it contributes to the present; the future is a rather dim unknown for which their best preparation is to become experienced total persons on their moving stage. At best, therefore, transmissive preparation—however important—is but a phase of total education. We shall see that it is better achieved as a by-product of education in present living than as the end product of schooling.

Developmental Education:
Emphasizing Creative Experience in Living

Developmental is actually the older type of education, just as it is also the more common form because it is the way of the home, the playground, the farm, and the shop. It can be misunderstood and mismanaged. Yet those who use it wisely are working in a long line of competent thinkers and practitioners. It also seems most nearly accordant with what modern studies disclose concerning the learning and teaching processes.

Briefly and in its essence, developmental education is a form of guided living in which a pupil, by the use of his developing powers within his environment, grows step by step into what he can desirably become. Development, we see, is the key word. This is a way to foster the constant growth of the total learner and advance of the social order.

Developmental education can be described more fully as experience in living and as creative experience.

EXPERIENCE IN LIVING

Education as experience in living—guided experience—means that the pupil is to be living now, intensively, in an educational situation which is to be as far as possible a segment of his real life. This is akin to the primitive way of learning by doing which is also the modern way in most activities except in school. It is the child's way of learning to skate; the older person's way of mastering his work. We have always said that experience is the best teacher. Now we are seeking to actualize that proverb in the school.

As a program of experience in actual living, developmental education strives to deal with the real life situations of pupils, helping them meet those situations with adequate adjustments and effective adaptations. The ideal school curriculum would be a series of actual experiences guided by every relevant resource possible. Then the teacher could sense the real material of his craft as pulsating and growing life. The pupil, too, could feel that he is living life at its keenest on the very growing edge of history. The whole result is to be learning experience that is vital, concrete, practical, energetic, and productive.

Meeting Need

Need is of highest significance in this type of education that could, not improperly, be called need-meeting activity. The "felt needs" of pupils can determine the purposes and procedures of learners and leaders. Let it be said at once, though, that a need is more than some superficial want; it is to be a substantial concern. Education that is experience in living, then, will be helping pupils find fulfillments for their substantial concerns. Only such education is lifelike, for to live is to be performing in a pattern of need-meeting.

Traditional education, too, has this factor of need-meeting but as a by-product; in developmental education a pupil's sensed needs are the foci around which the learning experiences gather. As an inalienable reason for this approach, education's law of readiness states that people learn most readily and permanently when there is aspiration, curiosity, inquiry, and quest.

There are limitations that suggest precautions. We dare not deal with superficialities. Fragmentariness must be avoided by recognizing the necessity to systematize and co-ordinate learnings from time to time. Because pupils may not be aware of basic needs we must sometimes lead them into deeper concerns, even help them articulate obscure ones. For Christian education we must deal with needs in their Christian dimensions.

Using Content as Resource

Both traditionalists and developmentalists use what we call content but they differ as to the meaning of it and the manner of its use. There are three possible meanings for the word. One usage is to denote subject matter, material substance that is external to the learner. Another usage refers to mental substance—internal content as psychological phenomenon. This internal content is usually seen as knowledge or the primarily intellectual components of the mental equipment. As a third usage, content can include components that are primarily emotional (attitudes) or primarily volitional (skills). The skills will be the accompanying technique or operative components of the total mental process; among the many are reasoning and judging ideas, controlling and experiencing emotions, planning and executing enterprises. This third usage of content covers the total psychology of the person and it is this wholeness with which developmental education aims to deal, not chiefly intellectual content represented in subject matter. However, the first usage will be largely the one in view for a few paragraphs.

Purpose with Content. Again too simply stated, traditionalists hold that mastery of subject matter is a pupil's chief business and the retention of such content is the most precious result of his schooling. For developmentalists, we have seen, the point of concentration is the growth of the learner in his current experience. Here subject matter—prominently the Bible—has its indispensable place as resource for help in meeting immediate needs. An element of it is to be retained, too, but as a by-product of actual use rather than by drill in anticipation of future use. Thus traditionalists use content in its logical form, especially to be memorized and later, it is hoped, utilized when need may arise; developmentalists use it in a functional manner, employing it when need for it is at hand and it can become naturally a component of the pupil's total activity system. In the latter case, content is serving an auxiliary function, being used chiefly as an accessory aid, adjunct, or handmaid. Thus Christian education will not be what is commonly called a content-centered or subject-oriented but an experience-centered or life-oriented program for integrated total response in the entire Christian activity system.

Procedure with Content: "Utilization" versus "Memorization" Emphases. The difference as to content's place also alters the emphasis in procedure. When content mastery is the purpose, that mastery is attempted by direct effort at it while the issues of life are to be solved as a by-product. When those issues get the spotlight and content is used as resource for their management, content mastery is largely a by-product. Since developmental procedure is laboratory work with "exercises" that are real, vital, actual as possible, the pupil is to make use of the resource today for the sake of today's living though we understand that there will be a certain amount of retention as a by-product for future use. We describe the procedure as an emphasis on utilization, the opposite way as an emphasis on memorization which most characteristically is provided by "direct drill."

Results of Content. Traditionalists are resting their case for education with a memorization emphasis largely on its value in preparation for life. Developmentalists are saying, instead, that subject matter as resource is to be helping persons live the highest type of life possible for them in their circumstances at the moment. They add that this is the way to lay foundations for the future; they would say also that the purpose of preserving the racial heritages can be achieved best by this procedure. When resources have been utilized for the effective meeting of needs confronted in problematic living, then they will be treasured. Thus, though pupils retain material best by the indirect way of use, there is a possible place for a supplementary element of memory drill—on Bible passages, for example. It is after a well-loved portion has had its deep meaning in terms of present life experience, promises to have further use, and is almost already at tongue's tip. Then the teacher may lead the pupils in a drill procedure that has some promise of leaving that material ready for recall and even for recall in the time of need for use.

CREATIVE EXPERIENCE

In developmental education, because it is to be creative experience in living, though necessarily guided, the pupil must be to a considerable degree on his own. This adventure in creative experience has many facets.

Dynamic Motivation. Developmental education waits as long as possible on dynamic motivation. Persons have drives that thrust them out for satisfactions, altruistic as well as egoistic. These activating forces within are to be the fundamental stimuli to pupil effort. This principle dare not be allowed to end in anarchy. Children and youth can become bored or frightened by too much freedom; coercion is needful in emergencies. Yet the ideal is independent decision in place of obedience, inner control instead of outward compulsion, self-imposed discipline. The leader need not abdicate but he is primarily a helper who counsels and encourages instead of dictating. The matter was well understood by a junior high pupil who was pleading, "Why don't they let you do what you're interested in? Then you'd do the work yourself and they'd just need to help you. That's it, why don't they just help you instead of always telling you?"

Pupil Purpose. Developmental education has high regard for the pupil's own goals. It wants him to judge for himself where his well-being lies and it allows his sense of need and interest to determine his work as fully as possible. The leader has a significant responsibility just at this point. A typical pupil has not seen all the values that he may serve, and cannot evaluate them with complete wisdom. He must have help to see and give proper weighting to what is pertinent.

Original Personal Results. Developmental education holds a creative attitude with respect to the pupil himself. It has no exactly preconceived notion as to his present behavior or future status although it does have standards and ideals for him. It wants his way as a Christian to be illumined by the clear light of the revelation that is in the life and teachings of Jesus Christ. Then it wants him to be himself at his best now and in succeeding days, growing stage by stage into the better than he can become. His unique qualities are not to be thwarted but encouraged to the extent compatible with long-range good for himself and others. His results are to be creative, at least as he views them. The pupil may utilize every resource of racial accumulation—that crystallization of past experience called knowledge not being excluded. Yet he uses the achievements of the past not merely to memorize, copy, or imitate them. He chooses from among them in a way that is creative experience in itself; then he adds his original contribution.

Self-directed Procedure. Developmental education encourages the pupil to devise his own ways of working but this is not to be an individualistic task. The community's desires and needs are always to be reckoned with. There is to be constant use of group procedure in arriving at the truth and implementing it. The democratic way of planning and attaining personal self-realization is to be stressed. Within the proper limits of that social setting, the pupil is allowed to have his say in planning, controlling, and executing his program.

Re-creation of Inheritances. Toward social inheritances developmental education holds the sort of creative attitude needed so sorely in a time like this. They are not only to be cherished, sustained, and utilized as resource, they are to be re-created. The need was expressed in this paragraph concerning Christian education:

> It is our obligation, as it was the obligation of our fathers in the Christian movement, to re-interpret Christian faith in terms of the living experiences of our own day, to discover its wider and deeper implications and to bring it into effectual relation with the issues of contemporary living. In doing so, we should constantly remind ourselves that there are depths of meaning in the Christian gospel that far outrun our limited capacities to apprehend them. Nor should we seek to bind our own conceptions of Christian faith upon the future. Rather, we should, by the understanding and appreciation of the great historic symbols, seek to use them without being bound by them and to free those who will come after us to explore the depths and the heights of Christian truth which belongs to the centuries and which cannot be fully stated within the limited framework of any given historic period.[5]

Guided Self-Education. Relying as it does upon the pupil's activity at each step, developmental education is essentially self-education. Self-control, self-reliance, and individual initiative, while sharing and progressively exercising social responsibility, are essential forces to advance enkindled life, foster awakened intellect, and increase productive capacity while accomplishing spiritual reformation and social reform toward increasingly abundant life for self and others. Yet the pupils are to have, throughout, whatever measure of guidance is needed. The school is a learning laboratory in which leaders arrange situations so that pupils

[5]*Christian Education Today* (Chicago: The International Council of Religious Education, n.d.), p. 12.

may have the most fruitful, creative experience. It is essentially a place for living—living at its best in a social center, a library, and a workshop. The teachers handle certain mechanical elements of the whole process. They guide the program to its principal track and keep it there. They make resources available. Meanwhile, they seek progressively to render themselves as unnecessary as reasonably possible. It is thus that a pupil is permitted to make a creative quest, although a guided one.

SUMMARY

Nobody has described the developmental way of education more simply, yet adequately, than Dr. Franklin Bobbitt when he wrote:

> The *purpose* of education is to bring each human being to live, as nearly as practicable, in everything that he does in a way that is best for him. The *method* of education is for each individual to carry on all his activities all the time, as far as possible, in the way that is best for one of his nature, age and situation. In the education of any person, the good life is both the objective and the process. The basic educational responsibility of the child or youth is to live the good life to the best of his ability; that of his parents and teachers, to help him do so. The educative process is what the child or youth does in living a good life. The teaching process is what parents and teachers do in getting him to live it.... To live rightly each day is the best possible way to learn how to live rightly each succeeding day.[6]

Contrast and Comparison: Traditional and Developmental Emphases

Diagram I represents an effort to summarize while contrasting and comparing the two emphases of education. It can be misunderstood; *"emphases"* in the caption is highly important. In the two vertical lines at the left and right of the two columns, the extreme points of view are mentioned only for the sake of completeness; neither is commended. There is no dividing line in the center of the page because each of the pairs of educational concepts (contrasting emphases) are not mutually exclusive sets of principles and procedures. In practice there will and ought to be some interchanges of component factors that represent the two types of education. People register for one political party or another but sometimes split the ticket because they approve planks in the other party's platform. Religiously, one may be Catholic, Anglo-Catholic, Protestant, or Orthodox. Yet he may sense a unity in certain phases and feel that one element of another's faith is serviceable to him.

[6]Franklin Bobbitt, *The Curriculum of Modern Education* (New York: McGraw-Hill, 1941), p. 5. Used by permission.

Diagram I

CONTRASTING EMPHASES OF MAJOR EDUCATIONAL TYPES

On the left: developmental and creative—constant growth of dynamic personality within developing group life.

On the right: traditional and transmissive—preservation, appropriation of the heritages.

Developmental		*Traditional*	
E	person-centered	content-centered	E
	creative learning	transmissive learning	
X	teaching as guidance	teaching as telling	X
	democracy	authoritarianism	T
T	importance of the how	importance of the what	
	inner control	outer compulsion	R
R	personal insight	thinking others' thoughts	E
	freedom	restraint	
E	social outlook	individualistic interest	M
	stress on present	stress on past	E
M	dynamic personality	static personality	
	activity	passivity	
E	curriculum as life	curriculum as text	
	inquiry, investigation	acquisition, accumulation	C
	current living	preparation for life	
	transformation	conformity	O
	flexible readiness	encyclopedic mastery	
R	socialized contribution	individualized recitation	N
	inventive production	imitative reproduction	S
A	free convictions and ideals	indoctrination	
	making decisions	accepting decisions	E
D	learning by doing	learning by memorizing	R
	flexibility of program	rigidity of program	
I	dealing with actuality	dealing with symbol	V
	psychological order of experience	logical order of presentation	
C	discipline by absorption in task	discipline by rule	A
	spirit	docility	T
A	discussion, research, social action	lecture, drill, textbook	
	rounded experience	knowledge and training	I
L	knowledge, belief result of action	knowledge, belief produce action	V
	self-development	passing examinations	
	education of life	education of the schools	E

Even so, a basic choice for one list of emphases is necessary. The millenniums of educational history seem to prove that nothing totally new will be discovered in the no man's land between the two. You can mix the components to have a blend—more of this or more of that—but you can't get a synthesis of the two theories that is a third. Also you can't go by one basic theory today and the other tomorrow. You can, in one hour, use a procedure that is more common in one outlook, the next hour a procedure more common to the other, your choice depending on what will serve best according to your basic theory.

Persons who deal in education must first see clearly; then they must choose positively and proceed firmly according to their choice. In terms of the diagram, while either extreme is to be avoided, leaders must take their orientation toward either the right or the left of center as regards philosophy and procedure. When we want to arrive at a northwesterly point we sometimes use some of the roads that lead to the northeast. In sailing we have a maneuver known as tacking with the wind. Yet there is never any doubt as to our general bearing. The orientation of modern Christian education is to the left of center. Yet, lest there be any mistaking, let it be repeated that this does not mean that no attention will be given to things in the right hand column; also one will not pursue any of the items in the left hand column beyond the fitness they may have for an educational situation at hand.

Actually, developmental education will usually be seen in a modified form—realistic developmental education we may call it. To know and appropriate it fully one must know it by participation as learner and leader—as the theory goes.

Limitations of Developmental Education

While developmental education demonstrated long ago that it is a practical way to accomplish the educational task, it is not an easy way and it must be used with judgment. It has suffered at the hands of detractors, also of practitioners who have not understood it or have misused it. Like any other form it has limitations that must be respected.

A mistaken attempt at developmental education could result in too little knowledge and too late. Under any type of education an effective learning must await some sense of need on the part of the pupil. Yet, it will be said rightly, the developmental leader cannot always wait until the learning is needed in the final way. Work at "first aid" is an excellent example. In such matters a teacher can only kindle the pupil's imagination to a maximum sense of future need.

When developmental education is misunderstood and wrongly employed, the valid goals of education may get lost in the process. There is danger of dallying with a superficial or trivial experience just because it appears creative—scribbling with crayons for example. Further, creative methods can be merely imitated without full understanding for adequate practice. As an instance, the discussion techniques by which groups are supposed to arrive at creative results in their common inquiries are frequently handled in a way that has been described well as the pooling of ignorance. This is a technique to be used when a real problem is clearly defined, adequate preparation has been made, and conclusions are sought and reached by persons who know how.

This type of education may be mishandled by clinging too closely to direct experience of immediate worth. Pupils need not be kept always on the lower levels of immediate experience only. They can advance to the plane of striving after deferred values if the values are in sight, though dimly. They can, too, arrive at the ability to do abstract and symbolic thinking. Developmental procedure can properly intellectualize the educational experience progressively as it proceeds to higher levels.

Likely the chief criticism against developmental education arises from error in its use at the point of control. This is not the alleged sort of education in which children "do just as they please." The approach is right in emphasizing intrinsic motivation; the discipline of creative and responsible living is infinitely to be preferred over the imposed discipline of the rod. Yet children, even older learners, may be immature, undisciplined, and inexperienced. They cannot see their highest good fully and dare not be humored in caprice or rebellion. Then leaders must exercise foresight, direction, even veto. Nothing in the approach, when properly understood, prevents such action. We have a dilemma because freedom can be misused so as to destroy the conditions that make it possible; nevertheless we must make the venture of freedom as far as possible because totalitarian control also will lead to ruin. Observing checks and balances, we proceed with caution. This is not a procedure for irresponsibles!

There are other points at which unguarded use of the developmental ideal may be wasteful. It may fail to reverence the past sufficiently, too readily neglecting or rejecting the racial inheritance. It may accentuate nonconformity. It may not sufficiently appreciate stability in the social order. It may neglect the tragical element. It may become too earth-bound and forget the factor of beyondness in complete experience. All of these, however, are only possibilities and not necessities.

A critique of traditional education would leave us with at least an equal number of limitations. In either case the limitations must be accepted along with the advantages. While the latter are exploited, the former will be guarded against.

WHAT IS CHRISTIAN EDUCATION?

As we move toward an answer for our question about the meaning of Christian education we must notice further that it is a form of religious education.

Religion and Religious Education

What is religion and what, as a result, is religious education?

RELIGION

There is likely no area of human concern in which there is more diversity of meaning and action. In the Christian sector alone religion means varying degrees and combinations of activities: abstaining from grievous breaches of the Ten Commandments; practicing family devotions and attending public services of worship; participating in church affairs; accepting certain beliefs; giving for the program of the church and to charitable causes; having some concern about those who are not in the fold and expecting a future phase of life.

Out of such a complex experience innumerable definitions have arisen and many characteristic ones could be quoted. For the purpose here, a further venture is made: *the religion of an individual or group is the system of activities which whether they are primarily intellectual, emotional, or volitional, arises in the relationships of that individual or group to its gods or God.*

This definition recognizes religion as an experience that occurs between man and deity when man's action is consciously an interaction with divine action. It further recognizes that religious experience may be known as an individual and a group phenomenon. It views the religious experience as one that involves whole persons in a total "way of living" where all life's activities are included directly or indirectly within the God-relationship. More particularly, the definition does not view religion as a disjointed or fragmentary relationship with deity; there is coherence and correlation among the specific religious activities.

RELIGIOUS EDUCATION

In the light of foregoing definitions of religion and education, we may first say simply that religious education is the learning-teaching process at work among those activities which emerge in the God-relationship.

More precisely, though, *religious education is that planned process in which learners, assisted by leaders: (1) perform the highest religious activities possible; (2) therewith acquire the corresponding desirable ways of acting; (3) thereby attain a progressively higher measure of abundant living within the relationship to God.* On this foundation we approach the definition of Christian education.

Typical Definitions of Christian Education

Again, there are many examples! The following have come from many sources in recent decades:

> By Christian nurture we mean the total effort of the Church to help each person to dedicate himself to Christ and to develop the understandings, the attitudes and the skills that he needs in order to be Christian in his personal life and in his relations with others.[7]
>
> The aim of Christian education is to help the child experience the fullness of Christian life in the church at all the stages of the child's development . . . primarily a nourishment of the child's soul—as it is at the moment when we come in touch with it. . . . All the basic truths of doctrine, the great realities of Church liturgical life, the moral and spiritual values of Christianity . . . have a meaning and a purpose for every kind of human being, at every stage of its development. . . .[8]
>
> To the Christian, education is that culture of the mind, the will and the emotions, which, whilst adapting a man for the exercise of a particular calling, disposes him to achieve an excellent personal and social life within the framework of that calling. The object of education is nothing else but human happiness.[9]
>
> . . . our task is to bring the individual Christian into the right relationship with the God of Jesus Christ, so that by grace the individual may do the task to which he is called.[10]
>
> The objective of religious education is the development of Christian personality through guided practice in Christian living.[11]
>
> The purpose of Christian education is to aid persons in their developmental responses toward encounters with God and to guide them in appropriating God's revelation in personal and social living.[12]
>
> Christian education is the process by which persons are confronted with and controlled by the Christian gospel.[13]

Developmental Definition of Christian Education

It is obvious that those definitions use, in general, the concepts presented in the foregoing descriptions of education and religious educa-

[7]Lee J. Gable, *Christian Nurture Through the Church* (New York: National Council of Churches, 1955), p. 11.

[8]Sophie S. Koulomzin, *Lectures in Orthodox Religious Education* (Crestwood, New York: St. Vladimir's Seminary Press, 1960), pp. 18, 19.

[9]Edward Leen, *What Is Education?* (New York: Sheed and Ward, 1944), p. 1.

[10]Randolph C. Miller, *Education for Christian Living* (Englewood Cliffs, New Jersey: Prentice-Hall, 1963), p. 54. Used by permission.

[11]Leon C. Palmer, *The New Religious Education* (Milwaukee: Morehouse Publishing Co., 1932), p. 30.

[12]George M. Schreyer, *Christian Education in Theological Focus* (Philadelphia: Christian Education Press, 1962), p. 8. Used by permission of the United Church Press.

[13]Paul H. Vieth, *The Church and Christian Education* (St. Louis: The Bethany Press, 1947), p. 52.

tion. We proceed in harmony with them to our definition in developmental terms.

CHRISTIAN EDUCATION IN GENERAL

Christian education will be religious education in which God is known in and through Jesus Christ. *Christian education, briefly then, is the guided activity by which persons live and grow in the Christian faith-life.*

In view of the recent theological emphasis it may be well to express our definition in these words: *Christian education is a process in which learners and leaders work together at enterprises in which God in his grace meets man in his need so that persons grow in Christian faith-living; the emphasis is on the step-by-step development of the persons as more devoted disciples and active apostles of Jesus Christ—even while they are being blessed in this relationship. More simply, Christian education is learner-leader nurturing of new beings in Christ.*

DETAILS OF DEFINITION

The Goal Is Abundant Living

The general goal of modern Christian education has been equated with the abundant life of persons. Recognizing that they desire the values of well-being for themselves and others, it seeks to help them attain those values. It is not content, however, with random or low values. While it permits some normal tendencies to find unhampered expression and requires that others must be curbed or at least redirected, it looks forward to fullness of expression in a life busy with choice activities that will be satisfying in the long run and in the highest ways. The objective guide and stimulus to its realization are such verities as the Bible and the church but there is also the inner Spirit of Christ.

Abundant life is to be interpreted with all the Christian connotations that arise from biblical associations, church traditions, and individual Christian experience. This is life as Christ would have it—the new life in Christ. It is the state into which the regenerate human spirit is born anew. It is life which finds its boon in discipleship and apostlehood. It is the life that is sometimes called fourfold, the kingdom life, the Way—the kind of life which is "found" by "losing" another kind. It is life of a type which is but foreshadowed until there is reconciliation of the human child with the divine Father by grace through faith in Jesus Christ. In its details it is a compound of the eight activities that will be mentioned later as general objectives of present-day Christian education.

The Substance Is Current Living

Modern Christian education, we have seen, deals in current experience, guided by Christian resources. Not chiefly a process of preparation for life either here or hereafter, it recognizes that the present moment has its values and that personality thrives primarily on these. It strives first, therefore, that pupils shall live richly and successfully hour by hour and day by day.

Yet thought is given to the pupil's future. Although the immediate emphasis is on the vertical section of the pupil's moving experience, there is a prime interest in the longitudinal section of his life. While Christian education busies itself about the former, it keeps concerned about the latter, just as the parent who is working daily with the present needs of a child holds always in the background of his mind his hopes for that child and shapes the present with the future in view. Christian education can hold this attitude because, if the present living of a learner is held high, the future tends to take care of itself. The pupil in his intense present experience of wholesome living fits his behavior into patterns that carry him into the future highly equipped. Actually there is no other way to equip him.

The Technique Is Performance

For its results modern Christian education looks to the truth of the old slogan, "We learn by doing," which could well be replaced as "We learn by living." It views any form of education as a co-operative learning-teaching process, the fundamental factor in learning being the performance of activities. The pupils learn to believe by believing, to trust by trusting, to serve by serving. It is the teacher's task to assist the step-by-step progress in believing, trusting, and serving. The deed is the thing!

Jesus Christ Is Savior and Lord

Throughout Christian education the ultimacy of Jesus Christ is to be recognized. Christ as God—Savior and Lord—is the acknowledged source and object of the Christian religion. He is Redeemer and Master. It is he who saves in every sense of the word; also he is the prime author of Christian doctrinal and ethical ideals whose precepts and example set the Christian's personality patterns and forms of thought, attitude, and conduct. Thus the person and work of Jesus Christ constitute norms, motives and substance for the outlook and procedure of Christian education. Its fundamental purpose is properly stated in terms of discipleship and apostlehood with him. Its methods are rightly conformed to his ways. Its basic resources are his life and teachings.

CHRISTIAN EDUCATION, SANCTIFICATION, AND EVANGELIZATION

Yet we are in peril if we overlook the other persons of triune God and neglect their works. God is also Father—the Creator and Provider. In particular, for us, God is Holy Spirit, too—the Sanctifier.

In this third person and work of God we have a particularly important concern of the Christian educator. Sanctification is being used according to E. C. Blackman in *The Interpreter's Dictionary of the Bible:* "The realization or progressive attainment of likeness to God or to God's intention for man. It may be regarded both as a status conferred by divine grace and as a goal to be aimed at."[14] Thus defined, sanctification may be called the Christian's progress in the race—a movement along the continuum toward maturity following the inaugural experience in evangelization. It stands, on the one hand, for the Holy Spirit's work by which persons grow in holiness following their regeneration. On the other hand it can mean the human experience of this work of the Spirit. Then it has to do with the increase in that new life in Christ which, always accompanied by weakness and failure, is never complete yet always subject to daily renewal. The increase, as sanctification, is an approximate theological synonym for education when considered as inward experience versus the outward, fostering work of the church. As a result, the Christian educator's favorite category of dogmatics can well be pneumatology. This *does not mean* that he will neglect Christology, including hamartology and soteriology. Educators must be always alert for that sequence of sin-guilt-repentence-forgiveness-reconciliation-renewal. It *does mean* that we shall be particularly concerned about the renewed-and-renewing-life-in-reconciliation.

This emphasis on sanctification is particularly needed at this time. Much of the writing today emphasizes redemption. We hear about the redemptive community, redemptive love, redemptive process, and more. Actually, God being triune, there are three persons corresponding to three works. These are clearly articulated in the Apostles' Creed where we confess God as the Creator, the Redeemer, and the Sanctifier. We would recognize the total person and work of triune God while we see the central position of Jesus Christ for the Christian church. Here we simply plead that Christian education, while it recognizes the significance of the second article of the Creed concerning God's work of redemption, does not forget creation (or re-creation) and will emphasize sanctification as its basic concern.

The Holy Spirit is he who calls people into his church. This raises the issue of education's relationship with evangelization. Sometimes the

[14]E. C. Blackman, "Sanctification," *The Interpreter's Dictionary of the Bible,* ed. George Arthur Buttrick (New York: Abingdon Press, 1962), R-Z, 210.

total Christianizing process is called evangelism and education is included as a phase of this process. It is better to distinguish between evangelization and education though the two may be viewed as correlative phases of evangelism if one likes. In evangelization the Christian enters the race—the Holy Spirit has called him and he is, shall we say, initiated into the church. In education, he is nurtured in his Christian status. This division may be pressed too far for the two are more like Siamese twins. So both education and evangelization are of deep concern to us and are not to be completely separated in our thinking. Yet we have an emphasis: sanctification of the evangelized within educational processes. We would recognize the total person and work of triune God while we see the central position of Jesus Christ for the Christian church.

Christian Education as Developmental Education

Unquestionably the current theory of Christian education is in the spirit of the developmental education described above at length. Yet we may wish to ask finally: "Does it meet Christian standards?" Even in the early years of this movement Dr. Bower wrote, in *Religious Education in the Modern Church,* a strong declaration that still rings true:

> It is little less than astonishing to discover how closely the technique of Jesus anticipated the best theory and practice of modern education. His placing of the supreme emphasis upon the personality, his insistence upon the central position of the growing person in the educative process, his basing his teaching upon the concrete and present experience of the learner, his insistence upon the issue of knowledge in the practical conduct of life, his organization of the school as an informal society of persons sharing a common experience, his basic assumption that we learn by doing, his admission of his disciples to responsible participation in his own work—these are almost precisely the focal points around which modern educational technique is in process of being reconstructed.[15]

[15]W. C. Bower, *Religious Education in the Modern Church* (St. Louis: The Bethany Press, 1929), p. 6.

CHAPTER III

HAVING OBJECTIVES

Providing for church schools to have, understand, serve, and reach objectives is a major activity of their leaders. The developmental education already described is a dynamic enterprise, "on the go," with an intent to arrive some place. Where? Remembering that education can mean either the result of a learning enterprise or the means employed, the question has two prongs. Primarily, what destinations will learners be aiming to reach and at what ends of the journey will leaders be working to help them arrive? Secondarily, what means shall the school be striving to make available for the attainment?

Objective is an "omnibus" word. We shall hope to escape confusion by using it only to designate purposes for educational work. Many general terms express the concept: aim, goal, outcome, purpose, result. By combining all of them, we have some such definition as this: *an objective is an educational aim, consciously understood and purposefully accepted by persons or groups as a desired outcome of endeavor, a goal to be reached, a result to be achieved.* Almost always we shall be dealing with what we shall call "personal" objectives but now and then with "organizational" ones.

THE NEED FOR OBJECTIVES

Do pupils and workers envision clearly the objectives of Christian education suggested in the definitions of Chapter II and work consciously toward them? Observation reveals widespread uncertainty. Beyond generalities, right enough in their way, a great body of church school people have been "going through the motions" with a limited consciousness of purpose. When twelve superintendents in a conference were asked to state the objectives of their work, only one made even a halting effort to respond. In the case of many teachers, someone asked them to take a class and they began to carry on the work in the way "they," the former teachers of these teachers, did it. Not seeing the angel in the marble, they just started chiseling away. Doubtless pupils have even more vague impressions about the reasons for their church school participation.

Observers who report on objectives in the church schools they visit often include statements like the following:

> The program was obviously determined by lack of objectives.
> An ample statement of purpose should be kept before all the people regularly, but isn't.
> They just teach "the lesson," that's all.

Under such conditions, desirable results are achieved largely by an over-ruling providence unless someone who established the tradition had a wise conception of the task. "Obedient purposelessness" has been a major weakness of the church school.

THE FUNCTIONS OF OBJECTIVES

Objectives can make five essential contributions toward effective Christian education.

Co-operation. They render co-operation possible. Twenty church school members, each going his own way, will scarcely accomplish anything spectacular; their separate results may even cancel each other or worse. They succeed by working as a team toward the same objectives, conforming to common aim with unity of purpose. Objectives, like lenses, can focus the disparate efforts of an individual just as they serve to co-ordinate group effort.

Economy. Objectives help to avoid error and waste. They save the time and energy of pupils and leaders who may otherwise be expending their efforts fruitlessly. As a student once put it, they keep you from "working around all day in a bushel." More than that, aimless working may produce the harmful result of disintegrated personality instead of unifying wholeness. Parents have sometimes questioned whether their children are profiting from church school attendance; a few have withdrawn their boys and girls because they considered it detrimental. This may betray a lack of the properly functioning objectives that are a necessary base for efficient learning and teaching activity.

Industry. Objectives that suggest values to be received will provide motivation to kindle the work attitude in both learners and leaders. For the athlete, the explorer, the scientist, the true worker in any realm, purpose releases power. The person who rises in the morning, knowing what he is going to do and why, goes about it with zest. That earnest vitality in church school work, for which so many have longed, may await simply a more widespread recognition of the real and important purposes which it can serve.

Standards. Objectives are standards for shaping and evaluating the various components of a school's operation. There must be anticipated outcomes for organizational, administrative, and supervisory procedures. The executive leader can build his organization carefully and administer it wisely only if objectives stand like a plumb line alongside his efforts. In his supervisory function he scarcely can devise, direct, or improve any processes until he knows what he is to produce. We cannot use a canning factory to build automobiles or revamp our manufacturing technique unless we know whether we are to build passenger cars or trucks. Teachers or other persons who construct and direct programs for pupils are similarly dependent on objectives as standards to determine the choice of materials or procedures and the sequence of their use for a session of a group, a unit, or the whole span of a pupil's curricular experience. Finally, objectives provide measures of failure or success.

Vision. "Where there is no vision the people perish," said an ancient sage (Prov. 29:18, KJV). Objectives put an essential foresight into the process of Christian education for both pupils and leaders. A church school that is not moving toward a horizon is in danger of becoming a merry-go-round. If education is the nurturing of desirable growth toward maturity, definite results cannot be expected without a clear view of the direction growth is to take. Piles of bricks and lumber, and a crew of workmen, mean little unless an architect has envisioned the prospective building.

TYPES OF OBJECTIVES

The objectives of Christian education are of many types, are expressed in various forms, and represent variant points of view. Some are stated in terms of the *learner,* others of the *leader.* There are *ultimate* objectives dealing with the final issue of the educational process and *proximate* objectives that refer to intermediate steps for the pupil as he moves towards his distant goal. *General* objectives attempt to gather up and express in perhaps a single sentence the total purpose of the process; *specific* objectives subdivide the complex. Lists of specifics may deal with half a dozen or half a thousand aspects of Christian experience; also they may apply especially to an agency or an age group. Distinctions may be made also concerning *comprehensive* and *particular* objectives or *primary* and *secondary* ones. The most significant variation among objectives concerns the *personal* versus the *organizational* type. The former designates some change which is to take place in the learner as a result of the educational process; the latter, organizational, looks to some achievement with regard to program, technique, finance, or management.

Personal objectives. While organizational objectives are important, the fundamental ones are those which state the outcome in terms of persons. Historically, these personal objectives have varied in their emphasis from age to age. At certain times the emphasis has been *ecclesiastical*—the purpose of preparing the pupil for membership in the church. Again it has been *evangelistic* with the salvation of souls in view, especially their conversion and preparation for the future life. During the nineteenth century and in many schools yet, a primary emphasis has been the *subject matter* aim of pupils well-informed in Bible, creed, church, and catechism. Still more recently *Christian character* and *social efficiency* were prominent. The present-day emphasis is on the concept of *abundant living* developed in these pages.

Organizational objectives. The following statement of objectives was pointed toward organizational achievements: "Nine goals were adopted by the congregation . . . for the year: (1) stimulating inactive members to helpful participation in the program of the church, (2) winning the unchurched of the community to church membership, (3) giving generously to the building fund, (4) continuing a special ministry to those in military service, (5) forming the new unified program for women and putting into effect certain other features of the church program, (6) organizing Scout troops for boys, (7) increasing enrollment and attendance in the Sunday school, (8) purchasing various projectors for use in visual education work, and (9) continuing generous support of benevolent objects." Such goals are needed, too, though they are secondary ones.

DETERMINATION OF OBJECTIVES

Precisely what shall the primary objectives of Christian education be?

The techniques of modern research have been let loose on a somewhat scientific determination of them. Workers at this task have held in view certain factors that should determine their substance, essence, or thrust. Other persons who deal with objectives need to keep these in mind.

Bible and Theology. While the demands of current experience deserve first place in determining objectives, "the heritages" will furnish essential guidance and substance. Of all heritages the Bible is supreme resource. It has not by any means been outmoded or reduced in value although extrabiblical materials are given a prominent place in an up-to-date curriculum. Theology too, meaning dogmatics and ethics—doctrinal teaching as to fundamental religious concepts and moral principles—is a closely related consideration. What we know about the nature and purpose of God and the destiny of man will loom large when we shape our objectives.

Christian Education. The particular character of our work is a necessary determiner, too. Only those objectives will be included that are a proper concern of a school and they will be those which enhance growth that is Christian. They will also have to suit various conditions such as staff, facilities, materials, and procedures in church schools.

Church. The church—one of the heritages though more than a heritage—provides by its history, nature, personnel, and mission a significant cluster of factors in the formation of objectives. They must be in harmony with the historic and present life of the church in its highest expressions of the faith. Participation in the body will be an essential one.

Home. Pupils live in homes that have religious influence upon them in one way or another; they have responsibilities within and for their own homes and for others. These must be recognized when objectives are established.

Persons. The learners themselves are the chief determiners. Objectives should be devised primarily in the light of their needs. Growing capacities, changing interests, and developing abilities of individuals are significant, too. Yet we are not to forget related persons, including teachers and other leaders, with their important concerns.

Public School. Church school agencies do not work alone. There is public education, also, that carries the major share of the educational load. Christian education does not need to duplicate this work; it does need to supplement and complement it. The church school can often parallel with profit the previous learnings as well as present experiences in public school.

Society. The social order at large is another determiner. A pupil undergoing Christian education lives in a cultural setting with a history and a continuity which influence him and which he will seek to shape. Objectives must recognize this twofold relationship of pupil and society.

Universe. In view of the space age developments bombarding our pupils it becomes increasingly necessary to take account of the physical universe in its scientific aspects. Objectives will recognize the great reaches of questing and learning in the physical sciences as well as the human. We need attention to both the infinitesimal and the magnitudinous of our natural habitat.

STATEMENTS OF OBJECTIVES

Under such general requirements numerous statements of the objectives of Christian education have been developed in recent decades. They represent varying educational approaches; they were prepared by various methods. Yet a remarkable consensus about their content will become evident as we see them.

General Objectives for Christian Education

Attention has properly been given to similar work in general education.

For a few instances to show the direction of that effort, we can go back to the "Cardinal Principles of Secondary Education" (1918). These dealt with activities that enter into "complete living" as distinguished from mental discipline and the acquisition of knowledge.[1] The Department of Superintendence (1928) dealt with the adjustments that an individual must make especially to self, nature, society, and God.[2] The Educational Policies Commission (1938) defined the purposes of education as self-realization, human relationships, economic efficiency, and civic responsibility.[3] The President's Commission on Higher Education (1947) cited purposes in terms of performance and behavior, not of mastering particular bodies of knowledge.[4] More recently the Horace Mann-Lincoln Institute based its curriculum design upon meeting "persistent life situations" which individuals and groups encounter in everyday living.[5] At the University of Chicago, The Committee on Human Development considered the objectives in terms of "developmental tasks" to be dealt with for reasonably happy and successful personhood.[6] A Mid-century Committee interpreted educational objectives in terms of "observable behavior."[7]

[1]U.S. Department of Interior, Bureau of Education, *Cardinal Principles of Secondary Education*. Bulletin, 1918, No. 35 (Washington: Government Printing Office, 1918).

[2]National Education Association, Department of Superintendence, *The Development of the High School Curriculum* (Washington, 1928), p. 51.

[3]National Education Association, Educational Policies Commission, *The Purposes of Education in American Democracy* (Washington: National Education Association, 1938).

[4]*Higher Education for American Democracy* (New York: Harper and Brothers, 1947), I, 50.

[5]Florence B. Stratemeyer *et al., Developing a Curriculum for Modern Living* (New York: Bureau of Publications, Teachers College, Columbia University, 1957), pp. 115, 149 ff.

[6]Robert J. Havighurst, *Human Development and Education* (New York: Longmans, Green and Company, 1953), p. 2.

[7]Nolan C. Kearney, *Elementary School Objectives* (New York: Russell Sage Foundation, 1953), pp. 7, 9, 37, 121 ff.

Clearly enough, the focus of attention has been shifting from primary concern for knowledge and mental discipline to the whole person engaged in complete living. That trend may have regressed somewhat under the initial impact of Sputnik but current objectives continue to emphasize the actual needs of individuals in a dynamic society. Properly, too, the all-around importance of fitness for group relationships is recognized increasingly. Throughout, too, "operational objectives" are of prime concern.

INTERDENOMINATIONAL WORK

Much of the earlier work for objectives in Christian education was done under the aegis of the International Council of Religious Education; since 1950 its successor, The Division of Christian Education in the National Council of Churches of Christ in the U.S.A., has been responsible. In 1928, Dr. Paul Vieth published, and thereafter the International Council promulgated, the statement most frequently quoted and widely used for three decades. The list dealt with goals in eight areas: God relationship; Jesus Christ; Christlike character; the good society; the church; the family; life philosophy; racial heritage.[8]

More recently, 1952-1958, a Special Committee on Christian Education Objectives, within the National Council's Division of Christian Education, produced *The Objectives of Christian Education: A Study Document.* It opens with a general statement of purpose and follows with six means for the attainment of it.

"The supreme purpose of Christian education is to enable persons to become aware of the seeking love of God as revealed in Jesus Christ and to respond in faith to this love in ways that will help them to grow as children of God, live in accordance with the will of God, and sustain a vital relationship to the Christian community.

"To achieve this purpose, Christian education, under the guidance of the Holy Spirit, endeavors:

"To assist persons, at each stage of development, to realize the highest potentialities of the self as divinely created, to commit themselves to Christ, and to grow toward maturity as Christian persons;
"To help persons establish and maintain Christian relationships with their families, their churches, and with other individuals and groups, taking responsible roles in society, and seeing in every human being an object of the love of God;
"To aid persons in gaining a better understanding and awareness of the natural world as God's creation and accepting the responsibility for conserving its values and using them in the service of God and of mankind;

[8]Paul H. Vieth, *The Development of a Curriculum of Religious Education* (Chicago: The International Council of Religious Education, 1930), pp. 64-74.

"To lead persons to an increasing understanding and appreciation of the Bible, whereby they may hear and obey the Word of God; and to help them appreciate and use effectively other elements in the historic Christian heritage;

"To enable persons to discover and fulfill responsible roles in the Christian fellowship through faithful participation in the local and world mission of the church."[9]

DENOMINATIONAL EFFORTS

The denominations, in designing their new curricula, have fashioned important statements. Two of these will exemplify the usual, basic agreement with that interdenominational one.

A Lutheran body presents this general objective:

. . . in accordance with God's revelation in the Old and New Testaments, in response to the Saviour's great commission, and by the power of the Holy Spirit, in order that men may live in Christ, the American Lutheran Church pledges itself in its program of parish education to teach faithfully God's truth—confronting persons with God what he has done for man, nurturing adults, youth, and children in their continued Christian growth, and guiding the Lord's disciples in their personal response and faithful witness in every area of life as they look forward to his return.

In the same document we have this pungent statement:

. . . we are to teach in such a way that the learners will get it and do something about it.[10]

The United Church of Christ announces this purpose for its curriculum:

The task of Christian education is to draw individuals into the reality of the Christian fellowship and to nurture them in the Christian faith and mission, so that, by accepting with gratitude and obedience God's forgiveness and power for new life, they will be enabled to mature as Christian persons and will become faithful participants in the mission of the church.[11]

The co-operating authors of *The Church's Educational Ministry: A Curriculum Plan,* working for several denominations, designate five areas of curriculum that suggest objectives in somewhat different dimensions:

[9]Commission on General Christian Education, *The Objectives of Christian Education* (New York: Office of Publication and Distribution, National Council of the Churches of Christ in the U.S.A., n.d.), pp. 21-22.

[10]*Foundational Statements for Curriculum Development in the A.L.C.* (n.p., n.d.), pp. 2-3.

[11]United Church Board for Homeland Ministries, *Design for Christian Education* (Philadelphia: United Church Press, n.d.), p. 1.

Life and its Setting: the Meaning and Experience of Existence.
Revelation: the Meaning and Experience of God's Self-disclosure.
Sonship: the Meaning and Experience of Redemption.
Vocation: the Meaning and Experience of Discipleship.
The Church: the Meaning and Experience of Christian Community.[12]

AN ACTIVITY STATEMENT

A listing that is in accord with the philosophy of Christian education presented in this book and will be used regularly here, grew out of still another body of study. It is stated so as to recognize (1) the learning by doing process in which the objective becomes at the same time the process, and (2) the nature of Christian education as continuous development toward what are continuing or "flying goals." It should be understood as a list of component factors in a total Christian experience which finds abundant life in the integrated system of activities they comprise. The list follows with major words arranged alphabetically; the words name entities with which a Christian learner has the relationships in which his life's activities arise.

1. Using the *Bible* fruitfully
2. Practicing effective *church* membership
3. Giving supreme loyalty to *God*
4. Maintaining discipleship with *Jesus*
5. Employing processes and products of *nature* beneficently
6. Co-operating in good will with *others*
7. Having personal acquaintance with *religion*[13]
8. Attaining the highest realization of the *self*

Age Group Objectives

The general objectives that pertain comprehensively must finally be related to particular times, places, and persons. There is need, most notably, for age group differentiation. Some learnings may be more ephemeral but many are continual. For example, an individual is developing his idea of God throughout life. Yet even that lifetime learning will have its special phases and significance at, for example, age ten.

The most complete statement of age group objectives is a denominational one, prepared in connection with the Long Range Program of Lutheran Boards of Parish Education.[14] It deals with each year of life

[12]*The Church's Educational Ministry: A Curriculum Plan* (St. Louis, Missouri: The Bethany Press, 1965), p. 16.

[13]This item, not usually included in such lists, refers to an integrated experience of total personal religion along with an ecumenical outlook that includes intelligent relationships with people of other faiths.

[14]W. Kent Gilbert, *The Age Group Objectives of Christian Education* (Philadelphia, 1958).

to age eighteen, then treats older youth and three areas of adulthood. It is organized according to understandings, attitudes, and action patterns that arise in the pupils' relationships with God (The Father, The Son, The Holy Spirit), Church, Bible, Fellow Man (individual, group), Physical world, Himself.

In 1958, a committee headed by Dr. G. Campbell Wyckoff within the National Council's Division of Christian Education produced *The Objective of Christian Education for Senior High Young People*. It consists of one inclusive statement and a list of five learning tasks through which that objective will be approached. The general statement follows:

> The objective of Christian education is to help persons to be aware of God's self disclosure and seeking love in Jesus Christ and to respond in faith and love—to the end that they may know who they are and what their situation means, grow as sons of God rooted in the Christian community, live in the spirit of God in every relationship, fulfill their common discipleship in the world, and abide in the Christian hope.

These are the five learning tasks that pertain:

> Listening with growing alertness to the gospel and responding to it in faith and love.
> Exploring the whole field of relationships in light of the gospel.
> Discovering meaning and value in the field of relationships in the light of the gospel.
> Personally appropriating that meaning and value.
> Assuming personal and social responsibility in the light of the gospel.[15]

OBJECTIVES IN A LOCAL CHURCH SCHOOL

Objectives can function only in particular churches, schools, and classes of individual persons who are undergoing Christian nurture. So the ultimate question becomes, what is to be the particular objective for and of this boy or girl, youth, man or woman here in this learning situation now?

General Objectives

A beginning at that more immediate and personal adaptation can be made by developing a statement of general objectives for the whole local school. There are four steps to that process: *formulation, adoption, publication, dedication.*

[15]Division of Christian Education, *The Objective of Christian Education for Senior High Young People* (New York: Office of Publication and Distribution, National Council of the Churches of Christ in the U.S.A., 1958), pp. 32 ff.

The executive may arouse sentiment for the *formulation* of such a document but preferably will let a demand for it come from his fellow workers. When once they have sensed the need, he may lead them to authorize a special committee which should include older pupils. The work may also be initiated and supervised by the congregational committee on Christian education. Any such group will study the various available documents, especially denominational ones. Then it will choose or revise one; best of all, it will create an original statement.

Whatever the method employed by the committee, its findings should be reported back to the entire group of workers. They will consider, amend, and revise if they see fit. Then there should be a wholehearted *adoption* by the school.

What is here called *publication* of the document is a continuous task. Every worker in the school should have a copy—not stored away in a memory book but kept available for frequent reference. It should be at hand, for example, to guide the teacher when preparing for class sessions. Parents and older pupils of the school, too, should have copies. Wall charts, mimeographed sheets, printed cards, and church bulletins are other means of keeping the objectives in view.

A school with objectives not functioning is little better than a school without them. It may be fully dressed to go somewhere but it is not yet on the way. The final step necessary is to secure every worker's constant *dedication* to their realization. Dedication may be certified by signing the school's constitution or a covenant for working in the school if that practice is followed. The objectives may be worked into the annual installation service for workers.

Specific Objectives

A school will need to determine specific objectives in the light of its general and comprehensive statement. These may be of the many types listed below. They will be suggested to no small extent by the curricular materials in use. Pupils, as far as possible, should have a part in the determination.

FOR AGENCIES AND AGE GROUPS

Numerous divisions of objectives among the several agencies of a church school will be necessary. In most churches for a long time to come the Sunday church school will carry the fundamental minimum of educational development while other agencies provide enrichment opportunities. One writer suggests for weekday work, a biblical emphasis; for Sunday sessions, churchmanship; for the vacation school, cooperative Christian living.

The objectives discussed thus far will have to be "broken down" for the various departments or age groups of the school. No piece of clothing will fit every person or any person always. Interdenominational or denominational patterns can be followed or a process of production similar to the fourfold one described above may be employed. Curricular literature will also provide guide lines.

FOR UNITS AND SESSIONS

The most vital need of all is to have definite objectives for each curricular unit and each session of the school, indeed for each person involved in the learning situation. Some individual objectives will be largely in the form of personal understandings between the teacher and the pupil.

Units are properly selected, planned, and conducted in the light of problems, interests, or needs of the group. Where printed materials are used, as they will be in most schools, serious attention will likely have been given already to specific objectives. Where units are planned creatively this kind of attention will need to be given by the group and its leader. The necessary unit objectives can be fashioned out of personal and social situations or selected from the printed materials for a particular emphasis in the light of those local situations. They should be subject to change, yet kept clearly in view by all members of the group as they proceed with the unit. They should also have positive relation to the total curricular program and the general objectives of the school.

Success or failure for all the effort with objectives will depend upon their utilization in the recurring sessions of the school. To say that pupils must always be lucidly conscious of their exact objectives, as they engage for example in a service of worship, would be absurd. It is more absurd to say that they need no clear-cut and continuous knowledge of purpose. As for leaders, every session pattern, whether written or prepared mentally, should be headed with a statement of the aim. Perhaps it is a worship service for which the statement may be, "The aim today is that these worshipers shall grow in the kindling and expressing of their trust in God." A teacher of a class may state in his session pattern, "Today the pupils are to be finding help for emulating Joseph's spirit of forgiveness more fully."

SPECIALS

National church bodies may have special objectives to recommend, perhaps annually. Locally a particular community problem or church situation may arise to suggest a special objective of some sort: reducing juvenile delinquency in the community; providing a recreational program for youth; resolving theological differences among the adults; introducing new forms and materials of worship; developing racial brotherhood. Some church schools have annual retreats in which they outline their special objectives for the year. A considerable number may be of the organizational type, goals for developing context in which personal goals may be attained more effectively.

The Pupil's Part in Determining Objectives

It has been said throughout that objectives are to be conceived in terms of helping pupils, also be related to their needs and graded to their capacities. Consequently, they ought to be determined as far as possible by the pupils themselves or in lively co-operation with their leaders. Many a church school leader would be shocked if he were to hear how far away from his pupils' interests his program has drifted! Pupil participation at this point would not only keep the program vital, it would also enlist co-operation in achieving the objectives. The total effect might be educational effectiveness beyond anything yet attained.

A junior high pupil was discussing his Sunday church school experience with his father. "We're having lessons about Moses and the plagues again," he said complaining. "I think Moses was a great leader of people, but we never go into that. I'd like to have some lessons on how to live. Instead, we just study those things that never happen any more anyhow. Why don't they let you study what you're interested in?" That lad was ready to sit in a planning session to determine objectives for a unit of study if no more. His general point of view should guide his leaders in planning for all his learning activities.

CRITERIA FOR OBJECTIVES

We can be overambitious with our objectives. Unless wholesome development proceeds at an appropriate pace, harmful frustration can result. Besides, we cannot possibly do everything in our precious little time; so, what we choose to attempt should be the best.

When we select among possible objectives, such criteria as those in the list below can be applied. While we may not secure a perfect score for many important ones, the score should be high or the proposed objective should be omitted.

Is it *Christian*: promising to have religious values in harmony with the Christian way of living?

Is it *correlated*: pertinent for past and present experiences in home, school, community, church, and church school?

Is it *fertile*: rich in leading on-and-out value; anticipating future experience while relevant to the present?

Is it *graded*: suited to the capacity and interest of the individual or group; difficult enough to challenge and easy enough for success?

Is it *practicable*: feasible under school conditions of time, equipment, and leadership?

Is it *progressive*: valuable in relation to changing culture, even creative while true to the heritages?

Is it *significant*: related in an important way to the larger aspects of life; not adequately provided for elsewhere?

Is it *social*: of general interest and concern to the affected groups?

Is it *vital*: considered worthwhile by students and teachers; closely related to situations and needs in present living?

Is it *worthy*: productive for growth in relation to method though chiefly as to substance?

To equip one of the giant new aircraft with the latest engines of propulsion, load it with cargo and passengers, then send it out without flight plans would simply not be done. Equally, in the church school, it is not enough to be leaving the place of arrival to chance. Objectives deserve consideration in all reaches of the church school, by all the personnel.

More than that the consideration must be continuous. The desired results of Christian education can never be stated with absolute exactness; religion is too complex for that. Neither can they be viewed in terms of a completely finished product. No person has ever envisioned, much less attained, full Christian stature. Besides, human personality, society, and the understanding of Christian living all are forever in the process of becoming. Concepts are modified; understandings grow; phrasing can be improved; new emphases arise; change is thrust upon us. Any list of objectives is subject to incompleteness and fluidity.

PART TWO

ORGANIZATION AND ADMINISTRATION OF PUPILS AND STAFF

CHAPTER IV

UNDERTAKING THE TASK

The church school has been viewed in its historical perspective and present status; the theory of Christian education currently shaping its practice has been examined; its objectives have had special attention. With this background there can be more specific answers to that basic question of our study: *What are the activities of a church school worker, either pastor, director of Christian education, superintendent, teacher, or other leader; also how can he be most effective in them?*

In this chapter and several to follow, we are dealing quite specifically with executive leaders rather than with teachers or other personnel engaged directly in the learning-teaching program. While the teaching type of leadership is not out of mind anywhere—the next few pages pertain closely—it will receive special attention later, particularly in Chapters IX to XII on program. Conversely, in those four chapters it will be remembered that an executive leader organizes and administers a school precisely for the program's effectiveness and he must supervise it.

BEING A LEADER

Recent years have brought us "new understandings of leadership."[1] Most of these have come from the military and industrial worlds. Since the contributions are being written into our church school publications they have begun to influence teaching as well as executive leadership.

Groups and Leaders

The new leadership practices grow chiefly out of what we have learned about groups—what a group is, how it works best and why. More can be said in Chapter X but we must begin here.

[1] For more on this subject see *New Understandings of Leadership* by Ross and Hendry (Association Press, 1957) to which indebtedness is gratefully acknowledged.

A true group is more than an aggregation of individuals; it is an inclusive entity constituted by the merger of individuals who are acting with a degree of common purpose. Such groups are best formed around tasks. While they can, and should, include personal development within their processes, the better church school groups will be not merely fields for cultivation but task forces. This accords with the concept of the church as the continuously ministering body of Christ.

How do such groups accomplish their work most effectively?

More is known now about group process. A principal datum is that results depend greatly on group dynamics and how they are ministered. A possible error must be circumvented immediately. By "group dynamics" we do not mean to name a handful of techniques. Group dynamics are the personal and interpersonal forces at work in a group. The term denotes what is happening by way of dynamism, pressures within social interaction and their results. Some of the dynamics can be helpful, others destructive. Effective leadership in a group requires control—not the gross manipulation but the management or perhaps one can say better the channeling—of these forces so that an objective is reached with the minimum of hindrance and the maximum of facilitation. If group dynamics are the winds of the group process, leaders set the sails. The effective leader is one who sets them so that the group is driven to its goal, not on the rocks.

What A Leader Is

Groups must have leaders; nothing has been discovered to suggest that they are unnecessary. One or more will be appointed, elected, chosen in some manner. Yet, in the newer view, leadership is a function of the group itself; we speak now of shared or group-centered leadership. Sometimes also, leadership is said to be a function of the situation in which the group finds itself. All this is to say that, while the group has a designated person as its leader, all its members are to share in the leadership as the situation shapes the need. From time to time one member will emerge as leader in a particular phase of the developing task, then another. This does not mean that the designated leader ever abdicates; it means only that from time to time he recedes into the background because the situation suggests this. Even there, however, he may exercise certain delegated responsibilities while he holds himself in readiness to be prominent again when he is needed in that way to help the group accomplish its purpose.

Once we thought that the necessary qualities of such a person were a somewhat mystical endowment, a gift of birth; a leader was a leader!

Perhaps there are innate character traits which do tend toward leadership in general yet the "great man theory" has been discounted. Now, when leadership is being recognized as a function of the group, we realize that anyone may have some of the necessary qualities. Likewise, because leadership is also a function of the situation, persons with differing characteristics fit the procedures of a given group at a given time. All together, leadership is not a matter of generalized character traits only; a leader must be a person fitted to a particular group and situation. Important for leadership selection and development, this allows us to believe that while the qualities of leadership with which one is born may be significant so is the kind of conduct that can be cultivated.

What are some forms of basic personality and types of cultivable behavior that mark leaders? The desirable leader is one who can be a member of the group, though beyond it, too. He has empathy, can identify with others and merge into fellowship relations with them. He will be considerate, with a practical readiness and ability to help. While he needs what we call geniality and enthusiasm, emotional stability is requisite also. General intelligence is not necessarily a major factor; competence for the particular task is the larger need. An ability to share his role, to step back when that seems indicated, to delegate— these are extremely significant. Foresight, imagination, and creativity belong also. For predominant mention, a strong leader needs a keen sense of purpose with which he can inspire and direct his group toward a goal that will be achieved as they work together with him.

What A Leader Does

The threefold responsibility of a leader is to act so that the group maintains itself, the task is completed, and welfare has been served. The task is properly a total group enterprise in which each one does his part when the times appear for him to serve, the designated leader constantly facilitating the achievement of the goals of each member and of all. One of his particular tasks is to establish the structure of the group's organization as trackage for the task's completion; he will also provide for a step-by-step schedule. He may often need to show people how to do what they want to do. He may sometimes have to furnish initiative but the preferred role is that of channeling group motivation. A related activity of no mean proportion will be to facilitate communication. Members of a group must understand each other, yet the lack of understanding about what seems to be very clear is sometimes amazing.

Another significant responsibility of the designated leader is the maintenance of the group—not that this is his task alone. The group must not break down but rather grow into greater cohesiveness. A leader will be alert at all times to see that the groupness persists, that tensions are made creative, that fellowship prevails. Basically, he must provide for satisfaction within the membership.

Here effective leaders will need to pay particular attention to individual roles. Certain types of individual behavior in groups have been identified as nonfunctional. A group may have the kinds of members who can be called "aggressors," "blockers," "playboys" or "playgirls," "dominators," "recognition-seekers." The major leader, with the aid of other members, will attempt to turn these persons into helpers so that they do not hinder the group's purpose unduly or spoil its co-operative fellowship, while they grow individually. Correspondingly, he will foster those who are playing such functional roles as: "initiator," "contributor," "opinion-seeker," "co-ordinator," "harmonizer."

Through such means a leader brings his group to the ultimate objective: welfare.

Variables in Leadership Practice

The nature of a group will shape the leadership requirements profoundly. A group's dynamics are particularly significant. Some groups will generate more tension than others; this may rise to sufficient height to make the goal almost unattainable, or it may be controlled so as even to contribute to maintenance, task, and welfare. Yet dynamism is only one of the many group variables. Some groups will require a more highly complex structure than others because of the task. Size is influential too; there are those who feel that for ideal work a group of ten is sufficient. In a larger group there is more demand on the leader but also more acceptance of his direction. In larger groups there must be more focus on the task and less on personal development; also the procedure will likely be more formal.

It has been hinted already that the basic attitudes of the group's members will be significant—what they expect, how they react to authority, who they are and what they want or like. Their previous experience will count. Some may be accustomed to working under certain conditions; they may be awaiting orders or they may be independent and so will chafe under authority. The life span of a group, whether short-term or long-term will have something to do with the kind of leadership needed. Whether the group is a compulsory or a voluntary one will also be a factor. Leadership must be adjusted to all such conditions.

Types of Leadership

It is customary to say that there are two types of leadership: democratic and authoritarian. Sometimes two extremes, one at either end of the continuum are mentioned: laissez-faire and dictatorial. Both are to be avoided in practice. Which, then, is better, authoritarian or democratic? If we represent democratic leadership on the left and authoritarian on the right of a diagram it would seem that the ideal for Christian leadership ought to be somewhere to the left of center. Much will depend, we have seen above, on the nature of the group and its task, especially on its previous experience. In general, the tendency now is to recognize the validity of a judicious variation. Sometimes more authoritarianism will be needed while the trend is toward as much of the democratic as possible under the circumstances. Perhaps the profile of a leader's progress will be a jagged line tending toward the left although it will sometimes swing to the right. Summarizing, there will be different leadership configurations depending upon the variables while the ideal remains in the democratic area.

GENERAL LEADERSHIP ACTIVITIES

Within the many conditions of "being a leader" there are ten general activities that will overlap the many specific items to be mentioned subsequently:

Counseling: A leader is at the wheel with many levers of direct control within reach. Chiefly, though, he advises, counsels, and suggests as workers and pupils face and solve their problems.

Deciding: He will have decisions to make though he shares them.

Doing: He cannot work solely through others. Some duties are exclusively his; he executes these responsibly.

Helping: He has the attitude of helper—helping pupils and especially co-workers personally and by means of his school.

Inspiring: He strives to meet that perennial need for morale by motivating and energizing people to keep busy and loyal.

Observing: He has eyes to see what his own pupils and workers, also others, are doing; he uses his observations to improve the school.

Promoting: He is a promoter in the best sense of the word; he handles the whole enterprise so that it expands for increasing ministry.

Sharing: He is not a one-man operator. Instead he shares his duties but more, he participates with other participants.

Studying: He is a student, as is proper of any member of any school; he studies the school, its people and its program, also the stuff of its enterprise.

Socializing: He works to achieve that happy situation found in a school that is, throughout, co-operative and united in fellowship and service.

ORGANIZING, ADMINISTERING, AND SUPERVISING

An executive leader of a church school serves in a threefold managerial capacity. He is *organizer, administrator,* and *supervisor*. When organizing, he is setting up in orderly form and maintaining in order the human machinery of staff and pupils who constitute the school. While administering, he is seeing to it that the machinery operates smoothly and efficiently. In supervising, he seeks to improve the processes so that the product of the machinery will be constantly better. Each of these activities will be defined more exactly soon.

First, though, it seems necessary to face the issue about the possible shape of things tomorrow. The growth of church programs with the rapid expansion of the accompaniments which have been called "machinery" is alarming clergymen and laymen alike. Already they complain that more than 50 percent of a pastor's time and too much lay time go to the maintenance of the machine. There are those who would simplify the programs and disband the ecclesiastical structure. However, there is little reason to think that any such revolutionary change will occur soon. Rather, there are massive pressures in an opposite direction. We shall likely need larger church programs and these will require more structure, not less.

Our particular concern is for church schools that may be responsible for at least half of the organizational, administrative, and supervisory task in the average church. Will the Christian educational program be reduced and the structure for it eliminated? Only a larger educational program will meet the future needs of the church. Cultural, including ecclesiastical, conditions, local and world-wide, will demand it. Church schools are becoming larger and will continue to do so. Population growth and consequent church growth is one simple reason. Another is the tendency to merge into larger units for at least supposed economy and better results. Greater scope of program with more time allotted to it is still another reason. Enlarged youth and especially adult programs, weekday as well as Sunday programs, are particular needs that will be met. It would seem that structure must inevitably expand, not contract.

Already a church school may have an enrollment of thousands and require hundreds of staff members although many have less than a hundred members. In any case, it is challenged to provide a program with the necessary structure. Already, too, executives have innumerable activities. Here are just a few, suggesting the scope and diversity:

Set up organizational patterns	Manage expenditures
Formulate policies	Operate an adequate record system
Work out program details	Recruit new leaders
Foster leadership education	Plan room assignments
Evaluate work of leaders	Arrange time schedules

These managerial activities and the many others can be classified in those three categories: organizing, administering, and supervising. They overlap, of course, and are in addition to what is specifically leadership in teaching.

Organizing

Organizing confronts an executive leader with two prerequisites. First, he must possess personal qualities with knowledge, attitudes, and skills such that people accept his leadership and share his responsibilities willingly. Second, his must be a dedicated and co-operative group that holds a basic faith and purpose in common. This leader and this group together must provide a structure, often called an organization. Sometimes a new one must be set up; usually an existing one is undergoing constant reorganization to meet new demands or effect improvement. The simplest organization would be just two persons working together toward a common goal and finding satisfaction in it. Obviously a church school cannot be so simple. Responsible parties, principally the executive leader, must provide a systematic arrangement of learners and leaders, placed in vertical and horizontal relationships according to a pattern that serves the learners' needs as it expedites them toward their objectives. Organization is usually guided by congregational and church school constitutions that should define the place of Christian education, outline the principal features of management, and mention outstanding procedures. The details of this task will appear in many chapters, especially the next.

Administering

Administering the organization is a kaleidoscopic task in which the executive performs the myriad activities of seeing that the purposes of the operation are actualized through the church school structure as an instrumentality. As another way of putting the matter, it is facilitating the activities of the entire school personnel—staff and students. It may also be described as managing the operations of the church school with the aid of such devices as a manual of operation, staff meetings, bulletins, memoranda, and personal advising. Again, it is employing procedures that will be discussed in following chapters in this Part Two and in Parts Four and Five.

Supervising

In his supervisory activity the executive deals with standards of product and focuses on production techniques. It takes place indirectly through more effective organizational and administrative activities. Its direct relationship, however, is to the details of procedure in the learning-teaching process. This aspect of an executive's responsibility will be defined more precisely and technically in Chapters VII and IX through XII. Briefly for the present, it means working with teachers and similar staff members for larger effectiveness in the curricular program, especially by means of session visitations.

PRACTICING CORRECT GENERAL PRINCIPLES

Just as there are principles of good government and of good business management, there are principles for good church school organization, administration, and supervision. Five will be mentioned.

Principle A. Keep the School a Church School

This dual topic has two emphases: keep the school a *church* school and keep it a church *school*.

Chapter I described the church school as a congregation working at its educational task. The school, therefore, should be under the control of the official board—of whatever name, "church council" will be used here—or the church school committee which the council appoints. The school's officers will be responsible to, and report to, those authorities. The program must be in harmony with and contribute fully towards the entire congregational program with its chief business the nurturing of the members. The pastor of the church will be the pastor of the school also. In return, the school can expect the entire church organization to recognize its vital importance, make full use of its function, support it with finances, and regard it with loyalty.

That church emphasis should be maintained; so should the educational one. Any leader is an individual who is guiding people. A church school leader is taking people somewhere with respect to Christian educational objectives. As an educator, the executive is dealing with people, especially the learning-teaching efforts of pupils with their teachers and officers. That relationship demands that he stress personal rather than organizational ends. His concern is for pupils who mean more to him than books, rules, or buildings. He is concerned with workers, too, whose Christian development should be more important to him than their promotion of his most cherished organizational plans. So a church school executive is both a churchman and a schoolman whose vocation is the Christian education of the persons under his care, fully within the church relationship and for the church's mission.

Principle B. Recognize the Purposes of Organization

Here we must observe that "organization" has more than one meaning. As verb it means an activity of organizing. As noun, it means the result of that activity, a structure.

A group can be "organized to death." This threat appears when the organization (noun) is unnecessarily complex, when simple processes are delayed by red tape, when the organization becomes an end itself instead of a means to render a service. By such errors organization (verb) can defeat its purpose and cease to be useful, if not a barnacle. Nevertheless, both the structure and the activity are necessary for at least two reasons.

First Reason for Organization. Organization—the verb or the noun —is *essential for group action,* action that affords opportunities which cannot be made available by individual effort. It gets the right people together in the right way to do the right things. It provides the means for pooling and using resources, distributing labor, arranging horizontally and vertically for leading and following, definitely fixing responsibilities with relationships. It masses effort at the necessary times and places, renders a united front possible, makes for continuity of programs. The group action thus made possible by organization provides for larger experience and greater service. In Christian education the four aspects of the curriculum—study and instruction, worship, fellowship, or service—require a group setting for their full operation.

Second Reason for Organization. As a second reason for organization, there are *values in organizational experiences* themselves—Christian educational values—particularly when the pattern and procedure make democratic involvement possible. Organization provides for people to fit into a program, to respond to expectations, to carry out responsibilities in and for the group. Such experiences contribute notably to the development of Christian personality that is to live more abundantly in a Christian community.

These, then, are two purposes of organization: (1) to render group action more effective in other educational results; (2) to provide in the organization itself an educational medium. Church school leaders will keep both in view especially because of the peril that organization, not carefully examined as to purpose, will be stressed for its own sake.

Principle C. Guide the School by Its Objectives

Both the general and the specific objectives of a church school will determine leaders' means, materials, methods, and measures.

Means. St. Paul's Church was planning an addition to its church school building. Should there be a fire place in the youth room? The young people wanted it; they had subscribed to the building fund and felt that their wishes should be recognized in these tangible terms. They argued that their discussion groups could be more informal, hence more productive, in a setting of fellowship around a fire. Older members of the church felt that this is not the way to spend a church's money. Should there be a fireplace in the new St. Paul's building? Yes, if it will advance the youth of the church toward those stated goals of a church school. Objectives should determine means.

Materials and Methods. Objectives properly determine materials and methods. One unquestionable objective in every church school is the growth of pupils in more effective church membership. But what is meant by effective church membership? Is the ideal member a staid, reasonably loyal, contributing attendant at most of the services of the church? Or is he a thoughtful and creative student of church affairs, intelligent as well as devoted in worship and aggressively active in the other enterprises of the church? It requires little imagination to conceive how the types of materials used and procedures employed in the church school should differ according to the purposes.

Measurements. What are the commonly accepted measures of church school success? Judging by the usual evidences they are quantitative ones, expressed by statistics of enrollment, attendance, offering, and the like. Probably not many church school staffs sit down at the end of the year to report the spiritual progress of their pupils. The Holy Spirit has been at work, with results in Christian growth. Spiritual temperature in the school has arisen appreciably; Mary has grown this way, John that way. A sound vision of such real objectives should determine the leader's measures as well as the means, materials, and methods to be used toward their accomplishment.

Principle D. Embody Essential Virtues

In his organizational, administrative, and supervisory work, a church school leader will stress five attributes:

Adaptability. An effective school must be adapted to the nature and needs of a particular group. There are general patterns to be followed, of course, but every church school is somewhat custom-made for a situation. While a program must take into account the ways in which learning takes place generally, it demands finally a creative adaptation to local concerns. The leader has a general background of understanding plus a particular knowledge of his own school as it is and a vision of what it could be. Then he nudges it toward that particular ideal.

Democracy. A church school in which there is consensus for all the leader's practices may be an attractive goal. Yet there are times when he must be sure he is right and go ahead. There are always those who resist change. The ideal leader tries to overcome resistance graciously but firmly, even as he expects to accomplish it slowly. He acts when necessary while democracy remains his goal—the sharing of plans, purposes, and effort by all parties, not a centralization of authority. Participants will have as much voice as possible within the dictates of wisdom and effectiveness.

Flexibility. The form and procedure of a school should permit adjustments to change. Every leader finds changes desirable with the coming of new pupils, new assistants, new programs; teachers should be alert to new and better ways. Consequently a leader will preserve maximum flexibility in order to meet these conditions. He will also provide maximum freedom for his workers and pupils to exercise individual differences. Specific rules are not to be exercised beyond their reason for being. The ideal is flexibility versus fixity on one hand and chaos on the other.

Simplicity. The church school leader seeking the largest returns for the least expenditure has no use for purposeless bric-a-brac. He exercises economy in organization with regard to the number of workers and meetings; he conserves the time and energy of his assistants. Values determine the structure, not the reverse. Practice is based on clear needs faced and met as simply as possible. The leader uses the most direct and efficient procedure; he does not mistake machinery for production or mere activity for achievement.

Practicability. The final measure of every organization is its working success. A leader of a successful organization must find the test of his principles in practice. So he will strive always to have a demonstrable reason for what he is doing. He has seen a thing done or has thought it through to its likely conclusion until he feels sure it will work.

Principle E. Employ Christian Educational Procedures

Every executive has the major duty of keeping the spirit of his purpose within the details of his processes. An important instance is the quality of his dealing with his workers who, actually, are not only his assistants but also in some respect his pupils. Thus another of his responsibilities is to deal with the staff so that desirable religious results are achieved. He selects a candidate with consideration for the religious good of that individual. He enlists a worker by appealing to his religious motives. In developing a worker he aims to foster that worker's spirituality, not only to improve his techniques. His supervisory counseling with workers' problems will be opportunities for spiritual as well as technical guidance. Committee work and public meetings will be shaped toward religious growth.

TAKING HOLD TO IMPROVE

An earnest leader who keeps reading the current literature on his work and observes outstanding schools will surely feel that his school can be improved. No church school ever has reached a zenith; there will always be goals ahead. Further, under the accelerating change in general culture and ecclesiastical affairs, there will likely be increasing need to reorganize, administer in new ways, supervise with regard to new materials and methods.

In most cases there will be obstacles. A frequent one is undue conservatism in the congregation. Many people distrust the newer ways of Christian education although other millions are waiting for leadership in these new directions. Tradition lays a heavy hand on many aspiring leaders. "We always have done it this way," they say, "why change?" In some places the trouble is sheer inertia. Expense may be a real handicap despite the fact that much can be done without great financial outlay. Lack of vision and, elsewhere, discouragement are potent forces. Besides, people so often oppose because they do not understand.

What is to be done?

Several of the one hundred writers of the letters mentioned in the Preface were asked: "How would you advise a novice to take hold to improve a Sunday church school?" Although they were thinking largely of a new pastor just coming into a congregation, and of Sunday church school work, the views apply widely. Their replies are mingled in the seven suggestions that follow.

Step 1: Secure and Maintain Solid Support

A church school leader cannot go it alone for improvement. "The leader's job is to develop an *esprit de corps;* he should conduct himself so that others will catch his spirit and want to improve." His school, usually his whole congregation, must be with him; he needs ordinarily to be working within the general trends of Christian education everywhere. In all matters of improvement it is necessary to "get everybody interested in making progress" and then to follow the leader.

The winning of confidence is essential. As one respondent has it, "When the respect and confidence of officers and teachers are won, desired improvements may be effected gradually with their co-operation." A particular way of winning the confidence of a constituency has been emphasized: "Remember that the church school has been functioning and doing lots of good. Be appreciative of all that has been done in the past." "Be friendly and appreciative of all the good things you see your colleagues doing." Especially important, the leader who wishes to secure support will be slow about voicing negative criticism of former leaders and of older equipment and procedures; there are those who may have labored valiantly for them and still like them. His purpose now is to harness the goodwill and effort that produced the present situation for co-operation in taking the next steps.

When confidence has elicited support, it must be maintained. The basic way to maintain support as well as gain it will be educational, of course. A leadership development program may be the best place to start. The executive can reach his constituency also through the regular sessions of the school and appropriate special services. A visiting speaker may reinforce his point of view. The proper use of Christian Education Week may help. Back of all else a church school leader will be sure he has his pastor's co-operation. They, best of all, can bring pupils, parents, and local workers into an improvement program.

Step 2: Work Co-operatively

A leader who wishes to improve a school will need to "be democratic, not autocratic." This involves more than just consulting and securing the approval of those who have responsibility. It means taking people into the game early and bringing them along from first to last. In a preliminary study, if not earlier, officers, teachers, and others who are anxious for change have been located. This can be a nuclear group who will enlist other supporters for the cause. All will continue to study and plan together. Always, plans that have arisen spontaneously will have the best chance to succeed. As one writer puts it wisely, "imposed change is not growth."

Step 3. Proceed Slowly

Church school leadership is not a job for either a revolutionary or an arch conservative. This work must go step by step though steps can be taken; one proceeds, but slowly. As one man wrote: "Do not be in too much hurry to change anything. Unless the situation requires immediate and radical treatment (and I believe such cases are quite rare) it may be that a few months, or a year, carrying on in the old way will injure no one."

In modification, not denial, of such statements, a school may be expecting its new leader to remedy some condition at once. When a situation is crying for prompt attention it is wise to act immediately. This will assure people that things are going to be better under the new leader and inspire confidence for following him further.

Step 4. Study the Situation

Ordinarily action should be preceded by an examination of past and present with a forecast for the future. Only by thorough study can the best means, policies, and plans be discovered. This requirement was mentioned by every leader who wrote on the subject of improvement. The widely varied suggestions included four principal ones.

Consider thoroughly the community and constituency. The particular church should have careful attention, beginning perhaps with a study of its constitution. Get acquainted with the school, its officers, teachers, departments, classes, pupils, as well as the equipment. Also, become thoroughly familiar with the program of the school including all the literature used in it.

Make a survey using interdenominational or denominational "standards." Some denominations have a self-survey instrument for a church school; this is a wholesome device for many reasons. As a principal one, it enlists the responsible and interested persons of the school itself.

Use the available resources in persons and publications. This will include the constant study of recommended books on Christian education and the reading of such monthly publications as the denominational church school publications and the *International Journal of Religious Education*.

Consult interdenominational workers such as the county or city officers and secretaries, similarly, the denominational field staff. Closely related: "Visit," writes a correspondent, "the finest church schools of your denomination and of others in the neighborhood. Pick up all the best points you find and endeavor to use them; see all the bad points and avoid those."

One pastor wrote this commendable precaution: "Be as analytical as the situation requires, but . . . watch out for the 'paralysis of analysis.' Better to make one or two improvements on the basis of your findings than to wait until you feel you know about everything and then do nothing."

Step 5. Plan in Detail

Building a tower without careful preparation (Luke 14:28, 29) is no more foolish than attempting to develop a vital Christian faith in persons of any age without regularly and adequately planning their program. The step is well summarized in this statement: "The most important thing is to know with a certainty where we are taking our followers. The second is to have a process or procedure by which our goals will be accomplished. This requires a plan, probably a long-range one with intermediate steps."

Extensive planning, such as for a building, begins properly with that study of the situation that includes some forecasting of the future. In this process the problem is defined and possible solutions begin to appear. Decision-making follows on the basis, probably, of alternative plans. Acceptance of a final plan is a crucial step. For far-reaching improvements it should have been submitted for suggestions by outstanding authorities in church school work. Then all the responsible local groups may revise it to satisfy as much justifiable criticism as possible. Those who properly act officially on such matters will give the final approval.

Step 6. Select a Point of Attack

It is often necessary to be satisfied with step-by-step progress in which parts of the overall plan are held in abeyance. So, after basic planning, a next step is to select the items that are to have first attention. Certain achievements are impossible except as a culmination of intermediate ones. There are points in which a beginning can be made. After success in the first enterprise, further ones can be completed and the whole goal reached by a succession of smaller steps. This is true particularly when large sums of money are required.

Probably there are very few schools that never tried to increase enrollment and attendance or improve physical equipment. Leaders too seldom, however, go on to the more important tasks of providing better leadership education, reconstructing the organizational setup, improving programs of instruction and study, providing better services of worship, introducing a larger program of service, offering larger fellowship opportunities, enlarging the whole program of educational work in the congregation including more time to be spent at it. All these are insistent demands and many are worthy of priority within the church school's program for improvement.

Step 7. Complete the Enterprise

Implementation is the "proof of the pudding" and the point at which the dish is sometimes spoiled. Careful planning should alleviate many of the common difficulties. Closely related, however, is this idea: "Be careful not to tackle too much at one time. It is better to do a thorough job and gain the support of the constituency for further improvement." Most important of all, a leader dare not grow weary in well doing. Some are constituted so that it is more fun to plan than to see change through to its conclusion. A still more difficult thing is to plod in the prosaic task of employing changed conditions continuously for the effective result that had been planned. Sometimes a plan will involve many steps. Then a time schedule for the various phases will need to be provided.

MEETING PERSONAL STANDARDS

As an undergirding for all steps toward improvement, several writers have voiced a sentiment that one expressed as follows: "Keep your big purpose before you—making the gospel effective in the lives of those who comprise your constituency. Never forget people; never forget the goals you are seeking in persons." It must be added that results in the lives of persons are strongly affected by a leader's personal influence. Thus is can be said that the first requisite of any Christian leader's work is to be himself at his possible best—just as a person though a competent one. Nowadays we rightly rate highly what may be called "relationship education," the informal and often wordless influence of a person upon persons.

Professional, General

There are standards of personal fitness to be met by all church school leaders—in this case, the executive. The first of three series may be called general professional standards:

Keeps growing as to the nature and purpose of his work.
Has a contagious enthusiasm for the job he has undertaken.
Uses creative imagination but gives careful attention to details.
Provides on his own part good workmanship and brings forth the best
    in others.
Has high regard for personalities of those he leads; wins their respect and
    confidence.
Encourages others to participate instead of his "running things."

Professional, Educational

A second series of professional standards of personal fitness are educational in character. The leader of a church school ought to possess a profound conviction that the educational method is a possible and desirable means to more abundant Christian living. He must be growing in his knowledge of theory and his skill at its techniques:

Knows the program as it is and as it should be.
Keeps aware of the nature and needs of persons and how they grow.
Encourages growth of workers in the school.
Accepts the kind of development he expects of others.
Makes constructive use of all available educational resources.
Does not let lesser enterprises get in way of the educational objectives.

Religious

But then an executive is a person, too. If he is to come to his full stature, discharging his responsibilities well and exerting a wholesome personal influence, he must give careful attention to his own growth as a Christian. One of the occupational hazards of this work is becoming too deeply immersed in the details of the job. In general, the executive holding a deep conviction about the superior worth of the Christian way of living ought to be achieving for himself a balanced and constantly growing experience as a Christian disciple and apostle. As J. B. Phillips renders II Corinthians 3:5: "It is God who makes us competent administrators. . . ." Thus a final group of standards of personal fitness may be called religious:

Shapes his work by Christian perspective and purpose.
Manifests wholesome character and exhibits Christian graces.
Keeps his outlook directly related to the distinctive mission of the church.
Has a basic commitment to the service of people.
Gives adequate attention to his own daily discipleship and apostlehood.
Is himself maturing toward the objectives of Christian education.

CHAPTER V

DEVELOPING THE EDUCATIONAL ORGANIZATION

This chapter is concerned with a church school leader's efforts at building or rebuilding the structure of personnel in his congregation's school system. There is a general, traditional pattern of organization; denominations recommend new forms from time to time. The older type may require modification; a new one will almost certainly need to be adapted. What are the principles that pertain and some possible structures?

STANDARDS

The standards for an educational organization arise out of the purposes mentioned in Chapter IV. As a generality, we organize so that persons may have benefits otherwise unavailable. First, organization is requisite for the group action by which we may provide better, larger, and more educational opportunities. Second, participation in organizational activity provides in itself learning experiences to develop the kind of person who can function appropriately in a Christian church and a democratic society.

The present structure for accomplishing these purposes in many congregations is a multiplicity of educational agencies, groups, or organizations that are operated by more or less remote control from officials of the church and exist as bodies largely isolated from one another.

Many a Sunday church school, for instance, is organizationally speaking as separate from the home church as if it were a mission in another part of town. In such churches the chief tie that binds their educational agencies to them is the fact that the same persons meet in the same buildings. Often, too, the separated agencies have no correlation with each other. The situation can be represented in Diagram II which re-

sembles a series of disjointed boxcars. Imagine a public school enterprise
which would have no more connection with local and state governments
than these educational units have with a congregation, and no more
relationship between its units—grade schools, high schools, colleges!

DIAGRAM II
EDUCATIONAL AGENCIES SEPARATED AND DIVIDED

| The Congre-gation | Sunday Church School | Vacation Church School | Youth Society | Women's Society |

Some measure of relationship to the congregation and a degree of
correlation between the agencies has been effected in certain other
churches. Yet the condition may be as confused as Diagram III suggests.

DIAGRAM III
EDUCATIONAL AGENCIES PARTIALLY INTEGRATED AND UNIFIED

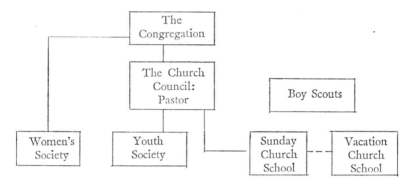

Do such organizational patterns serve the two purposes of organization as fully as possible? Scarcely, especially when we apply those "correct general principles" for the entire organizational, administrative, and
supervisory work of the leader according to Chapter IV. In particular
they do not keep the school a church school and do not, in a maximal
way, embody such essential virtues as comprehensiveness and simplicity.

For developing a congregational unit of Christian education, two
clear-cut requirements arise:

Standard I: *The educational organization should be integral with the basic
organization of the congregation, not separated from it.*

Standard II: *The educational work of the congregation should be unified in organization, not divided.*

How shall these standards be met?

INTEGRATING THE EDUCATIONAL ORGANIZATION

(with the congregational structure)

A separateness of church and church school results from history on the one hand and theory, or lack of it, on the other. We meet again the historical obstacle that the Sunday school agency arose in a lay movement outside the church establishment and so may remain largely a detached appendage. As for theoretical hindrances, the close identification of church purpose and school purpose has not always been sensed. Many have viewed the church too exclusively as an agency for evangelization whose primary purpose is to "save souls" and the purpose of the school is something entirely different, perhaps to build up the saved souls in knowledge. Most seriously, as some have seen it, the school's purpose is not nearly so important as the other. The truth is that, since we are total personalities, salvation and sanctification are quite interdependent in a Christian's experience. Also there is educational evangelization and there is evangelistic education.

Thus the time has arrived to realize the inseparable relations of church and school in the common task of winning persons and developing them for Christian mission with attendant welfare. Let education be included among the constituent functions of the entire church program. Let the pastor, among his many responsibilities, be the prime leader of the educational enterprise. Let a church school be truly the congregation at work educating itself. Then, let us have corresponding organizational arrangements. What we seek is not some loose federation of purposes, functions, services, and agencies, but collaborating cells built into a system of organs comprising the continuously ministering body of Christ.

In order to achieve that end the organization may well take the form represented in Diagram IV below or Diagram V on page 88. The latter represents the relatively complete and therefore a somewhat elaborate situation. Yet there can be all the simplification and modification necessary for a small church while moving toward the purposes of (1) eliminating the separateness of educational agencies and (2), as we shall see later, unifying the agencies. A possible structure follows:

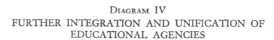

DIAGRAM IV
FURTHER INTEGRATION AND UNIFICATION OF
EDUCATIONAL AGENCIES

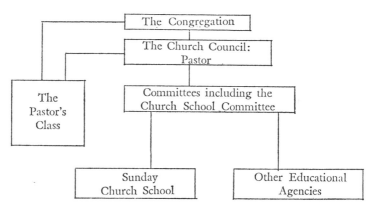

Overhead Personnel

Diagram IV, in part, and especially V to follow, show how Standard I, calling for organization that is integral with the basic organization of the congregation, is to be realized through properly devised overhead administration. It is charted completely in Part One of the next diagram.

THE CHURCH COUNCIL

The overhead management for the educational work of a congregation's church school—the personnel above the level of the immediate operation of the school—begins properly with the official administrative body of that church. The "constitution and by-laws" for congregations in one major denomination lists among the duties of what it calls "the church council": "To provide schools and facilities for Christian education for children, youth and adults."[1] That is an extraordinarily simple statement; yet it does make clear that the church council is to exercise general oversight of the entire church school work and foster it on an official basis. The council will operate largely by delegating its powers to the pastor and others working under its direction, particularly the church school committee with a director of Christian education or general superintendent of the school. Directly, though, it ought at least to consider major policies and problems, hear reports at appropriate inter-

---

[1]"Constitution of the Lutheran Church in America," *Official Documents of the Lutheran Church in America* 1960 (Philadelphia: The United Lutheran Publication House, 1960), p. 88.

vals, give basic attention to adequate financing and physical facilities, also make appointments or nominations of principal officers. All its practices should work toward the growth of the school and the efficacy of its program.

THE PASTOR

A hands-off policy on the part of a pastor is lamentable whether it is by his choice, the school's independence, or the congregation's demands. A minister is the duly constituted head of the parish; certainly he should be head of its school. In one way or another, by himself or working through associated leaders, he will lead the educational program. As a first responsibility he will spiritually guide and inspire the school. Further to fulfill his role he will at least help to shape the school's major policies, deal with its urgent problems, correlate its activities with other agencies of the church and with homes, introduce ideas that come to his attention for its improvement, foster its growth, and be always building a favorable educational consciousness in the parish.

Beyond these generalities the pastor may need in many situations to serve functions that are described later as the work of a director or a general superintendent. In a smaller or newer congregation he may himself work at many of the actual tasks: help to enlist pupils, recruit workers, choose literature. Increasingly, though, such work is delegated to another staff member, the pastor holding himself fully responsible for the efficiency of the delegated work.

A desirable trend would be an increase of direct teaching by pastors. This practice seems to be more common in Europe than in the United States; yet in America, too, pastors can find extraordinary value and satisfaction in meeting people—of any age—in school sessions. Also desirable is an emphasis on the teaching sermon in which the pastor deals with the needs of people, laying alongside them a freshly interpreted passage of scripture. He can also be a teacher in pastoral calling.

Clearly the pastor, to no small degree is "it" in education. In this connection it is worthwhile noticing that thought and effort for church renewal today is highlighting the pastor's educational role. Always, recognizing the basic importance of the teaching office in his ministry, he can be expected to keep an ardent educational commitment fresh and informed.

THE CHURCH SCHOOL COMMITTEE

Moving down the organizational chart, the next unit of overhead personnel is variously called church school committee or something similar. By whatever name, this standing committee should be established by every congregational constitution. Just why some churches have committees to look after the purchase of fuel, maintain the property, care for the finances, and provide for music but none to oversee the congregation's large and vastly important educational work is quite past comprehension.

Such a committee affords many advantages of which these are significant examples:

1. It symbolizes that the Christian education belongs within the total mission of the church. This dignifies the work in the eyes of the entire constituency—parish and community, council, workers, parents, and pupils.

2. It provides a group outside routine duties of the school to consider policies broadly and to implement programs co-operatively. Ideas can be exchanged and experiences shared; co-operation for new ventures can be secured.

3. It gives workers the understanding support of a responsible body that authorizes their work and hears reports upon it; it can muster outside support for the school.

4. It makes certain difficult decisions and actions easier for the pastor or superintendent because it is less personal; it can help to alleviate tension and friction.

5. It provides for continuity in policies and programs, inside or outside the congregation and beyond the change of elective officers.

6. It furnishes an agency through which the congregation can participate in co-operative programs beyond itself.

7. It correlates, by its very membership, educational functions within the school, with other agencies in the church, also with homes and community.

The following paragraphs will answer major questions about the personnel and procedure of a church school committee.

Who? The committee should be large enough to be comprehensive but small enough so that meetings with reasonably full attendance can be the rule. At least five to seven members are recommended to represent the interests suggested below (in many cases one individual will qualify in two or more ways): (1) the pastor, ex-officio, as responsible educational head of the congregation and the member perhaps best informed in general on Christian education and, in particular, concerning the parish and its needs; (2) one from the church council; (3) one from the missions or social service area; (4) at least one parent; (5) one with special knowledge of education through public school study and experience; (6) one with administrative responsibility and experience in

Christian education; (7) one or more teachers; (8) at least one with leadership education courses or higher study; (9) at least one pupil from the youth division.

How? The committee will be elected by the congregation, appointed by the church council, or appointed by various participating educational agencies. The members are wisely designated for three years, the various terms of office expiring at different times to avoid radical change of personnel and so allow for carefully considered programs to be continued. The operation of the committee will include: organizing itself with chairman (not pastor) and secretary, assuming delegated responsibility, studying its work, hearing and making reports, giving special attention to communication for an understanding of purposes and programs. Such a group can quickly decline into uselessness unless it has vital work to do and meets regularly to do it.

A church school committee, particularly in a large church, will have subcommittees. One plan of administration lists a special subcommittee on leadership education. This is meant to lift that enterprise into first prominence. The plan mentions other subcommittees which, in small schools, can be personal responsibilities of the members as follows: audio visual aids; enlistment; missionary education; library; stewardship education; worship education.

DIRECTOR OF CHRISTIAN EDUCATION

The executive officer of a church school committee will be, when possible, a director (or minister) of Christian education. This is a staff officer for whom an increasing number of congregations provide; some, indeed, have more than one. Elsewhere the need has been met in a partial way: two congregations support a worker co-operatively or a worker serves on a part-time or volunteer basis. If a competent, employed person is impossible to secure, then a general superintendent of all educational work, with requisite time and competence, should be appointed or developed.

Need

A pastor is responsible for ministering all the works of the church, not only education. But a man can scarcely be equally effective in every form of endeavor or have enough time to bring all of them to maximal effectiveness. More thought, study, and energy are necessary to provide the leadership talent needed, especially in a large church. Such a church needs a director of Christian education or comparable staff member.

More such workers should be available. Among the young people of the churches there must be thousands who would respond to a proper appeal, at least if what may be called the working conditions were made reasonably favorable. Some of these young people already have the essential qualifications or could shortly prepare themselves. People from public education are being used and others could be recruited. However, professional working conditions need to be established.

Duties

A director of Christian education is somewhat like a superintendent of schools in a community. He may do some teaching and handle many details of management but mainly he is responsible for seeing that everything needful is done. The specific functions vary with churches and denominations, yet many are common to most situations. Under the church council and pastor, also with the church school committee, he will lead in these major activities:

1. Developing basic policies for the educational program, having a fundamental theory of Christian education for himself, and helping others to form one.

2. Planning and replanning, with other workers, a comprehensive and balanced educational program in line with the mission of the church.

3. Integrating and unifying the many educational activities of the church. The director should relate his work to all age groups and agencies unless appointed to selected ones.

4. Interpreting the educational activity to the church as a whole, especially to the church school workers.

5. Supervising the "teaching" program. The director is a leader of teachers, chiefly to help them carry on their activities more effectively. He leads especially in evaluating their work.

6. Adopting curricular materials consistent with the policies, standards, and program of the denomination.

7. Discovering, enlisting, and developing leaders for the church; providing both pre-service and in-service leadership education.

8. Helping the church know what building and equipment are needed for education; also working with the officials to find ways to make best use of present buildings while securing new facilities if needed.

9. Helping church groups realize their responsibility for reaching more people, also helping them enlarge their programs to meet more of the needs of the growing constituency.

10. Knowing the people of the church; calling in homes, especially in relation to educational work.

11. Promoting co-operation with other churches of the community; encouraging participation in denominational, inter-denominational, or interfaith or civic programs.

12. Keeping himself and others vigilant about objectives at all significant points.

13. Establishing helpful personal relations throughout; cultivating the fellowship of the school.

14. Promoting adequate financial support for the school; assisting with matters pertaining to the budget.

15. Providing for adequate records.

16. Fostering use of standards and similar measures; undertaking or guiding important surveys and researches.

17. Being an educational counselor; helping on unusual problems, especially concerning pupils and curriculum.

18. Being the linkage between congregation, church council, church school committee, pastor, and school.

Relationships

The effectiveness of a director will depend greatly upon the relationships that are established and maintained. The official call should include a job analysis with a statement on these relationships. The entire congregation should support the call to service. It should provide salary and other benefits commensurate with years of preparation and experience had, the standards required, and the responsibilities assigned. A director cannot work effectively unless he has a budget. It is proper that there be secretarial help, living quarters, expense account especially for car usage, pension provision, and money for growth experiences as well as representation at denominational and other conferences.

The official body of the church will have major responsibility for the director's program. He should be invited to attend its meetings, make reports, and counsel on important decisions. The pastor will be recognized always as chief executive of the church, responsible basically for the total program including the educational phase. This relationship must be kept particularly close and harmonious. To this end a clear division of labor is quite essential. If there are other staff members of pastoral or directional rank, the responsibilities of each must be clearly defined and respected. The director, as the executive secretary of the church school committee, works with the chairman in outlining agenda for meetings, makes reports and recommendations on educational policy, program, and operation.

Within the school itself, the relationship to a general superintendent will necessarily be a close one. The exact activities of each will vary according to denomination and local church, yet in no case will the director take over the superintendent's tasks; the two will simply share the work in the way that will achieve highest effectiveness. Outside the local situation the director should be acquainted with the provisions of the denomination for directors. He will know the overhead personnel as fully as possible and try to represent the educational standards of the church. He will also establish working relationships with neighboring congregations, denominations or interdenominational agencies and workers.

The School Itself

Perhaps an ideal form of Christian education would be simply the immature members of the Christian community living and working with the more mature, each ready to help the other in real experiences, especially crises. Yet Christian education will likely continue to be ministered more or less exclusively in groups of pupils organized in schools —pupils with a staff immediately in charge.

How will the schools be organized?

THE PUPILS

We meet again the fact that Christian education is in a state of transition. Congregations have still those several school agencies, each existing in more or less isolated or independent status though there has been movement toward the unification we shall be describing in detail a little later. We must therefore consider both the older and the newer types of pupil organization.

It seems best to see the older structure in a typical, well-organized Sunday church school; the Sunday phase of a total church school now may or may not now have a similar structure. The usual groupings have provided for divisions, departments, and classes. These were in some cases formerly, and are frequently now, organized according to the ages of the pupils though the trend is toward public school grading. It is wise to observe carefully the names for the groups; these should be used uniformly so that all workers can understand each other. The basic principles for grouping will be considered in Chapter VIII.

In a school of 500 pupils with appropriate equipment the pupils may be grouped as follows:

Divisions	Ages	Grades	Departments	Classes
Children's	1, 2, 3		Nursery	As
	4, 5	1st, 2nd yr.	Kindergarten	
	6, 7, 8	I, II, III	Primary	
	9, 10, 11	IV, V, VI	Junior	

Divisions	Ages	Grades	Departments	Classes
Youth	12, 13, 14	VII, VIII, IX	Junior High (Intermediate)	
	15, 16, 17	X, XI, XII	Senior High (Senior)	need-
	18-24		Older Youth (Young People)	
Adult	25 plus		Adult (young, 25-35 middle, 35-65 older, 65 plus)	ed

A typical school of 100 pupils, meeting in one room, may be grouped in this manner:

Kindergarten Class	(ages through 5)
Primary Class	6, 7, 8
Junior Class	9, 10, 11
Junior High (Intermediate) Class	12, 13, 14
Senior High (Senior) Class	15, 16, 17
Youth (Young People's) Class	18-24
Adult Class	from 25

Some congregations are using now a 2-2-2 grouping with three, rather than two, departments for the elementary school age. Now the trend is toward single-grade grouping with self-contained rooms and largely independent sessions although a curricular sequence is recognized as a necessity. As schools increase in size they tend to go by single grades. Buildings are being constructed with closely graded programs in view. Adaptations of the pupil groupings to local conditions are always necessary because of numbers, building, available staff and, to some extent, tradition of the congregation. As a basic principle the needs of pupils in the program should be the ruling consideration. It will be advantageous to keep the usual framework and terminology in mind so as to approximate it whenever desirable.

THE STAFF

By pastoral and other leaders who may be starting a new school or, more typically, reorganizing an old one, two major principles concerning the staff structure should be followed assiduously. The first is *adaptation*. As a chief requirement the staff must be suited to the attainment of the school's objective in the most complete way. Just as with pupils, it must also be adapted to such local conditions as size of school, nature of the building facilities, leaders available in the congregation, the traditions of the community and the standards of the denomination. A second principle is *economy*. A leader will plan to have an adequate staff but he will include no more members than necessary to do the work effectively.

The following outline suggests the possible staff members from which choice can be made according to those principles—no school will have all:

> *Essential Adult Staff* (depending on size of school)
>> General Officers: Superintendent and Assistant or Associate; Secretary; Treasurer (as minimum)
>> Divisional, Departmental, or Grade Officers (usually as above)
>> Agency Officers (possibly as above)
>> Music Leaders: Chorister; Pianist
>> Teachers (with associated workers)
>
> *Optional Adult Staff* (depending on program and available leaders)
>> Supervisors: Divisional; Departmental; Grade; Activity (such as recreation, service, missions, or drama)
>> Absentee, Enrollment and Supply Secretary or others
>> Age Group Co-ordinators
>> Audio-visual Co-ordinator
>> Librarians
>> Ushers and Aides
>
> *Staff Committees* (in larger schools; their functions in small schools will be carried out by entire group excepting special committees)
>> Executive (for routine business)
>> Standing (as example: Pupil Program; Membership; Personnel)
>> Special (such as budget or publicity)
>
> *Pupil Officers and Committees* (general, divisional, departmental, grade, and class, depending on local conditions)

UNIFYING THE EDUCATIONAL ORGANIZATION

We have already mentioned that problem which educational leaders have been lamenting for several decades: too many educational agencies with all their officers, committees, memberships, and programs. No one is to blame for the present situation; it just grew up like Topsy. When, perhaps a century ago, it became clear that the Sunday school alone was not adequate to meet the educational needs in the church, leaders began to develop the various allies for the purpose. Each has made its contribution and is continuing to do so. Nevertheless, there has been too much overlapping of objectives, duplication of programs, overstimulation of pupils and workers, neglect of certain areas and groups, fragmentariness or disunity of experience and, at times, conflicts in the services attempted, even rivalry for loyalty. Too many agencies can get in the way of one another administratively while their multiplicity is an obstacle to best results with their various programs.

Unified organizations have been attempted or effected and unified programs are in operation, at least to some degree, in congregations and denominations. These are steps in the right direction. A chief deterrent is the normal resistance to change. There remains, too, a certain amount of organizational structure largely for its own sake; it may be due to personal loyalties which institutions command.

A Unified Church School

There is but one ideal way to accomplish unification, namely, to develop one inclusive or unified church school. There are possibilities for temporary expedients while working toward the ideal—several will be mentioned a little later.

Among the various efforts at unification no one particular pattern can be described as a customary type. A somewhat imaginative form will be presented for consideration with the understanding that local churches or denominations may keep the picture in mind as they develop something of the sort to fit their particular needs.

PUPIL AND STAFF STRUCTURE OF UNIFIED SCHOOL

Represented in Diagram V, Part One, the pattern includes the integrated overhead administration previously described so that this school will realize Standard I; then it shows how to realize Standard II. After repeating that integrative top level organization a new unit in the organizational chart is added. This is the church school council with "all officers—general, divisional, departmental, class; supervisors; teachers (with committees such as executive, leadership, membership, program)." This symbolizes that there is to be only one staff for all administrative and teaching leadership and, as a first unifying factor, this staff will be organized into the church school council which operates under the overhead administration. Its major functions are suggested by the committees mentioned.

Next, the pupil groupings are listed. It will be noticed that there is no listing of several church school agencies. There will be only one series of groupings as the total pupil structure for the congregation's educational work—no more.

DIAGRAM V

AN INTEGRATED AND UNIFIED CHURCH SCHOOL

PART ONE: UNIFIED CHURCH SCHOOL ORGANIZATION

THE CONGREGATION

THE CHURCH COUNCIL with PASTOR

THE CHURCH SCHOOL COMMITTEE with DIRECTOR

THE CHURCH SCHOOL COUNCIL (STAFF)

(All Officers—General, Divisional, Departmental, Class; Supervisors; Teachers)
(with committees such as executive, leadership, membership, program)

THE PUPILS

Divisions	Ages	Grades	Departments	Classes
Children's:	1, 2, 3		Nursery	As
	4, 5	1st, 2nd yr.	Kindergarten	
	6, 7, 8	I, II, III	Primary	
	9, 10, 11	IV, V, VI	Junior	
Youth	12, 13, 14	VII, VIII, IX	Junior High (Intermediate)	need-
	15, 16, 17	X, XI, XII	Senior High (Senior)	
	18-24		Older Youth	
Adult	25 plus		Adult (young, middle, older)	ed

PART TWO: UNIFIED CHURCH SCHOOL PROGRAM

(showing relation to "church services" also)
Units of study-and-instruction, worship, fellowship, service for eight objectives
of Christian education and six works of the church in groups indicated:

SESSIONS

	Sunday	Weekday	Vacation	Home
Nursery	Nursery	Nursery school	As weekday	Program conducted at
Kinder-garten	A. M. Two hours	Kinder-garten	Local or community	home fostered and su-
Primary	school	Local church	vacation	pervised by
Junior	session	school week-	school	Church
		day sessions	sessions	School to in-
		or attendance		clude:
		in commu-		Literature
		nity school		

	Sunday	Weekday	Vacation	Home
Junior High	A. M.	Confirma-	Summer	Visitation
Senior High	One hour	tion classes		
Older Youth	or more	Local church		
	school session	school week-		
	(one hour	day sessions		
	church serv-	Business	Camps	Parent and
	ice)	Project		
	P. M.	Social and		
	One hour	Study meet-		
	or more	ings		
	school ses-	Conferences	Conferences	Pupil
	sion			
Adult	A. M.	Clubs	and	Classes
Young	As above	Societies		
Middle	P. M. (one	Study groups		Meetings and
Older	hour school	Project groups		
	session or	Conferences		
	church serv-			
	ice)		Assemblies	Projects

Throughout: leadership education opportunities for all types of church work; also Christian family life education

PROGRAM OF UNIFIED SCHOOL

Although a unified organization is receiving primary consideration, we must consider also a unified program briefly in order to evaluate or perhaps even to understand the unified organization. It is presented in Part Two of Diagram V. Just as there is to be but one organization, there is to be only one educational program in the congregation. It may meet in Sunday morning sessions, Sunday evening sessions, weekday sessions, vacation sessions, and home sessions. Yet it would be but one program. To make the plan complete, the program should, like the organization, be integrated with the total congregational program. Only this would meet fully the ideal of the church as a school, according to Standards I and II.

The basic idea of the unified church school is to have one school, one set of pupils, one staff, with diversified sessions to provide for all present activities and more if needed and possible. There will be exceptions only for special reasons and for unusual purposes that may arise. The meeting of pupils in the same basic groups with essentially the same staff of leaders is meant to center loyalty instead of dividing it, and allow the pupils to complete larger units of study without the interference of fragmented groupings and schedules. It should eliminate the enormous

waste in our present overlapping agencies which consume time so vora-
ciously for pupils and staff by useless repetitions and duplications along
with a complexity of schedules. Possibilities of meeting the objection
that we cannot find personnel with time have been discovered.

Steps Toward Unification

A school need not travel the whole way to that goal in order to have
some of the advantages. There are halfway stages.

A first step which many churches could take toward unification is to
correlate their Sunday church school work with that of other educational
agencies. Relationship between the Sunday church school and weekday
church school of a congregation can exemplify some points at which
correlation is needful and possible. Shall the two schools have the same
objective or different ones? If different ones, how shall they be distributed between the two? Shall they use similar or different materials and
which school shall use each? Shall the same teachers work in both?
If so, with the same pupils? Shall their enterprises be different, similar,
related?

In many situations a beginning at unification can be made by merging two or more organizations. A city church had a junior choir and a
junior missionary society. Then the director of Christian education was
asked to start a weekday school, and it was suggested that a junior youth
society would be a good thing. Instead of trying to work with four
organizations, he developed a weekday church school which had a missionary emphasis at least once a month, used forty-five minutes weekly
for junior choir rehearsal and did additional weekday work to a total
of two hours on Saturday mornings. Not ideal, it was a step in the right
direction. Somewhat similar planning may result in a weekly or monthly
church night, a family night, a Sunday evening program for youth.

Relationship to Common Services

This chapter has been pointing toward a fourfold ideal. A first goal
and the one chiefly mentioned was an educational *organization* (1) integrated with the total congregational organization and (2) unified in
itself. But, in the study of that goal a second and possibly more important one became apparent, namely, a *program* that is (1) unified in itself
and also (2) integrated with the total congregational program. It is possible now to take the last step in considering that total complex.

TEACHING-PREACHING SERVICE

It concerns a possible relationship of the Sunday sessions of the
church school to the common services which would unify these major

congregational endeavors. While this is not the province of the church school leader specifically, he may see reasons to promote some such arrangement. The basic idea is a unified Sunday morning program in which the teaching-preaching activity would be combined in one two-hour program. For example, members of the congregation through the elementary years would have a two-hour school session while their elders have one hour of school and one of common worship (see Diagram V above).

There are those who see some such relationship of the present teaching and preaching services as a crying need of the church. It would, indeed, move us toward wholeness in church programming. It would further realize the concept of education as one of the church's methods for its total task.

Additional problems would be solved. One example will suggest others. A visiting preacher arrived at his appointment ten minutes before the announced time of the service. The walk that led to the building was crowded with two streams of traffic: one "going to church," the other "going home from Sunday school." Speaking to a member of the church council, the visitor said, "Why doesn't the church plan a two-hour program for its people each Sunday morning; then lead them to think of their Sunday morning attendance in those terms instead of attendance at one or the other of two services?" "I never thought of that," was the reply. (The combined teaching and preaching service will be mentioned again in Chapter XVIII.)

JUNIOR CHURCH AND FAMILY PEW

Not a few congregations have planned for a children's service to be conducted parallel with the main common service. Proponents of the idea believe that it is fruitful in educational value. It can be seen, however, to have the fault of prolonging the unfortunate idea of separation of church and school. In addition, it has often been guilty of seeking to initiate children into practices more suited to adults. Such an extended session of the church school as that described in Chapter XVIII seems preferable.

Childhood memories may be suspected though they are vivid. Yet one man feels certain that his time could have been better spent in some other way than disturbing his parents in the family pew—and perhaps others. He did not learn to appreciate the liturgical service. The sermons puzzled him as did the scripture readings. He was interested in the organ; how did it work? He remembers best the pastor's way of making announcements, "God willing, there will be Lenten services next Wednesday at seven o'clock." It was a long hour, defensible only because in that one-room rural church it was impossible to provide a parallel educational program, even if somebody had thought of it.

Many church leaders are now fostering the family pew concept; along with this should go, then of course, an emphasis on full family attendance in graded classrooms.

Current upheavals are resulting in some radical experiments. They should be devised with care, watched with interest, and wisely evaluated. Good may come of them.

CHAPTER VI

ADMINISTERING THE STAFF

A half century ago, in a book entitled *How to Teach Religion,* Dr. George H. Betts used this dedication: "To those who have in their keeping the religious destiny of America—the two million teachers in our church schools."[1] Now the noted author would be able to mention twice as many teachers and commend their significance for the whole world order. They are equally significant for the church schools themselves. Wholehearted, intelligent, and skilled leadership with vision is known as the paramount need throughout the world-wide program of Christian education. Every executive knows that his school rises or falls with the competency of his staff. His management of the staff is correspondingly significant.

ALLOTTING DUTIES: JOB ANALYSES

A major responsibility of the church school leader who is charged with the organizational, administrative, and supervisory functions will be the appropriate distribution of the specific tasks of the staff among the several types of worker. What duties fall usually to each? Every school should prepare its own job analyses and perhaps publish them in its manual of procedure. Selected items, especially of outstanding or unusual character, will be listed here.

General Superintendents

In most church schools the operating responsibility will belong to a general superintendent, working under the pastor, church council, and church school committee. Yet, in a growing number of instances, there will be a director of Christian education or equivalent staff person by whom many of the duties will be discharged. Then a general superintendent looks to that officer for direction, as counsel and guidance to

[1]George H. Betts, *How to Teach Religion* (New York: The Abingdon Press, 1919).

carry out his responsibilities more efficiently but not to do his work
for him. If there is no director the superintendent will have many of
a director's responsibilities.

REQUIREMENTS

The duties, broadly, are two: providing for the school when it is
out of session and governing it when in session. The task, properly
conceived, is not primarily the conducting of services of worship though
that may be necessary until other leaders have been developed. Basically
the general superintendent is really a school superintendent in charge
of a system, the leader of a group of principals, teachers, and pupils.
He deals primarily in personnel management. That fact determines
many of the personal requirements; outstanding ones have been mentioned in Chapter IV where general standards for any church school
executive are outlined. The more technical aspects of the task are being
considered throughout most of these twenty chapters.

As a person, the ideal incumbent—man or woman—will be an outstanding member of the congregation, with authentic Christian experience and deep commitment. This suggests that he will have the attitude
of a servant of servants—sharing in a ministry. Not the least of personal
qualifications is a capacity for entirely co-operative service under the
pastor, the director, and the church school committee. Throughout, it
is "our school" and not "my school." Such personal requirements are
in addition to over-all organizational, administrative, and supervisory
ability.

RESPONSIBILITIES

Specific functions of a general superintendent will vary considerably,
depending on organizational structure recommended by the denomination, size of the church, professional personnel on the staff and extent
to which the church school is organized by age groups or agencies subordinate to the general superintendent. Outstanding responsibilities may
include:

1. Seeing that personnel are aware of the educational philosophy, objectives, plans, policies, and standards of the school and that they
   carry these forward to results.
2. Working co-operatively with the associate, agency, and age group
   superintendents.
3. Attending to pupil administration items: membership, attendance,
   punctuality, and grouping.
4. Promoting home-church and other outside relationships.
5. Seeing that all staff positions are filled by persons with the most
   adequate preparation possible; providing for in-service supervision;
   nominating for vacant posts.

6. Making sure that all workers are provided with approved curricular resources and are using them effectively.
7. Arranging for general meetings or presiding at them (these include workers' conferences, special day services such as Christmas).
8. Observing the groups at regular intervals, giving attention to pupils' and teachers' needs.
9. Attending to any needs about building and equipment and providing for their best possible use.
10. Formulating a budget for an adequate program and supervising its implementation.
11. Submitting interpretative reports to the proper persons or boards.
12. Seeing that the work of the school is promoted in the entire constituency and community.
13. Building fellowship among workers and in the school as a whole.
14. Conducting evaluative studies.
15. Enlarging the program as needed and possible.

The method of naming a superintendent varies from church to church: elected by the congregation as a whole or the church school; appointed by the official church school committee or by the minister. Anything resembling a popularity poll is out of place. The recommended practice is to elect or appoint on an annual basis, subject to re-election or appointment.

With such important requirements and responsibilities involved, tragedy is revealed in an observation report which states: "The superintendent holds his position really because no one else will accept it."

Age Group Superintendents

Again, numerous conditions, especially size of the school and its facilities, will determine the duties of a divisional, departmental, or other age group superintendent. As schools grow larger, the work of a general superintendent will become chiefly directing and co-ordinating the efforts of these workers who do for an age group what a general superintendent does for a small school. In schools of moderate size or small ones, an age group superintendent may have a less prominent position because the general superintendent manages many features of the work. He will be like an associate superintendent representing broadly the interests of the particular age, perhaps looking after promotion, suggesting plans for improvement, leading the pupils in special enterprises. In any case age group superintendents work in a two-way channel of administration, unlocking the doors for greater service by both administrators and teachers. They help general overseers fulfill their responsibilities to the teachers, and at the same time help teachers meet their needs.

While these workers need attitudes and have duties similar to those of general superintendents, they need the special attribute of co-operativeness with those under whom, through whom, and for whom they work. They will be special students, too, of the psychology of the age group and the curricular program on that level. A particularly needed capacity is to win the confidence of fellow workmen so that they can feel free to share problems as well as successful experiences. They should also be particularly sympathetic to the problems of pupils in their particular group.

Age group superintendents in the fuller sense are executives who operate their own groups within the approved policies and program of the total school, directly responsible to the superintendent and through him to the director and committee on Christian education. All that has been said of the general superintendent may well be said of each head of a given group. Some special concerns include:

1. Being alert about, and reporting to the general superintendent, any needs for curricular services or related facilities.
2. Being sure that the age group is properly graded and that appropriate materials are provided regularly.
3. Insuring adequate teaching staff for each session.
4. Arriving early and making sure that all is in readiness; being watchful about the time schedule.
5. Planning for special activities in the group, such as special days.
6. Overseeing enrollment procedures and assisting in methods of handling the attendance records and offering.
7. Seeing that absentees are followed up, new pupils are recruited and are integrated into the school.
8. Guiding new age group workers to understand the special objectives and materials for pupils of this age.
9. Planning for co-operation with parents.
10. Arranging for evaluation of the teaching program; promoting improved teaching procedures.

Activity Superintendents

These officers care for particular types of educational procedure. Some possible positions would be superintendents of dramatics, stewardship, handwork, music, or special day programs. One author mentions supervisors of study, worship, fellowship, and service. However, according to the newer concept of curriculum all those activities are to be included within integrated units of activity, avoiding fragmentation of the program. Under that limitation, such leaders as the following may be used: superintendents of worship who seek to lift the level of worship experiences in all agencies; recreational leaders who develop well-rounded programs of fellowship; persons skilled in community enterprises who can superintend service. A closely related work is done by occasional resource leaders especially in the instruction and study area. Church schools have used this type of worker scarcely at all in proportion to the important services they can render.

Agency and Associate Superintendents

If the church school has not been unified there will likely be superintendents of such agencies as the vacation church school. Even in a unified school, some person will be needed, whether called a superintendent or not, to head each agency. These persons will look to the general church school superintendent or beyond that officer to higher personnel for direction. Their specific duties will be determined not only by the staff arrangement but also by the nature of the agency; many of the principles and responsibilities just enunciated for general superintendents will apply.

AGENCY SUPERINTENDENTS

Vacation Church School. This important once-a-year program, too, will be in immediate charge of a superintending officer with age group colleagues whose relationships and duties will be similar to those in Sunday church schools. Yet particular attention should be given to the special nature and objectives of a vacation-time school (see Chap. XIX).

Weekday Church School. If the weekday school is a local one, the procedures will be much the same as for the vacation church school; again, however, particular attention will be given to the special nature of this agency—for example, the school-like character of its program (see Chap. XIX). For a weekday church school conducted on an interchurch basis, its superintendent will serve under the community administrative body but also be relating the enterprise to local church programs.

Youth and Adult Groups. Usually a youth group will have adult advisers. If the group lacks basic correlation with the regular church school program, the advisers should co-operate with the church school's youth division superintendent. Some adult groups outside the Sunday church school may be under their own leadership to the extent that they are guided only by the overhead personnel. Correlation with the whole church school program may be accomplished by the adult representative. Better, all such work will be administered by the one youth superintendent and one adult superintendent of the unified school.

ASSOCIATE SUPERINTENDENTS

General, agency, or age group superintendents may have assistants.

A better title for this officer is "associate superintendent." In most cases there will be at least one. Too often the office has been merely an honorary position or its incumbent has been designated "to fill the office of superintendent in his absence or inability to serve." However, specific responsibilities can be assigned to this incumbent so that he can be constantly on the job and not just a "pinch hitter." There should be a job analysis including a statement of the relationships with the colleagues.

A superintendent should let an associate become a full member of the staff. Even anticipating the time when the associate may need to step into his chief's shoes, he will help him to get a necessary breadth of experience and be in readiness. As partners, the two may divide the duties in both planning and operating the school. Sometimes the associate may be leading a session with the superintendent; at other times he will handle that task and enable the superintendent to concentrate on some other responsibility. Together they would provide for the leadership of the classes; look after the welcoming of pupils; have oversight of latecomers; provide for substitute teaching; maintain good order; and achieve smooth progress for the program. Each cares for the other's work in case of absence; the two co-operate in planning on both short and long-range levels, also in evaluating.

Secretaries and Treasurers

A secretary or treasurer can be a most useful officer in building up the school and helping other workers meet their responsibilities more effectively.

SECRETARIES

While an average school may have one secretary with limited responsibilities, a large school may have several in addition to its general secretary. These may be divisional, departmental, grade and class officers or they may have such special responsibilities as those of membership secretary or others.

Duties. The duties of a secretary of whatever type, will include some combination of items from the following list:

1. Handling correspondence.
2. Keeping records of the several types and caring for record systems. Preserving historical items.
3. Ordering supplies, storing and distributing them.
4. Following up absentees or arranging for the follow-up.
5. Handling enrollments or withdrawals.
6. Preparing and making reports of many sorts.

7. Taking minutes.
8. Keeping lists of prospects.
9. Seeing that class offerings are turned over to the treasurer.
10. Distributing communications.

Still more that a general secretary, with possible associates in larger schools, could do is suggested in Chapter XV under *Gathering and Using Data.*

Problems. In their duties with regard to statistics, secretaries meet problems concerning membership, attendance, and punctuality. Recognized practice would say that a member is a member when he has signified his intention; also he retains that status until he indicates that he has withdrawn or it is otherwise known that his membership has ceased. Under that definition, the full enrollment of the school can never be expected to attend; there will always be someone who actually cannot be present. Statistics of "average attendance" therefore will give an unnecessarily gloomy picture unless some adjustment is made. One plan is to distinguish between "attending" or "active" membership versus "non-attending" or "associate" membership. Sometimes persons who have not attended for three sessions are included in the latter categories and the average attendance is computed on the basis of the "attending" or "active" membership. For punctuality statistics, no leeway can be allowed; unless the leader is present ten minutes before the time announced for the session, he is not fulfilling his obligations. If the pupil is not present for the first minutes of the session, he is late, no matter what his excuse may be.

Educational Outlook. Secretaries, like all other officers of a school, are to be educators. It is their function to inform, guide, and move the leaders, pupils, and entire constituency into better practice. On attendance, as an instance, they assemble the facts and report them—so that attendance will improve. The reports may show the pupils and parents how lax they have been, show the leaders that their program needs to be improved, or show the congregation that new equipment is needed. The secretary's work is not completed until such use of all the data with which he deals has been made.

TREASURERS

A treasurer can render an equally important educational service in addition to the collecting and disbursing of the pupil's offerings. In most schools the treasurer will simply receive the funds and disburse them according to a budget and procedure determined by the proper authorities. More can be involved. This work, especially in terms of education for stewardship, is described more completely in Chapter XIV.

Music Leaders

The importance of music in a church school can scarcely be over-emphasized; the need for excellent leadership in that field is correspondingly important. Every music leader is to be essentially a minister of music whose task is to cultivate this area as another aid to Christian growth.

A pianist should be the best available; this is not the place to give young music students some practice at playing in public. Perhaps the contract of the employed church organist, if there is one, can be extended to playing for the church school. In fact, the church organ, if it is located suitably, may well be used for certain school services. Pianists should prepare themselves for each session, not merely appear. This is recognized in the report of an observation which reads, "It would be better if the pianist would familiarize herself with the music before she arrives." There may, of course, have been the difficulty described in another report which states: "The music could be improved if the pianist were co-operative. She is a pillar of the church who will not be ordered around—which is her interpretation of any suggestion for improvement." A closely related need is emphasized by a report which says that the pianist's preparation in advance would "make it necessary, of course, for the superintendent to select the hymns in advance."

Leaders of choirs or of hymn singing, too, should be the best available persons. This does not mean they need to be highly trained musicians. The more basic requirement is an understanding of their real function as leaders in the pupils' development at feeling and expressing religious sentiment in music. In Chapter XII a period of "large group instruction" will be suggested in which there can be study of music and preparation for worship. At that period the leader of singing can interpret and teach new hymns and provide for other development in music. During the worship services themselves he will efface himself except to carry the singers along by his voice. Beating time in conspicuous fashion, exhorting people to "sing out," announcing novel ways of singing, humming, whistling, and the like will be taboo.

The phonograph and tape recorder provide striking new aids for music leaders. We are equipped now, as never before, to cultivate this educationally neglected aspect of the church program.

Librarians

Many church schools have had libraries for a long time. The importance of the library is increased under newer trends in curriculum where reading, researching, and reporting or related techniques are being recognized for their true value in Christian education. Once they were largely of a general nature, similar to public libraries, or they provided inspirational literature of a religious character. More recently they stress providing books for educational and other work in the church.

The librarian of the future therefore will not merely keep records of books. He will know his resource materials. He will co-operate with the teachers and other workers to build intelligently and promote vigorously the use of a body of reading and reference materials to serve all the members of the school and church. Books on the Bible, theology, ethics, the church and its enterprises will be included. Resource materials for worship services and fellowship events, as well as books on the theory of these activities will be there. The librarian will be building a file of materials that pertain to social trends in which Christians are interested—and fostering their use. Essentially he will be a superintendent of the reading resources of the school.

Audio-visual Co-ordinators

This officer is a relative newcomer on church school staff listings but a needed one. He may serve as a member of the church school committee in order to participate in planning for and the use of audio-visuals as an integral part of the entire school program. In larger schools he may also be chairman of an audio-visual subcommittee. Basically, he will know as thoroughly as possible the whole area of audio-visuals, particularly their educational value and utilization. Special attention will be needed for the items that accompany the curricular units used.

Specific duties can include these possibilities:

1. Furnishing full information to all workers concerning audio-visual recommendations for curricular phases.
2. Supervising any necessary assistants to provide preview guidance and other help for the best use of all resources.
3. Maintaining an effective system for requesting materials desired and for ordering, utilizing, and returning them. This will require a permanent record of materials owned or rented, also a calendar of dates and places when they were used.
4. Conducting leadership work for all workers so that they may be fully prepared to assist their respective groups. A course or workshop should include "how-to" items for the effective utilization of audio-visuals from an educational standpoint.
5. Selecting and training projectionists and assigning them to leaders and groups as needed.
6. Maintaining equipment in good working condition and arranging for adequate storage.
7. Providing "library" arrangements for materials.

Ushers and Aides

The smooth management of a school of considerable size may require the help of ushers and similar aides for the sessions. Depending on the nature of the building and size of the school, the following are possible duties: greeting workers and pupils as they enter; welcoming visitors and guiding them to appropriate places; introducing newcomers to the enrollment officer; keeping doors closed during worship or otherwise caring for latecomers; distributing programs or other literature; arranging chairs and other equipment; seeing that all persons have hymnals or other materials needed; caring for bulletin boards; ringing signals; distributing communications from the officers to other workers.

Teachers and Their Supervisors

Teachers are rightly regarded as the front rank members of the staff on whose shoulders the issue as to the quality of the school lies finally. We shall see that supervisors are essentially helpers of teachers.

TEACHERS

Paramount among teaching duties, of course, are preparing for the Sunday or weekday sessions of their groups and conducting these. Chapter X will discuss the nature of that task in more detail. It will, further, emphasize the fact that under developmental Christian education, the work of the teacher has broader dimensions than commonly supposed. Even under traditional education, teachers dare not feel that their responsibilities end with no more than preparing for a class session and conducting it.

When a general superintendent was arranging for an address to his teachers concerning some things that would make them more efficient, the prospective speaker asked him to propose topics for discussion. He responded with a list of five: "Ask them," he said, "either to be present when the time comes for them to do their work or get a substitute—at least advise the superintendent if they must be absent. Ask them to manifest an attitude of hearty willingness, not going to their work in an unhappy martyr's spirit. Ask them to be punctual, always a little ahead of time for the session so that they can help the pupils get situated and prepared for worship. Ask them to be workers all the week long, calling, phoning, or writing to their pupils, taking hikes with them, providing parties for them, and seeking new members with their assistance. Ask them, finally, to be present for all meetings, in particular those in which we are trying to advance their improvement in the work."

Among the responsibilities to be mentioned in job analyses the following are mostly of the type that would sometimes be overlooked:

1. Keeping familiar with the educational philosophy, objectives, plans, policies, standards and materials of the school and working by them while maintaining a flexibility to meet special needs.
2. Having a general acquaintance with the whole church school organization and administration.
3. Participating in the home and school program—regularly attending parent-teacher group meetings and activities; visiting pupils in their homes; making the visit useful for learning-teaching purposes.
4. Giving regular and serious attention to professional improvement.
5. Being a full-time participant in the work and services of the church.
6. Remembering that pupils and their Christian growth, not materials, are the center of concern.
7. Striving continuously to understand: how persons learn, age group characteristics, special needs of a given group and of the individual pupils within the homes and communities in which they live.
8. Learning how to use the Bible effectively in everyday life.
9. Starting to prepare the session's lesson early in the week, being watchful throughout the week for additional resources, keeping alert to new methods.
10. Studying the unit as a whole in order to put individual sessions into proper framework and knowing how the particular course fits into the whole curriculum.
11. Making careful lesson plans in writing, keeping in mind individual and group needs but being alert to important moments for spontaneous activities.
12. Being present ahead of time every Sunday morning, arranging materials before the class session, remembering that teaching begins when the first pupil arrives.
13. Keeping personal records of pupils and the work with them.
14. Observing comparable groups in other church groups and in public schools.

Many plans have been tried to make sure that a fully prepared teacher will be present each session to lead each class. When everything else has been done another means is to have workers called "associate" —not "substitute"—teachers. Their names should be listed with those of the regular teachers. They should be supplied with the same materials and be invited to all the regular meetings. They should not merely substitute in the event of an absence but assist regularly and sometimes have practice in full leadership. They can grow into team teaching (see Chap. X).

SUPERVISORS

The precise meaning and techniques of supervision will be described in the following chapter. Pastors and directors often serve in this capacity, yet special supervising personnel are being introduced in an increasing number of schools. Churches are using other workers with related or somewhat similar functions. "Counselors" are to help persons of one or all age groups with their more crucial problems. "Church visitors" call on the constituency. "Youth workers" have special responsibilities with workers and pupils of the high school age and older youth. "Age group co-ordinators" are recommended for larger programs.

Committees

Staff, and pupil, committees will be needed or perhaps arise spontaneously among the personnel. Several important ones have been suggested in these pages beyond the major church school committee. Some, especially standing committees specified in the constitution of the church or church school, will likely be appointed or elected on a rotating basis. Their duties should be clearly specified in a manual of procedure. Care must be taken lest other committees, some of them unnecessary, proliferate and continue to exist beyond their need for existence. Nothing is more useless than a nonfunctioning committee unless it be one that exists perennially in a *status quo* attitude. On the other hand useful committees can be serviceable not only for the work they do but because they let people learn through their work. Executive responsibilities include administrative attention to committee structure and advisement for committee action.

SELECTING STAFF MEMBERS

Many church school leaders have relatively little opportunity to select workers. When a new staff member is needed they ask (or beg) the one person available. For those who can select their workers, what types of persons shall they choose?

General Qualifications

Shall the workers preferably be men or women and what is the most desirable age for the people who are serving in the various positions?

AGE AND SEX

Several surveys have disclosed the general facts about these and other qualifications at the time of the studies. As for trends they indicate that the median age has been rising somewhat and there may be a slight increase of male workers.

When the Indiana Survey[2] was made in 1919 approximately 2,000 workers in 250 schools in that typical state, and in typical counties and towns of that state, were interviewed. It was found that 73 percent of them were women and 27 percent were men. The average age was about 37 years, one-fourth being under 27 and one-fourth above 47.

In 1949 a denominational study of 922 teachers revealed that the average teacher was a woman, 45 years of age. "Only one teacher in 7 was under 30 years of age; about one out of four was 50 or above."[3]

In 1960 another denomination researched its situation somewhat more intensively.[4] The sample for this study included approximately 2,000 teachers in more than 100 carefully selected congregations. Three-quarters of the teachers were women, one quarter were men; the percentage of male teachers increased in the upper age levels. The median age was 38 years, three out of four of them fell in the age group 26 to 55.[5] Five years later, on the basis of 800 questionnaires, the ages of leaders had risen slightly and the number of male teachers had increased slightly.

It seems generally agreed that the median age could well be younger and that a larger number of men would be desirable on all age levels.

Personality Qualifications

It seems agreed also that deep, broad, and vital Christian experience is a top demand on church school workers. As a student observed in one school: "A step in advance would be to secure teachers devoted to Christian principles in daily living." Those who hope to lead others preferably know of themselves the experiences into which they are trying to lead their pupils. Only religious knowledge, assent, and confidence gained through a vital practice in Christian living will meet the need. Among all desirable characteristics this is one that stands out most prominently. Several hundreds of college students described their "best" Sunday church school teacher by listing his or her outstanding characteristics. Many qualities were mentioned, among them: broadmindedness, conviction, enthusiasm, conservative spirit, earnestness, friendliness, honesty, faith, optimism, idealism, understanding, love. One other appeared always and usually first: Christian sincerity. Learners do demand

[2]Walter S. Athearn, E. S. Evenden, W. L. Hanson, William E. Chalmers, *The Religious Education of Protestants in An American Commonwealth,* The Indiana Survey of Religious Education, I (New York: George H. Doran Company, 1923), Part 5.

[3]Lewis J. Sherrill, *Lift Up Your Eyes* (Richmond: John Knox Press, 1949), Chap. 5.

[4]W. Kent Gilbert, *The Leaders for Whom We Write,* Long Range Program Series on Curricular Development, III (The Boards of Parish Education of the American Evangelical Lutheran Church—The Augustana Lutheran Church-The Suomi Synod-The United Lutheran Church in America, 1960).

[5]Verner Hanson, "Editorial," *Resource* (November, 1965).

of their leaders a hearty effort to act in the ways they urge. They will of necessity be members of some church, preferably the one in which they serve. Two other components are particularly needful for such a time as this: a zeal for constant growth with a willingness to study without stint; also a special measure of creativeness is required in the current educational approach.

Educational Qualifications and Experience

Regarding general education in the secular schools, the Indiana Survey showed that an average worker in 1919 had eleven years of schooling though 39 percent had less than ten years. The denominational study in 1949 reported that the average teacher had been in college for one year. Yet 3 percent had not gone beyond elementary school, 50 percent had attended college from one to four years and 8 percent (likely pastors) had undergone additional study. In the denominational study of 1960 the median educational level was graduation from high school. However, when the similar study was made five years later, 27 percent of the teachers had completed college, compared with 18 percent previously. Now, too, only 11 percent had not yet completed high school while 20 percent had been in this group five years earlier. The educational level is rising.

It has been assumed, doubtless rightly, that the more education workers have, the better qualified they are. Yet, it should be recognized that schooling does not necessarily insure education and there is education in living, reading, studying, and traveling. This sort of education, plus the largest amount of schooling, would seem to be the desirable standard.

Presumably the most acceptable worker has also the best possible religious education. What are the facts about our leadership here? No precise statistics seem to be available but one study shows that more study of Bible, theology, and Christian beliefs rated high among the expressed needs of teachers.

Another factor in cultural qualifications is professional education. A considerable number of church school workers are public school people with the appropriate degrees and so have had a variety of courses in general education. In one study, however, it was discovered that while some teachers had taught school for a time the larger percentage listed Sunday school work as the only teaching experience. The most highly qualified church school worker, other things being equal, would be one who has had strong professional training in Christian education. Data on this subject, reported in the following chapter, shows a grave weakness here.

We would choose ordinarily a candidate who has had the broadest possible experience in church school work itself, both as pupil and leader. One study indicated that the median church school teaching experience of its personnel had been six years. In almost all cases these teachers were active church members and had been in the educational programs of the church before they became workers. Second place in selection might be given to a candidate with public school teaching experience. Still another type of experience that fits people for successful and efficient church school work is parenthood. Many of the finest church school workers have been recruited among the parents, including fathers, who are sincerely interested in having their boys and girls undergo the best possible Christian development.

Obviously, church schools need to give urgent attention to the leadership problem.

PROVIDING STAFF MEMBERS

A church school executive has a thrice twofold goal of both a continuous and an adequate supply of capable workers: first, for immediate needs; second for future needs. The immediate needs, again, are twofold: regular workers and associate, assistant, substitute, or reserve workers. The leader should be ready to fill vacancies as they appear, not merely have to plug holes in the dikes. A perennial problem is how to secure them all and keep them all. This is even becoming more acute with the mobility of population; some church school staffs are like a sieve. Someone has said that there is the equivalent of a complete turnover in church school staffs every five years. Increased enrollments and the growing complexity of the task are further hurdles. An article not long ago was entitled, "More than a Half Million New Workers Needed Annually."

A Personnel Committee

Usually the basic duty of providing the necessary and desirable workers belongs to the church school committee. It may delegate this responsibility to a director of Christian education or to superintendents; also, while the committee as a whole can develop policies and make plans, the detail work may be assigned to a subcommittee. Best, perhaps, one personnel committee for the entire congregation would be charged with these typical problems of discovering, enlisting, and developing leadership for the whole church: Where can prospects be found? What qualifications are essential and what are the jobs? What plan shall be followed for enlistment? What are the motivations for service to which appeal will be made? What are to be the conditions of the service? How shall the talent be developed?

A committee on personnel for the church school might proceed as follows:

1. Educate the whole constituency on the importance of Christian education, the need for workers, the opportunity and privilege of such service.
2. Plan for a continuous program of leadership development that will include pre-service work including involvement from earliest years.
3. List kinds of positions to be filled and the qualifications required.
4. Canvass the constituency to discover who may be available, now or later.
5. Select those who are to be invited into leadership positions and extend the call.
6. Appoint the persons properly and initiate them into service appropriately.

Sources of Workers

Five sources of worker supply are the congregation in general, various adult classes and groups, the youth group, parents, and the community. The church membership roll deserves attention first. A church, if vital, should be able to develop members capable of propagating its mission and impelled to share its gifts. A questionnaire to be used with incoming and present members of the congregation can provide such information as the following: How long a church member? Types of church work and number of years engaged in it? Experience in church school work? Types of service preferred? Special preparation? Opportunities for training desired?

Adult classes, presumably having the most widely experienced and adequately qualified persons in their ranks, should be fruitful sources although one may have hard work getting some of them to give up the comfortable listening to their teacher's lectures. New members of the congregation, not already laden with other responsibilities, may undertake this task as their particular form of service. Women's societies and men's clubs should be canvassed also. Certain young adult groups are taking up study for leadership as one of their major enterprises. Youth are getting preparation in vacation church schools and camps as well as their other educational agencies; even high school students are having classes that ready them in substance, spirit, and perhaps methodology. Very often these people have a fresh attitude toward service. Parents sometimes accept responsibilities for the sake of their children or because they have a normal interest in Christian education as a result of their parenthood. There may be those in the congregation who have served once and now are able to return. Camp graduates are particularly promising candidates.

If such sources do not yield the necessary workers, there are possibilities in the community. A person not engaged in his own congregation's program may help, at least in an emergency. Specialists for certain specific needs may be willing to enlist for a ten-week elective course. Sometimes persons away from their home churches, such as students in a college town, can be enlisted. Yet such sources are not the final answer to the leadership problem. Congregations must develop their own leaders—some even have a waiting list, at least one church is known to give its workers a sabbatical leave occasionally.

Enlisting Workers

When the potential workers have been located they must be asked intelligently and invited persuasively.

It should not be assumed that people lack the desire to serve; it is better to believe they have it. Then why is it difficult to enlist them for this work? They may not realize the importance of the work, or it may appear uninteresting to them. Some are not actually qualified and know it; others have not yet discovered their abilities and may lack confidence. Many do not know how to start and so, properly, fear failure. Perhaps a few remain unmotivated for service of any type. With such an array of possible obstacles, a careful procedure is needed to enlist a prospective worker. Suggestions follow.

Lay sound foundations. An interested pastor will regularly teach and preach the needs for Christian service and the possible satisfaction in it. Teachers can present the same ideal to classes where prospective workers are studying. Case reports of boys and girls needing guidance and accounts of lives reoriented through the work are valuable materials for these purposes.

Make the proper approach. It is unwise to ask for volunteer leaders except perhaps in a leadership class. Difficulties can arise if a teacherless class is asked willy-nilly to suggest someone. We may get the kind of person we want to avoid: the emotionally unstable, the wrongly motivated, the hobbyist or controversialist with an ax to grind. Personal solicitation is always proper and usually necessary. The approach should be serious, not casual. Let a convincing leader confront a qualified prospect with a specific need. And not on the telephone; this job is worth a personal call if it is worth anything. The approach is not properly made if it minimizes the task by saying, for example, that it will not take much time. It should take time and the right people prefer a real challenge. Almost needless to say the job and its conditions should be clearly defined, the job analysis presented.

Appeal to the right motives. Why are people willing to serve in a church school? According to various studies the leading motives are church loyalty, love of children, joy of teaching, commitment to service for society, service to God, personal enrichment, and the evangelistic attitude. Some desire to help others learn of God, Jesus, the Bible; want to lead others to accept Jesus Christ as their savior; want to guide others into everyday Christian living; enjoy teaching, find challenge and satisfaction in it. Leaders of classes below grade 7 tend to choose different reasons for teaching than do leaders of classes of grade 7 and above.

Offer the best possible school. Schools with reputations for doing good work can challenge a prospect to share in a rewarding task. Such a school will exalt the work as it deserves; it will also provide desirable working conditions. A prospect has a right to expect the necessary help to do the job well: personal guidance when needed; the best facilities possible including all necessary resources; an element of freedom to work with spontaneity; a full share of involvement in school policy. In a good school, too, members of the church school staff will be protected from excessive demands; they are carrying a big share of a church's leadership load; the tasks should be shared equitably.

Appointing Staff Members

When workers who meet the standards as fully as possible have been selected and enlisted they should be officially appointed. By whom and how? In many schools appointment will be made by the church council, the church school committee, the pastor, or general superintendent. In other cases the school may wish to proceed more democratically. Let the next person or group in authority above the staff member under consideration make the nomination; let the group to be served elect the member. This would mean that overhead personnel may make nominations for the general superintendency and the workers of the school will elect. Also, a superintendent may nominate prospective teachers for the older classes and the members will vote on the nominees.

Whatever the manner of appointment, a candidate's willingness should be ascertained in preliminary conference. In many cases we are asking people to attempt what they have never done before; they must discover new interests and capacities. The appointment should be for a definite period, preferably one year. It will be understood that thereafter the worker can withdraw or the school can elect another worker if either party wishes.

Inducting Workers

An important ingredient in good church school management is an impressive service of installation, dedication, or consecration with members of the congregation, parents, and pupils present, the pastor leading the service. Each worker declares his intent to give faithful service; those to be served, including the whole congregation, avow their purpose to support earnest effort.

A worker's installation should be preceded and followed by a helpful introduction to the work. A teacher who is plunged into his job abruptly and then allowed to work without guidance or assistance will do one of three things: get discouraged and quit; go back to the methods used when he was taught; work his way through to effective dealing with the job. An understanding superintendent gives a new worker plenty of time to examine related books and materials. He presents the worker to his group under favorable circumstances. After the initial guidance, "first aid," if necessary, is administered promptly. Following up on new workers, inquiring into their problems and offering help, would save many and develop all for greater efficiency.

Significant help can be provided in a manual of procedure, already several times mentioned. Statements on such items as these would be useful:

1. What the objectives are.
2. Who should be consulted when problems arise.
3. How materials can be ordered.
4. Where audio-visuals are obtained.
5. What to do about absentees.
6. How to keep the records.
7. Whom to call for a substitute in emergencies.

After a new leader has been serving for some weeks the supervising officer should make periodic visits. As one last suggestion, it would be a good thing for members of the church school committee to take turns at being sponsors for new workers.

Retaining Workers

When all else has been done we want to keep our workers—with a few exceptions.

In public schools, staff members are retained partly through improvements in the program and facilities, salary increases according to a set schedule, tenure provisions, retirement benefits. Few if any of these enticements can be offered in a typical Christian educational program where volunteers comprise the majority of the personnel. Nevertheless there are steps to be taken. To have the worker properly selected, enlisted, appointed, and inducted is half the battle. Yet there are important suggestions for the other half.

"Contracts" or Covenants. There is a growing custom in which each member of the staff signs an instrument of commitment. This procedure cannot wisely be forced upon a school but staffs have voluntarily adopted it when brought to their attention. It makes for understanding of the worker's responsibilities and provides a stimulus where enthusiasm may lag. Also, any compact should include a statement of the school's obligations to the worker.

Providing for Leadership Development. Every church school owes its staff members any possible opportunity for advancement in their competence. Chapter VII following will deal with the subject.

Remuneration. With most schools the question of paying the staff is only an academic one for no money is available. In other schools the workers, especially superintendents and supervisors, sometimes teachers, are paid or could be. Thousands more of our congregations could at least be employing full or part-time directors. Perhaps the great body of our workers, though, wish to accept this voluntary opportunity to express their Christian faith-life along with fellow members who are working at other tasks. Similarly, the learners can profit from uplifting contacts with persons who, as typical lay Christians, are freely sharing their faith-life. One thing, however, can be done for all: provide excellent working facilities, helpful books, fees for attending conferences, tuition for study at camps, and the like. Somewhat related, perhaps "rest" Sundays or two or three weeks of vacation can be arranged occasionally.

Recognition versus Criticism. One writer has said that the church school leader should have two eyes to see much, but only one mouth to say little and that little, mostly commendation. More often than realized, commendation could lift a weary spirit out of apathy or error. Some years ago a cartoon featured a demure lady of uncertain years with a comment: "Few people know that little Miss Wiley has been teaching a class of girls for six years without missing a Sunday." Yes, few people know. Doubtless, too, many a "little Miss Wiley" does not much care. Yet the roll of the school staff can be published in the church bulletin; the annual induction can take the form of a recognition service; outstanding achievements can be brought before the school, the parents, the entire congregation. At least, the superintendent can appreciate his workers' efforts and let them know that he does; so can pastor, parents, and others.

Worker Determination. We want workers to manifest intelligence, initiative, interest, responsibility, and co-operation on the job. Allowing them to help determine the program themselves will go far toward accomplishing these desirables. They need to belong and share as fully as possible. Letting them decide upon policies will enable them to understand the policies better while it elicits their support. Workers cannot show initiative unless they are given freedom within responsibility. When they do, the enterprise becomes peculiarly their own responsibility. Then they are interested, and co-operation is generated.

Reassigning and Dismissing Workers

An executive sometimes faces the problem of reassignment or dismissal. Patience and forebearance are always in place. We are sometimes surprised when we discover who, really, has been most useful. Yet a worker might fit another age group more advantageously or be able to render better service in some other line of church work. For the good of themselves and the work, these persons should be reassigned. The purpose should be shared as fully as possible between the parties.

The dismissal of a staff member is particularly unfortunate and difficult. It should be made only when the worker is quite incompatible or incompetent, and the rarest of tact should be used. In view of the difficulties, constitutions should provide orderly procedures for the regular change of workers. The annual election or appointment provides a natural means of terminating service.

CONTROL WITHIN LEADER RELATIONSHIPS

Here control refers to the means employed for harmonious, collective efficiency—achieving the maximum of goal with minimum of expenditure and, as far as possible, without friction. Control is necessary within any organizational structure and under any type of administrative system. Moreover, we have here not only a necessity but also an educational objective: people must learn to control and be controlled. They can grow within shared responsibility. It is, as we shall see, a downward, upward, and outward as well as internal operation. It is first self-control, then control in terms of superior, co-ordinate, and subordinate workers. It is best achieved by inner dynamism which the executive helps to create.

Responsibility and Authority

Some responsibilities are natural—the very job suggests and requires them. Others are officially designated or delegated. An executive on any level—a teacher or pupil leader, too—may place a responsibility into the hands of some person or a committee, even issue a directive under appropriate circumstances. This church school leadership task requires persons to allocate responsibilities, to accept them and be accountable for their fulfillment.

Every responsibility carries with it a need for authority; every responsible person must exercise a measure of it. It is best exerted by means of personality and competence but there is no escaping the necessity. There are higher and lower levels of authority as well as relationships on the same level. Even in Christian circles there are, by the nature of things, superiors and subordinates although the status may alternate continuously.

Staff and Line Functioning

Here the distinction made by Bower[6] is useful. An organizational structure provides both horizontal and vertical relationships. So there is staff functioning and line functioning. Staff functioning takes place in the horizontal relationships. The several age group superintendents, for example, do not have authority over one another. They confer and advise; they must co-ordinate in mutual consideration of one another's opinions.

Line functioning occurs in the vertical relationships. An executive, such as superintendent, has line functions, with authority. His responsibilities reach down the line of authority so that he has an element of directive force for those beneath while they, in turn, have responsibility upward. An age group superintendent has authority for issuing directives to a secretary just as he may receive directions from a general superintendent.

Decision-Making and Communication

In church school leadership, just as in any other, decisions must be made within the lines of established authority. Consensus will be favored or voting may be necessary. There are occasions, however, for individuals to make decisions. The time element may require immediate action. Also some decisions do not merit extended discussion; we need not and should not bring trivialities to a conference table. In general, decision-making processes need to be speeded up.

Once decisions have been made they should move promptly into accordant action. On the one hand, somebody must see that they are

[6]Robert K. Bower, *Administering Christian Education* (Grand Rapids, Michigan: Eerdmans, 1964), pp. 36, 37.

implemented and take steps if there is any failure. On the other hand, all up and down the line, provisions are necessary for obedience to the proper authority.

Failure in action may be due to slothfulness or disagreement; more often though, the trouble is inadequate communication. There may have been incomplete instructions or insufficient attention to instructions. Communication must be clear, rapid, and effective. Chief aids to control, therefore, are communication devices. Especially in a large school, an organizational chart that shows the lines of authority will be helpful. Job analyses are essential. A post office for memoranda and letters about changes in procedure is a simple aid. Mimeographed reports, for example on the budget status, can be provided. The manual of procedure, several times mentioned, will be indispensable.

CHAPTER VII

DEVELOPING THE LEADERSHIP

Everywhere, really everywhere, it is recognized that a first charge on church school executives is to provide for an increasingly competent staff. What can be done? But first, how well prepared are present workers and what are they doing about opportunities to improve themselves?

A comparison of surveys undertaken through the years is revealing. Findings of the Indiana Survey[1] of 1919 showed that the great majority of workers interviewed were not specially prepared for their responsibilities in any way. Next to none had taken professional courses in religious education. Very few had ever read a professional book. Only 125 of the 2000 had graduated from leadership schools in 21 years; only 83 were enrolled at the time.

The denomination that studied its personnel situation in 1949[2] found that the average teacher who participated in the survey had never taken a formal course in leadership education but did attend a workers' conference when possible. Of the 922, almost 70 percent did not list a single course in leadership education; the others had taken an average of 3.2 courses. That average teacher was described more specifically as follows:

> In preparing for her Sunday school group she spends a little less than an hour a week, usually on Saturday night. In her preparation she relies almost entirely on the quarterly and the Bible. More rarely she examines a commentary, or turns to some other kind of written help. But beyond this she seems to do no other reading in connection with her teaching for she does not recall having read either a book or a magazine article for help in her teaching during the past year. She has never taken a formal course in leadership education. She goes to the Workers' Conference, however, when possible.[3]

[1]Walter S. Athearn, E. S. Evenden, W. L. Hanson, William E. Chalmers, *The Religious Education of Protestants in An American Commonwealth,* The Indiana Survey of Religious Education, 1 (New York: George H. Doran Company, 1923), Part 5.
[2]Lewis J. Sherrill, *Lift Up Your Eyes* (Richmond: John Knox Press, 1949), Chap. 5.
[3]*Ibid.,* pp. 132-33.

In the 1960 study by another denomination[4] half of the teachers reported that they had no special preparation before they began their careers. More than a third of the leaders reported no in-service education since they began to teach; teachers' meetings were most often mentioned by the two-thirds. About half of them had participated in one or more training classes, courses, or programs at the local or co-operative level. Two-thirds received the denominational journal regularly. At the time of this denomination's study five years later, a strong leadership education program had just been concluded; so statistics on that subject were not compiled because the situation was abnormal.

Those reports indicate that there has been advance though not nearly enough. Dr. Lee Gable has rightly said: "One of the most glorious chapters in the story of Protestantism is the contribution that volunteer workers have made."[5] Yet Christian education needs to take with utmost seriousness the history of public school leadership education. The first state normal schools were launched more than a hundred years ago. By the end of the last century good beginnings toward adequate preparation of administrators and teachers had been made. Now, throughout major areas of the United States, except emergency conditions, no child studies on any level under a teacher who has had less than a college education or its equivalent and many have higher degrees. As a result, the public school systems of most American communities are a source of pride where pupils show interest in their work and have confidence in their leaders. We, too, must have stronger leadership, more intelligent in educational theory and more skillful in procedure.

Incidentally, a special problem can emerge here: disparity between the preparation, outlook, and practice of leaders in the church school when compared with those in the public school. Church school teachers who are also public school teachers have sometimes faced a great gulf between the respective approaches in the two types of school. Pupils, too, may find themselves in a rather unfamiliar world when they leave the public school room and go to church school. People with one foot in an airplane cannot travel well with the other in an oxcart. New curricular series may relieve the tension but will have to be kept up to date.

As there has been progress, however limited, in leadership development during recent decades, there is promise in the programs now underway. The greatest obstacle is general lethargy and self-complacency. The church

[4]W. Kent Gilbert, *The Leaders for Whom We Write,* Long Range Program Series on Curricular Development, III (The Boards of Parish Education of the American Evangelical Lutheran Church—The Augustana Lutheran Church—The Suomi Synod—The United Lutheran Church in America, 1960).

[5]Lee J. Gable, *Christian Nurture Through the Church* (New York: National Council of Churches in the U.S.A., 1955), p. 60.

does not demand better leadership; church schools may not provide opportunities; leaders often do not accept their responsibility to grow. Perhaps when all parties to the situation realize that teaching religion is an infinitely more subtle and complex process than teaching "the new arithmetic," they will insist that teachers of the former subject be at least as well trained as teachers of the latter. Then we, too, shall be making more use of advanced leadership development programs.

NEEDS

Two kinds of special effort at the improvement of leadership are needed: (1) *a pre-service program of means for preparation of those who have not yet begun their work;* (2) *an in-service program of means for workers already at work to improve their performance.*

Before considering the many special means for meeting that dual need, it must be noticed that the church conceives leadership improvement differently now at two points. Once we used the term "leadership training" but that has a too narrow meaning as a rather mechanical drilling of people in technique. While this work has a place, a broader goal is in view. Later, the term leadership education was used, and still is, but that term tends to emphasize courses. These, too, remain important but we think now of many additional means, some of which are more serviceable for our purposes. The favored term is now "leadership development" because we have in view a leader in the large sense of the term; not merely a technician, such a person must be a fully developed individual with cultivated knowledge, concern, experience, skill, and personality. Quite specifically, leadership development works with objectives that deal with content as well as method and beyond this with Christian manhood and womanhood. As a second difference in the present outlook, the improvement of leadership has in view the whole scope of church work and every type of church worker including, for example, the church councilman. Yet the majority of church workers are those engaged in educational tasks; so leadership development programs continue to deal largely with that work.

MEANS

Here, of course, the major subject is the improvement of the church school staff although leadership development throughout the church is not out of mind. Fortunately, the widest variety of means and agencies is available. Some are of a group nature; others are more personal. Of the latter type, supervision—that third major responsibility of the executive—is most significant.

The General Curriculum

All other agencies are in addition to the important leadership development that takes place in the general program of the school. Major work at preparing leaders is done there although the fact may be rarely recognized or specifically utilized. From the earliest age, future candidates for the educational staff are learning basic facts they will need in their later service—Bible, church, and Christian conduct. Each small task performed for the school at any age is a step in developing leadership responsibility and skill. In all their church school experiences and relationships pupils are gaining some sort of educational outlook and learning some type of educational procedure. Those are the foundations on which the special forms of later leadership development are built.

Group Agencies: Wider Community

Conferences, conventions, and institutes on church school work have been held through more than a hundred years and continue to be one form of leadership development. Although the big convention idea seems to be declining, each year provides a series of interdenominational and denominational gatherings to serve the church schools of regions, states, counties, cities, and general church bodies. Programs of these meetings have leaned toward general themes and inspirational speeches; there is a trend now toward biblical and doctrinal papers. Yet the practical is being stressed in specialized group sessions such as departmental conferences. There the workers can ask questions and share experiences about their immediate situations. Another promising development is the introduction of newer procedures into the program itself—film presentations, panels, forums, and the like.

The executive's basic problem is to make sure that something gets done as a result of attendance. A woman who had been attending conventions for two decades said she always comes home with enough good resolutions to revolutionize her department; alas, though, those resolutions evaporate one by one. That woman's pastor, director, or general superintendent could help by calling pre- and post-convention meetings of the delegation. Before the convention they would go over the program and plan what they will look for and do. Then, back home, they will decide on one or more things to undertake and carry through to completion.

The *summer assembly, camp, or school* agency is most widely represented in numerous interdenominational or denominational camps. There the workers in attendance live for one or two weeks in out-of-door surroundings while they study under outstanding leaders. The typical program is varied. The classes are often in the First or Second Series of The

Leadership Curriculum. There are worship, dramatic, and recreational activities under expert guidance.

Much of the improvement in local church educational programs during the last decade or two can be credited to the camp leadership education movement. Camp experience is singularly well adapted to the needs of workers who can and will study for a short period under ideal circumstances. The leaders are usually of high rank. There is concentrated work, relatively free from the usual distractions. There is rich fellowship with choice spirits in both faculty and student membership.

Colleges, seminaries, training schools, and universities are contributing especially to the development of higher leadership for Christian education. This work is largely a product of the present century, paralleling the progress of the so-called modern movement and in no small sense responsible for its continuation. Colleges often provide courses in which prospective lay leaders may prepare themselves for educational service. Seminaries are helping the oncoming pastors gain an advanced educational outlook and be equipped to carry forward the educational work in the parish which they are called to serve; some have advanced programs for unordained workers. Denominational and interdenominational training schools have provided directors of Christian education, deaconesses, and parish workers who can give expert guidance to educational work. Universities offer programs in which teachers of teachers may do advanced study and others may prepare for such highly specialized tasks as planning curriculum, organizing denominational forces, and serving as general secretaries. They have also fostered research which has worked back into leadership competence. The contribution of such agencies is restricted chiefly by the unfortunate lack of recruits.

Home study and correspondence courses are offered by some of the denominations. They make it possible to engage in leadership education wherever mail is delivered. There is now some similar work by radio and television.

Laboratory schools and workshops are relative newcomers in this area. They are operated as separate units or as features within, for example, a summer camp. Well done, they are leadership development at its best. Workers have personal experience in the same procedure they will use in leading others in learning by doing.

A laboratory school may be an every day school engaged in experimental or, for our concern, practice work. More likely it will be a special week, in charge of national workers and with a complement of pupils and learning leaders. It is based on the principle that teachers learn realistically in a combination of observation where they see skillful workers in action and can themselves participate under expert guidance.

The workshop, too, is a means of learning by practice in actual experience, though too often it has been just a new name for a conference. It is properly a limited enterprise of actually developing specific ideas, plans, and materials or of threshing out to solution a particular problem. What are we going to do about departmental discipline? How shall we eliminate drop-outs? Let's prepare a different kind of Christmas program. We need a script to go with last year's slides for publicizing this year's vacation school. There is typically a continuous period of time, concentrated and uninterrupted.

Group life institutes, intensive experiences with group process, are perhaps the most recent means for our purposes and they are mushrooming. They may be of a few days' or weeks' duration. The emphasis is on experiencing group relationships under shared leadership. A major result can be an awareness of group dynamics with attention to their effect and to planning for the management of them. Institutes are important for understanding and practice within the current emphasis on small group process as an educational matrix. Yet personal development of leaders is being stressed in them.

Group Agencies: Nearer Community

Nearer community agencies of leadership education include many of the above types but especially local conferences, conventions, and institutes and leadership education schools or classes on the local level.

First and Second Series courses come to mind first of all when the term "leadership education" is used. They belong in *The Leadership Education Curriculum* promoted interdenominationally by the former International Council of Religious Education, now by its successor The Division of Christian Education, NCCCUSA. Approximately forty denominations co-operate as do state and local councils of churches. The work is done in classes or schools of many types. The interdenominational program will be described with the understanding that denominations have adopted and are promoting vigorously the same type of work with similar standards and procedures. There are two levels of courses, First Series and Second Series, in order of advancing requirements. There are also "experimental courses."

The *First Series* courses are meant for beginning students and young workers or persons with limited time. At least ten hours of work are to be done for each course, usually five hours in group sessions and five in out-of-class work. Recommended texts are to be used wherever possible. The class should be enrolled with an accrediting agency, either The National Council's local unit or the denomination. A Course Card of Recognition will be issued to each student who completes the course. Such First Series courses as the following are listed: *Personal Religious Living; The Life and Work of Paul; The Program of My Church; The Children We Teach; Youth at Worship; Planning a Vacation Church School.* The courses may be taken by individual study or as informal group work, in an institute or camp or through a workers' conference which uses a course as part of its program. Usually, though, there is a special "leadership class" for the purpose in a local church or a community denominational or interdenominational school.

The larger proportion of nearer community leadership education is done in schools or classes working on the level of *Second Series* courses. This work is for those who are ready for the more advanced materials and are able to expend the requisite time. The courses must continue for at least ten fifty-minute periods. The sessions can be arranged on a great variety of schedules so as to be completed in five days, two weeks, six weeks, or twelve weeks. Many communities have fall and spring semesters of six weeks each. In all cases it is expected that there will be an hour of outside work for each hour in class. A Second Series class for which a Course Card of Recognition is to be issued must have an instructor who is certified by National Council or denominational leadership headquarters; a school which offers several such courses must have an accredited dean. Approved texts or equivalent materials are specified. Those who contemplate establishing such a school and those who teach in one will need to secure the national or denominational bulletin for their guidance and consult the appropriate offices of national or state secretaries of leadership education.

Local Church Agencies

Agencies for leadership development distinctly under local church management are in many respects the most important of all. While the previously mentioned agencies suit leaders of leaders particularly well, these local ones fit the rank and file more closely.

GROUP TYPES

The most formal local church agency is a *leadership class for present workers.* Though a class of this sort may be done on The Leadership Education Curriculum basis or under denominational auspices, one planned and conducted locally, if done with similar or higher standards, has advantages. It enables workers to meet their precise interests and needs with their particular equipment, leadership, and pupils. If the workers are involved fully in it, the planning and conducting are of high educational value in themselves. The pastor should be the leader if no other is available. It provides him a unique opportunity to guide the educational progress of his church; under any circumstances he should be an active participant. The list of courses presented in the interdenominational or denominational leadership bulletins will suggest units of work; printed resource materials such as leaders' guides and textbooks will be listed there, also. A program that deals with real problems is the desirable approach.

Another local church agency deserves more attention than it receives: *church school class or department work* for future educational workers. The few pastors who report more trained workers available than they can use have almost invariably employed this means. In such church schools there may be a leadership education division parallel to the youth division. In one instance, a general invitation is given for enrollment and selected young persons are urged to enter. Thereafter, they have two years of study, observation, and practice. At the end of that time they graduate and are placed, when possible, in a position of leadership. Then another class is started. Current camp programs and vacation church school literature are stressing this leadership development for future workers.

Somewhat related to the above, there are various types of volunteer and informal *study groups*. A small number of people can gather periodically to study available material on current problems or hear an outside speaker on some vital topic. Also related is a *coaching conference* for a unit overview on lesson preparation. Once a month or more often, certainly once a quarter, the staff of a department or school can work on forthcoming materials.

Another valuable form of local leadership development is available to congregations through *visits by professional or semi-professional leaders*. Major denominations have field secretaries of Christian education who regularly observe or survey in local congregations, then hold conferences and make recommendations. They may study the whole program or some feature only, such as children's or youth work.

A different form of leadership development, available for every church school is *guided reading*. A church school workers' library, however small to begin, can be established. Lists of recommended books can be secured from denominational houses. A librarian may be needed to promote the reading or promotion can be undertaken by the pastor, director, or superintendent. One school maintained a reading program in which a kindergarten department superintendent led all the workers and mothers in reading a series of books on the religious training of small children. A book table is a regular feature in some church schools. Public librarians will co-operate where intelligent use of books is made. Every school should place *The International Journal of Religious Education* on its budget for the superintendents and similar leaders, also the denominational educational periodical for every worker.

A *monthly workers' conference* can be one of the most pertinent units in the improvement program. Properly, it would be a meeting of all the workers of the church for inspiration and study to the end of larger effectiveness in the total program of the church. Because of our special interest the appropriate successor to the typical "Teachers' and Officers' Meeting" is in mind. Those meetings have been given over usually to routine business with a discussion of problems relating to the Christmas program, the annual picnic, increased attendance, reward systems, and the like. A monthly workers' conference may take care of such items, but should never be devoted solely to them. Instead, it will attempt to lift vision to higher goals and increase effectiveness in attaining those goals.

The program should be fourfold. It will include devotions, not perfunctory but employing and indirectly demonstrating improved procedures in planning and conducting worship. There will be business limited to important issues, the routine items having been cared for by the proper officers or an executive committee. Nothing will kill the whole idea more surely than an undue waste of time on business. Fellowship is just as important here as anywhere else. There may be a simple meal together or refreshments.

Yet the study feature is to be the heart of the meeting, with topics of immediate and practical interest though an adequate treatment may take the group into so-called theoretical considerations. A general presentation or study may be followed by age-group conferences or interest-group meetings for the workers in particular areas. The topics should be chosen by the group under guidance that will help them have a balanced program. Good suggestions will come from the denominational and interdenominational journals and various books that publish suggested programs. Topics like the following may be fruitful: What are our real objectives? What shall we do about "homework" and "memory work"? Are we holding and serving our young people and what can be done about it? How can we help our pupils appreciate the true meaning of Christmas? What does teaching really mean?

The ways of handling the topics will vary with the resources at hand and with variety in view. They may include discussions, lectures, outside speakers, research with reports, book reviews, and studies of textbooks in the Leadership Education Curriculum or denominational equivalent. The new leadership education kits of filmslides, filmstrips, sound filmstrips, and recordings may be the greatest boon yet. They enable a leader to present pertinent items in realistic ways he could not duplicate in any other manner. They provoke discussion and, all in all, provide an unexcelled launching platform for progressive action.

A regular meeting time should be established and rigidly adhered to. The most important means of securing attendance is to provide a program that makes every worker sense an opportunity. Each one should feel, too, that he is expected, and missed if he is not present.

A recently popular group leadership development agency is a *retreat*. It can combine the *evaluation conference* idea with a *planning conference*. The church school committee can be in charge with all branches of the church school planning the program.

INDIVIDUAL TYPES

Among other and effective ways of improving the church school staff are several personal means. Basically, any leadership development program should result in continuous self-education.

Here as elsewhere there is no better way to learn than by doing— *apprenticeship*. We have long recognized the value of "training on the job." Many present workers have begun that way. Quite young people, junior highs for example, have been called in to help with younger children. By that means they get acquainted with pupils of a given age and see the program in operation. Beginning with rather simple tasks like handling chairs, greeting pupils, assisting with coats and hats, they gradually assume more difficult tasks such as telling a story, leading conversation, and guiding handwork. Incidentally, this is not, if properly handled, taking them away from their "lesson"; it is working with realistic lessons. Likely, though, they should remain on the roll of their usual classes and after a time go back to that regular work if not forward into educational service.

An apprenticeship should involve some introductory study and always be coupled with careful coaching and guided study. The coaching can be quite informal but real. Simple suggestions can be given in advance, and the worker can be commended or cautioned after the work is finished. Continued reading, too, can be related to specific problems that have arisen although in time it is broadened to cover more background.

Apprenticeship may be an accompaniment of a specific leadership education course. Then it takes on the character of the "practice teaching" by which public school teachers have been prepared. *Practice teaching-leading* is regularly a part of the program in churches that maintain a leadership education division, department, or class. After preliminary study, members of the group are assigned to experienced leaders who give them opportunities to teach or lead in other ways. Meanwhile they are under the guidance of their leadership education teacher who confers with them personally and conducts evaluation sessions in which the members of the group may share their experience and arrive co-operatively at solutions for their problems.

Among individual agencies of leadership development, personal *reading* must have a large place. A magnificent number of books and journals are now available. They must be made readily accessible and their use encouraged by pastor, superintendent, librarian, and other interested persons. Somehow we need to help workers understand that this is not only a part of their responsibility but also a splendid part of their privilege. When one begins to be more intelligent about his task it becomes more meaningful and interesting just as it is more effective.

Doubtless *weekly preparation* should be included as a form of leadership development. One study showed that teachers spend an average of two and a half hours preparing for each Sunday session. That is not enough time, yet it has educational value in content terms if no more. It can be made more valuable if the school will provide abundant helps, also if teachers learn to prepare written session patterns.

The word *observation* covers a considerable variety of means for individual development. Workers may visit other schools to see the equipment and observe the work being done in organization and administration, curriculum, worship, and the like. The idea is to see and carry home the fruits of observation to make it effective in the home school. Ordinarily, good situations are observed; even so, the observer should be helped to recognize what is bad. Arrangements should be made in advance for persons who will guide the visitors and help them avoid disturbing the work. Observers should have previous direction concerning definite things to look for, and should have an opportunity to discuss their visit. Visits to public schools as well as to church schools can be very helpful.

Demonstrations are sometimes arranged in conferences and conventions. They have the disadvantage of staging so that the situation is unreal and leaders as well as pupils are under strain. Nevertheless those who observe, if wisely guided, may benefit. The demonstration should be preceded by a discussion of the prospective session and followed by a conference to consider its procedure and results.

Finally, workers may employ *personal rating scales* and *survey schedules* now available for discovering their strengths and weaknesses. *Parent-teacher meetings* and *home visitation* have a place among agencies for leadership improvement. Still another means is the *orientation conference* to acquaint new workers with their tasks.

Supervision

A final means of leadership development, an individual one, in-service, on the local church level, deserves special attention. Though it appears last in the listing here, that position is sometimes the emphatic one. This agency deserves that prominence because it provides the most intimate, down-to-earth assistance.

The church school executive, as Chapter IV defined his work, is supervisor as well as organizer and administrator. Supervision has sometimes been made synonymous with the whole complex of management. Obviously that is not the meaning here. The task was defined very broadly as "improving the processes so that the product of the machinery will be constantly better." More narrowly, the supervisor is a master technician available to help specifically those who are less mature in their experience. Certain other names help to describe the task: "teaching consultant"; "helping teacher"; and "worker counselor."

With that purpose of improving the acts which occur when a learner meets a leader, it is more narrowly the personal guidance of workers, on the job, for the improvement of their work and results. Somewhere it has been popularly defined as "two or more people tackling a problem that otherwise one would have to face alone."

Pastors are constantly serving as supervisors in the broader sense. They supervise when they consciously take hold of the local situation at any point to effect improvement in the learning-teaching process. In the more narrow sense they supervise when a worker comes to them with a specific problem and they together study the various solutions of that problem until some improvement is effected. One director of Christian education serves his supervisory responsibility chiefly by visiting each worker of his school once a month for a two-hour conference.

The fundamental approach of a supervisor is made through the learning-teaching act. Of course, teaching in this case is broadly viewed as guidance in any area, session, or circumstance, not simply classroom instruction. The supervisor is interested in what takes place when leaders meet their pupils in a unit of activity. How do they study, worship, serve, or conduct fellowship? How do they work at a unit of activity? How can their performance and consequent results be improved? In particular the supervisor seeks to work with problem situations. There he observes symptoms, diagnoses causes, and suggests remedies.

The characteristic technique of supervision is threefold. It includes: (1) a preliminary conference with the worker involved; (2) a visit at the session in which the worker leads; (3) a conference with the worker after that visitation. The preliminary conference is meant to enable the worker and the supervisor to arrive at mutual understanding about the goals and plans for the session and the purpose of the supervisor's visit. The visit itself should be conducted in an unobtrusive manner so that all the conditions remain as normal as possible. Always the visit should continue through the session. In the post-conference meeting, the good features of the session receive paramount consideration with mutual agreement upon the steps of improvement to be undertaken. Follow-up is essential until satisfactory results are evident.

In effecting remedies for a situation, the program of improvement may extend far beyond the supervisor's immediate range of effort. Here he meets his broader task. It may include working for improvement in such areas and through such means as the following:

Using standards and goals for the school and tests and measures for pupils.
Reorganizing.
Suggesting better administrative management.
Providing more adequate financial support and improved facilities.
Educating the entire constituency of the congregation about its school.
Building better relations with the home.
Developing an improved curriculum.
Fostering the appropriate forms of leadership education.

All supervisory processes must be conducted on a democratic, co-opera-tive basis for this is not something into which people can be forced. A pastor, director, deaconess, or superintendent may foster it. It will succeed most surely when it is provided because of a demand from the workers themselves. It should be supported and directed by a responsible body such as the church school committee. The whole congregation should under-stand the work of the supervisor.

MOTIVATION FOR DEVELOPMENT

Providing various means for the improvement of church school staff members is one thing; their use of those means is another. The statistics cited earlier show a pitifully small proportion of workers profiting by the vast efforts to help them grow in their competence. The following sugges-tions are meant to help the church school executive meet that frequent plaint, "But they don't come."

1. *Set an example.* Here is another place where the leader must lead. His reading, study, attendance at conferences, camps, schools, classes, and the like will be contagious.
2. *Help workers be convinced of their need.* This sense of need may begin with a conviction about the importance of educational work in the church. It passes on to a recognition of need for progress in that work. Finally the individual worker should see a definite point at which he needs help.
3. *Show them that they can grow.* While some workers may think they have already attained their maximum competence, others may humbly doubt their capacity to be helped. They must be enticed into experi-ences that really serve their practical needs.

4. *Assure them they will not be embarrassed.* This assurance may require a promise that they will not have to take an examination, make long talks in public, or give answers that may be wrong. Yet the time should come when they can appreciate the help realized through full participation.

5. *Help them see that the work can be interesting.* Leadership education is not necessarily dull. Many people love to sharpen their wits in a study experience. Here is a challenging field for self-realization.

6. *Help them develop a hunger for such a program.* An outstanding camp is an ideal place to catch the spirit. Perhaps the more hesitant can be taken to visit a camp or at any rate meet an enthusiastic camper. Visiting a superior class or school may be helpful, too.

7. *Make the means practicable, readily within reach.* Place, amount of work required, and time schedules are important considerations. In some cases, too, financial problems must be eliminated.

8. *Make sure that the experience will be satisfying.* It should be planned to help the worker have larger satisfaction in his work. This requires especially that he have opportunity to deal with practical problems on specific points of felt need.

9. *Plan for appropriate recognition of progress.* Course completion cards, credits, certificates of progress or diplomas, and recognition services have this purpose in view.

10. *Build workers into the fellowship of the cause.* Association with important leaders will have value for this motivation. Each one should see himself as part of an important movement in which honored persons are working.

A STANDARD

Out of the many forms of leadership development listed and discussed above each Sunday church school executive or responsible group should plan a complete program for the improvement of the staff. Its nature will vary with the size of the school and many other conditions but it should include every present and prospective worker and provide the maximum opportunity which can be made available and will be used by the workers.

A minimum standard would seem to be: *some definite leadership education experience for every present worker each year and some definite preparatory possibility for prospective workers each year.* If possible, these enterprises will include regular credit courses in addition to the more informal means of improvement. The emphasis can best be placed upon growth "on the job."

CHAPTER VIII

ADMINISTERING PUPILS

Major items in our work with pupils have to do with what is typically called curriculum, discussed in Chapters IX through XII. In this chapter only selected topics concerning administrative management of pupils are considered.

GROUPING

Pupils must be grouped in even the smallest of schools. A standard pattern, according to the diagrams of Chapter V, includes divisions for children, youth, and adults—in larger schools, nursery, kindergarten, primary, junior, junior high school, senior high school, older youth, and adult departments—with their various classes. These divisions and departments correspond to the major phases of the life cycle: childhood, adolescence, and adulthood with their customary subdivisions. Some schools now have primary, middler, and junior departments for elementary pupils, each including two school grades; most recently there is that strong trend toward grouping by single grades. These contemporary developments are breaking up the traditional patterns. Executives do not need, however, to undertake crash programs of change. It is better to keep informed, watch emerging changes, and be prepared to suit the school's conditions at any given time.

Purposes of Grouping

We group pupils not merely to meet some prescribed standard of organization. Educational theory and practice require us to form homogeneous units. More effective education takes place when people of similar purposes, kindred interests, and like experiences meet in groups of their own kind. We do not want passive recipients who are to learn by sitting and listening; we do want active participants who learn by guided living in situations organized for purposeful, democratic activity. Therefore persons are placed in the groups where they can do what they rightly want to do and where they can work co-operatively to attain their objectives. Too, pupils need to develop a capability for working in groups; so they must be put where they will feel reasonably at home.

For schools that recognize these purposes fully, the typical organization of divisions, departments, and classes may be too rigid. Consequently, in this treatment of the topic, flexibility will be emphasized. There are occasions when pupils will grow best if exceptions are made. Function, place, time, process, or facilities may cause us to cut across usual lines. People can profit by work with a variety of ages and academic backgrounds; experiences of sharing in worship, fellowship, and service may require rather variegated groups. At other times, a group may better be organized on a highly selective basis.

Bases of Groupings

The usual bases for differentiation in grouping are age—often school grade now—sex and interest. Frequently, for example, the children nine, ten, and eleven years of age are placed in a junior department. Calendar age is not the ideal basis for classification although it has often been adopted as the most practical one. There may be, theoretically, a religious age which we may some time be able to determine. Meanwhile, there is reason to believe that the religious age will normally correlate rather well with the mental age. So church schools increasingly follow the public school grade for grouping the younger pupils. For older pupils, their interests in particular subjects or particular social situations may provide the best basis. Much can be said in favor of recognizing the interests of pupils, even younger ones but particularly adults, who can form spontaneous interest groups. While it is unwise to disturb venerable adult classes that prize their fellowship, we can make a varied program available for those who want it.

Sometimes boys are separated from girls and men from women. Various reasons are used to justify this sex segregation: the differing physical and social, or even religious, maturity at certain ages; the desirability of male teachers for boys, female teachers for girls; specialized interests and needs. In all probability, though, the practice grew out of an ancient tradition by which men sat on one side of the church and women on the other. That custom, the vogue when Sunday schools originated, is being discarded except where a type of activity has special relevance to one sex or the other. It creates an artificial situation which suggests that Christianity is something apart from day to day living. Boys and girls work together in public schools; they do now and will continue to live together in homes; their religious experiences are not particularly dissimilar. Coeducation minimizes instead of emphasizing their differences. It allows the sexes of the congregation to get acquainted with one another. They do not differ much in the ability to get good ideas and both are broadened by sharing them.

Size of Groups

The proper sizes for groups is another important consideration. How big is too big and how small is too small? There was a time when exact specifications had been worked out. Now we recognize that the preferred number depends on such criteria as objectives, equipment, methods, discipline, and leadership. The trend is twofold: to form larger groups with small subgroups for small group process.

The large class, with subdivisions when conditions require it, has merit but large classes are not to be undertaken as an escape to something easier. While a good teacher in an adequate setting can accomplish more with a large class than two or three less qualified teachers with parts of it, it must not be so large that the teacher cannot keep personal contact with each member. Also big classes demand appropriate types of teaching, division for certain procedures and purposes, perhaps use of a team of workers. Too many classes are too large under their circumstances. Classes must be small enough so that each member can be active and at the same time large enough for people to have a sufficiently varied program and breadth of relationships. As a final standard for decisions about grouping we can ask: does this plan provide the best feasible way to develop the well rounded Christian living of the pupils involved?

Promotion

Promotion provides for a regular progression of pupils from one group to another. There should be a sense of advancement in church school just as in public school. Further, there should be variety of experiences with different groups and leaders. To remain throughout the larger part of one's church school experience with one teacher, or in a particular class, can be a calamity for a pupil. In larger schools pupils can be promoted from one class, grade, department, and division to another. In the smallest schools there can be a promotion every three years or as often as a pupil is ready for another major group.

In Christian education there can be less rigidity than in public schools—even they are breaking the lock step. We are emphasizing that a church school pupil, particularly an older youth or adult, should ordinarily be permitted to shift from class to class, even department to department, for the unit of activity in which he is most interested or in which his need can be met best. Yet a time should come when the various units of activity have been brought to a stage where there can be "promotion day."

Shall the teacher be promoted with a class? In many schools the answer has been affirmative; teachers have remained with groups for many years, even through their entire church school experience. But those pupils have had only one interpretation of Christianity and one Christian personality influencing their lives! It is perhaps best to have a teacher remain with pupils through the three years of a typical department. This avoids the lack of variety just mentioned and the further problem which arises when pupils change teachers every year so that neither they get well acquainted with their teacher nor their teacher with them. By this three year cycle, too, a teacher can become somewhat of an age group specialist.

STANDARDS FOR PROMOTION

Any advancement should properly follow the attainment of standards and these should be in terms of objectives reached, not just attaining an age or being allowed nominal progress.

Some schools have announced, for example, these "Junior Department Requirements": (1) know the Ten Commandments; (2) recite the Christmas and Easter stories; (3) know The Apostles' Creed and Lord's Prayer; (4) name the books of the Bible in order. Are such requirements desirable? They put an emphasis on a too limited portion of our total objective and there is another fault. It was Promotion Day in a midwestern city. Members of the junior department were brought before the congregation to recite the memory requirements for advancement to the intermediate department. More than half of them did not meet the stated standards, yet they were being promoted. That was no less than immoral and irreligious.

We may question whether we can ever have real standards for promotion in the church school even if it is agreed that we should. For something of the sort, it is possible to have suggested "achievements" in each group and let pupils who complete them be promoted with citations on their certificates.

PROMOTION DAY

A special Promotion Day gives significance to the beginning of work under new conditions, provides a degree of recognition for work completed, develops in pupils and leaders a feeling of progress. Its deeper significance may be in the fact that the school must reclassify its pupils and start them anew with the groups and activities that are more appropriate to their progress.

The day ought to be celebrated with a service of definitely religious character and one that recognizes Christian educational ideals. It certainly should not become what one harrassed worker called "commotion day." Parents may be invited and it can be Church School Day in the congregation. "Diplomas" can be used; classes will be moved actually up to their new positions where they should be thoughtfully introduced so that they can begin to feel at home. Such criteria as the following are applicable: Will the day be worthwhile educationally, memorable? Will it produce school spirit? Will it provide another wholesome religious experience?

SPECIAL CASES

The grouping of adults often creates difficulties. The problem is how to conserve important fellowship values while meeting levels of ability or types of interest and need with satisfying learning experiences. It is best to establish the basic differentiations: young, middle, and older adults with the usual age specifications. In some church schools, particularly where the population is mobile, this will likely serve. Elsewhere churches have sometimes found it best to start a new adult class from time to time and let it continue as long as it persists. However, if the classes are large and self-perpetuating they need a variety of self-liquidating groups alongside. This bifocal approach may be the solution where classes that have existed for a long time do not wish to break the social bonds permanently. Let the group have basic work and fellowship together, along with parallel elective units for which people do not lose their membership in the larger group.

Every school has its quota of exceptional pupils. Some are subnormal. Where shall they be placed and what shall be done about promoting them? Sometimes special provision is made for the unfortunates in the school itself, in a special school, or in their homes. They do create social problems in the typical school but it may be argued that their presence provides a special opportunity to exercise the right sort of Christian compassion and helpfulness. It is best, if reasonably possible, to let them stay in their age range.

At the other end of the scale, there are superior pupils who are out of step with their age group because of greater ability and advancement. These, too, create problems. Again, the general principle is to keep them in their own school grade. There they can be given special class responsibilities or be assistants for suitable work in the school's management.

SECURING REGULAR ATTENDANCE

Regular attendance is important. Frequency of repetition of experiences, other things being equal, is essential for learning. Effective unit procedure requires everybody to be present. Irregular attendance breaks the fellowship among students and with the teacher. How can we overcome the customary low percentage of regularity?

1. *Have the best possible school.* Poor program with inferior leadership heads the list of deterrents. There is significant meaning in the papers of pupils who wrote on "Why Children Do Not Go to Sunday School." One said, "Because those who go are not any different from those who do not." A high percentage of attendance can be attained only when every member makes satisfying and stimulating progress—noticeable progress—toward desirable objectives. To depend on institutional loyalty is not enough though a sense of obligation is wholesome in its way; a concern for the "record of our class" and the "good name of our school" is not to be deprecated. Yet, until each child, young person, and adult, along with every officer, teacher, and parent finds the church school the most worthwhile activity for that hour, there is grave doubt whether any outstanding improvement in attendance records can be achieved.

2. *Surround the pupils with friendship.* Lack of hospitality is probably second among reasons for irregular attendance. A young woman made a glowing report of her reception when she visited a neighboring school. She was greeted at the door, ushered to the proper place, guided through the worship service, and welcomed in a class. She says that she will always be interested in that school. Contrast that experience with the coldness newcomers meet elsewhere. Visitors enter the room, look around for the most inconspicuous place to sit, feel unwelcome stares of curiosity, wonder about the proper thing to do, then await the close of the hour in order to escape. One objective of a church school is to foster Christian fellowship. People learn to practice fellowship by experiencing its worth to themselves and being led by their teachers and officers to shed its grace upon one another in the school. That "oneness" or "groupness" comes best as a by-product of an all-around human concern but direct cultivation through a hospitality committee, "greeters," or sponsors for new members, may prove beneficial.

3. *Have a common attendance goal.* A definite goal for attendance is recommended. When a school devises its target, the average during the past year should be computed; then it can consider some percentage to achieve. It may be reasonable to begin at 75 percent instead of a usual 65 percent. The goal should be accepted by the congregation, too, so that everybody will be working toward it. Progress can be visualized in graphs pasted on bulletin boards and printed in congregational bulletins.

4. *Care for the absentees.* The school's secretary, possibly a special absentee secretary, will usually prepare lists of absentees after each session. These should be followed up promptly, preferably by the teacher although

class members can often be the most persuasive solicitors. Cards or letters may be sent after the first absence; telephone calls may follow continued absence; a personal call should be made if the absentee does not return promptly. Personal interest is what counts most. Whatever the exact procedure, a definite plan is necessary.

The reason for an absence is perhaps more significant than the fact of it. If there has been only a minor problem a demonstration of interest and a word of encouragement for the absentee to return is enough. Often, however, more basic causes are involved. Is the pupil disinterested? Is he uncomfortable in his group? Is his work not meeting his needs? Does the leader fail to understand him and minister to him effectively? Are there home conditions that could be changed? Does he need help with transportation? Are all the school's facilities conducive? The threefold prescription for the ailment is to build preventives, attack causes, and undertake remedial measures.

5. *Reduce drop-outs.* The percentage of pupils who eliminate themselves from our schools appalls every leader who knows the statistics. According to the findings of one study, made some years ago but there is likely little change, the peak of attendance comes at about the age of twelve. From that time the exit sign is up until at age twenty only a few remain. The causes and cures should be studied by each school for itself but some are universal.

The tradition of quitting in adolescence is strong. Adolescents may think of church school attendance as an adult infringement on their freedom. Too many youth classes, as examples, are "the same old thing" because the method has not progressed with a pupil's promotion from the children's division. They want to be moving into authentic adulthood; the school has not come to their aid. Closely related, adults do not set a favorable pattern; many do not find church school membership essential for their lives; some are bored, apathetic, and indifferent. Youth too often hear that "Sunday school is for children." Their elders should be challenged.

The school needs to be the kind that everybody can take seriously. To the immediate point it must maintain a program and provide leadership for a growing experience which is adapted to life's changing interests and avoids the monotonous repetitions which too often characterize the program. It is helpful to secure the participation of the pupils in the development of school policy and program; they can help manage their learning with leaders who understand and are skillful. Too, pupils must be worked into the whole church program as integral parts of its ongoing functions. New curricular materials, incorporating these ideas and properly used, are bringing back some of the alienated drop-outs with their friends,

6. *Secure home co-operation.* A chief factor in regularity of attendance is the sentiment of the home; improvement can be accomplished in part by building that home base. Have provisions been made for the parents and older persons in the home to have an ongoing program for themselves in the church school? They, too, must be participants. Does the school meet at times and under other conditions which are favorable for home co-operation in attendance? Has the home been kept fully informed of the work of the school so that it is interested in that work and will be co-operative in carrying it on? Does the school aim to help the parents with certain problems of the children so that they welcome this opportunity for assistance?

7. *Send periodic reports.* Later chapters will say that reports to the pupils concerning matters that may include attendance are commended by those who use them. Perhaps, too, there should be reports on the parental as well as the child members. These may open the eyes of everybody concerned and challenge everyone for more regular attendance.

8. *Recognize commendable achievement properly.* Artificial incentives are to be avoided in all church school work. This prohibition includes attendance pins and any similar devices. Do they have permanent value or lose their impact promptly, except on a few individuals? Do they put the emphasis on the wrong values, maybe foster rivalry, pride, and alienation? Can the system be administered fairly? The likely answers are not encouraging. The proper inducement is improvement of one's own or the group's achievements in things for which the program exists.

Doubtless, though, Christian living leaves room for some modest recognition of genuine achievement. A person who exercises his Christian responsibilities with vitality deserves the commendation "good and faithful steward." That kind of award may be given best through a kindly word by teacher, school executive, or pastor as well as by peers.

9. *Avoid contests.* Various publishers of church school equipment have nearly exhausted human ingenuity to discover new forms of contests. There is more than one fault about them all. They concentrate attention on winning the contest—not the proper motive for religious work. They set group against group in competition whereas the only rivalry appropriate in Christian institutions is that of a group against its own record. Besides, too, there are always the losers as well as the winners of the contest! Contests expend time and effort in ways not fruitful for Christian growth. They can do actual harm. It is better to trust that people want to meet the demands of opportunities that are worthwhile.

10. *Educate everybody involved.* All procedures of a school, including attendance promotion, should have the educational thrust. Consequently in matters of attendance it is desirable to share the figures and facts among

pupils, parents, teachers, officers, and any others involved so that they understand the situation and can respond to it appropriately. This means, for one thing, helping the entire membership understand the difficulties created and losses sustained by irregularity. It is hard to administer, learn, and teach with a third of the membership absent. A church school session held weekly for one hour, at intervals of seven days, is a meager enough program to care for such high interests. If people waste that inadequate provision by attending a limited percentage of the time they make a thorough educational job almost impossible. We can educate for the values of regular attendance by using the congregational bulletin; leaders can emphasize the matter in the special programs the school offers from time to time; periodic calls in homes can be utilized.

SECURING PUNCTUALITY

Who would venture even to guess the percentage of people tardy for church school sessions? When five, ten, or fifteen minutes are lost by tardiness a good portion of the already limited opportunity is wasted. Also the program is weakened for everybody. What shall be done?

1. *Make the opening minutes worthwhile.* Again a vital program is the essential. The session must begin when the pupil arrives, with his leaders on hand to greet him and follow with pre-session conversation, fellowship, and work. One pupil can be given some task to help with the work of the school, another may start some piece of work on the day's unit.

The formal school session will often open with worship. This should be a real experience, not just a routine. Three hundred workers in a large institute were asked to tell how many of their pupils arrive on time. The leaders of only one school could report in numbers as high as 80 percent. Among the reasons for that percentage, they mentioned first the choice services of worship conducted by their superintendents. To feel that you will miss something worthwhile if you are not on time is the highest incentive to be there even early.

2. *Set a goal.* Just as for regular attendance, schools should study the problem of punctuality and establish a goal. They may begin by aiming at having 75 percent of their people on time. The point is to start at a figure which can be reached in a reasonably brief period of time, then move forward step by step. The ultimate is perhaps represented in the public school's punctuality record of approximately 98 percent. Progress toward a goal, in this matter too, should be made concrete by interesting charts or graphs presented and discussed in the school.

3. *Have the staff on time.* We cannot expect Jimmie and Mary to come on time if their teachers and officers will not be there. The attainment of

any punctuality goal depends heavily on the earnestness with which the workers themselves accept their responsibility. One Sunday church school published a memorandum on a leader's duty to arrive ten minutes early. It stated that 93 percent of the cases of lateness are inexcusable. Every officer and teacher was directed to be at his post of duty by nine-twenty; anyone coming at nine-thirty, the scheduled hour for the session, would be considered ten minutes late. The bulletin presented a long list of reasons for being early, chiefly the sense of sincerity created by those who are on time versus the lack of confidence cultivated by those who appear careless.

4. *Start promptly.* Don't punish the punctual by waiting for the tardy! Besides, when we know that a certain program will start on time without fail, we aim to be there promptly. If past experience teaches us that we shall waste our time by punctuality, we wait until we know the business will start. So does the church school membership. The leader who is working for punctuality will start on time if nobody is present but himself.

5. *Close the doors.* This seemingly harsh rule is not to be carried out in a spirit of effrontery toward the dilatory but of fairness toward the prompt. The typical church school opening service is a time of confusion caused by people who arrive late. They step over other people's feet as they get into their places and distract attention generally. They make it impossible for the members who came on time to have a hearty experience of reverent worship if this is the activity. Meanwhile, too, all are learning bad habits; promptness is sound education for proper churchmanship.

Depending on the arrangement of the doors, late pupils may be ushered to a position at the back of the room where they can be given books and enter into the service from that point. Or, it may be necessary to have ushers in a hall to keep people quiet until the opportune moment has arrived for them to enter their room.

Five additional suggestions were made under securing more regular attendance. These pertain equally to securing punctuality: (6) *secure home co-operation;* (7) *send periodic reports;* (8) *recognize commendable achievement properly;* (9) *avoid contests;* (10) *educate everybody involved.*

HAVING "DISCIPLINE"

A university student of Christian education, observing a teacher at work, heard her scold the pupils twenty-three times in nineteen minutes. A pastor whose church school building was just across the street from a public school building asked, "Why do they behave so well on the other side of the street, but so badly here?" Yes, why is disorder almost an epidemic in church schools?

Concern over the discipline problem is proper for two reasons. First, order creates the conditions under which good work can be done but disorder makes full accomplishment of the school's objectives impossible. Second, so often overlooked, disorder provides bad character training whereas good character training is the purpose.

The meaning of discipline needs to be clearly understood. An ideal school is not one in which pupils are regimented into military precision and where the proverbial pin can be heard to drop. It is a school in which there is no confusion except a normal by-product of work going on busily to achieve proper objectives. There is discipline where the members of the school are working by inner control which grows principally out of their assurance that values will follow. We have gone beyond those thirteen "Rules of This Sunday School" reported in *The Teacher Taught* of 1839 where this one was printed in capital letters: "I MUST ALWAYS BE STILL."

Reasons for Disorder

Bad order in a church school may come from many sources. One is a *generally disruptive condition*. Tradition may be responsible. If a boy became a pupil, let us say at twelve years of age, and entered a class where the other children misbehaved, his misbehavior is to be expected. General contagion often works to this same end. Someone in the room starts something, nobody stops it, and disorder spreads. The workers themselves may have low ideals. Many grew up in a school where poor discipline prevailed. They may not realize that they can insist upon a greater degree of seriousness and elicit a finer spirit of co-operation in real work toward objectives.

Much disorder arises from *inadequate equipment*. The typical equipment breeds a degree of excitability: a crowded building with too many or too large classes; poor seating, lack of teaching aids, insufficient quantities of materials.

Another source of disorder is *laxity on the part of staff and parents*. Tardy leaders are an occasion for trouble to begin. They cannot exert their influence for order from the beginning. Unprepared workers are another major cause of disorder. If a teacher does not have a general background of understanding of his work, if he does not know what he is going to say or do, he will neither do nor say much that is worthwhile. So the pupils find something more interesting to do. The habit of irregularity on the part of the teachers is particularly distressing. When somebody from an adult class is called to act as a substitute teacher, but is unprepared for the day, unacquainted with the pupils, and not particularly skilled in teaching, good order can scarcely be expected. Another frequent source of disorder is an unfavorable home condition; lack of intelligent parental concern and co-operation shows.

The prime cause for disorder is, of course, an *inadequate pupil program*. Bad discipline tends to vanish when the program interests pupils and meets their needs. If a pupil finds the work uninteresting, irrelevant, beneath his dignity, above his understanding; in short if it does not enlist him in co-operative participation he will turn his attention elsewhere. More simply, the grouping may be bad. Finally, adult domination versus pupil determination is too prevalent. Pupils do act better when they feel that the school is in some measure their own and they are personally responsible for its good effectiveness.

With so many obstacles we should obviously not be too ready to ascribe disorder to perversity. We too often misunderstand. Normal exuberance can be taken for misbehavior. Also there can be an inverted manifestation of need for love, security, and self-appreciation. These are not excuses, though, for inaction.

Securing Order

An effort at discipline should meet these criteria: Does it harmonize with ideals being taught in the school; is it Christian? Does it represent a positive and constructive approach rather than a negative and repressive one? Does it proceed by indirect means as far as possible? Does it appeal to the highest values the pupil can understand? With these standards in view, certain steps for improvement can be taken. Manifestly the first will be to correct those unfavorable conditions: disruptive elements in the school; inadequate facilities; laxity of leaders and parents; a weak program. Other possibilities follow:

1. *Maintain morale.* In efforts at discipline no pupil's self-respect is to be sacrificed or his good will destroyed. On the contrary, every attempt will be made to build up morale on the part of all. If teachers set the pace for work, interest, and good will, the pupils will catch the spirit. If the executive has a genuine and stable enthusiasm, the contagion will eventually infect some of the most unpromising pupils.

2. *Insist on good deportment.* Under the conditions existing in most schools, some distraction and confusion cannot be avoided. So, although the ideals ought to be high, they dare not be unreasonable and the workers should not be fussy or officious. A school sociologist, talking on problems of discipline, emphasized firmness. "A firm hand is to be kept on the throttle when necessary and no foolishness is to be tolerated," she said. When plans have been made and regulations established, they are to be carried out with no backing down unless it is clear that wrong would be done. Meantime the leader aims to keep his self-control. Friendly understanding belongs with firmness and vice versa.

3. *Gain pupil co-operation.* The best approach for improved discipline is to deal with the real thing: the work and the satisfactions that accompany it. But this suggests that the school itself assume responsibility for good order. It is everybody's school; as much self-government as possible is proper. It is best to let the pupils consider the need and set up their own regulations. Then they will be more ready to obey them and see that others do. Classes can profit by setting aside regular lessons for a session to discuss the subject and make plans for proper school etiquette. They could arrange a program about it: a panel, stories, dramatizations, role-playing. Self-rating charts or records could be devised. One school improved after it heard a tape-recording of its confusion.

4. *Make social approval and disapproval work for order.* The opinions of peers have high potential for control. Too often those who misbehave get the group's attention. They may feel they are being admired for the "courage and manliness" they are showing in their defiance. Pupils can avoid laughing at foolishness and thereby quench the folly. Leaders must utilize group capacity for self-government.

5. *Don't plead, scold, or threaten.* Reprimands, ridicule, and sarcasm often yield negative results; to expect, suggest, and discuss is more promising. Most pupils appreciate a leader's faith in them. They should be approached with the attitude of helpfulness and with the expectation that they will co-operate. Good humor is important. The unfortunate time may come when definite instructions are necessary but the fight-it-out attitude, the final showdown has no place in a church school. Leaders can do more by a tactful and good-natured spirit, accompanied by mental alertness in handling a situation at the beginning before it becomes serious.

6. *Make individual adjustments.* There will always be problems of adjustment with that one or two in a dozen. Friendly conference is often sufficient. Some cases of hostility, we may discover, are the result of righteous grievance, in the school or at home. As a first suggestion for the control of the persistent cases: get acquainted with them. Giving them a big brother or sister has often helped. The basic suggestion for dealing with individual discipline cases is to make the school wrecker a school builder.

It will be noticed that many of these suggestions for better discipline require an awareness of group dynamics and skill at channeling them for group maintenance as well as task attainment. It is also observable that discipline problems can be turned into important learning experiences. Fundamentally, discipline is not something a teacher accomplishes, it is something pupils learn, the teacher helping them. The basic motivation is a readiness for freedom in something better than disorder; disciplined behavior carries the privilege of winning freedom through it.

FOSTERING OTHER FAVORABLE RESPONSES

Essentially, this chapter has been dealing throughout with means of securing favorable responses on the part of the constituency: attendance, punctuality, good work in favorable grouping, interest in progress and good order. Among other desirable responses are such things as general enthusiasm, readiness to serve, initiative, co-operation, interest, and support. All these are complex; their nature and the methods for securing them are not simple. Two major suggestions will be made beyond that inevitable having a program that everyone finds worthwhile.

Providing for Pupil Determination

To provide for determination is to make arrangements by which each pupil participates in selecting the objectives he is to reach and the procedures by which he approaches them. It is to think of pupils as persons who are directing their own education with teachers and officers to help.

Even the smallest child can become involved. He can have some small task in the nursery department, something that he would like to do. A little later the child may take his part in the session program. As he advances in years and ability he will participate in a decision, conduct some portion of a program such as a service of worship, even vote on an important policy like controlling the expenditure of money. Meanwhile, too, he has been taking his full part in completing the current unit of activity and selecting what is to follow as the next unit in the sequence. Meantime his leaders will have been the responsible heads of the program, shaping it so that it will not drift off into wastefulness; yet they have taken their roles essentially as coaches and guides who provide for profitable educational experience.

A pupil's first step of a more formal sort in determining the work of the school may be service on a committee; another would be representative on a young people's council or the church school council. In time he may become a member of the administrative staff.

Organized classes may foster self-government, develop individual initiative and personal responsibility, satisfy social tendencies, enhance esprit de corps, and foster school loyalty. However, it must be asked whether the school is already over-organized, also whether the class organization is really contributing to morale, whether its attitude toward the whole school is helpful. Classes should not be organized unless definite objectives will be served.

Knowing Pupils

In all these procedures a church school leader needs to know his pupils. He will need to know them in general, the characteristics common to their age group. He will need to know their individual situations at home, at school, and the like. Finally, the leader will need to know the individuals as persons so that he can work with them in the spirit of true fellowship in service. Pupils need to know their leaders similarly.

This knowledge can be mutually cultivated. There should be cards or letters of congratulations and good wishes at appropriate times. Members of the school should be cordially invited not only to its various affairs, but also to all the activities of the whole church. Books can be shared. Young people should be helped with their choice of lifework. New pupils in the school deserve special attention. The ideal is an abundance of fellowship between all youth and all adults for the social, intellectual, and religious sharing of personality appropriate to Christian learning.

PART THREE

SUPERVISION OF THE PROGRAM AND TEACHING IN IT

CHAPTER IX

PROVIDING A PUPIL PROGRAM

Whatever an executive leader does in organizing and administering a school (Chaps. IV through VIII and XIII through XX) is meant basically to provide a route on which learners can move toward objectives. The following chapters IX through XII, will bear on the activities of those leaders while it deals especially with "teaching-leaders" and what they do with what is usually called the curriculum.

That word is not used in the chapter title because of the wrong meaning sometimes attached to it; instead we use "program." "Curriculum" is too often taken to mean a package of lesson books and related materials that arrives in the mail. The meaning here is broader and different. Lesson books are only "curricular materials," pupil and leader guides. The curriculum is all that the pupil does under the guidance and with the help of his peers, parents, and other leaders, especially his teachers. Properly, it includes four major types of learning activity or, better, four phases of it: study-and-instruction, worship, fellowship, and service—all to be undertaken in units within a program unified in itself and integrated with the total program of the congregation.

These matters that pertain directly to curriculum are of foremost importance. Other concerns of church school leadership are subordinate in the sense of ancillary. The center of effort for all leaders is directly or indirectly to the end that the program of pupil activities is as productive as possible for growth in the new life in Christ.

Rightly understood, curriculum is a good word. By derivation it can mean "race-course." Thus the curriculum is a path along which the pupils are being guided "to the wire." We shall find later, though, that it includes not only the track on which a pupil runs, but also the race he runs and the personality change that takes place in the running. To define: *curriculum is a sequence of activities through which a learner is guided by leaders so that desirable sorts of change take place in his living and greater abundance of life results for himself and others.*

146

THE NEW CURRICULUM

Recent years have been an era of quiet revolution in curriculum theory, design, writing, and practice. The ferment is world-wide. Even in the chapter on history (I) we began to notice already what American denominations have been doing and what has been done by regional agencies in many centers around the world under the aegis of the World Council of Christian Education.

Recent Developments

Dr. A. L. Roberts has summarized the situation admirably in an article whose very title describes it: *The New Day*.[1] He says that this is a time of "the most widespread curriculum efforts in the history of Protestant religious education." In a period of less than twenty years, the major Protestant denominations in the United States have been recasting their curriculum concepts. More money, more personnel, more technical proficiency than ever before have been brought to bear.

TRENDS

Dr. Roberts and other writers have mentioned numerous trends within these curricular developments:

1. Christian nurture is the responsibility of the whole church, beginning in the local congregation but reaching upward into the highest levels. All the church agencies must participate in curriculum designing and production.
2. Curriculum must be built with careful thought as to the nature of the church and its mission; it must involve persons and groups fully in that mission.
3. Curriculum planners must utilize the best insights about human development revealed in such relevant sciences as psychology, and sociology, and especially the broad field of education.
4. Because Christian growth is a lifelong task, the full age span must be covered by the curriculum, with adult Christian education having a key role.
5. An adequate curriculum will provide for full participation by parents and put a strong emphasis on Christian nurture in the family.
6. Curriculum designing requires careful concern for pupils' relationships in current experience—social as well as personal—but themes on Jesus Christ, Bible, and church should be constantly recurring notes.
7. Profound study, including scientific research, on curriculum development is essential. Evaluating the effectiveness of curriculum is a necessary component. Experimentation should precede publication of materials.

[1]*International Journal of Religious Education* (October, 1963), pp. 7-9, 43. Published by the National Council of Churches of Christ in the U.S.A. Used with permission.

8. Curriculum must provide for interdenominational and interfaith experience; a full Christian faith-life cannot be developed in isolation.
9. Besides curriculum programs for the average pupil and situation, provisions should be made for exceptional persons and situations.
10. Individual church schools must consider customary concerns in developing any original designs and must make necessary adaptations of denominational programs so that printed materials are used effectively in a particular place. The real curriculum is what happens in a given school or class.

EXAMPLES

How these principles have been working out in practice can be exemplified in brief descriptions of three curricular series.

Seabury Series

New curricular ground was broken in 1955 when the first materials of the Seabury Series[2] appeared (it is noteworthy that the series is now undergoing a third revision). Dr. David R. Hunter states in the *International Journal of Religious Education*[3] that this curriculum differs from anything previously produced for Episcopalians in three ways:

1. It espouses a *"new theory of learning"* that is "theologically rooted." The basic theological assumptions are: "... that what is being communicated in Christian education is the gospel,[4] that the communicator is God himself, and that the context of this communication is the covenant community...." Gospel is defined as good news. The author continues concerning the resultant learning theory: "For the builders of this particular program it meant that the learning they sought, the apprehension of the gospel, would be most likely to occur through maintaining an adequate balance of past, present and future . . . a balanced exposure to the meaning of God's action in all history."
2. The *"organizing principle"* was "religious issues." "Such broad issues as freedom and authority, right and wrong, and decision-making became the operating areas of the course." The intention was ". . . to allow teachers to determine what they would do on a given Sunday. . . ." They were to be ". . . sensitive to what was happening in the lives of the learners now, and select content accordingly. . . . Only enough lesson plans were included to serve as a training device for enabling teachers to make their own plans."
3. In a *"holistic concept of the church,"* the Sunday church school was conceived ". . . not as an entity in itself but as an integral part of a parish program; a part which is dependent upon the whole with the whole dependent on it."

[2]Now *The Church's Teaching for Closely Graded Church Schools.*
[3](January, 1964), pp. 14-15, 34. Published by the National Council of Churches of Christ in the U.S.A. Used with permission.
[4]Defined as good news "that the triune God has acted, is acting now, and will continue to act in people's lives, and that he waits and works for their response."

United Church of Canada

A less well known "new curriculum" is the work of the United Church of Canada. Peter Gordon White, in his report on the work,[5] says that the entire church was involved from local churches to administrative bodies and theological seminaries. The curriculum was an accompaniment of a general desire for what we typically call renewal of the church. White's article contains this interesting sentence: "The word began to spread: 'We can't live a faith we don't know; we can't know a faith we don't live'!" To this the author adds, "Nor can we teach a faith we don't live. If it is not in us all propaganda about 'nurturing children and youth' is a flight from reality."

After four preparatory years in local churches the "New Curriculum of the United Church of Canada" was inaugurated in 1962, with work for adults. Thus it gave prior attention to the necessity for a mature, adult context for any successful work in Christian education. The first cycle of teaching throughout the church school was concluded 1964-65-66. The annual themes in a three-year, cycle-graded program are: "God and His Purpose"; "Jesus Christ and the Christian Life"; "The Church and the World."

The Lutheran Church in America

A curriculum project for the Lutheran Church in America began in 1956.[6] The program was to:

(1) include all age levels from early childhood through adult; (2) coordinate in one curriculum the work of all educational agencies of the parish, Sunday church school, weekday church school, vacation church school, leadership education, church camps and the Christian family; (3) be fully field tested; and (4) serve the church's needs from the mid 1960's through the mid 1970's.

A first step was to consider and "blend" understandings in theology and education. Early productions were objectives, including an extraordinarily complete manual on needs in terms of age group objectives.

What may be called the organizing principle of this curriculum is a co-ordination of "continual life involvements" and "continual Christian learnings." As a member of society each ". . . individual becomes involved in many situations and faces many demands and responsibilities" that are in common with others. These situations become "recurrent opportunities

[5]"The New Curriculum of The United Church of Canada," *International Journal of Religious Education* (July-August, 1964), pp. 22-23. Published by the National Council of Churches of Christ in the U.S.A. Used with permission.

[6]W. Kent Gilbert, "The L.C.A. Parish Education Curriculum," *International Journal of Religious Education* (April, 1964), pp. 6-8, 23. Published by the National Council of Churches of Christ in the U.S.A. Used with permission.

for learning . . . they provide 'take hold points' at which education can occur most effectively." A given situation involves relationships—with God, the church, the Bible, fellow men, physical world, and self. It is at such points that continual Christian learning takes place.

The first new LCA curriculum materials were introduced in 1964 and 1965; they include not only printed publications but also audio-visuals. Most of the courses that reach the churches will have been field tested in sixty-two pilot congregations. Provisions for evaluation have been built into the series and far-reaching researches toward revision are already initiated.

BASIC THEORY

A view of curriculum that has been developing within Christian education, especially since 1925, was shaped to no small degree by the work of Dr. William C. Bower.[7] It is clearly represented in the series described above as well as others; Dr. Bower's central word, "experience," is employed frequently in the recent book, *The Church's Educational Ministry: A Curriculum Plan* (p. 648, for example).[8] From his point of view, the curriculum is that part of the pupil's stream of experience which is brought under consideration in the school for enrichment of meaning and increase of control.

Curriculum in Terms of Life's Experiences

A pupil is passing through certain experiences in his complex of life situations in which he has problems for which help will be useful. The church school is equipped in leaders, materials, and procedures to assist him at needful points. So, selected experiences are brought under consideration in the school for educational results. The curriculum consists of the learner-and-leader dealings with those experiences.

In that view any curriculum is a series of educational events involving many components: (1) the material, historical and contemporary, employed—content; (2) the techniques concerned in using it—procedure; and, (3) as a basic ingredient, the pupil's "becoming" in, with, and through the above—experience. In Christian education the events can be described in an additional way; they include four aspects: (1) the topic studied, the pupil's work studying and being instructed, and *primarily* the reconstruction taking place in the pupil as he studies; (2) the worship service in which the pupil engages, the communion with God which he enjoys, and *primarily* the change going on in him as he communes; (3) the social affair planned for the pupil's enjoyment, the fellowship he has

[7]William C. Bower, *The Curriculum of Religious Education* (New York: Charles Scribner's Sons, 1925).
[8](Bethany Press: St. Louis, Missouri, 1965).

in it, and *primarily* the social development which he is undergoing as he participates; and (4) the service enterprise which the pupil undertakes, its performance and *primarily* the growing of his personality as he does his good deed.

However, that analysis suggests a fragmentation which falsifies the concept to that extent. Learning takes place holistically, not in isolated fragments, although each whole must be broken into manageable bits. The curriculum properly is comprised of units of work with interrelated aspects. Study-and-instruction, worship, fellowship, and service are properly woven as varied colors into a total pattern that constitutes the design of the experience.

All in all Bower, with those who have followed him, considers the curriculum as life—life undergoing reconstruction, life in the process of being enriched and controlled, being made richer as to meaning, being socialized, being brought under control to larger self-realization.

> The experience curriculum will, then, consist of a body of carefully selected and organized experiences lifted out of the actual, ongoing life of the person or of the social group; of a critical study of the situations themselves for their essential factors and their possible outcomes; of the ideas, ideals, attitudes, and habits that have emerged from the past experience of the learner and of the vast stores of historical subject-matter that have descended from generation to generation and that contain in organized and available forms the best that the race has thought and felt and purposed.... one will find a body of experience that is feeling its way from point to point of meaning and control as it moves out into the uncharted areas that skirt its everwidening frontiers, and a rich body of source material in which the learner may see his own experience reflected and interpreted, and by the aid of which he may deepen his own insights into reality, widen the range of his own outlook upon life, and bring his own experience under conscious and certain control in the light of the most dependable knowledge, the worthiest ideals, and the highest purposes of the race.[9]

Curriculum as Life's Activities under Guidance

Here, curriculum was defined earlier as a sequence of activities. That definition is not meant to be different from Bower's in its essence or functioning. It uses different language to be in harmony with the terminology and educational theory represented throughout this book. "Activities" is considered preferable to the more vague, subjective, and passive word "experience." Life is a network of activities; we learn through performing them. By our terminology both the abundant life objectives and the living under guidance method of education employ the same concept—activities. There is to be no dichotomy between purpose and process.

[9]Bower, *op cit.*, p. 179.

But curriculum in terms of activities, too, is concerned with the pupil's moving stream of experience. The pupil desires, and the church school leader aims at helping him, to move from his present status to a more desirable one. The two participants have a mutual purpose for the pupil to live his Christian life on a higher level than at present, with the corresponding increase of abundance. The pupil is to change so that he will be performing more desirable and satisfying Christian activities. Since he will learn through, in, and for doing, the means by which he moves toward his higher achievement is the performance of ever-increasingly desirable activities. Certain activities in his total system of current living can be influenced by the school. They become his curriculum so that the curriculum is a sequence of constantly improving activities.

THE PLACE OF THE BIBLE

Bible lessons have been viewed so long as *the* curriculum that the use of the Bible in the new curriculum needs immediate attention.

Functional Approach

When the Bible is used to promote growth in the direction of the objectives of Christian education, it is being used educationally. What is perhaps the dominant pattern of usage can be called *factual* approach in which the emphasis is on hearing, mastering, and remembering what the Bible says. The particular form of use now gaining world-wide currency can be known as *functional* approach. This means to employ the Bible purposively in relation to the life's activities of persons so as to effect their Christian growth and enhancement at definite points of current need. History discloses that this is a way Jesus used the Old Testament and the early church used the then new New Testament. It has appeared throughout later church history, too.

Simply, biblical materials were written with the intent that they should function in the faith-living of those to whom they were addressed (the Corinthians, for example). Succeeding centuries have proved that they still have potential for that purpose. So in education we strive to set up conditions in which the ancient writings can act—it is better to say, God acts through them—in situations similar to the originally contemporary ones. Accordingly, in the functional outlook and procedure the Bible is utilized as supreme resource to show direction and give support to the ongoing Christian faith-life of persons and groups. It shows Christian people the activities appropriate to their abundant living and moves them to perform them. The Bible that came from God, through life, is to go back into life again.

The particular manner of functional use can be expressed by a contrast. In both the older and newer types of curriculum, the purpose may be that pupils shall "live the Bible way." In the older curriculum, the hope is that those who know the Bible will live according to it. In the newer curriculum, the approach is as if to say: "Here we are with this problem in living; what shall we do? Let us see what help the Bible can furnish. We shall utilize it in action."

The focus in the former case is the Bible; in the latter, persons within their life situations. Perhaps better, the starting point in the factual approach is the Word in its written form; it begins with the Bible. In the functional approach we begin with the persons in whom the Word is to live again. Then, basically, there is to be an impartation of divine life, ministered by the Holy Spirit as the Bible's pages are read, studied, taught, and exemplified, also accepted and obeyed.

General Potentialities in Biblical Usage

When the Bible is utilized functionally in the new curriculum as supreme "resource," we go to it as to a storehouse of materials for fostering Christian growth with consequent increase of abundance in living. Specifically, it can aid development in the primarily intellectual area where it provides meaning, deepens insight, furnishes standards of appraisal, and shows direction for effort. It can aid development in the primarily emotional area as it subdues or stirs feeling, provides proper outlets for expression, restrains or liberates the spirit. Also, it can aid development in the primarily volitional area by developing purposes, reinforcing motives, lending steadiness, and releasing power. In totality, it integrates wholesome personality.

These potentialities of the Bible to effect educational results are called "teaching values." Teaching values are means that produce growth, namely, change in knowledge, attitude, skill; they foster development toward objectives. Teaching values of the Bible, then, are potentialities resident in a passage of Scripture to effect educational results as they interpret, evaluate, redirect, and empower human experience. They are like naval craft which come alongside other vessels to render some special service: to put aboard a pilot; to bring a doctor; to supply food, water, or fuel; to put out a fire; to pass a line for a tow; to ease the ship into a berth. In functional use of the Bible, similarly, its teaching values are brought to bear upon human activities.

Exceedingly important, though, many teaching values are implicit, not explicit in words. They appear as significant overtones and undertones. Closely related, this is not to be a prooftexting type of biblical usage; real teaching values are to be discovered by sound interpretation and brought to bear as resources. Also, many portions of the Bible are so complex as to require rather exacting study on a content basis before they yield their values for effective utilization. Unconsidered use of such material may result—does often result—in grievous error. There is a place for essential content study. This should be understood, however, as a secondary and not the primary level of functional utilization of the Bible.

More Specific Potentialities in Biblical Usage

The Bible can be utilized in that functional way for a minor purpose— enrichment, and for a major purpose—control. Those two interact, each being in some degree a by-product of the other. The minor purpose is to *enrich* the Christian life of persons and groups. Biblical materials may serve to enrich pupils so that they have somewhat more abundant life whether or not the material controls their conduct to any considerable degree. In some detail, these values lodge in such categories as: vocabulary, imagery, fund of knowledge, sense of beauty, devotional attitude.

The major purpose in educational use of the Bible is to *control* the Christian life of persons and groups. Objectively, first, biblical materials may serve to help pupils by guiding them in the performance of Christian activities through *examples-in-performance* (Christ's prayers) and *statements-of-principle* (the Ten Commandments). Second, biblical materials may serve to help pupils by stimulating them in the performance of activities as it shows *values* and *penalties* (the Beatitudes) and brings *sanctions* and *disapprovals* ("Thou shalt not . . ."). As a third service of scripture, it is empowering pupils so that they accomplish what they have been guided and stimulated to do.

THE PLACE OF THEOLOGY

By theology we mean here the conceptual formulations of religious experience we know as dogmatics and ethics. How should it be used in Christian education? Theology's proper relation to Christian education is not the same as that of the Bible but similar to it. Its status is not equal because it is largely a derivative from the Bible, along with additional historic and present experience of the church and its people. First, our educational theory and practice should be informed by dogmatics and ethics. Second, to the point now, they are appropriate curricular resources —important though secondary ones—for learners and leaders who are working at enterprises in which a gracious God meets needy man for growth toward Christian maturity.

Historically, though, we have used doctrine mostly as content to be mastered. With theology as with Bible, the custom is to have pupils read about it, study it, listen to lectures on it, and memorize its propositions. There has been here, as with Bible, a tendency to get this material to our pupils as soon and fully as possible with the expectation that what they get into their minds early will remain and somehow guide their thinking and practice. Naturally, disillusionment has often followed. People have not remembered and they do not act in proportion to the effort expended. So, as with Bible, a reorientation is taking place. This is toward using theological materials, too, with a functional outlook and practice. Theology, too, is to be used directly for its services toward our various objectives —resource for living now.

Such an approach does not rule out specific studies in dogmatics and ethics within our programs at one time or another, on any level, in one form or another—when relevant to observable need. There can be sessions, units, or courses for children, youth, or adults. However, we can go much farther than simply to conduct such studies on a factual basis. Our individual learner must be developing a sound faith at which he is arriving personally and inwardly, not merely accepting by intellectual assent. Although he is not by any means to ignore the church's teachings, he is properly led chiefly at theologizing — dogmatizing and ethicizing — rendering doctrinal or moral decisions rather than memorizing doctrines and principles. The formulated materials will serve him as guides as he moves toward his own dogmatics and ethics.

As to both Bible and theology, therefore, the trend is toward functional usage. We start our educational process with the recognition of pupil needs, understood as substantial concerns in the religious realm. They may be superficial at the beginning; indeed they may be only "hidden hungers." Nevertheless, we start where learners are, touching perhaps only a leaf of the total need though we expect to proceed to the roots of it. Then we minister the healing water of Scripture, along with derivative representations of it, bit by bit as they may serve, even until deep calls unto deep.

CURRICULAR ACTIVITIES IN UNITS

Curriculum, as previously defined, properly includes all the guided Christian educational activities of a pupil not only in the church school but also outside it. The Christian learning activities which a pupil performs in his home, public school, place of work, and community, in so far as they are affected at all by guidance, are a part of his Christian curriculum. Increasingly, church school leaders realize that they must do more about pupils' lives beyond the walls of the church if objectives are to be reached.

Yet the curricular activity for which the church school leader provides more directly is, of course, living the Christian life under guidance in the church school. In practice, it embodies those four major aspects of curriculum: studying and receiving instruction about Christian matters; worshiping in Christian modes; enjoying fellowship in Christian groups; serving at Christian enterprises.

The meaning and directing of those four types of pupil activity will receive detailed consideration in Chapters X, XI, and XII. Since, however, they will be handled as interrelated phases of curricular units in a total pupil program, "units" need definition now: their management can be considered later (Chap. XII).

Though the Christian curriculum is properly a total program of the four interrelated types of learning activities it must be apportioned; we cannot be doing everything all at once. So, for convenience as well as effectiveness, the portions are managed by pupils and leaders as "units of activity" or simply "units."

What is a unit? One of the best descriptions was given earlier by Hewitt[10] who thought of each church school group as being engaged with a "slice of life." Each such slice of life would deal with some center of interest, and that center of interest be developed through "major activities or experiences, or units of work."

We shall define a "unit of activity" as *an educational enterprise which is to develop as a constellation of interrelated religious activities centered around some specific objective of Christian growth.*

In the light of that definition a church school becomes a group of persons engaged in units of activity moving forward with desirable results in Christian growth. Also, the task of the leaders of the school is to provide a series of well-selected and efficiently managed units for everyone.

PROVIDING A TOTAL CHURCH SCHOOL PROGRAM

In Chapter II a Christian's life was described as a system of activities of a certain type. The individual activities, it will be recognized, are legion. Chapter III grouped these as eight major and comprehensive activities called objectives. Living a Christian life consists in performing all of these on the highest level possible for the person in his present situation. In Chapter II, also, Christian education was said to consist in making such changes in an individual's system of activities as will result in greater abundance in his Christian living. The same chapter showed that the method is performance, learning to do by doing, or better, by living. Thus

[10]Mildred Hewitt, *The Church School Comes to Life* (New York: The Macmillan Company, 1932), p. 50.

the activities of a Christian faith-life are at once the objectives and the process of Christian education.

The Need for Program Building

It was inevitable that this chapter should define the curriculum of Christian education as the sequence of these pupil activities. They are performed, it has appeared, while living the Christian life in the home, at school or work, throughout the community as well as in the church. Those performed in the church school are broadly the ones which emerge in the processes of studying and receiving instruction, worshiping, fellow-shiping, and serving within organized units. Now we see that a major responsibility of church school workers is clearly to arrange for the initiation, continuance, and completion of a series of units of activity.

A DENOMINATIONAL PROGRAM

That responsibility is met most often by a school's adoption of the denomination's curriculum with its series of materials. The publishers are then directed to ship a set of supplies at proper intervals.

There are good reasons for using denominational curriculum materials. Many can be cited; they center around the major fact that denominational ones are those most likely to involve learners responsibly in the mission of the church. Here is where an individual will meet all phases of a definite church's history, heritages, structures, personnel, needs, services, and works. It can be seen in its relation to the universal church but it enables the learner to have an essential concentration.

Yet, although those published materials have been prepared with careful research and even experimental testing by expert workers who adjusted them for typical pupils at the various age levels in the average situation, a considerable amount of dissatisfaction will be encountered. Pupils are individuals, not averages; groups differ; times change. A third of the pupils of the class will find the materials too easy; another third will find them too difficult. Half the class may be deeply interested just now in something else. An up-to-date teacher may find the helps too old-fashioned; the traditional teacher cannot approve "this new-fangled stuff."

AN IDEAL PROGRAM

Such facts suggest the need for a custom-built program designed to fit a particular church school. It would help each pupil there to meet his immediate needs and fit his personal attitudes and interests, taking account of his full life. It would consider each group's particular outlooks and problems. It would recognize differences in the ability, interest, education, and outlook of the leader as well as of the pupils. It would fit the school's tradition, equipment, administrative policy, and organizational setup. It would consider new issues constantly appearing in an infinitely complex, varied, and fluid social order.

The ideal program would be always in process of building, constantly under reconstruction—to a considerable degree not only a year-by-year but a week-by-week affair. "To a considerable degree" is used since there is no need, and certainly it is not desirable, to lose foresight and sequence out of the process. When a family goes on a vacation tour, it may spend the winter laying out the major lines of its journey although it will be making adjustments day by day and hour by hour en route. The curricular program can have general outlines shaped long in advance while lesser adjustments are made as it proceeds.

It may be observed that providing an ideal program would be a task for experts. Yet, is it the right way? If so, more experts are needed. Besides if there are no people with time and ability to do such a creative piece of curriculum construction, efforts can be made in that direction.

Finally, it is important to realize that something of this sort is the kind of thing that is being done, or has been done, by denominational and interdenominational staff workers around the world in the present ferment of curricular revision including design, writing, publication, distribution, introduction, supervision, and evaluation. This is the way trainloads of printed materials were fashioned except that they were accomplished one step away from local church schools although schools were represented in the process in many ways such as experimental testers. While, for the typical church school the prepared materials will be adopted, it can be understood in the light of the foregoing description how they may be used flexibly and with as much adaptation and creativity as may be possible.

Providing for Particular Schools

Realistically, we know, most schools are not ready for ideal procedure. There are four types. (1) Those which build their programs creatively, perhaps prepare some of their own guides, and select special materials as they proceed in the various units of activity. They will follow the sort of procedure suggested above, at least with modifications. (2) Those which have accepted the ideal but serve it only as far as possible. They may outline their programs, then select printed guides from various sources to serve the program they devise or employ creative units where there are workers who can manage them. (3) Those where some standard series of guides, usually a denominational series of lesson materials, has been adopted with the idea of doing some creative unit now and then or substituting some elective guide to meet a special interest or need. (4) Those which adopt and use an established series of materials just as they have been planned by the publishers.

Only those schools with personnel having the necessary capabilities should undertake anything more difficult than the third procedure listed. Many, however, could venture that far in the direction of the ideal type of program. Once the need is understood and accepted, instances will be found in which some larger or smaller thing can be undertaken. There is no need to wait for the day when it will be possible to go "all out" for a total homemade design. One does what one can do now.

The responsible leader with the ideal before him will not, like a certain pastor, insist that a teacher must always use just the prescribed lesson for the day exactly as provided in the denominational publication. Instead, when a Junior teacher comes to say that the boys of his class need different lessons, he will help that teacher find what is needed. Wherever, indeed, a few workers have the capacity for even a limited amount of constructive work, he will welcome their endeavor.

MATERIALS IN THE PROGRAM

In every program there is need for various resources. Main items will be the pupil and leader guides for completing the units of activity, "lesson books."

The full adoption of developmental theory and practice with creative use of the various techniques would require more. Something in the way of a library for pupils and leaders is one requisite. It could contain reference books of a general nature as well as books dealing with specific areas of related study: Bible, history, biography, literature, psychology, sociology, missions. There could be, also, journals dealing with current developments and a filing cabinet containing a wide variety of pamphlets and clippings. Films and recordings could be available there. Further, this could be the place to store and consult the records of procedure in previous units in the school: analyses and descriptions of life situations; the resources already used; the data gathered; the principles arrived at; the experiments undertaken and the results achieved. If churches cannot themselves maintain library resources, the members can share what they have. School and community librarians will usually welcome requests from church workers.

Prepared "Lesson Materials"

Almost every school will be selecting some form of printed guides and their accompaniments. These should be selected democratically. When feasible the pupils as well as their teachers will participate; for major choices the administrative staff and the parents should join the task force. First, of course, the objectives should be well understood by all, just as the conditions of leadership, equipment, and the like must be kept constantly in view. Then samples can be secured from publishers for examination. The executive himself will make certain that he is fully informed and that the best criteria prevail as the final selection is made.

THE INTERNATIONAL UNIFORM LESSON SERIES

Many Sunday church schools in the United States, Canada, and elsewhere are using what are familiarly known as "uniform lessons." They date, as we have seen in Chapter I, from 1872. The original idea was to have everybody studying the same scripture selection each Sunday.

Now the National Council of Churches of Christ has the Committee on the Uniform Series which develops outlines for *Internationl Sunday School Lessons: International Bible Lessons for Christian Teaching, Uniform Series*. The committee represents approximately forty denominations. In its annual meeting the members prepare outlines for the lessons of subsequent years. These outlines include lesson titles, scripture texts, memory selections, and devotional readings; there are also suggested lesson emphases for the handling of the materials.

In recent years the Committee on the Uniform Series operates on a principle which has modified the uniformity idea considerably. It seeks to make suitable adaptations of a basic text to the three age groups: Primary-Junior, Intermediate-Senior, and Young People-Adult. The gradation is achieved by planning the outlines on a common core of scripture for each Sunday with particular blocks chosen out of it for the several groups. The lessons are based on a six-year cycle (1969-74 for example) which aims to cover all the portions of the Bible that are specially promising for group study. At least one-quarter each year considers the life and teachings of Jesus.

When the outlines for a given year have been completed they are printed and furnished to the various denominations or to independent publishers in this country and in other parts of the world. Writers and editors then prepare the familiar quarterlies.

The approach in the uniform series is from the study of the Bible more than from the development of the pupil although the latter concern is not lacking and some publishers are stretching the series in the life-oriented direction. The lessons do have certain advantages. As originally planned, they allowed a whole school, including the homes represented, to be working in a measure of unity. So they tend toward systematized instruction that can be—if it is—integrated with worship, fellowship, and service. Their widespread use makes possible the provision of more than ordinarily specific and abundant teacher and pupil helps. They solve many publication problems especially for smaller denominations. They fit certain schools, particularly smaller ones, with the minimum of difficulty in grouping.

Yet, especially as developed by some publishers, there are points at which uniform lessons may be rated as the least desirable instruments for use in study and instruction. Even as improved in 1945 the lessons continue to be fragmentary, disconnected, material-centered, and less effective because of the transmissive techniques they induce. They have had a tendency to foster superficial moralizing about biblical verses instead of penetrating insight into the problems and possibilities of Christian living with scriptural assistance for it.

GRADED LESSONS

The last decade has seen an enormous increase in the use of graded lessons. While there are many types, closely or broadly graded, the general idea is to provide separate, and supposedly better adapted, lessons for each grade or larger age group. Until recently the Division of Christian Education provided outlines which were used by many publishers of such lessons. Now the denominations, particularly the larger ones, have designed and are producing their own graded series.

The denominations' work is, in many cases we have seen, guided by careful research studies meant to reveal the range and details of experience in the several areas of relationship met by the pupils for whom the curriculum is being provided. Then resources of content are similarly researched for the appropriate helps.

The National Council of Churches has been responsible over several years for a series of studies on which denominations have drawn heavily in the above-mentioned curricular researches. Several denominations have worked together in the development of a curriculum design that is to be used widely. Work on this design was carried forward through the *Cooperative Curriculum Project*. Results of first stages of the work are published in the book, *The Church's Educational Ministry: A Curriculum Plan*.[11] The emphasis in this project has been the way in which "the gospel" speaks to the "persistent life concerns" of a learner. It is recognized that learning takes place at the "crossing point" of the gospel with these persistent life concerns.

As a result of the serious work that has been done in planning and developing graded materials, based on research, most graded series offer decidedly improved materials. They approach what the church has to offer without fragmenting it so much. They are as closely as possible adapted to pupil interests and needs. They introduce materials from many sources, biblical most of all, but extrabiblical also. They take into consideration

[11](St. Louis, Missouri: Bethany Press, 1965).

developmental education and make use of what we know about the procedure that is suited to the learner at a given time. There is no little recognition of what we have learned about groups and their work.

ELECTIVE UNIT GUIDES

Many of the presses now have available what are often called simply "electives" for use in church school agencies, particularly for the youth and adult groups. If a group wishes to study, for example, the choosing of a vocation, some work of the church, or a particular part of the Bible, it can secure the leader's guide and pupil's manual for that study. These materials merit the wide usage they are receiving. They often approximate the best school procedures in learning and teaching. They can be chosen to serve genuine interests; they can help to meet real individual and social needs. This elective usage can foster initiative which should lead on in many cases to the situation in which a group can prepare and pursue its own elective study with the resources and procedures it has selected.

Criteria for Selecting Materials

Numerous topics crowd into the picture when we determine the criteria by which materials are to be selected. Elaborate studies and schedules are available but simplicity must be maintained here. Too often price is made the fundamental consideration. Church schools exist for educational purposes, always a costly matter; thrift is commendable yet a few additional budget cents or dollars spent for better materials may prove to be one of a church's best investments. As for other criteria:

Is the basic educational theory correct?

Do the materials represent a sound biblical and theological outlook, and are Bible and theology wisely employed as resources?

Do they represent the best of Christian experience—past, present, and prospective?

Are they harmonious with the objectives to be served, do they provide for ample attention to objectives, and do they promise to be effective in attaining those objectives?

Are they manageable under the conditions (leadership, facilities, time) in which they are to be used?

Do they guide learners and leaders in the most forward looking educational procedures which can be employed in the situation?

Are the items of the highest possible quality in literary form and physical makeup?

Are they rich and ample in basic substance and in variety of pupil and teacher helps for all four aspects of the curriculum?

Do they provide for sequence but also flexibility?

Are they adaptably relevant to particular pupils' vital needs on a broad spectrum of relationships?

Do they co-ordinate the work among the various agencies of the total church school? Closely related, do they integrate with the congregational program and ecumenical outlook?

Do they provide for constant evaluation and finally for revision?

Using Materials

However fine the materials selected, the manner of using them will enhance or hinder their efficacy. The more basic things regarding use are discussed in later chapters, particularly the next which deals with teaching. Several incidental but significant factors will be considered here.

INSTALLING NEW MATERIALS

When new materials have been selected, care must be exercised for their careful introduction. Whether the new materials are a whole new series, a hymnbook for the school, or a course for a class, all the participants need to have the reasons for the choice well in mind so that the initial reaction will be favorable. Should any considerable part of a group make up their minds that they do not like this new thing, they spoil the possibility for the best results. Denominational staffs have gone to extreme lengths to prepare the constituency for their revised programs.

One of the most important demands at the present juncture in Christian education is to interpret the underlying philosophy of the materials. Not long ago, a pastor introduced a new series in his weekday church school. The leaders had been accustomed to the type of texts which duplicated the Sunday church school work in content and employed a pronounced sort of transmissive theory with memoriter procedures. The new series represented the denomination's most progressive publications. Wisely, the pastor distributed the new leader's guides well in advance of the first session. Within a few days one teacher came exclaiming, "Just look, I can't do this. We need maps, and blackboards, and tables. Besides, I don't know how." Then and there the pastor undertook to show that leader, and later all the others on the staff, the meaning of the new ideas in Christian education. They responded favorably, caught the concepts, and did well with their new type of work.

That anecdote leads to an incidental statement: the frequent complaint that the new materials require better teachers. This is not altogether justifiable. What is a good teacher? One who gets results? Is it easier to get results by the new methods? Workers may need to be re-educated, it is true, but given that requisite, the same workers can, as a rule, do better work with the new materials than with the old. Besides, and most important, all have some background of experience for them. If no more, this is the way of education in the home, on the street, in the office or shop—almost everywhere except the school. Further, a growing number have experience as pupils and teachers in public school where things are increasingly being done in these ways that may be new to others.

HANDLING THE MATERIALS

Once the materials have been selected and installed, how shall they be handled? For example, shall the books be given to leaders and pupils for permanent possession or shall they be the property of the school to be used over again? The question is often debated pro and con, but the basic principle is easily established: handle the materials so that they will produce the greatest possible educational result. If they have been prepared for pupils to use and keep, then give them to the pupils, but follow through to see that they are used in the way intended. If they were prepared so that the disposition is optional, and there is no serious financial stringency, we can get religious literature into the home this way. Teachers' materials should always be made the property of the teacher so that passages can be underlined, notes written on the margin, pupil reactions and suggestions for procedure another season noted in blank spaces. In all cases, neat and thrifty care of property should be encouraged.

TIME SCHEDULES

Whatever the material provided, proper scheduling is a significant factor. Executives must see that it is as ample as feasible and is utilized for maximum learning.

Here we shall think of a Sunday church school schedule but the general principles will apply in other agencies. The majority of schools meet in the morning for one hour although many are increasing the time. A typical schedule may be:

Worship, 20 minutes
Announcements and similar matters, 10 minutes
Class session, 25 minutes
Closing assembly, 5 minutes

Such a schedule raises serious questions about length of session, balance of worship and study, value of closing assembly and the like, even on the traditional level. With the "new curriculum," it is unsatisfactory. There must be work time, if possible, and considerable flexibility so that various aspects of the unit activity may be completed without too much regard for the ringing of bells. The proportionate arrangements of activities, the way time is spent on a given unit and like issues need to be worked out by the persons involved. Adjustments to age levels are a paramount issue.

In the present development of curricular theory and practice, certain general trends in the use of time are noticeable. Schools are lengthening the session, some to an hour and a quarter, an hour and a half, or as much as three hours. Attention is being given to a measured amount of the "large group instruction" discussed in Chapter XII. "Opening exercises" that wasted so much time are anathema although worship experiences of a proper sort are deemed appropriate. The closing assembly is often omitted. There is a strong tendency also to modify the proportion of time given to worship and study; the details are given in Chapter XI.

Everywhere time needs to be economized. An efficiency expert would pale at the manner of using session time in the typical church school. Whether the schedule lasts one hour or three hours, there is not a minute to be wasted by insufficient planning for sessions or ineffective procedures in them.

CHAPTER X

GUIDING PUPIL ACTIVITIES (I)
(Especially Study and Instruction)

The program of pupil activities described in the preceding chapter, although built and going, must be guided. In that task an executive leader has many and varied responsibilities. Some may be quite immediate ones in which he deals directly with the pupils. In most of his duties, though, he works through other staff members, particularly teachers. All his organizational and administrative activities have an important bearing on teaching; the supervisory task described in Chapter VIII is intimately related. Essentially, though, the topic in the present chapter is leadership in teaching. Yet more than usual is meant by that expression. We shall let teaching include all formal and informal guidance of the pupil in study-and-instruction, worship, fellowship, and service activities within the school sessions or outside. First we shall consider the learning cycle, the sequence of pupil activities which results in educational growth, later the parallel teaching cycle or sequence of teacher activities by which a learner's activities are guided.

LEARNING

Since we shall say often that to teach is to help folks learn, it is essential in teaching to recognize how pupils do learn. As another way of putting that essential: teachers must understand the process pupils employ as they deal with learning activities.

Description of A Learning Activity

A "learning activity" is an activity, we have learned, to be (1) introduced into or eliminated from the learner's system of activities or (2) increased or decreased as to the frequency or facility of performance in the learner's system of activities that is his life. We shall examine some details of its character.

POSSIBLE LEARNING ACTIVITIES

From one point of view, the major learning activities in Christian education are identical with the four aspects of curriculum discussed in the four chapters of this Part Three. They are also, in general, the objectives according to Chapter III. In more detail, here are samples from a long list of possible ones:

Appreciating (music, poetry, scripture, and the like)
Discussing (includes conversation, conferences and others)
Evaluating (ideas, plans, activities of self and others)
Giving
Handling materials, tools, objects, equipment
Leading and following (as officer, committee member, or member of school)
Music, making (includes study, practice, composition)
Reading biblical and other materials
School management (fitting into and helping with)
Serving in social ministry
Worshiping and conducting worship services

The basic pupil procedure in learning, we must say again, is performance of such activities.

TIME ELEMENTS OF A LEARNING ACTIVITY

In the simplest activity performed—and more complex activities are largely combinations of smaller ones—there are three types of elements when considered as to time relations: *preparatory, consummatory,* and *anticipatory.* Preparatory elements grow out of native readiness, past experience, and current insight. They carry the learner up to the performance of an act. He performs it, the consummatory element. Then there are left in his physical and mental structure the anticipatory elements which become preparatory to the same activity or a related one on a later occasion. When it is said that we learn to do by doing, it is meant that we make use of preparatory elements of an activity to carry it to performance and by the performance store up anticipatory elements that will function in a subsequent enterprise.

A six-year-old girl composed a hymn—words and music. Back of it was a long line of enterprises in which she learned to do the various preparatory elements of the consummation by doing them.

At an early age she had sat with her father at the piano stool enjoying the Christmas carols. One day she started singing them with him. Then he guided her fingers to play a few measures of "Silent Night." Later she decided to learn to play "Come Hither Ye Faithful" and worked at it until she was able to pick out the tune.

Meantime she was being introduced to poems she learned to love.

Soon she decided to do a poem herself. Her father encouraged the impulse by writing down her production. Frequently thereafter she had poetic moods in which she would place pencil and paper in her father's hands for her dictation. Composing poems doubtless suggested the composition of piano tunes, brief at first. Later she invented her own form of musical notation so that her tunes could be preserved.

In each of the separate steps described above, preparatory elements growing out of a previous activity led to consummatory ones and they to further anticipatory ones. Finally the various streams of anticipatory elements merged and a poem became a hymn with a tune composed to fit it.

That is the way a pupil learns. Also, it is the way a teacher teaches ideally—being at hand to provide help for a questing and creative spirit.

STEPS IN A LEARNING ACTIVITY

At several points in the example described above, one observes the young composer working through these steps in a complete learning activity:

1. Being aware of the situation
2. Discovering the possible activities to perform
3. Evaluating those possible activities
4. Choosing an activity for performance
5. Desiring to perform the activity
6. Resolving to perform the activity
7. Outlining the procedure
8. Providing the conditions
9. Executing the activity
10. Experiencing satisfaction or dissatisfaction with results
11. Evaluating the activity in retrospect
12. Planning to repeat, alter, or discontinue the activity

A good way to conceptualize the steps is to imagine how a service enterprise would be undertaken in a church school. The steps may overlap in a given case or some may be omitted; the order may not be always the same; nevertheless, the list is representative and complete for a typical learning activity.

Contributions of Basic Learning Theory

Exactly how does a pupil learn basically—psychologically and sociologically? How does he acquire new understandings, develop better attitudes, improve his patterns of action? No one knows how long learning theory has engaged human thought; it has had particular attention during the last half century. Yet when anyone but a specialist delves into the voluminous literature he finds unbounded complexity. We need an overall picture but who can organize, codify, integrate, synthesize? The complexity increases as we recognize that personality theory, indeed all the behavioral sciences, have contributions to make. More recently, too, Christian educators have been trying to reconcile learning theory with theology.[1] Years ago Hilgard[2] examined a selection of theories and found worth in all but had to conclude: "The next twenty years may lead to a clearing of issues. . . ."

Now, though, while we do have building blocks, who will erect the building?

Despite the immensity of the task, we are moving. Usable insights have been discovered. Many are incorporated in the literature and practice of Christian education in general and they appear here from point to point. Among the most prominent new insights are the findings about group process, the "learning by wholes" concept that underlies unit procedure, the importance of nonverbal learning in our relationships. Now, too, we know more about the inner dimensions of human experience as revealed in depth psychology. Now communication theory and language analysis also offer us significant help.

Careful study of the newer literature on learning theory discloses the continuing worth of elements in an early theory termed connectionism or associationism. Its implications deserve caution in use and we should remember that notable additions have been made. Yet Thorndike's "laws of learning"[3] remain fundamental. According to those laws the effectiveness of a learning activity is in proportion to the three factors listed below with a statement of their ways of working.

Readiness, the learner's state of preparedness or unpreparedness for the change. If the learner is "ready," the change will take place with relative quickness and permanence; if he is "unready," the change will take place not at all or slowly and impermanently.

Effect, the amount of satisfaction or annoyance which the learner experiences in making the change. If there is much satisfaction, the change is more quickly and permanently established. If there is much annoyance, it takes place slowly and impermanently; results may be negative.

Exercise, the frequency or infrequency with which the learner practices the change. The more frequent the practice (positive or negative), the more quickly and permanently the change takes place; the more infrequent the practice, the less quickly and permanently.

However, the operation of those laws is subject to their interdepend-

---

[1]Robert R. Boehlke, *Theories of Learning in Christian Education* (Philadelphia: The Westminster Press, 1962).

[2]Ernest R. Hilgard, *Theories of Learning* (New York: Appleton-Century-Crofts, Inc., 1948), p. 360.

[3]Edward L. Thorndike, *The Psychology of Learning,* Educational Psychology, II (New York: Teachers College, Columbia University, 1913), p. 23.

ence. As examples, there are important correlations of effect with readiness and of readiness with exercise. For teaching purposes, though not as a statement of the laws in sequence, a formula can be stated: strike while the iron is hot; foster practice with satisfaction; let annoyance attend the wrong.

TEACHING

The learning cycle, obviously, is not simple; neither is that sequence of teacher activities by means of which the learner's activities are guided.

Descriptions of Teaching

Very broadly, when we teach we create situations that make it possible, even enticing, for a maximum of pupil learning to take place.

TEACHING AS HELPING PUPILS LEARN

We can describe teaching more exactly in many other ways. Earlier pages described the teaching function in monosyllables: *to teach is to help folks learn.* "Learn" means to change, develop, grow, mature. This is the process that includes initiating new activities, eliminating old ones, increasing or reducing the functioning of an old one. "Help" means guide— guide in a creative experience of living. We have seen earlier (Chap. III) that "experience of living" means doing real things and "creative" means putting the emphasis on such factors as dynamic motivation and self-directed procedure as far as reasonable.

In the light of the learning process, as described earlier in this chapter and elsewhere, the nature of the teaching task can be made still more clear. It is to help pupils do and, while doing, to change—a process ideally represented in coaching the direct performance of a real task. It is to assist pupils while they complete a unit of work, providing the necessary guidance and stimulation for seeing it through. It is to make available an effective setting of time, space, material and social relations for an educational experience. It is to help revive anticipatory elements which become preparatory for the consummation of a learning activity, help provide conditions for the consummation, help husband the anticipatory elements for later preparatory use. It is to lend the helping hand at each of the various steps of a complete learning activity. It is to help the pupil observe the laws of learning.

TEACHING IN TERMS OF OBJECTIVES

It is possible to describe teaching also in terms of objectives. One of the teacher's first tasks is to help the pupil locate and define the highest objectives. While a pupil's own objective is to have first consideration, it is to be chosen always in the light of the best social checks, including the teacher's views. The teacher needs to know and take account of the pupil's present interests and likely needs in the fields of human relationships involved; then he helps the pupil interpret the situation and choose his goal. After that choice has been made the teacher helps the pupil to win through to it.

TEACHING IN TERMS OF GUIDANCE

Guidance is likely the best synonym for teaching. So we describe teaching when the general task of guidance is pictured. The following are important items among the innumerable activities of guidance which a teacher may be called upon to perform:

Helping each pupil to do what he needs to do most.
Knowing each pupil's experience, interest, and capacity.
Being one of the learning group in the highest sense—the more mature member of a fellowship of learning.
Imbuing pupils with spirit.
Giving special help to those with special problems.
Securing voluntary acceptance of responsibilities essential to individual and group success.
Arranging time schedules.
Calling forth ideas from the group.
Helping keep the focus on real goals with step-by-step progress toward them.
Seeing that equipment and materials are provided.
Sharing personal experience with pupils.
Opening up new activities.

TEACHING IN TERMS OF PRINCIPLES

Finally, teaching may be described by its principles. Each type of education has its own outlook. In the developmental view teaching proceeds on the platform outlined in these short paragraphs:

The basic purpose of a teacher is to help pupils learn by the most efficient technique.

The basic procedure in teaching is not teacher-telling-pupil but leader-guiding-pupil-in-performance.

The basic unit of a teaching experience is not a "lesson presented" but a pupil activity guided.

The basic organization of a teaching task is not a textbook to be followed but a unit of work to be completed—an objective and all that is done for its attainment.

The basic control the teacher uses is not dictation and compulsion, but counsel and eliciting of inner discipline.

The basic pupil function on which the teacher depends is initiative, not imitation.

The basic stuff of the teacher's craft is not some social inheritance such as a book or an institution but the growing life of a pupil.

Principal Ways of Teaching

Many terms are used to describe the procedures a teacher employs; "methods" is perhaps the favorite; "techniques" is another. A competent teacher at work in a classroom is an exceedingly versatile person doing many different things, always adapting to the ever-changing situation and personnel. The task, really, is living with the pupils in ways by which they can learn most rapidly and effectively. So "ways of teaching" seems best as a general descriptive term. Each "way" involves detailed techniques which vary from situation to situation and sometimes comprise a rather precise group which may deserve to be called a method.

Listing of Ways of Teaching

There are many "ways of teaching" and no two lists will be the same. The list below aims to be rather complete. It is arranged alphabetically as to chief words.

1. Cultivating *appreciation*
2. Making *assignments*
3. Utilizing *audile and visual aids* (in general—details follow; creative work)
4. Supervising *case* method
5. *Counseling* (includes pastoral calling)
6. Providing *demonstrations*
7. Leading *discussion* (includes buzz groups, brainstorming, conference, conversation, debate, forum, panel, round table, symposium, and other procedures)
8. Coaching *dramatizations* (formal and informal; includes pageantry and puppetry)
9. Conducting *experiments* (social service or other—the laboratory idea)
10. Directing *games* (play, in general; includes use of toys)
11. Developing *group process* (in general)
12. Guiding *handwork* (includes art activities, construction, crafts, and hobbies)
13. Arranging *interviews* (includes use of resource persons)
14. *Lecturing* (includes commenting, also use of resource leaders)
15. Securing *memorization*
16. Leading *music* (includes creative work with music)
17. Employing *natural* objects
18. Guiding *participation* in administrative affairs
19. Using *phonograph* recordings
20. Holding *planning* sessions (and evaluation sessions)
21. Guiding *prayer* experience (includes participation in special services and programs)
22. Providing for *programmed learning*
23. Employing *projectors* (slide and filmstrip, motion picture)

24. Doing *questions and answers*
25. Using *radio and television* (includes production)
26. Fostering private *reading* and public reading or recital (includes work with contemporary literature)
27. Using the tape *recorder*
28. Directing *research and report* (includes seminar and other forms of group inquiry, such as committee work)
29. Conducting *reviews* (reinforcement exercises)
30. Guiding *role-playing* (includes psychodrama and sociodrama)
31. Coaching *speaking* (choral or other)
32. Telling *stories* (includes anecdotes and illustrations—sometimes open ended)
33. Directing *supervised study* (also home study)
34. Directing *surveys* (includes questionnaires and opinion polls)
35. *Testing*
36. Conducting *textbook-study-and-recitation* (includes "socialized recitation")
37. Taking field and museum *trips*
38. Employing *visual aids* (not otherwise mentioned above, such as chalkboard, charts and graphs, displays and exhibits, flannelgraph, picture study)
39. Conducting *workshops*
40. Guiding completion of notebooks, workbooks, or creative *writing*

TEAM TEACHING

To have two or more teachers working co-operatively with a group of pupils is a growing trend. It fits work with children particularly well but there are interesting possibilities for youth and adult work also. The teachers plan, study, teach, and evaluate as teams. One may serve as a "leading teacher," but not necessarily.

When selecting a team, attention should be given to the variety of special interests, skills, and aptitudes of the prospects. A good team may combine, for example, skills in music, storytelling, projects, Bible interpretation, and worship. Each should be ready to become a leader in the learning situation as a particular need for a given competence develops.

The pupils can be grouped in fairly large classes. It has been said that "a safe guide" is to have six to ten pupils per teacher. There can be considerable diversity of membership if, for certain parts of the program, a large group is divided into smaller ones with particular capacities, interests, and work to do.

A leading teacher with, let us say, two helping teachers would perhaps be responsible for the "all-together experiences" such as worship, introducing a new unit, announcing plans for activities; yet each may have this opportunity from time to time. When teachers work with individual interest groups or at tables where children need considerable guidance, the tasks may be shared equally. All can, too, share responsibility for out-of-class work, home contacts and the follow-up of absentees. It will be understood that the whole team has planned the entire program together so that each knows what the other is doing and why.

Many advantages are claimed for team teaching:

Pupils can have the experience of working with, and are exposed to the influence of, more than one person.

Pupils can have broader contacts through their work in a larger and more varied group.

When the strongest teachers have been designated as the leading teachers, all the pupils receive the benefit of the more competent leadership.

Certain special abilities and skills of teachers can be utilized to the greatest advantage.

Pupils may have a greater variety of activity and have some freedom in the choice of their activities.

Uneven growth patterns in children can be taken into account. Adjustments can be made for slow or fast learners and those with more or less previous learning.

This can be an informal type of leadership development because the less mature may team with more mature teachers.

It is unwise to attempt this work unless the relationship between the members of the team can include an unusual amount of Christian understanding and fellowship. Teachers must respect and accept one another as unique individuals, not being afraid of exposure to embarrassment. Only good natured tolerance, humility, and deep commitment will hold a team together.

LEARNING-TEACHING AS GROUP ACTIVITY

"Group" is a major word in Christian education now. It appears in numerous terms such as group dynamics, group life, group procedure, group process, group relationships, group therapy, group work. Already we have met it prominently in Chapter IV when we discussed "being a leader" of groups. Group process, the basic fact, has been viewed in its relation to executive leadership for organization, administration, and supervision. But the process is specially significant for learning-teaching, classes being the groups chiefly in mind here although our group theories and practices pertain to any form of curricular activity.

What does this stress on the group mean for learning and teaching?

What Is A Group?

We have observed that a group is not merely several individuals assembled; rather, it is a collective personality. Members of a group create a new entity as they meet, organize, decide on program, plan the details, get at the work, complete it, and evaluate it. Yet, while group behavior is more than the mere sum of the behaviors of individuals who constitute the membership, we must not lose sight of the individual behavior. Ten persons in a group are not ten fingers at the piano, but two hands with each finger individually and in its subgroup doing its part in a co-ordinated way to make music that satisfies the participants and their beneficiaries.

A mature group at its best possesses such characteristics as these:

1. Identifiable membership; the members know they belong while outsiders do not.
2. Group consciousness; members are aware of a unity.
3. Fellowship; there is a series of relationships that pleases the members.
4. Interdependence; members interact and by interaction enhance one another.
5. Ability to communicate; members can reach common understandings and feelings.
6. Relatedness of purpose; goal drives, looking in similar directions, are shared.
7. Concert of action; there is joint commitment in participation.
8. Emphasis on parity; each member is significant to the others.
9. Self-analysis; the group and its members can study themselves in their relationships.
10. Collective achievement; there is consummation of a common goal.
11. Interpersonal cultivation; the membership grows by relationship in its *diakonia* and *koinonia*.

What Do Groups Accomplish?

Numbers of pupils and shortage of teachers make grouping a necessity. Yet we are interested in group work because of the contributions to individual Christian growth and social good that can result.

Every complete group has three responsibilities: task, welfare, and maintenance. These are interdependent and overlapping but, to separate them for analysis, a group needs:

1. To accomplish things in general and something in particular—*task*.
2. To satisfy the concerns (meet the needs) that each individual brings into the group and to make available an overflow of satisfaction for other persons influenced by the group—individual and social *welfare*.
3. To develop and maintain working relationships with an accompaniment of fellowship—group *maintenance*.

For Christian education these three activities, separately and together, can serve the basic purpose of satisfying growth for each person touched by the group's activity, within but also outside of it.

TASK

Task orientation is a fundamental need of any Christian learning group. The task can be solely a learning enterprise but the best tasks may be those for which learning is a by-product of something that is beyond learning only. A service enterprise is an admirable type. Tasks can provide groups a focus for effort; they also elicit effort. Because they can ordinarily be accomplished better by groups than by individuals, each member can have his part in an activity bigger than himself and an achievement beyond what his own could be. Group tasks can be therapeutic although we are interested chiefly in nurture, not healing. When two or more people are busily at work, the actions of each are influencing the others. These interactions are significant in themselves for learning; they are powerful influences to modify undesirable behavior, intensify effort in approved directions and achieve needful self-control.

WELFARE: PERSONAL AND SOCIAL

Any learning, even learning in groups, must be self-assimilated and personally manifested. So, group process has to do especially with individual welfare. Yet certain needs in individual lives can be met better, often only, as people work in groups. No man lives, really lives, to himself alone. Persons have potentialities for which a full development requires group experience. A group provides the social setting in which to discover and try out and develop many an individual's potentials within the group's challenges and possibilities. It is likely true that most of our valuable learnings take place in groups—in homes, in casual gatherings, at work or play, especially in classes within larger school groupings.

Also Christians are members of one another; an isolated Christian would be an incomplete one to say the least. We live in groups, at home, in church, and elsewhere; our faith-life must be manifested in social relations. Various learnings in Christianity by their very nature—love, for example—are accomplished in face-to-face group relations that are realistic Christian activities. The same example suggests how group process operates for the social welfare.

It is right that much of our school learning is undertaken in groups. Yet, as a precaution, learning privately is not to be neglected. We have not sufficiently provided for individual learning enterprises in typical church school programs. Because Christian growth takes place in two ways, namely, learning alone and learning together, both have their place in a complete program.

MAINTENANCE

The third responsibility of a group, maintenance, means much more than having it hold together until its task is completed. For the group, just as with an individual, maintenance is on-going life with health and satisfaction. It cannot be entirely a by-product although what is done for maximum welfare through an exciting task will be the best guarantee for maintenance. Other factors of immediate significance for maintenance will be the control of the dynamics, the facilitation of communication, the heightening of morale, the wisdom with which structure is devised, and the care with which personality is recognized, employed, and served.

How Do Groups Act?

The basic problem any group leader faces is, again, awareness of and management of group dynamics (see Chap. IV). Previously we examined this phenomenon for the executive leader's guidance; now we are thinking of it for learning-teaching effectiveness.

An effective class must be a true group, not just an assorted collection of pupils but one of those collective bodies working at shared purposes and growing interdependently in the process. As such a body there will be dynamics in it, a grid of forces will be operating. They cannot be turned off or on at will; they are there—forces as real as any in the physical world. They operate for results, good or bad. The group maintains itself or disintegrates; there is fellowship or hostility; members and related outsiders have satisfactions or grievances; work gets done or not; there is desirable learning or perhaps undesirable.

FORCES AND ROLES

What are these forces with which we must deal?

They will vary—no two groups are alike. A few of the variable factors have been mentioned earlier; a more complete list would include such as these: (1) clientele of group (age, social class, maturity, educational attainment); (2) experiences of members in other groups and in this one in particular (especially with authoritarian or democratic control); (3) functioning of leaders and actions of members; (4) hedonic tone of meetings; (5) nature of task (educational goal); (6) setting of meetings; (7) size of groups; and (8) timing of enterprise.

The particular forces operating in a group are manifested in the roles played by the members regularly or on occasion. Some have been mentioned earlier. There are others, even more pertinent for the learning-teaching process. These are considered functional: clarifier; co-ordinator; elaborater; encourager; evaluater; follower; information-giver or seeker; opinion-seeker or giver; pace- or standard-setter; peace-maker. Teachers will recognize these positive roles, and the serviceable forces they represent, for what they are and encourage those who are taking them. But persons also play nonfunctional roles, representing disruptive and destructive forces. Teachers will try to thwart those who take these roles and avert their deleterious effects: aggressor; balker; clown; discourager; idol;

playboy or playgirl; power-wielder; recognition-seeker; scapegoat; special-interest-pleader.

CHARACTERISTICS OF FORCES AND THEIR MANAGEMENT

The forces behind those roles have representative characteristics. To a degree they are uniquely those generated when these certain persons get together in this particular situation. Basically, they are driving toward welfare for the self and others. Some, it is true, turn out to be self-defeating and group-destroying, so are frustrating to the group and leader; others are cohesive instead of disruptive and, therefore, pleasing. All require individual adjustments as well as appropriate management. They are affected by nature of goal and precision of its definition; they will mass behind a task that is a substantial concern. They need to be informed, also managed, controlled, ministered, or channeled—as much as possible by all the members and not only by the designated leader.

A complexity in group action is added by the human tendency to form permanent or temporary subgroups. In large associations there must be committees or even natural subgroups that can contribute to productive interaction as they co-operatively add to the effective completion of a task. On the other hand, individuals may begin to cluster around a subleader to form a satellite clique, with undesirable results. Destructive counterforces can develop between some subgroups as well as individuals. Fellowship can be broken because there are favored insiders as over against isolated outsiders.

How Do Groups Learn Effectively?

What can be done to facilitate learning in groups? All that is known about the individual learning process anywhere will apply here. The difference is that people are not being individuals alone; they are learning together. Subject to the social interaction for better or worse, they have the inherent advantages and disadvantages of it. Personal growth will be subject to limitations while it takes advantage of possibilities. Each pupil must subordinate himself at times for the common good but that, too, is a form of learning. There may be competition, hostility, disruption, aggression, domination, blame, sarcasm, recrimination, breakdown of communication. Learning how to meet these negative experiences, even if it exasperates or frustrates the learner, can be in itself an important form of learning. Some people are able to come awake within tension.

Groups are effective learning situations for the possible kind of social learnings mentioned, along with individual learnings, under certain conditions:

> When the group was well formed in the first place so that its members are capable of fellowship within their collaboration for results.

When the group faces, is concerned about, and works together at that threefold obligation: task, welfare, maintenance.

When the spectrum of group variables is not too broad. Yet diversity can often be shaped into better learning if the members understand that there will be individual variation in what is given and what is received, also when they accept the limitations as well as the advantages of their differences.

When members are being satisfied without expecting too much for themselves and while trying to provide much satisfaction for others.

When there is interpersonal attractiveness the power of groups to alter behavior is closely related to this factor.

When the sense of belonging is strong and members feel accepted and secure; also when the group is valued beyond itself.

When each individual can sense his growth, even if it is occurring within an element of struggle.

When the members have full participation in deciding on the task—what to do in general and subtask by subtask.

When group members, as far as possible, understand group process, are aware of the dynamics operating, and pupils, like the teacher, are playing up the constructive roles and playing down the destructive ones.

When there are shared objectives for action and norms for evaluation, strong and sure sense of purpose so that procedure can be spontaneous.

When there is learning atmosphere, esprit-de-corps, morale to which all are contributing.

When everyone participates in the teaching leadership as he is able.

When the members know each other, barriers down, for interaction; also when the group leader knows and is known by each so that all have the confidence of all.

When everyone's special interests and abilities are getting the best possible chance for realization. When individuals have a chance to express themselves freely.

When the leader understands the individuals and when the group relationships are adequately interpreted by the leader.

Teachers in Effective Group Process

What was said earlier in general about "being a leader" will pertain here, though with variations. In classroom leadership situations, just as in others, the leadership function is properly group- or situation-centered though there will be a major leader, the one we call teacher, who also lets others "teach" in one way or another.

What is true anywhere about the teaching process will still be true for Christian education. What is new nowadays is the requisite of an informed awareness of group process functioning and especially of group dynamics operating. Now we recognize that "teacher" has special obligations, principally helping the group accomplish those three responsibilities: (1) task with sense of achievement, (2) welfare (individual and social) with satisfaction, and (3) group maintenance with fellowship. In these areas the teacher wisely seek appropriate answers to such questions as these:

1. Is this a true group? What (or who) are the subgroups and how are they functioning?
2. How does this group differ? What can be expected because of the particular group variables?
3. What should this particular group accomplish that can be done better because these individuals comprise this group?
4. Is the leadership conscious of the way the group is feeling as well as what it is doing?
5. What forces are operating in the group? Why? How can they be channeled for good? Is the leadership (pupil as well as teacher) controlling impulses, pruning some and watering others?
6. How are the members acting individually (up to their best)? How are they interacting (as well as should be expected)? What roles are the pupils playing? The teacher?
7. Is the teacher sharing the leadership while fulfilling the special obligations belonging to his status—fostering self-government but also exercising any needful authority for larger interest of total achievement?
8. What are the horizontal relationships among pupils? Vertically, how do they rate one another? Are group tensions working toward objectives?
9. In general, is the leadership co-ordinating the powers and interests well for both individual and collective ends?

Ways of Teaching in Group Process

Under the impact of what we are learning about group process as a matrix for Christian growth, certain changes in Christian learning-teaching are taking place. It seems true that the individual-centered approach for learning has been giving ground to pupil development in group situations. It is also true that the teaching process is moving away from formalistic and authoritarian procedure toward an emphasis on democratic group participation. This can change the details of technique in older ways of teaching, also foster new ways.

The more typical ways of teaching still have a place. As an example, lecturing may be used under appropriate conditions—when it is the best way to get needed information to people. The teacher may have more time than others to assemble data more fully, integrate and organize it better, present it more clearly; he may be speaking out of experience that is his alone. However, this does not mean that the lecture will be a mere recounting of what the teacher has learned. He will try to involve his hearers as he proceeds. He will also arrange for "feedback" at points during a lecture or after it.

Yet modern teachers seek to use the more active, creative, and participant ways of teaching. A favorite way that fits the group process notably is group discussion procedure in its many forms: brainstorming, buzz groups, conferences, conversations, debates, forums, panels, round-tables, symposiums, and others. Much of the current group process teaching takes the form of problem-solving and decision-making for the group task. Ways of working for these purposes include interview, research and report, role-acting, the use of films, and other such devices. These are typically accompanied by discussion with an effort to reach conclusions worthy of conviction and action. Still other ways of teaching emphasized today include dramatization — especially informal — also games, handwork, studies by individuals or committees, surveys, trips, and workshops. Procedures of these kinds enable people democratically to analyze situations, collect data, explore alternate answers, choose solutions, plan action, and evaluate results. They can also strengthen fellowship, resolve misunderstandings, develop common goals, engender enthusiasm that builds morale, facilitate planning, and increase productivity.

More formally, of course, teaching in church school means dealing with the four classic aspects of "curriculum": (1) study and instruction; (2) worship; (3) fellowship; and (4) service. These will be treated one by one in the remainder of this chapter and the next, in each case with an emphasis on a leader's activities in relation to them—the executive leader, but especially in supervision, mainly the teaching leader.

DIRECTING STUDY AND INSTRUCTION

Study-and-instruction is a twofold way of dealing with the primarily intellectual factors in curricular units. In study, the pupil takes the spotlight; in instruction, the teacher. Always, though, the pupil's learning process is the central fact. There can be no true instruction by a teacher unless the study attitude is present in the pupil. Study, therefore, is the more significant of the two components while instruction takes the lesser role as the effort to render the pupil's study more effective.

In actual practice, study and instruction are centered usually around "lesson materials" so that a leader's task—executive or teacher—in directing this aspect of the curriculum will ordinarily be shaped by the type of materials used. The various possibilities as to materials were discussed in the preceding chapter. Here a general point of view must be taken with the understanding that the leader will adapt his activity to the problems and possibilities that arise under the conditions in his school. Always it is expected that the school is not confined strictly to a particular set of lesson guides when the larger advantage can be served by another type or by creative work in program building.

Study

Properly, study is the pupil's whole fact-finding, data-gathering, deliberating, and problem-solving process with respect to that creative experience of living with which he is dealing in his unit of activity. That is much more than the usual meaning which is largely concerned with mastery of materials only. Nevertheless, study must be taken for the moment as usually conceived so that a leader may direct it into better usage, making it truly the conceptualizing phase of a unit of activity based on the principle of performance—living and learning in the church school.

Among the activities through which pupils achieve Christian growth, the study of Christian topics has always been viewed as an important one. It remains important for three reasons: (1) people learn to study by studying and study is a significant Christian activity; (2) the knowing has some value in itself; and (3) most important, knowledge elements are necessarily involved as a phase of other Christian activities. Yet church school pupils do not, according to their teachers' reports, give themselves to this activity with any great diligence. How shall church school workers get their pupils to study—really—the Bible and subjects like the history, organization, work, and worship of the church, as well as the special problems of morality and belief? That continues to be a problem although there are heartening signs of gain with new materials and methods.

STUDY OUTSIDE OF THE SCHOOL

Under typical conditions, the problem was how to get pupils to study their lesson books at home before they came to the sessions of the school. Many persons now question not only the possibility but also the desirability of fostering home study on that basis. Almost inevitably only a few members of the class have done their home work. Those prepared pupils answer or ask questions while the unprepared sit as more or less disinterested onlookers. Worse, if the teacher works with the unprepared, the others start some activity of their own. We probably cannot expect too much else. Where are pupils in all their educational experience, save in church school, supposed at intervals of seven days to get out a manual, read a few pages on a subject, and memorize the answers to some factual questions or think superficially about some problems? They are accustomed to dealing with real books, often a considerable number of them, and proceeding generally in a quite businesslike way.

Yet there can never be a religiously literate people and spiritually regenerate race without a great program of study among Christian people. Perhaps the result can be attained by supervised study described below, by such methods as research and report, and by direct effort to foster reading broadly. A certain percentage of qualified pupils will "look up things" and make a report to the class when proper plans have been made. Others, properly guided, will do post-session study of things in which they have become interested and about which they want to know more. Not a few will read a good book highly recommended by a leader whom they like and respect. Perhaps the new "programmed learning" concepts and practices will become prevalent in church schools as another form of study procedure.

SUPERVISED STUDY IN THE SCHOOL

Excepting rare classes, general study of the lesson could be done better at a period of supervised study in the church school schedule. In some cases, the whole session could be a supervised study experience. On a minimum basis the teacher would guide the pupils for ten or fifteen minutes of reading the helps, referring to maps or other materials and getting themselves ready for the subsequent discussion. This procedure does not apply to all age groups and cannot be undertaken easily in the one-room school. It will fit best those schools that have extended the time for class sessions. Denominations have revised some of their lesson materials in this direction.

Whatever the particular means, it is important to initiate and guide programs of study so that the typical Christian learns how to continue some personal self-education throughout his life, making personal use of the vast range of available resources in the field of religion and related subjects. This is in addition to the necessity for study in the school because of its relation to all other activities there. Supervised study may be the best means now in sight for both results.

Instruction

Being instructed about Christian matters is the type of pupil activity for which the most ample provision is made in typical church schools. Thus the directing of this activity in a pupil program is one of a leader's major responsibilities as things now are.

But instruction has a tendency to crowd out all other considerations in the process of education. When people think of education, they seem to think first of a teacher instructing a group. That view is trebly short-sighted. *First,* teaching and instruction are not coextensive. *Second,* education is not primarily teaching, but learning. *Third,* study is but part of the learning process just as instruction is only a part of the teaching process. Again: there are four aspects to the curriculum of Christian education and the basic procedure in all units of learning is complete *learning by doing.*

THE PUPILS UNDERGOING INSTRUCTION

Instruction has been considered usually in terms of "presenting a lesson," viewing it solely from the teacher's standpoint. The newer approach is from the pupil's angle. He is being instructed, himself engaging in instructional activity. The teacher, as instructor, is only helping him with his process.

Roughly, the instructional techniques by which pupils proceed in their units of activity parallel the ways of teaching listed earlier. Most of them are of ancient origin. Many are old in church school work, but several are relatively new. In the former class we have listening to lectures, memorizing, answering and asking questions, listening to stories, and reciting from textbooks studied. While these still continue to have a place in church school practice, recent Christian education tends to reduce their frequency while it emphasizes such as dramatizing, discussing, doing handwork, reading, researching and reporting findings. One of the most amazing developments in the history of Christian education is the present use of audile and visual materials and equipment for seeing and hearing in new ways that captivate interest, give more accurate understanding, stir feeling, increase retention, move to action.

THE TEACHER INSTRUCTING

The precise instructional techniques teachers employ to assist their pupils in effective study, broadly conceived, are suggested by those ways of teaching. "Lecturing" can provide a rather simple example of what teachers do as pupils learn by instruction. The pupil is working on a unit of activity meant to answer his question, "What shall I do on Sunday?" and get him started on better and more satisfying use of the day. That unit will have as its central feature the doing of the right things on Sunday. Nevertheless, thinking the right thoughts about the matter is a part of the doing. Consequently, some preliminary exploration of principles is in order, and that may involve study and instruction. The pupil wants to know, for example, what light can be shed on the matter from the Bible. Using a concordance, he finds such a passage as "The sabbath was made for man, not man for the sabbath . . ." (Mark 2:27).

"But what does it mean?" he asks the teacher. The teacher may reply that you cannot answer a question like that on the spur of the moment. He'll prepare to speak on it next Sunday if there is not time or material for the student to study the matter himself. The pupil comes next Sunday presumably with a questioning and ready mind. He'll ponder as he listens. That is the pupil's technique under lecturing. The teacher will have prepared himself by study, planning, outlining, and making notes for an informal lecture which he will deliver according to the techniques of lecturing insofar as he understands and accepts them as good procedure. That is his body of instructional techniques.

The example illustrates that present tendency in the use of techniques, namely, their creative use. The larger meaning of creative use of techniques has been discussed, particularly in Chapter II. It is made effective in the teaching which results when pupils ask for guidance to do something they want to do as they move toward their objectives. They may ask, "I'd like to know more about that, please tell us," and an informal lecture follows. "I want to look that up," and a plan of study is arranged. "Let's have a play about that," and a dramatization results. "Please tell us a story about that," and there is storytelling. "I love that verse, please help me memorize it," and the teacher conducts a drill. "This is what I want to make," and a handwork enterprise follows. "I feel like writing a poem," and the way is cleared for a poem to be produced.

Not to be forgotten when thinking of study and instruction, schools that use developmental education will have pupils working at units of activity in which the major procedure is direct performance of activities although as many kinds of instructional techniques as may be necessary will be employed. Since pupils learn to do by doing, instruction is to be employed only as an aid to final doing and, while pupils are guided in doing by instruction, schools which stop with the teacher's performance of instructional techniques may not have completed their educational task at all. The pupil's part in the process is the vital thing.

Summary

Any executive leader's task of directing study and instruction is clearly a large one. He will foster in his school the creative use of the modern techniques insofar as he can believe in them. He will provide the conditions under which they can be employed, and encourage and develop his teachers to do effective work with them. Undergirding that effort, he will help his teachers to see that teaching is really something bigger than what they have typically understood by instruction. From the teacher's point of view, the major effort is to coach and direct the performance of Christian activity using instruction as a significant activity to be employed as necessary.

Executing a unit of activity, including the planning and evaluating stages should, also, involve the other aspects of curriculum—worship, fellowship, and service—in an interrelated experience of great variety. The next chapter will consider these three aspects of the activities within the curricular program. The following one will deal with nonclass aspects and the management of total units of activity.

CHAPTER XI

GUIDING PUPIL ACTIVITIES (II)
(Worship, Fellowship, and Service)

"School" and "teaching" may sometimes still suggest little more than study or instruction but recent decades have worked vast change in the actual situation. Now public school programs include numerous features beyond those typical classroom experiences. Similarly, church schools recognize the essential places of the additional aspects of curriculum that are the topics of this chapter: worship observances; fellowship events; service enterprises.

We are concerned about these activities in terms of Christian growth through, in, and for them. Growth takes place *through* each—pupils move toward general objectives as they have experiences of these kinds. Pupils also expand their capacities to find increasing abundance *in* the activities themselves. Finally, they develop abilities *for* promoting higher types of worship, fellowship, and service in their church groups.

It is difficult to conceive a vital church school that is not urgent about nurturing the devotional life and providing fellowship and service experiences. Yet these areas are relatively neglected. Almost everywhere improvement is needed.

DIRECTING WORSHIP

Clearly, worship can be a paramount instrumentality for fostering central elements of Christian growth. It is also a significant area for development in the ability to have increasingly higher experiences of it. Skill at planning, conducting, and promoting more vital services of worship is another important objective. Yet typical church schools have long held "opening exercises" that are dull, monotonous, unprepared, and conducted without much thought of their educational value or even their religious significance.

Half the corporate worshiping our people do is in their educational programs. For at least half our people their first experiences of group worship are in church school agencies. Almost the only place where people will have education in worship is the church school. Nearly half the time in some schools is scheduled for those "opening exercises" that include elements of worship though they may not be really worship services. Here is a conspicuous area for renewal in the church school along with general renewal in the church.

Definition of Worship

Nothing is more needful for both leaders and learners than a clear concept of worship's meaning. What is it?

Worship is an activity that includes, when complete, six components: an outreach of the self toward God; a felt inreach of God toward the self; resultant communion; some thought about things of God and godliness; an emotional reaction to the same; and, above all, some response in peace, purpose, or action. With that basic definition we may say that church school worship observances are to be experiences, planned and purposeful, in which human concerns are brought into God's presence and commitments are made in the light of his revealed nature and will.

This definition is avowedly a dynamic one, life-related. It would not eliminate the objective reference to God but does not neglect the subjective reference to man in his world. Someone has said that a service of worship resembles the withdrawal of paratroopers for a briefing. They leave the field and go to a center where they are re-invigorated in mind and spirit; then they will be dropped behind the enemy lines again. Similarly, the life of a Christian encompasses withdrawal and engagement.

We need "practice of the presence of God" and "companionship with the Divine Spirit" but this is not complete without an identification of the human will with his. There is innate worth in meditation and the expression of sheer joy, adoration, thanks, and praise. Confession and assurance of forgiveness are essentials; life would be incomplete without supplication and submission. Yet after, above, and through all these—there is also a proper concern for deliverance into fresh effort at new life for self and others. Worship is properly realized in some change outwardly as well as inwardly; lacking this ethical phase it can become pagan, the "empty phrases" Jesus mentioned in connection with prayer (Matt. 6:7). There is peril if the sanctuary becomes a retreat from life.

Instead, let it be a center where life's highest values are recognized in clear consciousness and appraised under God's light, where determination is heightened for life's reconstruction and where enterprises for its enhancement are accepted for planning, beginning, and concluding.

Yet our primary concern in educational agencies is not worship for worship's sake alone or even its appropriate results. It is principally for that three dimensional growth. However, we recognize that growth takes place only through worship that is real, just as all other full-fledged learning comes through actual doing. Worship in a church school agency should of itself be moving, satisfying, and productive; it should also have results in growth. Today the pupil worships at the highest level possible for him under the circumstances; simultaneously he becomes ready for the still higher experience of meeting God in the fellowship of believers tomorrow and thereafter manifests his increasing Christian maturity. Too, the pupil becomes increasingly able to help others worship, not only as a fellow worshiper with them but also as a leader for them. Thus the ultimate standard as to form and content in all that we attempt to do for worship experiences is REALITY—reality, including its overflow in mission.

This does not preclude direct study and instruction as to worship. There can be studies of hymns and the music for them, of prayers and their sources, of liturgical forms in churches where these are used. Yet, these will be done within other activities, not in the worship services themselves.

Planning a Total Program of Worship

The directing of worship in church schools should begin with the planning of a rounded program of worship experiences for the entire congregation: private and family observances, as well as corporate ones. While the pastor and other leaders will need to consider the whole congregational situation, purpose, and practice, the church school representative will stand primarily for that educational ideal of growth through, in, and for worship.

One result of such planning could be a clear understanding of the mutual relationships of all services but also the special contributions to be made by the church school agencies:

Additional experiences of worship.
Breadth of experiences, especially beyond the typical, formal ones.
Education for worship through worship itself and by direct study and instruction about it.
Experiential worship (individuation of occasions).
Graded worship.
Leadership opportunities with guidance.
Small group worship experiences.
Spontaneous worship.
Variety of worship forms, including perhaps unusual types.

Time for Worship in the Church School

What follows has mainly in view a typical Sunday church school with a more or less formal service of worship in the morning session, likely at the beginning of the hour. Yet current trends favor, especially for the younger children, spontaneous and informal moments of worship at any appropriate point, quite regardless of the clock. Also, certain schools have worship at the end of the session. This allows for preparation during the session. Too, worship at this time can be an integrating activity that sends pupils out with a rounded inspiration in both the lesson and culminating worship experience.

In any case, what proportions of time should be given to the worship phase of a session?

Preschool Age. Worship for nursery and kindergarten children should most often be spontaneous, with no set schedule or form. They will sing and pray as the program brings them naturally into a few minutes now, additional minutes later.

Elementary Children. These pupils can begin to have a more definitely scheduled service with annual progress toward a more formal order though a degree of informality must never be lost. Primary and junior pupils should begin to plan and conduct their own services; complete education in worship requires that people can be "producers" as well as "consumers." Worship should not take, ordinarily, more than a fourth of the time of elementary children or the high school youth mentioned next.

High School Youth. Beginning not later than this age, pupils will be attending the common services of the congregation for their major experiences of formal worship. If they do not have other opportunities to plan and conduct services, a part of the Sunday church school time should be used for that. If the congregational services do not provide variety, that element should be a principal charge against the church school program. All persons need an opportunity to develop a broad outlook about types of worship and the total program of a congregation should minister to divergent tastes.

Older Youth and Adults. For these students of worship, ten minutes well done, should ordinarily suffice. This leaves more of the session time for instructional purposes; it may also encourage, instead of possibly discouraging, attendance at major services. Even a brief service can furnish some of the necessary variety.

Planning Church School Services of Worship

Worship experiences in the church school can be rich. Careful planning would be a significant contribution toward quality. This would be in contrast with the typical lack of preparation beyond random selection of hymns, reading of the next responsive selection in the hymnbook, and calling on the pastor for prayer.

The need includes general planning for the year, more detailed planning for the quarter and meticulous planning for single services. The resources are available; there is an abundance of books about the subject and even more volumes of materials for use in the services.

There are three primary considerations when planning a single service: the *elements,* their *selection,* and their *arrangement.*

ELEMENTS OF SERVICES

The climate for a service of worship is an intangible factor but it can contribute greatly or detract heavily. It will be an amalgam of numerous conditions. There will likely be a church school tradition as to the general attitude, good or bad. Physical facilities are important: good architecture, decoration, equipment, furniture, heating, lighting, pictures, and symbols. There is a quality in a leader's manner or the pupils' demeanor that can inspire or frustrate worship. Fitness of the service for the mood, need, and purpose of participants is paramount. Throughout, careful study is necessary to seize and promote every favorable condition for the incoming of the Spirit to the worshipers and for the Spirit's outgoing through them. Six tangible elements can be employed in the services.

Devotional Arts

This element refers to a variety of things "seen and heard": pageants, stories, sermonettes, objects, pictures, extrabiblical literature, and others. There are excellent possibilities in the projected picture as a focus for worship and in recordings. When well selected and presented, all these can be extremely effective; they are especially useful for variety.

Liturgy

In one usage, the term is equivalent with worship, if not all the Christian life. Then it ". . . expresses the fact that worship is a present *experience*—the action of Christ in the midst of his people and the action of Christians in response."[1] The term is used here in its narrower sense of "ceremonial forms." They are at the pole of formal expression in the verbiage of others versus spontaneous, individual expression. Services in many church schools are conducted according to the liturgies of a hymnal or some modification of them. They are convenient, orderly, and uniform. On the other hand, their repetition may engender monotony and disinterestedness. Too often their purpose and meaning are not understood;

---

[1]Alfred Shands, *The Liturgical Movement and the Local Church* (rev. ed.; New York: Morehouse-Barlow Co., 1965), p 22.

the verbiage may seem like a foreign language. While their character is historic, it can seem so archaic as to be irrelevant. More simply, these orders can make leaders careless about their preparation.

Proponents of liturgical services argue that we must start children early in this type so that they will learn to use it in congregational services. But we cannot be really educated for a particular form of anything merely by ceaselessly repeating it! Actually, we may but learn to dislike a form of worship, perhaps worship itself, if it gives us spiritual malnutrition in a form not suited to our taste, vocabulary, and need. Also children may but acquire adult habits as a sort of veneer and so develop into the spectators at worship of whom we already have too many.

If liturgies are used, thorough education of pupils and leaders in the meaning of the forms is essential. It is most important to recognize the seasonal variations for the sake of variety, provide for progression in age group adaptation, give attention to the leader's expressiveness in reading and employ every available means to meet the immediate experience of the worshiper.

A form of worship should provide a highway on which to travel with one another to the place of communion with God—communion, with an aftermath in mission. It may be that this can be accomplished better, at least for some, and particularly at certain ages and under certain circumstances, through informal services. It may be better to reserve liturgical services as something special to be done under the pastor's leadership in the congregation's common services with all the fittings of chancel, choir, and the rest. It may even be true that people can be led best into the effective use of the formal liturgies by arriving at the result indirectly and step by step, through other orders.

Actually, research is profoundly needed to determine exactly what forms of worship provide the maximum of reality for the people. What happens, really, to children, youth, and adults who participate in liturgical services and in contrast, nonliturgical services?

Music

The musical element is likely the chief of all means for creating and releasing religious sentiment. Substandard quality in so much that is used in church schools is correspondingly distressing. Only the best musical, literary, educational, and religious standards should prevail in its selection and rendition. Hymnals demand care in choice and then wise handling in use. Hymns deserve similar attention in selection, study, playing, and singing. The best of the new hymnals provide helps; leaders should make use of these and other aids. A much greater variety of music, both vocal and instrumental, is possible and would be welcomed.

Functional Outlook. An interest in music as music is wholesome. Yet in church schools we are concerned primarily about Christian growth *through* music (to guide and stimulate Christian living); growth *in* music (to enlarge appreciation and increase responsiveness); growth *for* music (to expedite effective rendition and participation). Religious concepts may be enriched by music, religious feelings aroused and expressed, religious conduct guided, motivated, and empowered, religious community shared. Such a functional outlook is realized when the leader inquires whether this is a learning situation where a song will be useful and if so, what song, used how. The proper approach was understood by a teacher who, when asked, "How do you teach songs to your children?" replied, "I do not teach songs, I use them for learning." Leaders and pupils should choose and use songs which "sing themselves out of their spirits," then "take the message on into further expression." Closely associated is creative procedure in which the pupils can sometimes "make up" music to express themselves.

Standards for Hymns. There are standards for measuring the educational value of a hymn. The *aim* should fit the objective in view. Are the hymn's *concepts,* both doctrinally and ethically, as wholesome and proper as they can be. The *motivation* that the hymn will likely arouse is naturally to be in harmony with the purpose. The historical *occasion* which produced the hymn will likely affect its relevance; so will the literary and historical *sources,* including the date and character of the author and composer. Other standards are summarized when the *theme* of the hymn is considered. Is it abstract or concrete, limited or broad, activistic or quiet, individual or social in outlook? Above all, does it embody an experiential relationship of pupils that is appropriate to the purpose of the occasion?

Poetry of Hymns. The literary form of a hymn deserves attention, too. How about its craftsmanship; is it worthy, ordinary, or faulty in rhyme, rhythm, sentence structure, and grammar? Is the message portrayed in the most adequate language possible and is that language suited to the age group? It is particularly difficult to find hymn poetry that fits the child and youth groups of our day. The visual imagery of many springs from backgrounds unfamiliar to the modern person. Closely related, the emotional quality of some hymns can be questioned; the general feeling tone they would create may stir improper emotions instead of proper ones. Above all a hymn poem should be true to, not untrue to, things as they are. Too often the ideas have been exaggerated and the images are painted too vividly for any relationship to the realities in which people live. It is a serious fault to sing about impossible or erroneous religious experience. Too often, also, poems are overburdened with ideas; they do not travel like an arrow to serve a purpose.

Studying Hymns. Hymns deserve study, as to words and music but most of all meanings and relation to life. Good procedure will include these steps: *Introduce the hymn.* Tell interesting facts about it and perhaps something about the purpose or relationship to the theme of the service and even the objectives of the day or the course. *Interpret the words.* In almost every hymn there are new and difficult words and phrases that need to be pronounced but mostly explained. Possibly the lines need to be read one by one and discussed. Nonreaders will need to memorize the words. *Stress the meaning.* The basically relevant message of the hymn must be revealed. *Teach the tune.* This may need to be done according to the step-by-step procedures that are familiar to students of music. We could add, *observe certain precautions:* do not tire younger pupils; conduct the study in the appropriate spirit; learn hymns outside the service itself; let leader and pianist be well prepared.

Offering

Offerings are received most fittingly within a service of worship. There is nothing educational about passing an envelope around a class just as the teacher is starting the lesson. On the other hand there can be high educational value in making the offering in a religious manner, within a setting of worship.

Prayer

Prayer, it would be expected, is often the heart of a worship experience. It should, accordingly, be the most carefully considered feature of a service. Casual calling upon the pastor, careless reading of some formal prayer, constant repetition of the Lord's Prayer exclusively—all these should be avoided. Let the leader set the prayer as a jewel in the midst of the service and be in itself a gem.

In prayer, even more than in music, only the highest standards are allowable and many will be the same. Particularly, the nature of prayers will be carefully determined by the age group of the pupils and, even more, by the occasion.

As a few emphases, prayers should be brief, with sincerity as their keynote. Variety of form and procedure is desirable; collects, litanies, sentence prayers, and silent prayers will provide dignified variety where prayers by leaders only have been the practice or vice versa. Creation of written prayers is useful. Informal prayer, like other features of informal or spontaneous worship, should be integrated with other forms of activity. Quite young pupils can lead in prayer and are able to serve beautifully if carefully guided in preparation and performance. Formal experiences of prayer in worship will be most effective if pupils have helped to plan for them and if they meet the basic standard of relevance as fully as possible.

Finally, it may need to be said again that in our church school services the special purpose is growth through, in, and for prayer. Closely related, the nature of prayer as an elemental feature in any religious experience suggests that it needs to be not only an element in services and a constant activity within the Christian faith-life but also a major subject for study.

Scripture

Perhaps the principle of relevance to age group, occasion, and purpose is violated most frequently when scripture is selected. Fitness of the language need not concern us so seriously any more; we have the children's Bibles and the modern translations which should be employed regularly. Words of introduction, explanation, or interpretation are not out of place instead of routine announcement of book, chapter, and verses in the use of devotional scripture. Sometimes the scripture may be made more effective by supplementation with a story or bit of modern literature that parallels the meaning. It is most important that the scripture be integrated into unity with the other features of the service.

Variety in usage can include free telling, musical setting, unison or antiphonal or choral reading, along with the usual responsive reading or reading by superintendents and pupils. Of utmost importance, the Bible is too significant a resource to be read so poorly as it usually is. Good reading demands preparation; this includes a mastery of all difficult words and ideas, also the practice of fitting expression. Fundamentally, readers must know and feel scripture before they can communicate its words.

There are still other elements of services: benediction, call to worship, creed, silent meditation, and more. Church school worship services will be enriched as all these materials are woven wisely and appealingly into constantly varied patterns.

SELECTING THE ELEMENTS

Out of the wealth of materials available it is necessary to select for each service of worship the specific ones best suited. What are the criteria?

Adaptation. Age, need, interest, and experience of pupils, including their experience in worship, will be a principal criterion. Developmental relevance is more important than ecclesiastical heritage. Where are these worshipers in their lives right now?

Completeness. There should be sufficiently adequate development of the theme for the day and inclusion of enough representative materials to make a finished product.

Familiarity plus Variety. We cannot worship well with the hymn we are singing for the third consecutive session or with one we have never seen before. The whole service should be neither so unchanging as to foster perfunctoriness nor so novel as to draw attention to the unusual features.

Fitness. This criterion asks whether the materials used are the best to foster the highest possible experience of worship here and now. It involves full consideration of the needs of the worshipers, the objectives, the quality of the materials, the circumstances in equipment and leadership.

Participation. Each worshiper should have full opportunity to be involved throughout the service. It is to be, as far as possible, not something done for him but by him. He will sing, not be sung to; pray, not be prayed for.

Unity. Every service should have a theme, usually one that expresses the objective. The hymns and other components will be gathered around the theme. As an example, quite obviously there should be genuine giving of thanks on a Thanksgiving Day Sunday; so "We thank thee, Lord" would be a fitting theme. "Let Light Shine in and from Us" would be fitting for an Epiphany occasion. Themes may follow the lesson for the day, the great holy days of the church year and the holidays of the national year; especially they should often pertain to vital pupil experiences such as, for the young, the beginning of school.

ARRANGING THE ORDER

When the materials have been selected as wisely as possible for the intended result, they must be put into the most suitable sequence. Four major principles will guide the arrangement. *Alternation.* Music and reading, standing and sitting, as instances, are mixed so that varied expression is achieved. *Climax.* The opening event is chosen with special care; then the service proceeds to its height. *Familiarity plus variety.* There is need for variation in the order to prevent monotony. One general outline may serve for a quarter if there is some change each month and a bit of variety each session. *Practicality.* Materials are to be used, only in the order that will "work" under the conditions. Awkward effects can be avoided by taking into consideration such practical factors as the physical movements of pupils and leaders, ability to read, skill at singing, and the like.

Conducting Services

When the program and the service have been well planned, artful conducting remains as an essential if the objective is to be attained.

FITNESS OF PHYSICAL SETTING

In too many schools, pupils of widely varied ages are crowded into rooms that are not conducive to worship. On the other hand, a few build-ings, newly built or remodeled, provide children's chapels as fully ap-pointed as the places of worship for the congregation's chief services. Some of these have been overdone; it may be desirable to withdraw pupils from the instructional setting occasionally but not too extremely. Schools need to provide what is not necessarily the most ecclesiastical setting possible but the one most compatible with the ideals of both worship and education.

It is written that Paul and Silas were able to worship heartily in a dungeon, but they had attained a degree of spiritual maturity scarcely typical of church school pupils. Hence, if any group must use basement facilities for worship, let it be an older one that will find the situation less distracting. Besides, the room may then be changed. There was one base-ment room, long used by children, that was unventilated, undecorated, and dimly lighted. Dampness, even, showed on the walls. Then circum-stances made necessary its use as an adult classroom. Before long it had water-proofed walls, softly tinted decoration, indirect lighting, and a rug on the floor.

An ideal room will be well lighted, with sunshine if possible; heating and ventilation will have requisite attention. It will be decorated in a dig-nified way, with windows neatly curtained or draped and pictures care-fully chosen. A well equipped room will have chairs of suitable height, rubber-tipped if there is no carpet—preferably not pews—a plentiful sup-ply of hymnals and Bibles and, important, shelves and a cabinet for putting things away. A prime requisite is a good musical instrument, kept in tune regularly.

There was a period in recent church school history, and it has not entirely passed, when altars were the thing. Something more informal, probably a special table, is better adapted to worship experience for most age groups. The appointments can be changed from time to time, depend-ing upon the season, the theme of the unit, and the session's objective. They can be made more relevant to daily life. Besides, it seems best to think of only a single altar or its equivalent in a church.

FREEDOM FROM DISTRACTION

Satisfying services of worship will be conducted under conditions in which attention is focused on worship alone. Thinking of a somewhat formal service for a group of considerable size, the leader must be prepared so that there are no delays after the service has started. The pianist needs a copy of the day's order so that she can proceed without hesitation. The pastor, superintendents, secretaries, treasurers, librarians, or sexton must all understand that their proper responsibility is to worship, keeping silent and not moving about until the service has been concluded. For this portion of the schedule the leaders are the figures on whom attention is to be fixed as they guide everyone corporately in communion with God.

If worship is conducted at the opening of a session, some plan to restrain late pupils from disturbing those who came on time is important. Simple justice demands it. Besides, orderly procedure would accomplish at least three things: raise the tone of worship; foster punctuality; educate members of the church for proper deportment in the adult common worship. Careful study of church school etiquette has been suggested already; also a practical help is to admit late pupils to the back of the room, if the building is suitably constructed.

Announcements will be excluded from a service and only an essential minimum of directions given. Hymn numbers can be posted on a hymnboard, written on the chalkboard, or mimeographed along with the complete service if it is different, as in many cases it should be, from what is suggested in hymnal or lesson book. The passing of papers or other supplies during worship is a gross misdemeanor. Talks by a staff member or visitor should be eliminated if they are not specifically worshipful in character. Stopping the pupils in the midst of a hymn to correct their singing is undesirable; let the hymn be learned in advance.

PROPER APPROACH

As the time draws near, it is necessary for worshipers to develop an appropriate spirit. For a service at the opening of a session the leader needs to arrive early. Other workers can help by being in their places, greeting the pupils, helping them get to their seats quietly, and providing them with the necessary hymnals or other aids. Women workers should remove their hats and coats and be at home; pupils, too, should have a place to get their surplus clothing out of the way. The earliest arrivals may help with arrangements. Some profitable pre-session activity is possible for all, even if it is but quiet conversation. Listening to music is another possibility— soft music on the piano or with recordings. Then, when the moment for beginning has arrived, a hand signal to rise, the chords of a hymn, or a superintendent's standing in his place should be sufficient.

LEADERSHIP AND TECHNIQUES

An ideal leader of worship possesses a rather rare combination of personal characteristics: dignity, reverence, self-command, sincerity, good voice, pleasing appearance, friendly disposition, quiet enthusiasm. Most of all, the ideal one will be the chief worshiper; he worships and the pupils follow.

The planning and conducting of worship should pass to pupil leaders, under adequate advisement; they can be rendered capable. Here, for example, is a youth group in its Sunday session on the day before Christmas. Plans have been made by the appointed members well in advance. As the visitor enters, he is greeted by a young man who ushers him to a seat. He observes a quiet orderliness enforced by the young people who know what they are about. Throughout the session the adults are inconspicuous, only a superintendent sitting near the back of the room and a few teachers in appropriate places. Preceding the service, the department's president requests a meeting of his group on a certain weekday night. Then the young people worship. One young woman takes her place as leader; another is pianist. The order of worship, headed by its theme, has been written on the chalkboard so that there are no announcements. The only spoken words are words of worship. They sing. A young man leads in prayer. Others collect the offering. Finally the young people go to their class sessions, spiritually uplifted. Already they are launched into the week's experience, ready to be guided further by the work in their classes.

Ten general suggestions for proper technique can be listed as a summary. (1) Know the purpose of worship in general; have definite and specific aims for each service. (2) Know the worshipers and be sensitive to their needs. (3) Know the materials available and the principles of combining them. (4) Enlist the co-operation of all persons involved. (5) Provide the most favorable setting possible. (6) Have preparations made thoroughly in the interests of poise, ease, and a finished service; then arrive early and be able to proceed with freedom of spirit. (7) Start promptly; keep moving quietly and reverently; lead the service to its conclusion and close it there. (8) Eliminate every possible source of distraction. (9) Expect order, and in all kindliness, tolerate nothing less. (10) Worship devotionally, though also educationally.

In all worship experiences, the ideal is achieved when outward expression and inward experience parallel each other.

DIRECTING FELLOWSHIP

From its beginning with Jesus and his disciples, the Christian church has been a particularly intimate social group. Within its membership men, women, youth, and children can experience a warmth of human interrelationship that is akin to the divine relationship in which they have their highest realization. We all sing heartily when the hymn is "Blest be the tie that binds our hearts in Christian love." Fellowship fits the meaning of church as communion of saints and of Christianity as love in its several dimensions. Without fellowship experience God's people cannot be living abundantly.

Fellowship in the Church School

This sense, spirit, and practice of fellowship is worthy of cultivation in our church schools. We rightly aim that Christian persons shall become more mature individuals *through* their experience of it, *in* their appreciation for it, and with skill *for* promoting it. Their education from fellowship to constantly higher fellowship for themselves or others, even others the world around, is not an insignificant component of an abundant life.

MEANING

Outside the church, what we have most in mind is typically called recreational activity. Yet fellowship is the more exact, inclusive, and desirable term for use in the church.

While fellowshiping is closely associated with play and the play spirit, it should not be despised or considered of little importance. Play is a universal and perennial fact of life, as old and farflung as the race. Martin Luther wrote favorably about education through play—we use it notably in the Christian nurture of small children. Yet as late as the 1850's, Sunday school leaders in a convention were debating whether it could be right for a Sunday school to have a picnic. It is a far cry from that debate to the present use of church game and other social rooms. Playing in the Christian group as a legitimate activity has been growing in favor; its fruitfulness for wholesome religious outlook and practice is appreciated increasingly.

NEED

The favoring trend will scarcely be reversed in view of present social conditions. Technological civilization is bringing even more needs in this area. Man's wrong use of increasing leisure can destroy him more slowly but as surely as nuclear catastrophe. Shorter working hours we have already; they will grow even shorter we are told. How will still more leisure be used? Idleness can lead to apathy and indifference; feverish pursuit of pleasure can become morally hurtful "recreation." At the same time the monotony of work in a machine age gives some people, it is said, little opportunity for expression. What will happen when we have still more machines? Yet our modern inventions and cultural developments can enrich life immeasurably. One can marvel at the immense opportunities in sight for helpful developments in work as well as play if they are seized.

What will the churches do?

Some of our Christian fellowship experience can be the by-product of study, worship, and service: the greeting and visiting many congregations enjoy after the benediction, or the "fun" people have while working on a pageant. There can also be planned fellowship. It may follow a worker's conference meeting when refreshments are served after the more formal program is finished; it may be a day's picnic or an evening's game or party. We are thinking here of an annual program that includes such activities but additional ones and more of them.

Educational Aim in Fellowship

It seems necessary to say that the fellowship program of the church school, though valued in itself, should have an educational result wrapped up in the package. The program is not to be merely "bait" for attracting and holding youth *in* the church. It is better to aim at conserving their leisure time against spending it to their moral, physical, and spiritual detriment. It is best to say: "If we don't cultivate the Christian fellowship experience of all our people we lose an opportunity to help them develop into the most wholesome Christian personalities they can be."

With this general aim we rightly emphasize the positive values that accrue by helping people turn leisure time into physically, morally, and spiritually profitable pursuits. As one specific value, church school programs should broaden people's repertoires by letting them glimpse good things they had not known in the field of leisure-time pursuits. In summation the fellowship program of the church should help people find life more abundant through happiness in associating with a Christian group so that they will grow *through, in,* and *for* it.

A Program for Fellowship

When a congregation takes seriously the fellowship aspect of its life it will have a total church program. Then it will want its church school agencies to notice this element in all units of activity and arrange for special events in which fellowship is a central interest. Six steps will be needed:

Accept the task. To have or not to have? Many churches have given little thought to nurture in fellowship; others have been reluctant to launch an adequate program. A majority need to consider its desirability, convince themselves of its worth, and determine to do whatever may be possible and most worthy.

Discover the facts. This second step refers to a study of the congregation's present fellowship value within the community recreational situation. In both areas the average church is due for some awakening! It will likely find that while the church has its doors closed six days a week young people, in particular, are being seduced by commercial interests for relatively useless if not dangerous forms of recreation. A world of youth needs, and some want, what the church could undertake if it would. Even where a church is trying to do something, it may find that it needs to raise the level of the quality, so as to serve a conscious purpose while not losing the spirit of the thing.

Organize for fellowship. The organizational structure should be based on a determination of the functions various persons and groups will serve. It will begin with an examination of the pastor's role, then of the places for other leaders and committees who will see to it that fellowship interests are given full place in the inclusive program building. When the pattern has been devised, it must be manned. There should be those who will care for interchurch co-operation and community relationships, especially with public schools. The principle is not to duplicate and to do jointly what can be done better in that manner. Locally, as usual, teachers will have a prominent responsibility and pupils should have their leadership capacities used.

Adopt standards. Here, as in certain other instances of church activity, standards have been relatively low. Some of our "drama," parties, and athletics have been cheap! Not only must the church avoid questionable practices but the fellowship activity should be of the finest types, conducted on the highest level of which the group is capable. Events must be practical, of course, the kind that the group can manage. They can, at one time, serve Christian development as well as wholesome pleasure and be educational in the sense that they lead on to finer things in the realm of fellowship and otherwise. As other proper tests of the program: Have the people learned to know one another at their best? Do they more fully appreciate the fellowship they have in the Christian church? Are they learning wholesome means of recreation? Have they had good fun? Have they been introduced to right social techniques? Are they becoming more loyal in their Christian commitment?

Provide a program with adequate leadership, equipment, and finance. A good program will include a wide variety of activities. Some events will be primarily physical: athletic games, sports, hikes, and the like. Others will be primarily mental or cultural: reading, dramatization, lectures, and study groups for pleasure alone, purely, or as well as profit. A third type will include social activities such as parties, socials, and picnics. A yearly calendar should be prepared, balanced as to the types of things included. It should include all the age groups and agencies and be graded to the interests of participants. There is a wealth of literature to assist leaders; the church could fill a library shelf.

As usual, no other consideration is as important as *leadership.* This priority is attested by congregations that built a gymnasium without providing for leadership and soon found it desirable to close the facility. While bricks are a valuable resource, they do not come first. Leadership does and one of the greatest weaknesses in the world of church leadership is the lack of proper supervision for leisure time activity. Further, we cannot hope that leadership will just come naturally; leadership development is essential.

It is possible to do fine things with little *equipment* and modest *financing* if the leaders are winning, wise, and competent. Yet most churches do need more equipment. Some should be homemade, if possible, as a service enterprise. The financing of fellowship is best done by a budget allotment although there are affairs where pay-as-you-enter may be appropriate.

Educate everyone. Our basic purpose is to develop our people for higher fellowship experience through better fellowship events. Simply, do people, in general, know how to enjoy themselves in ways appropriate to the churchly atmosphere and purpose? More broadly, do they recognize the awful wastage as well as the mighty potential in the better uses of leisure time? So we have our educational task.

Guiding Fellowship Events

An executive's major efforts in the fellowship area will be making sure there is an adequate program, supervising leaders for the fellowship aspects of the units, and seeing that fellowship leaders in general are developed. Yet, many will be required themselves to preside at a banquet or manage a picnic or see that a party comes off with the right sort of good taste and good time for all.

As with any other curricular activity, there is a body of specific techniques. Some will apply to any type of fellowship activity; others to certain ones only—physical, mental, cultural, or social.

1. Keep this aim in view: joyous, wholesome, leisure-time activity that will also build for well-rounded Christian personality and conduct. Remember, these are to be learning experiences, too.
2. Understand principles; know resources for games, stories, and other activities; know the group—size, nature, and interests; take care of individual variations.
3. Use fellowship attitudes: tact, wit, cheerfulness, friendliness, sportsmanship, spirit of fun; bring to bear such skills as athletics, teaching of games, singing, storytelling, leadership in general.
4. Be prepared, in general and for each item of the event. Don't have to hunt for ideas, rules, or equipment while participants wait; have extra ideas on tap.
5. In planning the event: get a theme and stick to it, but have variety in the program; visualize things beforehand; put games in psychological sequence, mixing active and quiet things; recognize the importance of

first items in the event; keep expectancy alive by making use of the surprise element; arrange for a sense of fellowship from the time the invitation is received; remember that decorations or refreshments are significant too; include plans for happy "cleaning up."

6. In conducting the event: use helpers—well prepared, too; get attention quickly and as quietly as possible, get it before speaking and hold it; don't let the group get away from you; secure discipline by group action; explain things clearly; keep things moving with only necessary relaxation and rest; get everyone into the fun.

7. In closing the events: there are those who feel that fellowship affairs should have their devotional moments, particularly at the end of a social party. Perhaps typical self-consciousness has disappeared as the play welded the group into a unit. This may offer an unusual opportunity to recognize the divine fellowship. There must be painstaking preparation—better not to attempt anything than to bungle it. The technique requires skill at moving the crowd by easy stages from one attitude toward another. By management of lights and music, illuminated pictures, straight from the shoulder talk, a brief story, heartfelt prayer, fellowship experience can be brought to its summit.

DIRECTING SERVICE

We saw earlier that there are six works of the church; the church school curriculum can be expected to deal with all of them, integrated within its units. Two are named specifically among the four phases of the curriculum: *worship* and *fellowship*, treated above. We come now to a phase that includes three of the six. The animating spirit of service is equivalent to a sense of *stewardship*; the practice of stewardship includes *social ministry*, we may possibly add *evangelism*, which in turn, may well be the highest form of service. Only *education*, of the six works, remains to be mentioned and our whole subject is that one, with the study and instruction phase as a specialized effort.

Meaning and Place of Service

"Service" is that phase of the church school program in which pupils learn as they contribute to the welfare of others by acts of helpfulness. Here again we have in view learning by doing with growth *through, in,* and *for* the activity. If sharing is a better word than service this is the program area where pupils learn by sharing. Also we are in the realm of stewardship—defined as fulfilling God's intent with all one is or has; so, learning by being good stewards of money, energy, time, and talent is still another meaning.

It seems proper to single out this activity for special attention in Christian education. The life of Jesus is often epitomized in terms of a servant ministry; naturally his teaching on service by word as well as example is to be recognized. If the church is a ministry, the church school learner and leader will undertake as many as possible of the tasks through which ministry is exercised. Regrettably, though, service has been largely subordinated to the least of all time and attention given it in a typical church school. As McKibben once wrote, "Church school workers in general are perhaps more lacking in appreciation of the general nature and significance of service training and expression than any other element in the total program. . . ."[2] That comment remains still a challenge, though new curricular series are redressing the neglect to some degree.

Our people may need to be initiated into the concept of the church as a task force. No one can measure the harm that has been done by two classes of people. One is the group who, rightly or wrongly, were accused of overstressing service to the neglect of other activities such as worship. The second deplorable group includes glib scoffers who refer to efforts for Christian social action as "works righteousness." Salvation by works is one thing; Christian work is another. Christianity can no more ignore social implications than individual expressions of the faith. In every age when the church has been vital her institutions and works of mercy have glorified the body of Christ.

Leaders and pupils who engage in service do need proper motivation. Throughout the Bible we are called to serve the neighbor; the gospels stress a neighbor's claim on our service. Service is implied in the doctrines of creation, of man's nature, of man's place in God's kingdom, and of God's will for human welfare and his goodness to us. Christianity is expressed in terms of love by God, for God, also for and by others. Proper motivation is an essential in our commitment to the Lordship of Jesus Christ.

Education in Service

There are two principal areas in which education *through, in,* and *for* service can take place: (1) participating in church and church school work; (2) engaging in social ministry.

SERVING IN THE CHURCH AND CHURCH SCHOOL

We have regularly given our pupils tasks to perform for the school as secretaries, treasurers, librarians, or ushers. Now and then we have allowed them to do substitute teaching or assist in groups of younger children. They have ushered or sung in the choir for the chief services of worship. But these activities have not always been viewed as education by participation in the mission of the church. If it meant taking them out of classes it

[2]Frank M. McKibben, *Improving Religious Education Through Supervision* (New York: The Methodist Book Concern, 1931), p. 140.

was stopping their education! Actually, we were coming closer to the basic truth about education; these services were the valid employment of doing as learning. By these means pupils have probably learned most of the things they really know about the church and gained most of the wholesome attitudes or useful skills they possess for church work.

Young people could well have much more to do in their churches and church schools. As a good goal, the young Christian completing his work in the youth division has had experience in all six types of church work. He has done all he can by way of holding office, serving on committees, planning and conducting sessions, and otherwise participating in the directing of units of activity, starting in the youngest age groups. He has engaged in congregational evangelism and had some experience in carrying mercy to the needy. He has had opportunities to promote Christian fellowship through assisting in recreational programs, club work, class, departmental, school, or church social events. He has become familiar with the stewardship work of the church by making his own financial contribution to its enterprises and other forms of participation in its program of support and benevolence. He has had some part in conducting worship services.

ENGAGING IN "SOCIAL MINISTRY"

Education in service that does not look beyond the local congregation or even the whole church is not complete. There should be units of activity that provide opportunity in each pupil's program to participate in the work of church organizations and institutions of mercy, also in established community agencies of social welfare. Even when using only the typical Sunday church school lessons this objective can be served. Occasional elective units should be offered in this area and no pains spared to carry out their suggestions of things to do—actually do.

It is best, of course, for the learner to have direct contact with individuals with whom he is sharing. One small group of young people will never forget their touching experience of delivering a Christmas basket to a barefoot, twelve-year-old girl who was bravely trying to take the place of mother in a one-room slum home. It was a complete experience in sharing; she shared her spirit, the young people shared their food. Yet, service should go further, into lively study of the community near and far with constant concern to uplift conditions wherever one's influence can reach.

Program of Service

When building a total church school program this service element will properly have a larger place than usual. The churches need a constituency that is more intelligent about service—its meaning as the sharing of well-being with all, its place in the Christian mission, the need and the privilege for reciprocal human relationships in the name of Christ. Proper attitudes are just as important—strong and abiding motives of good will and devotion that lead to unfailing action. An ultimate requisite is skill, the ability to carry forward, perhaps even in full time service in this area. Throughout the service phase of our program, that possibility of lifetime vocation in some specific form of ministry can be an ultimate objective.

As a basis for such a program, church school workers ought first to make an inventory of what they and the community are already doing in both the areas, local church service and social ministry. Next, the available resources and the needs for service should be surveyed. Then the school is ready for such steps as the following: educate *about,* while inspiring *for* it (an inventory of people's interests will show readiness for this); develop policies and practices for serving; secure support for the budget and from it as one phase of service; provide opportunities for service, with materials and personnel for guiding it; correlate all plans within the church and related community and integrate with all phases of the curriculum; give guided practice in it.

ENTERPRISES AND CRITERIA

A central problem in a program of service is providing opportunities to serve beyond the contribution of money into dealing directly with the actualities. Giving is highly important and there are many things which no one can do except by his gifts. Yet the leader will concentrate on providing specific enterprises that make this aspect of the pupil program a truly creative, personal experience. Clarice Bowman[3] has been able to list nearly a hundred possibilities in the categories of churchmanship, reaching the unreached, building brotherhood and warm friendship, lifting moral standards, serving the local community.

From within those categories leaders will need to make selections. They can choose more wisely among the possibilities by checking the enterprise against these criteria:

Acceptable, heartily approved by the group?
Actual, not just something to do?
Adapted to the group, attainable by them?
Balanced, a part of a program that will include various types and outlooks, needs and peoples?
Correlated with other aspects of curriculum, part of a unit?
Educational, fertile of understanding, attitude, and skill?
Helpful, really not pauperizing recipient or givers?

[3]Clarice M. Bowman, *Ways Youth Learn* (New York: Harper and Brothers, Publishers, 1952), pp. 150-60.

Important, dealing with urgent need, necessary enough to be challenging?
Manageable, practical?
Planned by group?
Progressive, part of step-by-step experience?
Studied, preceded by careful study, even a survey?
Valuable in genuine sharing?

With selected enterprises as building blocks, workers and pupils can develop a comprehensive program for the school that will integrate with that of the congregation, denomination, and world-wide church. It should be comprehensive for all age groups and adapted to them. It should be flexible enough to include all reasonable interests. It should represent balance among the competing demands for enterprises to be undertaken in the home, the church, the community, and the world.

Standards for a Service Enterprise

Conducting a service enterprise is a more than ordinarily serious task. These are important principles to recognize:

1. Appeal to spiritual motivation.
2. Use direct procedure; connect giver and recipient personally whenever other principles will not be violated.
3. Guard the best interests of both giver and recipient.
    a. Avoid as giver: formal, perfunctory giving; blame or patronizing; sense of superiority; sentimentality.
    b. Avoid for recipient: defense and escape; dependence or parasitism; loss of proper pride; simulation of need.
4. Go in the attitude of Christian fellowship.
5. Follow through; don't start and then give up.
6. Make it a creative experience.
7. Remember that the best service is preventive service.
8. Recognize that in many instances it is best to work with the regular social agencies.
9. Be assured of competent guidance.

CHAPTER XII

CONDUCTING OTHER GROUP SESSIONS AND DIRECTING UNITS

In the three preceding chapters leaders' basic duties in the pupil program as a whole and in each of its four major aspects have been treated. Yet the subject must be continued. Several kinds of group meetings lie somewhat on the borders of the main stream of curricular endeavor. These less typical, though important, activities are here called "other group sessions" though it is desirable to minimize their "otherness" and integrate them into the basic curriculum as fully as possible. They are to be the first topic of this chapter; as a second topic and a final consideration under program, unit management will receive attention.

OTHER GROUP SESSIONS

Any church school leader—executive, teacher, or pupil helper—has occasion to conduct certain special meetings of various groups. This is an activity in which significant productive service is possible. A leader's competence in handling business or committee meetings, leading large group sessions, even announcing the numbers of special day services, can shape favorably the attitude pupils, parents, and church members hold toward him and the school. More important, an executive will often be in charge and these events can be teaching opportunities; also as supervisor of other leaders he will be continually concerned to improve their performance.

There are "practical" principles to guide a leader for making the most of any group meeting:

Provide for something worthwhile to happen.
Be prepared with a program thought through and worked out.
Arrive early and start the meeting on time.

Win the members to the program; don't try to drive them.
Suit the occasion with appropriate dignity, reverence, or good humor.
Keep the program moving.
Don't talk too much; listen also.
Be tactful in handling difficult problems and persons.
Observe the special requirements of the particular type of meeting.
Achieve the chosen purpose as far as possible.

Large Group Instruction

"Large group instruction" refers to a portion of a church school session in which an entire grade, department, division, or school engages in some activity that is largely study and instruction. A typical instance would be the time when a department has had its opening worship service but is not yet dismissed for classes. With proper purposes and procedures this nonclass work can be a vital factor in the whole program; more schools could use the idea advantageously. In alphabetical order below several older and newer possibilities are considered.

"THE LESSON"

In some schools, especially when closely graded lessons were not so prevalent, it was customary for the superintendent to introduce the lesson or review it in a departmental assembly. Many teachers did not like the practice. They expected to conduct the session in their own way; they preferred to prepare their own introductions and finish with their own conclusions.

Yet it may be desirable occasionally to have a resource leader make a presentation that will bear on the later work of classes. Perhaps a superintendent will agree with his teachers that he will present a particular subject. A teacher or pupil who has traveled to the scene of some biblical event may tell the whole group about it; other life experiences may be shared similarly. The most legitimate employment of large group time for the lesson is to have the pupils work at some activity related to the class session but not a duplication of it.

MISSIONS

There may be individuals in the church who are missionary enthusiasts or specialists but all Christians are to share the responsibility and satisfaction of working in the enterprise. In an earlier day, church schools would have "Mission Sunday," perhaps once a month, with a missionary story and a missionary offering. While we may still have special occasions to foster missions, we are to lose no opportunity throughout the year. Now all our teaching is to be permeated with the mission emphasis and we have special courses on it.

In the light of those ideals, every church school leader is properly a missionary educator. Clearly, too, this work will be done in more ways than having a special program once a month. Study and instruction, worship, fellowship, and service elements in all units of activity will have the mission flavor and special units for all age levels and in all agencies will center on the activity. Yet this does not set aside the possibility of good to be accomplished by occasional large group instruction with a mission story, a mission exhibit, a film presentation, some work for a mission enterprise, a visit by a missionary. There can be special times, too, for direct giving to mission causes. Properly, all types of missions, American as well as overseas, will have their fair place.

STEWARDSHIP

Stewardship activity and learning, like mission, nowadays permeates the entire program of the church school. A time may come, too, in courses, units, and lessons, for special consideration of the giving of time, energy, money, and talent. There will be occasional calls for personal service and perhaps special contributions to social enterprises. Time must be allowed in connection with the church school financial program for all members of the school to participate in budgeting, pledging, and hearing reports of expenditures. Basically, we learn to give and we give to learn.

USING FILMS AND RECORDINGS

Getting teachers to use the numerous audile and visual aids now available has been a problem in some schools. In others there are obstacles to be overcome by those who would use them gladly if the conditions, such as building facilities, were more favorable. Large group instruction time may be the way out. A film can be viewed or a recording heard, with classroom discussion to follow.

WORSHIP PREPARATION

Outstanding contributions to worship experience can be made in periods of large group instruction. Worship services themselves should not be interrupted for guidance in such things as the rendition of hymns but occasional periods of ten or fifteen minutes in an age group assembly can be scheduled for these purposes. Pupils can consider the meaning and significance of worship; they can memorize portions of future services; they can study the words and music of hymns and learn new ones.

Special Day Services

It would be interesting to know just when church schools began having Christmas and Easter services and fascinating to see one of those first programs. Some of us remember early ones in our own Sunday School days. We may picture, for example, a tall cedar in the chancel of a country church, decorated with popcorn strings and tinsel, real candles twinkling like the stars outside. Near the tree was the shepherd scene on green paper grass, with toy sheep and miniature shepherds and a sister's doll bedecked in angel's wings poised above it. The church was packed to the doors while everyone sang the carols, heard the children speak their pieces and do their exercises, listened to the preacher and choir outdoing themselves in speech and music.

Those fond recollections suggest the extraordinary possibilities in these programs. They bring the whole church fellowship together, often by families, in a common experience that can strengthen the ties. They put the children in the limelight. Pupils co-operate to do things for others; it is an outgoing religious experience as well as an intaking one. The church becomes important for the time; enthusiasm is aroused and loyalty expressed. The content of the program is made vivid and the memory remains.

There is no lack of occasions for special emphases—days, weeks, and seasons such as Lent: holy observances, celebrations of an ecumenical, interdenominational or denominational nature, affairs that are shared by church and world. This is only a sampling from the available list:

Christmas	Easter	Rally Day
Thanksgiving Day	Children's Day	Week of Prayer
Reformation Sunday	Independence Day	Youth Week
Universal Bible Sunday	United Nations Day	Christian Family Week

Discriminating judgment must be exercised. If a church school observed everything it would not engage in much but fanfare. There should be comprehensive, congregational planning so that balance is achieved in the total program and so that conflicts between the various groups are avoided. As a prime criterion the events chosen should advance the school's objectives. Also, while there must be variety in a program, we do not want to interrupt our routines without valid reasons.

PURPOSE

If there is any one supremely important need concerning these events it is that leaders and pupils will consider the proper purpose. When a group of some fifty workers was asked, "What is the aim of special day services?" the first answer was, "To show off the children." Others followed: "To make some money"; "To draw the parents who never come otherwise"; "The children like them." Christmas, Easter, Children's Day, and similar programs have no real excuse for being unless they are Christian learning experiences. They should be planned and conducted so that each "performer's" growth in grace is furthered and each hearer—pupil, parent, friend, visitor, church member, or worker—is nurtured.

The proper purpose will need to be recognized in selecting the features that constitute the program. Songs, "pieces," exercises, pageants, plays, or whatever else must be chosen not because they are "cute" or merely attractive in any other way but because they allow the participant to express his religious feelings in a manner that will share his experience with others. Purpose can be guiding when parts are assigned and rehearsed, too. There are ways of asking people to take part—better, offering them parts—which suggest the spirit in which you would like them to perform. That spirit can easily be lost, however, in rehearsals that are conducted in the typical bedlam of such occasions. A worker presented the proper ideal when she told how the pageants she conducts are rehearsed with the reverence of a full performance.

TRENDS

Recent years have seen different types of programs developing. The play or pageant tends to displace the agglomeration of "pieces," exercises, and songs. If the latter are used they are chosen and arranged in a structure that has some unified impact under a theme. The "White Gift Service" at Christmas suggests this form. Projected picture programs at Easter and Christmas have been employed effectively but a "spectacle" should not take the place of pupil participation in a "presentation."

There is a wholesome tendency to combine educational programs with adult congregational services. In this way, that traditional Children's Day observance, with children parading across a rostrum, can become more productive for lifting up the significance of children and their work. As an instance, children can develop the parts of a service. One grade may prepare a call to worship; another may create a litany to be used by the congregation; some class may write the prayer. Children can select the hymns that are familiar and loved by all. Under competent leadership they can even compose an anthem for the children's choir to sing. The minister can add a short, appropriate sermon whose text and theme the children suggested.

This kind of program provides for creative teaching and learning in its preparation; it gives teachers an opportunity to interpret and explain meanings. There can be a relaxed atmosphere for pupils, teachers, or parents without anxiety about performances. The entire congregation can be together. The children will have shared the results of their learning and given public expression to their faith through their "production." Their personal offerings of materials have been considered worthy for use. They should feel evidence of the loving concern of their church for them just as it has felt a justifiable pride in them.

Incidental Teaching: Collateral Learning

There are times when a leader is engaged in activities that may seem not at all related to the learning-teaching process as we usually conceive it; yet they may be more important than some of our most carefully planned learning procedures. We call these instances incidental teaching, the other side of collateral learning.

All pupils should arrive early; some will come unduly early. This is an opportunity to lengthen the session. To be sure, leaders must arrive still earlier and be ready with pre-session activity. They can put some of the pupils to work, valuable work educationally, helping to make ready for the session. Others can read from a browsing table, look at pictures, start completing some enterprise, consult an atlas or encyclopedia, present a question that arose during the week, perhaps go to a music corner. There is also post-session work to be done, valuable though it may be largely housekeeping. Pupils can put away the items of equipment that belong in cupboards or cabinets. They can clean up scraps of paper or the like and in other ways put things in order so as to leave the room "shipshape."

Before and after sessions is an excellent time for incidental cultivation of that Christian grace of fellowship. Each pupil deserves a hearty greeting from as many leaders and pupils as possible. There are special opportunities for fellowship when a new pupil or visitor attends; nothing will do more to make one want to come again although that is not the chief purpose. Pupils should be sent home with the gracious good-bye that is an informal benediction.

Business and Other Staff Meetings

One of an executive's concerns will be the monthly or similar staff meetings in which business is to be transacted or other business meetings of pupil and worker groups. These are significant as educational events beyond the business transactions which may themselves be important.

"How can we get our workers out for teachers' and officers' meetings?" That question is raised in almost every church school conference on administration. Leaders say they have enough trouble getting the people to attend regularly for the teaching sessions, much less for staff meetings. The best answer is to raise a better question: "How can we have more profitable meetings?" That goal is not easily attained. The general principles listed earlier are not simple in practice. Typical meetings tend to degenerate into a pronounced informality which drags them out interminably. Unless the superintendent talks, most of the talking will be done by one or two others and there is often a hobby-rider who is difficult to handle. The business may be relatively unimportant, anyhow. What to do?

Several answers can be proposed, besides recognizing group dynamics in all group procedures. First, do not have a meeting unless there is worthwhile business to transact; most people already have too many meetings to attend. Routine matters can be handled better by an executive committee so that general meetings will deal only with policies of larger import. Second, see that an agenda has been prepared, then followed with dignity and precision. Third, make it a habit to follow parliamentary practice, using Robert's Rules of Order when appropriate though a recent trend favors consensus except where official action is taken. Fourth, view every formal monthly or quarterly meeting of teachers and officers as an educational opportunity. It can be said again that monthly workers' conferences should have a fourfold program including worship, education, and fellowship along with business.

UNITS IN THE PROGRAM

We have seen that a church school pupil is to be completing successive units of activity in which he learns to perform Christian activities by performing them under guidance. Studying and being instructed about Christian matters, worshiping in Christian modes, fellowshiping with Christian groups, serving at Christian enterprises are the major interrelated factors of units and these make, with the additional activities mentioned above, a total program.

Few curricular series are written now without employing the unit design. Thus it has become essential for any leader, including an executive, to understand unit procedure. If it is not now being used in his school, he may wish to introduce it. If his teachers are using it, he may need to make adjustments in schedules and facilities. His workers as well as his pupils will expect him to be familiar with the type of work they are doing so that he can understand and appreciate it. He will himself want to be informed about unit procedure so that he can help to make it more effective through his supervisory work.

Meaning of Units

A unit is an educational enterprise which is to develop as a constellation of interrelated religious activities centered around a specific objective that pertains to Christian growth. Cully's dictionary has said it in a different way but with the same intent: ". . . a cluster, group or chain of experiences in a specific area, carefully planned and guided to help a person grow as a child of God."[1]

This general way of organizing the learning-and-teaching procedure has been in the vanguard of educational thought and practice for a generation and its validity for directing learning effectively is widely accepted. The essential concept is the handling of pupil work in meaningful wholes of complete and real experience. There can be a varying number of sessions all having a oneness in the attempt to fulfill a given purpose. One session builds on what has gone before and prepares for what is to come until the goal has been reached.

Unit procedure is meant to be a lifelike way of learning. Just as in life, the pupil is challenged by something he must do to satisfy some aspect of his personality and meet the social demands upon it. He must analyze the situation, gather data and deliberate about them, then decide how he will act. He carries his strategy to its conclusion and gets his result. In retrospect, he evaluates his achievement, perhaps also his process, and links it all with prospective experiences.

Completing a unit clearly involves much more than appears on the surface in typical thinking about a pupil's "going to church school." It is not just presenting himself, singing a few songs, keeping quiet while someone prays, listening respectfully while someone reads scripture, hearing the lesson story, perhaps answering a few questions about it, putting an offering in the envelope, tarrying a moment for another hymn, then leaving.

This is having a particular sense of need, a problem, an interest about which the pupil feels keenly and wants to do something. It is defining the issue, then sharing that center of concern with a group of pupils and with leaders. It is planning to see the issue to a conclusion, with the problem solved and the need met. It is studying about it, worshiping about it, fellowshiping in the process, serving in relation to it. It is doing things, fitting into situations, arriving at some goal. It is learning to perform in many areas and one in particular. Then it is getting ready to do the next thing, something about which a new concern has developed, likely in the process of dealing with the former one.

Groups in a typical church school will most often be following the denominational schedule of units and the groups will be employing printed guides for pupil and leader. A few of those guides may do little

---

[1]Carolyn Wolcott, "Unit of Study," *The Westminster Dictionary of Christian Education,* ed. Kendig B. Cully (Philadelphia: Westminster Press). Copyright © 1963, W. L. Jenkins. Used by permission.

more than use the word "unit"; sometimes, also, it is used for a subject-matter division. Too often, too, teachers have no basic understanding of the meaning of a unit or no experience in the related procedure; consequently they follow the book slavishly and do not accomplish the full purpose. As an opposite error they will disregard the book to do things their own old way. In those cases, one of the executive's supervisory tasks will be to help his teachers study the underlying theory and master the details of unit management. These details are described below in the form to be followed when groups are doing creative work but the same general procedure is represented in the better printed guides.

Unit Management

The management of a unit includes four stages but a class does not necessarily finish one stage at a time; the four may overlap; also, no two will develop in exactly the same way. Only a general picture can be painted.

FIRST STAGE: PREPARING AND BEGINNING

In a well-planned curriculum, the units of activity follow one another in a related and cumulative manner. As pupils and teacher work with a present unit, they discover their next concern. Consequently, preparation for a subsequent unit will take place during a former one. "Let's do this next," one pupil may have said, and the entire group accepted the idea. Then they started to clarify the new issue and plan the work.

Beginning refers, of course, to the opening sessions in which the new unit is initiated. The pupils are to get a clear understanding of the new learning situation and their mutual and individual objectives within it. Past experiences that will contribute to the enterprise can be associated with the new work. Meantime, the teacher is ascertaining the pupils' abilities, needs, interests, knowledge, and experience in general.

This general overview may be developed in detail by discussion, reading, viewing a film, hearing a recording, or having an informal talk by teacher or resource leader. Then the specific work to be done and methods to be employed by the entire group, its committees and its individual pupils, can be outlined tentatively. That may result in a written or mimeographed statement of specific problems, objectives, activities, and assignments.

The real work of the unit is about to begin. Everyone can co-operate to assemble the materials and make other arrangements for the various experiences in view. This working together with a close correlation of all individual or small group enterprises, is important in all stages but particularly in this getting the unit on the road. Success with a unit calls for unity.

Many of the processes in this stage will have to be repeated at intervals. Reclarifying problems, re-examining objectives, further planning, arranging for additional experiences, and finding more materials will go on continuously.

SECOND STAGE: WORKING

The purpose of the working stage is to see that group and individual interests and needs are finally met as fully as possible. Meanwhile, too, initiative should develop and self-direction should grow through abundant opportunity for creative achievement. General habits of good work and proficiency in the use of techniques and materials are important by-products.

Now the teacher proves his real ability to guide and help pupils. "Ways of teaching" will be selected and employed so that individuals and the group make the most effective attacks upon the various angles of the problem.

Preferably the pupils will be encouraged to ask for suggestions on content or method. Then, it is to be hoped, they will attend carefully to plans which the teacher helps them arrange and submit their results for correction of error or for approval. Throughout, though spontaneity is precious, it must not result in hasty enterprises for what is trivial, irrelevant, and ill-considered.

Members are to share their findings and otherwise help one another toward the best possible results. Each should feel his obligation to contribute something real to the periods of discussion; anyone should be ready to give a demonstration, make a report, or share his personal experience. Those same purposes pertain to committees, too.

One responsibility of the teacher, as difficult as it is important, is to control the use of time. Pupils always need help to estimate the time in which to complete things and keep themselves on the main track so that they meet the schedule. It is possible to fritter away a session doing practically nothing. The pupils may become interested in following some tempting bypath but there is peril in overexpanding the unit. If some highly important new subject develops, it can be the center of the next unit. Thoroughness and definiteness within the time limits must be emphasized; it is better to omit some phases and complete others.

THIRD STAGE: CONCLUDING

"Concluding" is more than ending the unit. It means integrating various aspects that have been considered part by part. It means bringing results to a vivid focus and working them into the permanent structure of the personalities and social situations involved.

In a final reorientation things may need to be summarized and reviewed. There may have to be special effort at final mastery of some knowledge, attitude, or skill. Wrong notions must be discovered and corrected, bad habits eliminated if possible. Notebooks, workbooks, and portfolios have value here. Discussion is an important means. Tests and measures are obvious techniques. Records of procedure and reports of conclusions are essential.

Above all, some provision to assure utilization of the results of the unit in future situations ought to be made. The basic idea is to do something of the nature which the unit was meant to help the pupils learn to do. Doing something for an audience or other group may serve this purpose. Demonstrations of the processes mastered, exhibitions of products made, talks, oral or written reports, dramatizations—all those are good. Has the activity been really learned? That question is answered in the affirmative when pupils have done things that promise further action in the future.

FOURTH STAGE: EVALUATING AND PLANNING

Concluding is followed naturally by evaluation and both of these by planning the next unit. Most directly, pupils can list the results of a unit in terms of habits, attitudes, and appreciations as well as knowledge gained. While the gains are to be for general growth as Christians they can properly include progress in learning procedure. At least an informal conference at the end of every unit or subunit is suggested. A pupil who participates in an evaluation session usually discovers that he has accomplished more than he had realized. This develops personal encouragement, enthusiasm for the school, stimulation for more effective work to come. Examination of the techniques employed in the process of completing one unit should expedite more effective work in the next one. It should be an important step toward the final product of the school, namely, an individual qualified to profit educationally from everyday experiences and to undertake efforts at Christian growth beyond the school.

The end of stage four, planning, will merge into stage one, preparing. At this point the teacher leads pupils to summarize their new interests and decide upon something to do next. If, of course, the pupil program is determined by the denominational outlines and published materials, this step will be the time to introduce the prescribed unit, see its value, relate it to past experience, and get ready for its effective use.

Repeating, this description of stages in unit management deals with creative unit procedure. While a typical school will have its printed pupil and leader guides, they have likely been designed according to the outline above. The treatment should clarify the idea back of them and enable an executive to see what his pupils and teachers are being guided to do. This should aid everyone to do unit work more effectively; in more advanced schools, a leader can encourage his people to proceed with units on the creative basis.

Example

The nature of a unit and its management can be illustrated to some degree by an example of one already designed and published. It is from *Is It Christian?*,[2] a twenty weeks' course for Sunday church school classes, grade 10. The materials are a teacher's guide and a pupil's book, also a three part sound filmstrip that depicts open-ended situations of teenagers with difficult problems.

There are five units, beginning with one called *Making Christian Decisions.* This basic study leaves the youth with a fundamental criterion for testing ethical issues: "faith active in love." Then the units deal with specific issues.

Unit III is entitled *My Crowd and I.* It is planned for four sessions; one is on *My Friends and I.* The teacher has been given the objective: that the activities of the session will help the young people to find, make, and keep friends on the basis of Christian love and respect.

The work is to begin with the biblical story of David and Jonathan; the teacher, or a student previously prepared, may summarize it. Then the class is to read selected comments of young people in "Elmtown," printed in the pupil's book. There is guidance for talking this over afterward or debating a selected question. A checklist that includes things we often hear about making and keeping friends has been provided for use at the end of the discussion. The students are to consider the different ways they marked the questions. There is also a list of ten true-false statements to help the group consider friendship in the light of Christian principles. As a device to bring the matter toward a conclusion, there are two letters supposedly written to a newspaper columnist by a sophomore girl in a small town and a fifteen-year-old boy in a big city suburb. The students are to take the columnist's role and answer these writers' questions about friends and gangs. As reinforcement for decisions that may have been made, or final guidance in making them, the session closes with reference again to the story of David and Jonathan. In subsequent

2J. Russell Hale, L.C.A. Sunday Church School Series (Philadelphia: Lutheran Church Press, 1964).

sessions other problems, such as *The Other Sex and I,* will be considered. There can be an evaluation at the end of the unit. The course continues with related units.

While obviously this is not the creative type of unit procedure described earlier, a teacher who is able and wishes to do somewhat more creative work can make free selections from these materials. Teachers who want or need it can have the specific guidance.

FROM THE OLD TO THE NEW

Obviously curriculum nowadays is different. The new series are working at least a modest revolution, perhaps slowly and often silently, sometimes arousing enthusiasm, sometimes creating tension. Many persons had wanted change; others still resist it. The latter would prefer traditional content emphasis, the teacher-telling procedures. What shall be done?

Change must be accepted as everybody's destiny. Patience is necessary and time will be required; nevertheless, there must be a beginning. The beginning may come from denominational pressure; it ought to come from congregational demand, especially from the church school constituency. The pastor, the church council, and the educational committee are key persons. The pastor must be sold on the new ideas—first, understand them. The education committee can do much to win the congregation's acceptance of the program by talking about it intelligently, distributing literature on the subject. The director of Christian education or the general superintendent will need to educate the whole church school as to the value of new materials and methods. His particular responsibility is to secure the approval of the teachers, see that they are properly prepared, and give them every possible aid. It will be necessary, also, to educate the parents. They want the best for their children; they will need to be shown that this is the best. Rooms may require adaptation to the new methods; additional equipment and supplies will likely be needed. These should be provided amply and promptly so that there can be initial success. Everybody should look forward to an evaluation of results with the expectation that their purposes will have been served more fully.

ADAPTATION TO SIZE AND LOCATION

Our general planning as to structure and program fits best, broadly speaking, suburban church schools with a few hundreds of members. The pupils and staff in view, again speaking broadly, are reasonably healthy and upright Americans of something like middle class income and culture. Yet some schools and people are not like that. Consequently, everything an executive or a teaching leader does is subject to adaptation for one reason or another. As instances, the organizational structure and manner of administration will depend upon size of school and type of community; also the program must be adapted to characteristics of particular pupils.

Midway through our pages it seems wise to deal with this subject directly. We shall have to say first that every church and church school is an individual. Then we can consider adaptation to size and location here, to special ministries for unusual persons and groups in Chapter XX.

Every Church an Individual

It is impossible to classify churches, hence also their church schools, exactly. Actually each is an individual with particular traits. Smallness or largeness and rural-ness or urban-ness are sources of individuality; there are others.

The principles of current Christian education are suited to this variety. If they are understood clearly and applied with common sense, special needs will be met in the ideal way. As just one example, a local church school will then have objectives that arise from the situation of its people, whatever their status or way of living. Nevertheless there are generalities about particular types of schools that deserve consideration.

Size of School

Some schools may be relatively small or large. Let it be said at once that small schools can be as exemplary as their larger counterparts. The large ones may number thousands in their membership and will likely be in a suburb or city of moderate size. The small ones are often in the open country or village though they may be in downtown districts of a great city. They have from twenty-five to one hundred members. They meet in a "one room building" with or without a small room or two, maybe in a basement. Probably there are several other small churches of other denominations nearby.

THE BROAD CONTRAST

It is not easy to specify characteristics of smaller churches in contrast with larger ones because there are so many other determining factors. However, such possibilities as the following have been suggested:

1. The small congregation is more likely to be like a large family; there is a less intimate group relationship in the large church.

2. Small congregations must plan in smaller terms; large congregations will be able to offer fuller programs.
3. The small church is more likely to be central in the lives of its people; people in the large congregation may have more outside interests.
4. Equipment in the small church is often meager; while some large churches are crowded, others are admirably equipped.
5. A member in the large church may have no particular interest in the church except for its ministry to him; there may be more sense of being needed in the small church and more zest in helping.
6. Where the membership is small, leaders may be overworked to the point of inefficiency; a large church will more likely have professional staff for its church school.
7. The leadership in the small church can know its following more intimately; large churches may have rapidly changing constituencies.
8. Finances may be more seriously lacking in the small church.

IMPLICATIONS

Those contrasts show both advantages and disadvantages for each church school, small or large. In the small school a leader's intimate acquaintance with other workers and with pupils' interests and needs, the smallness of groups, perhaps a family spirit, the sense of having a significant place—are genuine assets. At the same time there are liabilities: too few leaders, overworked; meager equipment; lack of finances; a possible tendency to be satisfied with things as they are. The leader of a large school must cope, most likely, with the opposite assets and liabilities.

It is probably easier to realize the church school as the congregation educating itself in a small school. The closeness and smallness of the group will make for actual unity whatever the structure. It is necessary to group the pupils in a small school in larger age ranges. The staff in a very large school may run into hundreds and can represent a high degree of specialization. Securing leaders is one of the small school's most serious problems but it must not be thought that increasing size will progressively solve the problem. The curriculum for small schools will be less varied, less formal, and more individual. Study and instruction cannot be so closely graded and may be more limited in types of procedure. Fellowship events may be more simple but inclusive. Service enterprises can be very personal. Leaders must understand that they cannot hew too closely to the established lines. Mergers of small schools are becoming common in order to provide a greater variety of opportunities. Large schools may alleviate some of their difficulties by establishing branches.

Location of School

Church schools are located anywhere along a continuum from remote rural pocket to deep inner city; intervening are the more typical village, town, suburban, and urban types. Change is the rule. Folk farming gives way to large-scale scientific agriculture. Highways and airways enable the urban characteristics to reach out like transforming tentacles to draw rural regions into some semblance of urban life. Public schools do their transforming work. Population moves toward the city for work and suburbs blot out farm land for building plots. Villages are drained or absorbed. Small towns become large ones just as cities become megalopoli. Cities may deteriorate; yet there is both city and urban renewal. We do know the trend—toward urbanization; indeed we now speak of metropolitanization. Dr. Walter Kloetzli reports that, ". . . by the year 2000 . . . ten gigantic super-metropolitan areas will contain one-third of the nation's population . . . Urbanites will compose about 85 percent of our national population."[3]

Not only are churches and church schools individuals; their locations represent a bewildering variety of particular conditions. We shall group the types as: (1) rural, including village and small town; (2) suburban, including small city; (3) urban, including the larger city and metropolitan complexes with (4) their inner cities. We can mention only a few general characteristics of each that may have some meaning for church school work.

RURAL VERSUS URBAN CHURCHES AND CHURCH SCHOOLS

The Broad Contrast: Rural Characteristics

1. The family unit is likely to be a more important factor in rural church life.
2. Most rural churches can have more vital civic influence.
3. Rural people may be more tenacious in holding to older theological terms and ideas, less disposed to change their methods.
4. A rural church may be more central in its people's thoughts and lives.
5. Rural people are often said to be more zealous of denominationalism, yet many of their activities might be done better on an interdenominational basis.
6. Typical rural adults are more given to church school attendance.
7. Rural people may have a stronger interest, readiness, and grasp in the spiritual area. Doubtless debatable, this is frequently expressed in such a quotation as: "Religion is considered more worthwhile . . .; practical Christianity is better practiced. . . ."

The Broad Contrast: Urban Characteristics

1. There is a big city tempo; church matters are likely to go at a swifter pace.
2. City church membership is more mobile; some congregations have to run to keep up with their membership losses.

[3]Walter Kloetzli, *The Church and The Urban Challenge* (Philadelphia: Muhlenburg Press, 1961), p. 2.

3. In the city a leader can likely be found or developed for almost any kind of task; yet there is a tendency toward noninvolvement.
4. City memberships may include persons of wider variety in economic, educational, racial, and vocational status.
5. A city church must give somewhat more attention to "finish" in its accomplishments.
6. Work, particularly for young people and women, will likely be very different in the city.
7. A big city church will likely provide more opportunity for a seven-day-a-week program.

Implications

Typical organizational, administrative, and supervisory principles will pertain and the basic plans of structure will be followed rather regardless of location except that people will be different and this may make a world of difference. Similarly, the usual general objectives and program will be the basic pattern. Yet extreme adaptations may be necessary in specific objectives, in program emphases and in ways of learning-teaching. As one example, so often mentioned, biblical symbols, language, and pictures are much more suited to the rural mind than the urban. Ethical issues, too, may manifest themselves in different ways. Perhaps, even the self-image and the God concept of a city-bred soul cannot be the same for the mountaineer. Again, the church school will need to exploit the advantages shown by the contrasts and minimize the disadvantages.

SUBURBAN CHURCHES AND CHURCH SCHOOLS

Shippey[4] says that one out of four people are already suburbanites. The percentage will likely increase. Suburbs are becoming characteristic of American culture; they have been called "the abode of American man."

Suburban Characteristics

We have already noticed that the typical church school is probably a suburban one; yet suburbs differ widely and, like the countryside or city, may change rapidly. In general, suburbs are urban satellites, dependent upon relationships with a great city. Their residents have usually sought them as a better place for themselves to live and to bring up their children. They may represent a refuge from minority groups, an escape from industrialism, or a mecca of comforts and conveniences. It has been said that the suburbanite symbolizes the successful citizen. But there are many types and these are becoming more varied—with resultant tensions, racial strife among them. There are persons with nonsuburban backgrounds, white collar and blue collar workers, the organization man and the pro-

[4]Fredrick A. Shippey, *Protestantism in Suburban Life* (New York: Abingdon Press, 1964), p. 119.

fessional man. Religiously, many are Protestant—sometimes but not by any means always marginal—along with similarly oriented Catholics and Jews. Perhaps less than the usual number are pagans.

Is it possible for the church to make suburbia a place where the best in Christianity meets the best in modern secular life for the coming decades? It is too typical to criticize what is called "suburbia" as if it were a specific entity; there should be more adequate studies of the general characteristics and the particular issues and problems of various types. Like everybody else suburban residents have their particular virtues as well as sins.

Implications

"Who is my neighbor?" becomes a primary question with which the suburban church can profitably deal. It must stand for the sacredness of human personality, faith in man as well as God, life motivated by love, the reality of Christian fellowship. Small group activity with community outreach can be emphasized. It has been well said for suburbanites that "nigh-dwelling" does not result in "neighbor-living."

Obviously the fellowship phase of the educational program will be significant in a suburban church. Let the church represent a concern for the community, implementing assiduously the spirit of neighboring. Yet the spirit must reach out beyond the self-complacency and crack the barriers of self-satisfaction. To meet the issues of tension will often be urgent. Ecumenical education may be significant.

Closely related, the service element can be emphasized. There is often wealth without much stewardship. Also fellowship can result from cooperative service. The stranger can be drawn into the service enterprise and through it into the church for all its activities and benefits.

Suburbs are the homes of families. The family program of the church school—both for Christian life in the home and toward that life—can meet need for reinforcement of home. The children's program will be important; there is equal need for a challenging program for youth to help them meet the trouble areas in their way of life.

Just because the suburban adults are often successful persons need not mean that they have no need for assurance, courage, and wisdom to meet their quandaries. Church school experiences can minister to their stresses. We need not assume that they have no concern for the spiritual element in their lives; they may be craving more adequate faith. Most of them are of a type susceptible to more knowledge through study of Bible and related materials. Skills of worship and personal prayer may be meaningful. They may be reading people. Church schools usually must be conducted on a high level intellectually, esthetically, and procedurally.

INNER CITY CHURCHES AND CHURCH SCHOOLS

In many smaller cities and even in portions of the great cities, certain strong churches persist. Their church schools may be very much like the larger and better rural or suburban ones. There is need only for the usual adaptations to particulars of membership, leadership, and the like. Yet, while some such churches have survived, others have succumbed to the blight of deterioration except as they have met new demands. Many have moved; others are merging. Still others are valiantly undertaking new types of ministry; in some cases their church schools may have dissolved into study groups, social clubs, and vocational or welfare services.

Inner City Characteristics

The inner city situation has been admirably described in a publication of the Division of Christian Education, NCCCUSA:[5]

1. Differences of race, ethnic group, politics, religion, etc.
2. Unemployment and economic deprivation.
3. Differences of language, symbols, etc.
4. Attractive qualities, such as basic honesty, freedom.
5. Lack of association or rapport with agencies or organizations.
6. Strong family solidarity—even when families seem broken by middle class standards.
7. Different expressions of morality.
8. Rigid value structures.
9. A limited view of the world—their world being bound to the inner city.

Implications

Inner city church schools must discover the role that is uniquely serviceable in their given location in this present moment. Probably they cannot have or use the typical building; in many cases community resources must be used—the "store-front church" is an example. This can mean that a congregational polity is no longer the effective framework for education; diverse groups may need to yoke together for the task. Quite concretely, too, the organizational structure and the literature of typical church school work may be utterly impossible. We may even need a re-examination of objectives. The following have been suggested as significant minima: (1) an awareness of the presence of God within the circumstances, however depressing; (2) a sense of meaning in life within a depersonalized society; people need a sense of importance to God and to brothers in the faith; (3) an experience of church relationships as a participation in the living body of Christ.

[5]*Ministry in the City with Children and Youth* (New York: Department of Educational Development, National Council of the Churches of Christ in the U.S.A., 1966), p. 14.

This work is a creative job with immense difficulties. Special development of an unusual type of worker is likely necessary. A particular difficulty can be the negative attitude of a constituent toward the church. Many carry false images of the church and its agencies. They don't know or don't understand what is being offered. They need an acceptance and lack of condemnation that a typical church member may not be able to muster. We must overcome the alienation that bars them from mainline church endeavor because of poor clothes, no money, and behavior that is socially unacceptable according to usual standards.

Christian relationships on a sound level must precede any of the typical learning-teaching experiences. Teaching and learning must be from life to life. We must deal with people as they are for an experience of Christian faith-living where they are. And it may be of a kind not mentioned in most of the books. Many can be approached through play. Summer is a particularly fruitful time for this work; vacation church schools, day camps, even summer Sunday church schools have been successful. A considerable number of children have been ready to come though they may lack education, discipline, and family encouragement. Adults can be interested in small group study using simple, short term guides. Signs of understanding and new forms of educational ministry have begun to emerge. Congregations have been able to transform themselves sufficiently to build bridges toward inner city situations. They have had to discover the mind of the inner city dweller and then fit it in order to serve it.

Two precautions seem pertinent: we must recognize that the disadvantaged and alienated are dispersed throughout the nation in country, small town, and city though congregated more noticeably in the great cities; also they are not all minority group people, many are longtime American white folks who have been overcome. Churches may have a particular service to render those of diverse racial backgrounds, but they have also the immense social responsibility to those of their own kind who are now in pathetic circumstances.

PART FOUR

GENERAL MANAGEMENT:
SELECTED ITEMS

CHAPTER XIII

PROVIDING PHYSICAL FACILITIES

We could estimate that each Sunday morning perhaps thirty million American Sunday church school pupils assemble in several hundreds of thousands of buildings and in at least three times as many rooms. They sit in millions of seats and use innumerable hymnals, lesson books, and Bibles. The facilities are widely varied in nature and quality despite the great volume of building that has occurred recently. For a few schools they are similar or superior to the best in public education but in many cases they are still meager. Happily, conditions can be improved in almost any school by cultivated vision and earnest effort. Jesus could convert the most commonplace surroundings into a thrilling classroom and it is not impossible for skillful workers now to have good results under severe limitations. Yet the Master's followers can profit from the best possible physical aids to do this educational work at its best.

What would be the ideal and how can we realize it?

PURPOSE

The first requisite is a firm grasp on a sense of purpose. It ought not to be said as one pastor wrote: "I think we have wasted money from time to time in some types of buildings because we forgot their purpose." Do congregations forget that their church school equipment is an instrument they are to use in educating themselves? Christianity must never be moored to a place but there must be places for its work. The church school places are to be settings where Christian growth is facilitated. The buildings and all they contain are to be silent teachers themselves while they serve as tools for the learners and leaders who use them. They should even entice people into them and allow people to get excited about the experiences there.

More particularly, we dare not lack a clear understanding about the dimensions of our work.

Our concern has its element of eternality, even otherworldliness, but there is more. Our doors must open into the world as well as into the church. We are interested in nurture not only for the life of the church's people themselves but also in a similar ministry among the people of the world. Always the religious have made pilgrimages to their temples but then, like Christ, have returned to their villages. While a church school should be a temple it should also be a drill hall for task forces, more like an armory than a retreat center. In general a building declares what a congregation believes to be significant in the Christian faith and life. It should speak to the community about a people of God concerned for Christian nurture toward the wholeness of every person of every age, always and everywhere. This purpose will determine how it houses and equips its church school.

MAJOR CONSIDERATIONS

When the fundamental *why* of physical facilities has been answered a hundred other questions follow. Many can be answered by the principle well stated in a mimeographed book soon to be published: ". . . form not only follows function, form nurtures function."[1] This is to say that an effective program of building and equipping produces a structure that does its intended work but more; it also produces a congregation that understands its educational task more completely and knows how to accomplish it more fully. New ways of working should be fostered by new tools. What are some of the major questions to be faced under that principle?

Who: Persons

Since the basic concern of a Christian church school is for the welfare of persons we ask first precisely who the learners and their leaders will be. Quite simply, how many pupils are there and will the school expand or contract in numbers? More fundamentally, we inquire about the forces molding people in the American environment today and how these may be utilized or how they must be sublimated or frustrated. What are the present patterns of life in the local community? What are they likely to become, what ought they be? In particular, for children and youth, what is the public school situation; for adults what are the conditions of work, housing, leisure, transportation, family life? Not incidentally, who are the expected leaders and what are their needs? We equip our school to meet needs of all these persons within their community which, also, we serve.

[1] From "Focus: Building for Christian Education," mimeographed edition, p. 55. To be published by the United Church Press.

What: Policy and Program

In due time we must translate our purpose into required spaces and fittings that will serve an intended policy and program. What educational theory and practice will be employed by our learners and leaders? Is the school to be a special place for living while learning, where life is not only planned but life happens? Is it to be a place where people will not only be ministered to but also have a launching pad for their ministering? Do we aim to introduce people into the full meaning and mission of the Christian community? What is to be learned and experienced: concepts, facts, attitudes, skills, and forms of ministry?

A particular program will be needed to fill the requirements of our educational policy. So we ask for what type of program we are building and how it will be organized. What is the present program, overall, age group by age group, phase by phase? Quite specifically what are the learning-teaching procedures to be and what material aids will be employed? Closely related, what is the expected organizational structure; how, for example, are pupils to be grouped?

A very special question just now is how the era of explosive change in which we find ourselves should affect our planning for building and equipment. What is likely to happen within the next two decades concerning persons, policy, and program? With the mobility of population, the people and neighborhood are likely to change; in what direction?

What may the future program be; what newer methods of learning and teaching can be anticipated? What new organizational structures may develop? Such far-reaching questions as the following have been raised about that future:

1. Will schools be centers where people really get involved in the crucial social issues of the day and do something about them?
2. Will they be places where presently neglected groups mentioned in Chapter XX find understanding help?
3. Will they minister to those who have enforced leisure time through early retirement, longer vacations, and shorter hours?
4. Will groups be meeting more often on week days—perhaps Sunday programs even become obsolete?
5. Will there be more paid workers?
6. Will there be more interdenominational provision or interfaith provision for at least some of our educational work?
7. Will we house ministries for unusual civic needs, provide for the preschool children of the community, as an instance?
8. Will there be more collaboration with public education; will shared time develop?
9. Will urbanization of an increasing population make a difference?
10. Will family living change?
11. Will there be more use of the mass media?

12. What new technological aids will develop? Will there be automatic devices to perform some learning-teaching processes; will linear print be outmoded and religious facts be communicated from an electronic storage center?

The prospects are exciting and doubtless some will come with accelerated pace. Yet we cannot be idle while we wait for the future to unfold; we can try to anticipate futureness while serving newness.

DEMANDS OF CURRENT TRENDS

Already observable trends, such as those mentioned in Chapter I and elsewhere are modifying the facilities needed. Recently, though, a man who had toured nearly twenty new buildings said they were built to house a program already outmoded. He called them "egg crate" structures, halls leading to little rooms—precisely what we do not need.

Already the school equipment is increasingly a setting for the inclusive educational work of a congregation that is expanding its reach and scope and enlarging its program. It will likely be more than ever a beehive of constant activity, no longer merely a place for "opening exercises" and classes held during one hour each week. It will house weekday and vacation church school and numerous other groups as well as Sunday school. It will also serve to reach out into the community and to bring the community in. Thus a church school's facilities must now be planned for a more varied type of sessions and activities, for a greater volume and variety of people.

Both the integration of church school into the basic organization of the church and the unification of the total educational enterprise have bearing on facilities, too. As an instance, the adoption of a unified Sunday morning program (Chap. V) would modify buildings somewhat.

A chief factor affecting physical facilities markedly is the expanding adoption of developmental education with its creative use of techniques versus traditional education with the transmissive emphasis. We now aim not only at knowledge and understanding of external substance; we also provide for dialog in which people will be meeting and relating to one another in the church and out of it. Above all, this kind of learning involves doing. Procedures are changing to think-plan-and-do-together from passive sit-and-listen-to-telling. Just as there is not so much fixity in the program there will not be in the building. It will reflect the emphases on pupil instead of leader activity, more informality, larger freedom.

More precise implications for equipment arise out of procedural changes. Unit procedure deserves first mention; the trend toward larger coeducational classes with small group process and team-teaching are almost equally significant. These, with wide recognition of individual differences in interests and needs that result in elective courses and interest groups require frequent changes of groupings as well as variety of activities. This suggests rooms of variable sizes and furnishings, doubtless a larger number than usual except as rooms are made adaptable to a flexible program.

A particular development of recent history is the demand for ample provisions to use audile and visual materials and equipment effectively—a demand that is almost sure to grow. The entire educational plant must be considered in terms of wiring, screening, darkening, projection, amplification, and storage; also machines and materials must be provided and stored.

BASIC NEEDS

Space! Adaptable, combinable, convertible, divisible, expandable space —with furnishings to match. Movable and removable and changeable furnishings. Multipurpose rooms, large enough for a great variety of procedures; double-duty rooms that can be shared for different days and purposes and sessions depending on need. Overcrowding is a cardinal handicap; so are solid walls instead of functional space dividers, movable screens, movable partitions, flexible partitions, changeable walling. Space!

Management

More particularly, the basic demands on church school facilities are provisions for management, for comfort and convenience and, fundamentally, space for staging and enacting the curriculum. Offices and committee or conference rooms are needed for management, the co-operative management by pupils and workers for the whole school, but also the organizational work of small groups. At least there will be office space for superintendents, secretaries, and treasurers. Comfort and convenience require cloak rooms, lavatories, drinking fountains, and an abundance of cabinets, shelves, and other storage space.

Curriculum

A broadly based modern curriculum demands appropriate space for each of its four phases. Study and instruction, we have seen, makes its demand for groups of varying sizes and shifting constituencies: assembly places for the entire school or large segments of it; well equipped classrooms of variable types and sizes, at least adaptable ones; corners for groups and individuals to carry on enterprises of reading, writing, construction, or supervised study. Special attention will be required for a present emphasis on art, dramatics, and music. Closely associated is the need for a library.

There is similar need of space and furnishings for worship, formal and informal, in large or small groups, broadly or closely graded—it may be in classroom. The fellowship aspect of the curriculum calls for such things as parlors, fellowship hall with stage and kitchen, play and scout rooms, possibly a fireplace or playground. Service enterprises especially, but other phases, may involve construction work that requires room and storage space for tools, supplies, and unfinished work. There should be plans to use the out-of-doors where climate and when seasons make it feasible; there may be a gardened spot for preschool children.

These needs will vary for the age groups. Briefly, preschool children require large spaces with abundant opportunity to be informal. The general effect is to be more like a family room. A recently constructed kindergarten room has six centers for nature, quiet reading, story-telling, music and worship, block building, household activities; all the furnishings are moveable. Elementary children will have space and furnishings much like the public school counterparts. Youth need the particular attention they have so often not received; besides well-equipped class facilities, space for counseling, dramatic work, music, art, and construction. Something like a youth cultural center—perhaps interdenominational—would be excellent. There they could enjoy good music, have a teen-age library, prepare snacks, be alone, or meditate. There would be an opportunity to lounge as well as to engage in physical activity. For modern adult programs we need more than the typical classrooms; there would be rooms for small or large meetings for a variety of electives, perhaps as seminars, and space for unusual groups meeting at unusual times—at breakfast or lunch, for example. Teaching resources other than the common ones, for all these age groups, are becoming more needful.

Schools will likely equip themselves somewhat differently as rural, suburban, or inner city churches, large or small. The relations to community service that will likely become more significant will mean something for the church school facilities. Homelike conditions are increasingly required as homes become more confined. A growing sophistication of leaders should enter into all the calculations.

Only an unusual congregation can provide all these facilities to the maximum, of course. Yet the total need can be kept in view, even in a small church. What the congregation has or can have will depend in considerable measure on the vision of its leaders. A cultivated vision becomes one of the requisite characteristics for those who are dealing with physical facilities.

BUILDINGS

Church school buildings are of two general types, except a third that may be called "haphazard." Too many have been improvised, built more or less as afterthoughts or perhaps rebuilt as necessitated without a carefully devised plan from the beginning. Often they have been copied from some church around the corner.

Types

Better buildings of the older type were erected on the Akron plan. This plan was originated, it is said, by Mr. Louis Miller, superintendent of the First Methodist Episcopal Sunday School in Akron, Ohio. While seated in a natural amphitheater watching his Sunday school pupils at a picnic, he conceived the idea that such an arrangement would be desirable for the school at work.

An Akron-type building is much like a theater. There is a superintendent's platform or stage on the first floor with assembly space in front of it and classrooms around the sides. The second floor is a gallery with classrooms built on a slope and open at least in front. All classrooms look toward the superintendent's platform, radiating from it like the spokes of a wheel. An Akron building, as its chief advantage, was meant to provide for "togetherness" and "separateness." In practice there is too much of the former and not enough of the latter. The mass meeting that results may engender spirit but is more conducive to noise and confusion than reverence and learning. It is gravely unsuited to current trends.

Buildings of the newer type—here called "large-small" for want of a better name—are characterized by large spaces for worship or large group instruction, smaller spaces for class sessions—more like a public school than the theater pattern of the Akron plan. It is giving way to more separateness and not so much togetherness. However, too many of the large and small spaces have been separated by permanent walls although there may be exceptions for the younger pupils. These often occupy rooms having a central space for worship or other large group activities, with screens or semi-permanent partitions to provide small group meeting places around the sides and one end of the room. The present trend in the erection of new buildings and remodeling of old ones is toward this large-small type with more flexibility about them now than formerly.

Our real need is creative genius to produce some functional development, the sort of thing we are emphasizing for better homes, offices, and factories. It would proceed from the view that there is a task to be done and ask what kind of equipment could serve the purpose most economically and efficiently. A clear vision of the task would eliminate anything bizarre in character and maintain continuity with the historic and ecclesiastical past. Yet there would be any change that would expedite the program toward objectives through more serviceable means. The worldwide emphasis on contemporary church and public school structures may gradually carry us into a new era though there is no little "church school building lag."

Basic Standards

For creating a new building or remodeling an old one, elaborate schedules of standards, and procedures, have been set up. They can be found in available books and pamphlets on church and church school building. Yet leaders who undertake an extensive building program should consult denominational and interdenominational committees as well as knowledgable architects and Christian educational specialists. With Christian education on the march, much earlier thinking and writing on the subject is obsolete.

Five important standards can be listed as generalities only; the details must be sought in fuller treatments of the subject.

Beauty. There is a close kinship between beauty and religion; the note of artistry must enter into the planning and construction of a church school building. Symmetry, strength, grace, and color can impart their ministry to a pupil's religious growth. It was realized by a five-year-old boy who, finding himself in a rarely beautiful church auditorium, said, "Mother, let's stay here where it is so soft and quiet." Cleanliness, orderliness, and good repair, it should be needless to say, are essential to beauty. The exterior with grounds and lawn, so often neglected, is almost as important a consideration as the interior. We do not need showcase buildings but the whole ensemble should equal or surpass to some degree the average home of the community. Everything should be an invitation to use for learning.

Utility. The artistic will rightly modify the merely practical but should not overpower it. A building may have something of the monumental about it, yet it should be more than a monument. Floors, ceilings, windows, and walls may be a symphony of beauty but chiefly an instrument for educational achievement. The artistic builder should not be blinded to his real purpose—the creation of an effective setting for the growth of persons in the Christian graces. It is necessary first to ask: What is or ought to be the educational program of this congregation? Then plans can be made with abundant attention to flexibility for the current conditions and adaptability for future developments. Utility as a first consideration, with beauty as its handmaiden, is the ideal. Let objectives determine means.

Comfort. Austerity has held a large place in religion; perhaps there is not enough of it now. Nevertheless people expect to be comfortable in church and pupils find a hindrance to their educational growth in the distraction of discomfort. Among the important factors in comfort is temperature. The heating system must be adequate for severest winter with provisions for proper control at all times. In summer the building should be capable of management to keep it cool—air conditioned if that seems necessary. Sound control may be more important; an item so often neglected is the acoustical treatment. Proper lighting is another major requirement, also adequate ventilating facilities to keep the air fresh at all times. Safety is requisite, too; no oversight should leave the pupils insecure because of fire or other hazards. As to size, there should be neither a sense of overcrowding nor of seclusion. Many of those ideals can be summarized by saying that a church school building should be at once a temple, a schoolroom, and a comfortable home.

Economy. Buildings are not good merely because they are big and costly. Indeed, they begin to lose their value as they draw too far away from the daily living conditions of the pupils or place too much strain on financial resources. There is point, too, in the query whether a church is not socially blameworthy for the undue expansion of equipment that is used with relative infrequency. Simplicity is a commendable keynote but the false economy of cheapness and artificiality should be zealously shunned. True economy comes from careful planning to accomplish the maximum service with a minimum of space, making every dollar buy the most in permanent values especially avoiding elaborateness. Multiple usage of facilities is a prime way to economize. A room may serve one function on weekdays, another on Sunday; one on Sunday morning, another in the evening. Special rooms for worship may be used on a platoon schedule. Two or three sessions on Sunday morning are not uncommon.

Adaptability. It is but a step to the ideas of flexibility already stressed. New forms of Christian education arrive with each new decade. The seven-day program of religious education is a reality in some churches, and will become more prevalent. Because of population shifts and church growth or decline a church school building large enough today may be too small tomorrow or vice versa. To create a building that can be modified session by session and through the years, that can take in more groups and persons while it renders more services, should be the ideal. We have to say again that no one can fully foresee the needs of the church or church school far into the future; we can embody adaptability.

Use

We have had an era of erecting new educational buildings and many of them met a considerable number of the desirable standards. We might have looked forward to a corresponding increase of effective church school work. Yet one thing was omitted from the calculations of some who built —they did not recognize that Christian education results most importantly from personalities meeting personalities while physical equipment, though important, is secondary.

In the years of postwar building, a man who was acquainted with nationwide church conditions said he knew scarcely a congregation that did not plan some form of building activity. However, when asked whether he knew any congregation that planned to add an educational worker to their staffs, he replied, "No, not one." Thus, numerous congregations erected their structures at a cost which exhausted their financial resources so that it was impossible to provide professional staff in the program for which the building had been provided. There is danger of making the same mistake again. Church leaders who envision more adequate educational work may wisely attend first to provisions for leadership.

The entire personnel will need to give attention to servicing the facilities. Pupils should be led to respect, preserve, and beautify the building and its grounds while using them for their fullest educational advantage. Workers must have eyes to see that housekeeping matters are not neglected and skill to plan for orderly employment of all the resources. Among the most concerned in the use of the building the sexton will be responsible for its cleanliness, good repair, heat, and ventilation. Provisions to facilitate all these services should be built into the structure.

FURNISHINGS AND SUPPLIES

When the walls, floors, ceilings, doors, and windows of a building have been provided, the church school leader has yet another responsibility: to provide proper furnishings and supplies.

Types of Furnishings

When the outstanding items of this nature have been listed, one is astonished at the large array of them, many being more or less essential. A check list follows with the understanding that, of course, no church likely will ever need or have all.

——*Bulletin and service boards:* necessary for displaying notices, pictures, poems, and similar materials.

—*Cabinets and shelving:* for storage of supplies, unfinished work and the like.

—*Chairs:* not folding ones that clatter, creak, and collapse, but substantial, stackable ones. There are definite standards of height, form, and type.

—*Chalkboards:* either permanent or movable types make available certain forms of learning-teaching not otherwise possible.

—*Cloak racks or closets:* without these, pupils create disturbances with hats and coats. Teachers, too, should have and use them.

—*Curtains, drapes, and shades:* control the light but also contribute to a homelike atmosphere.

—*Display cases and tables:* for archaeological artifacts, old Bibles, completed work.

—*Dramatic equipment:* a fully equipped stage with costumes and properties, or simply the sheer requisites for informal dramatizations.

—*Easels:* being portable they are sometimes more serviceable than chalkboards.

—*Fellowship furnishings:* easy chairs, lamps, and the like for a parlor; kitchen and pantry facilities for serving; games and related equipment; craft tools and supplies. Youth like a fireplace.

—*Floor coverings:* new types of tile unless there are hardwood floors, then rubber runners are desirable. Rugs are preferable in social and children's rooms.

—*Library facilities:* shelving, tables and chairs.

—*Maps and charts:* these make concrete and real the biblical and missionary facts and scenes. How can one study Bible without maps?

—*Musical instruments and supplies:* good pianos, in tune! Why not use organs for the children, too? Record players.

—*Offering plates:* to receive the offering in a worshipful manner.

—*Office equipment:* it is difficult to imagine a modern educational program without typewriter, duplicating machine, and files.

—*Outdoor equipment:* some churches have playgrounds or scouting and camping programs which require appropriate equipment. Tools are necessary for a garden or landscaping.

—*Phonographs and tape recorders:* there are recordings for many purposes, especially for studying church music.

—*Pictures:* well-chosen, good reproductions, placed at the proper height and location. A related need is a file of mounted pictures for class use. One superintendent visited seventeen young people's rooms and saw not one picture on the walls.

—*Projection machines and materials:* machines and a library of filmslides and filmstrips. Visual and audile aids have major importance.

___*Public address system:* in larger schools this equipment is essential; educational uses for it are multiplying.

___*Radio and television set:* these aids can be useful, particularly for weekday sessions. Television will be more widely used for church school purposes.

___*Screens:* these or other forms of partitions for small groups are an insistent demand.

___*Servitors:* may be built into the walls so that materials can be passed into and out of classrooms without creating a disturbance.

___*Signal system:* only if needed as, for example, in a large school.

___*Sink and work table:* many handwork enterprises require these.

___*Tables and desks:* tables for the pupils have been popular but there are age groups and activities for which chairs with tablet arms are preferred. The leader's needs must not be forgotten.

___*Worship furnishings:* preferably simple provisions for a worship center.

Types of Supplies

After the building has been erected and furnished, a next step is to provide all the necessary supplies. First concerns will be Bibles, hymnals, and lesson books with their accompaniments. Strangely, Bibles are sometimes neglected. One school insisted on the name "Bible School," yet a supply teacher one Sunday could not find one except on the pulpit. A plentiful supply of hymnals of high musical and religious quality, kept in excellent repair, should be conveniently at hand. Lesson materials for teachers as well as pupils, of the best available types, should be supplied in sufficient abundance to permit full usage by everyone. Reference materials are requisite, too. Examples of other supplies are record-books, paper, scissors, pictures, and similar items needed for handwork, many things for dramatics and recreational activities. Now, too, we must think of materials for recording.

Standards for Furnishings and Supplies

The first standard for furnishings, naturally, is *utility*. Leaders will strive to provide for their school whatever will serve toward the highest attainment of its objectives. This means that the furniture, for example, should be comfortable, durable, attractive, of a kind that fosters orderliness and quiet. (It seems necessary to add, not cast off furniture.) *Economy* can be served by portable, multi-purpose things. The do-it-yourself movement belongs in the church, too; homemade equipment constructed by volunteer labor can be a form of service enterprise. A repair shop is significant. Crowded conditions can be eased by easily movable, stackable, and storable furnishings. Improvising with what is at hand is another virtue for church school people.

Among standards for school supplies five can be mentioned:

Condition. No ragged, torn, and worn Bibles, hymnals, or lesson books should be tolerated if they can be replaced; at least they should be kept clean and mended.

Fitness. The supplies should be as closely adapted to the school's purposes as possible. Only the finest treatment of Christian topics should be studied; only the choicest hymns should be sung. All should be carefully chosen to fit the ages and interests of the pupils using them.

Quality. It is regrettable if we cannot use attractively bound and well printed textbooks with the best of religious pictures.

Quantity. One visits schools where supplies are so limited that halfway through the term there are not enough books. "They take them home and leave them," someone laments. "What if they do?" one may reply. "At least a piece of religious literature got into the home." Enough should be ordered to take up the slack.

Thrift. A church should, and usually must, be economical in its use of supplies but the virtue can be overdone. Expenses are moderate at most. It seems foolish to do everything else, then fail at this one vital point of providing needed materials.

Use of Furnishings and Supplies

Leaders will need to give careful attention to the manner of using their available equipment. A first consideration will be an effective and pleasing arrangement of furniture in the various rooms—a combined educational and housekeeping problem. The items of cleaning, repairing, keeping in good order, and conserving are further responsibilities. In a well-regulated school, pupils will be as careful of the furnishings and supplies as in a home. The carelessness that prevails in some schools is another evidence that somebody has not given thought to the bad educational results of a program conducted under those conditions. Reverent regard for the church's property is a proper objective.

RENDERING PRESENT RESOURCES MORE EFFECTIVE

Vision has been several times mentioned as a requisite in the providing of physical facilities. A man who visits many of them said he had never stepped inside a building without seeing some condition that could have been improved if taken in hand by a leader who envisioned the possibilities.

The typical leader is prone to let the real or assumed limitations of the present building restrict his program. Some daydreaming about the things that would be done if the school had the requisite equipment would be wholesome. Then, with the main outlines of an ideal program in mind, the school can make an inventory of its present resources and determine what forward steps can be taken. Frequently some slight adjustment is possible as a first step. Then larger things can be done, one by one, until the maximum possibility is exhausted.

Often a way can be found to do what has seemed impossible. A nook for scouts, a place for a stage, room for the nursery age group, provision for a social center for youth or adults—sometimes these have been arranged in relatively meager surroundings by somebody who had in mind a full picture of the needs of a complete church school plant. Since it is not necessary to carry on the whole educational program under one roof a neighboring building can be used. Another important way out is to use "the main church" for church school purposes. Small churches do this regularly and many larger churches might. Multiple use of other rooms will help, too.

There was a certain primary room. Its possibilities were good. But two discarded sand tables stood at one side. There were at least a half-dozen different types of chairs, many needing paint and repairs. When the children worshiped, they sat facing the light from a half-dozen unadorned windows. There was not a single attractive thing about that room unless it was the collection of pictures cut from old charts and hung on the panels of the doors dividing it from another room. But someone had a vision.

The women of the department painted the chairs green with black stripes and put curtains at the windows. They brought plants to provide a bit of green on the window sills. They tore down the charts and put a few attractive pictures on the wall, planning to change them with the seasons of the year. They faced the chairs away from the light and arranged the other furnishings to give the room a homelike appearance. The result was a chain reaction that swept through the whole school.

SECURING NEW EQUIPMENT

Many church schools have long been planning a new or remodeled building and others need one without daring to hope for it. There are few schools, indeed, that do not need some new items of lesser equipment. How shall they proceed?

To start is the important thing. An executive's basic approach is to sell the school to its congregation, develop a deep loyalty to the school, and arouse contagious enthusiasm about it among pupils, workers, parents, and friends. The next step is to make the constituency conscious of the school's need. If it is a new building, he will work first with the pastor, church council, committees, and influential members of the congregation. If it is a smaller item, he will likely work more directly with his helpers and pupils.

After creating sentiment and securing a realization of the need, representative leadership may be required. If a large building project is in view, there will be a building committee. This committee, doubtless appointed by the congregation, should include the best possible talent with liberal consideration for their educational point of view. In smaller projects other workers, pupils too, may be the committee.

Planning will follow. As many members of the constituency as possible should have an opportunity to share. In the case of a building program, an architect will be chosen. Caution is necessary for the architect may have no knowledge of current Christian educational theory and practice. He may be guided by his boyhood experience in Sunday school or the numerous Akron-type buildings he has seen. Insistence on the use of skilled advisory assistance of Christian educational specialists is vital. From the beginning all parties should understand that the building is to provide for a total educational program and that some adaptation of the large-small plan is to be followed.

Throughout, attention must be given to financing. Again, the important thing is to start. A fund for such purposes will always win support. It can begin to accumulate by freewill offerings in general or at stated times or seasons; the ideal way is to place the item in the church or church school budget.

The small proportion of money spent on Christian education in general and on equipment in particular is pitiful. More money would be a capital investment with immeasurable returns for the church. Yet, money is not as important as faith and imagination. So often one hears, "But we can't do that," followed by some explanation, such as, "We're just a one-room church." "But," one wants to ask, "are you sure you cannot do it? Have you tried? And do you need to remain a one-room church? Isn't there some way to carve out or add an educational room or two?"

A schedule of activities for those who are conducting a more elaborate building program is available from overhead agencies; some will apply to smaller projects.

A world of weary adults may rightly wish to rest its soul before a monumental altar, elaborately adorned. Yet the over-indulgence of that tendency may be a major ecclesiastical peril of the next few decades. One cannot forget the Ladies' Aid Society that purchased an expensive carpet for "the church" while the Sunday church school grievously needed new hymnals but there was "no money" for them. Christian education can succeed more brilliantly when it is equipped more generously.

CHAPTER XIV

FINANCING THE SCHOOL

The financial phase of church school work too often receives little attention except that teachers collect offerings in classes and treasurers expend the funds received. Yet, when a conference of some fifty workers considered the subject, they found it bristling with such problems as these: What system for securing adequate funds is best? How can a school increase its income? Shall a congregation use its church school as a source of revenue or support it? Who rightly controls the use of funds? How shall the money be administered?

PRINCIPLES

Those problems suggest the need for sound financial policies and programs with efficient management under proper control.

Policy and Program

It is assumed here that policies and programs will be determined by purpose and proceed on proper motivation. Most importantly, the approach will be educational. Also, the gathering, care, and expenditure of funds will be managed in a manner appropriate to church practice which will include good business procedure.

As a basic principle for policies and programs an executive needs chiefly to remember that his is a church school. This can mean three things: (1) the practices will be both educational and churchly; (2) because the school is the congregation at its educational work the latter will be financially responsible for it; (3) because the school is a congregational agency it will serve the church fully and, in particular, be educating the constituency in the financial phase of Christian activity. In addition, beyond details of operation to follow, purposes and motivation are highly significant.

246

Management

Within that fundamental outlook the task is to support an educational program adequately and efficiently. The factors will be somewhat like these:

Consider the program to be supported.
Have correct purposes.
Develop the budget.
Raise the money educationally, with stewardship motivation.
See that the things for which the money was provided are done.
Practice economy.
Account for the funds carefully.
Report the results.
Evaluate in terms of objectives reached.

Throughout the management, good business methods will be used, not for their sake alone. Lacking them, we are not doing good educational or church work; they belong in good stewardship.

Control

Who should control church school funds? Justice would answer immediately: those who give. But it is rarely so in practice. Very often the controlling officers are the church council's men and women. These officials may wish to determine what offerings are to be asked and how moneys are to be handled and expended. One can understand their desire to raise and use the income of the church expediently. Certainly, too, their authority and responsibility should not, under any conditions, be disregarded. Yet they may not be education-minded persons. As an example, one church council refused to allow a weekly allocation of 25 cents for a vacation church school out of a weekly church school offering of eight dollars. Within the realm of possibility, givers properly have the fullest measure of involvement.

PURPOSES

Most church school financial problems begin to solve themselves, as do so many others, when objectives rule. The fundamental intent is to support a high grade church school. Yet, to recognize that the financial program has, beyond meeting monetary needs, both educational and religious purposes is a great gain.

The Financial Aim

Obviously, the school needs money for operating expenses and benevolent work; at times, too, capital outlay is necessary. The adequate provision of these funds is an important charge upon the executive and his people. A mistake is made, though, when the financial aim is put foremost. It is not to be neglected but a too direct and single approach from this angle is self-defeating. On the other hand, when a Christian educational service is emphasized, the necessary resources tend to appear.

The Educational Aim

The financing of a school is a learning-teaching opportunity as important as many others. Finances can teach. Christianity is a religion of serving and there are some services that cannot be rendered except by money. Hence the giving and spending of money can be viewed as an integral activity of a good curriculum; it belongs in the significant phase of service. The church school financial program should be a laboratory experience for one form of Christian service.

There should be curricular guidance as to needs for funds, plans of giving, habits of giving, and manner of spending. More exactly the procedures with church school funds should educate pupils to *give* for *certain causes* in *certain ways*. To give—regularly, freely, and cheerfully in proportion to income and needs. To give for the maintenance and benevolent enterprises of the church or other worthy objects. To give in the regular manner of the congregation—perhaps making a pledge in an annual solicitation and using customary offering envelopes weekly—with full participation in the procedures. This recognizes the definite relationship between church financing and Christian growth—pupils are to grow through, in, and for it. It is proper that education of this type is prominent in new church school curricular materials; we meet it on many pages.

The Religious Aim

Church financing is basically a spiritual matter, yet that characteristic is the one most often neglected unless it be the educational note. Giving a church school offering is too seldom treated as a religious act. It should be done as an element in worship observances, perhaps with a proper consecration of gifts On this point it is a privilege to quote from a student in India:

> I like the way we do there in India. We have one Sunday a month set apart for offering. The children and parents are told previously. In fact, on Sunday before the offering, announcement is made to the church during the morning service so that pupils can come prepared. The members of the staff and the pupils follow the superintendent in systematic order making a procession around the altar with singing praises to God from

the church hymnal. Then, when all have gone back to their respective seats, a passage is read from the scriptures followed by prayer. After this we have the class as usual.

The religious aim is related to the objectives on churchmanship. How the church acts may be as important as what a pupil hears or reads about it. A congregation teaches by the way it gets its money and uses it. Its budget speaks of what the church is and wants to do. What it does about financing its educational work is a significant index to its purpose for being. Its own financial practices must match what it tries to teach in other ways.

MOTIVATION

Each pupil should be led to make his offering as a component of his total stewardship activity. The motivation should be based on the divine call to serve, even sacrificially, for the material and spiritual welfare of everyone—a goal to which we are committed as Christians.

Many motives for giving are less than the highest; some are unworthy. The latter type includes giving on a transactional basis—payment for value received or to be expected. There may also be a feeling that God must be appeased, won over, or at least not offended. Other motivations may be commendable in their way, for instance giving out of a sense of duty. Gratitude is a higher form of motivation. It sees that God has been gracious; Christ gave all. Divine benefactions move us to serve divine purposes. Loving compassion is the highest of such motives. In it there is no fear, no waiting for a return, no driving element of duty; we are impelled even when outward reasons for gratitude may not be apparent.

The fundamental motivation is in practice of stewardship, that work of the church which is the fulfilling of God's intent with all one is and has. Stewardship has been too narrowly defined in terms of church budgets but they are not to be excluded. God is the owner of all; man is the trustee. An offering of money is a return of the Father's own goods—a portion of what one has in trust—to the Father for special causes among his children who are needy in body and spirit. This is being and manifesting oneself as a steward, a manager of a bit of God's resources.

SYSTEMS

A typical financial system is an independent church school treasury or perhaps a series of separate agency treasuries to which pupils contribute each session, often by dropping their money into an envelope passed around in a class session. Special day offerings on Christmas, for example, also offerings for designated causes like a particular missionary objective are common. The birthday offering is a popular device. There may be special school or class funds, possibly raised by such semi-commercial enterprises as dinners, candy sales, or bazaars.

Obviously these methods do not meet fully the educational and religious standards mentioned above; in many cases they do not even meet the financial need. There is a better system: to include the educational program in the church's total budget and have only one treasury.

Unitary Congregational Treasury

As a long range ideal, a unitary treasury for the entire congregation is probably the most desirable system for the church as well as for the church school. It lets the whole church testify to the integrity of Christian education as one of its central ministries. Above all other means, it educates for churchmanship.

By this system the church school expenses are paid out of a single church treasury to which each person in the congregation, young or old, contributes. Every member of every constituent group on reaching the prescribed age, makes a pledge and contributes in a weekly envelope, at any session of the entire church program he chooses. Very important, the plan presupposes a careful consideration of a well-planned budget for all the congregation's six works.

There are necessary precautions: safeguard the intention of the donors; give organizations appropriate responsibilities that will elicit interest; watch lest centralization makes things impersonal; do not let gifts simply disappear; do not allow extreme individuality about the use of gifts; permit groups to support causes of their own choosing occasionally although such funds should be channeled through the regular treasury.

The advantages of the unitary system are many. *First,* it is the only method by which a broad gauge educational program can be financed. Already some churches recognize that the educational services of high quality cannot be a source of revenue or even be dependent on self-support. Rather, they are to be viewed as the major investment opportunity of the congregation. Are any schools except church schools expected to be money makers or even to support themselves?

Second, the unitary treasury is the only sound plan educationally. A pupil learns to give from the beginning as he always will give, not to *our class, our department,* or *our church school* but to *our church.* No financial loyalty is being developed but the permanent one, namely, to the church in which all members provide for all. Again, the pupil gives not for one but for all the works of the church. The youngest child, from the beginning, participates in the church's total life. Having a part in the missionary and other benevolent work, the expenses for the professional ministry and the physical upkeep, as well as the educational program, the pupil can begin early to take an active interest in all those activities. A church-school-centered interest is avoided while an expansive educational opportunity is made available.

Independent Church School Treasuries

Although those who have a unitary treasury system commend it and it is being adopted widely, it is unfortunately viewed in some quarters as too impractical for one reason or another. We must therefore consider also the management of a separate treasury for an entire church school or one of its component agencies.

A diagram (VI) modeled after an actual design, shows the operation of a unitary treasury.

DIAGRAM VI

OPERATION OF A UNITARY FINANCIAL SYSTEM

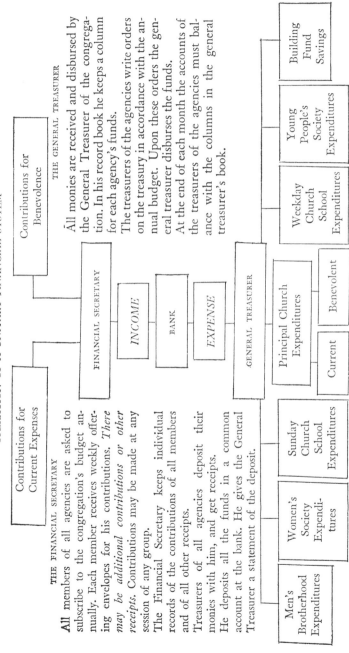

Contributions for Current Expenses

Contributions for Benevolence

THE FINANCIAL SECRETARY

All members of all agencies are asked to subscribe to the congregation's budget annually. Each member receives weekly offering envelopes for his contributions. *There may be additional contributions or other receipts.* Contributions may be made at any session of any group.

The Financial Secretary keeps individual records of the contributions of all members and of all other receipts.

Treasurers of all agencies deposit their monies with him, and get receipts.

He deposits all the funds in a common account at the bank. He gives the General Treasurer a statement of the deposit.

THE GENERAL TREASURER

All monies are received and disbursed by the General Treasurer of the congregation. In his record book he keeps a column for each agency's funds.

The treasurers of the agencies write orders on the treasury in accordance with the annual budget. Upon these orders the general treasurer disburses the funds.

At the end of each month the accounts of the treasurers of the agencies must balance with the columns in the general treasurer's book.

FINANCIAL SECRETARY

INCOME

BANK

EXPENSE

GENERAL TREASURER

Men's Brotherhood Expenditures

Women's Society Expenditures

Sunday Church School Expenditures

Principal Church Expenditures — Current / Benevolent

Weekday Church School Expenditures

Young People's Society Expenditures

Building Fund Savings

The three goals—financial, educational, and religious—give us a ready suggestion: make the methods as much like the approved church methods as may fit the situation. For one item, a school may use weekly church school envelopes. Sometimes these are used only by children not yet confirmed or otherwise received into complete membership in the church. Older pupils may have two sets of envelopes, one for the school and another for the church although this is not advised. Pledges and records may or may not be used.

BUDGETING

The well administered school will operate on a budget that provides for its annual requirements to be secured and expended systematically in accord with advance consideration. Its groups will pool their needs and resources. As they deposit agreed sums in a treasury, they will in turn disburse what is allotted to them in advance consideration. As a principle, under any system, contributors, as far as possible, would have had a voice in the whole procedure.

Procedure

Under a unitary treasury system, the church school committee would be the responsible agency for developing the church school's portion of the budget. Then the council, in preparing a total budget for the congregation, would consider and approve church school recommendations or send them back for correction. Finally, that total budget would be considered for adoption by the entire congregation.

Constituent church school agencies, departments, or classes may have their subcommittees on budget. These groups will send their recommendations to the overhead budget authorities and finally vote on the result. Any committee's routine for budget preparation would include the following steps: receive requests from appropriate groups; study requests to determine the most important needs in relation to likely funds; estimate what the group can contribute; prepare a proposed budget for consideration and adoption.

The groups who participated in budget preparation will thereafter have the maximum authority they have proved their ability to use in administering the items designated for them. Everybody who is old enough then shares in meeting the budget as well as making and in expending it. Only this effort to realize the democratic ideal will accomplish in the fullest way the educational objectives of a financial program.

There should be appropriate standards for the budget. It must be realistic. Properly, it will be based on personal giving rather than money-making projects. Needs for the coming year will be computed on records of previous expenditures and receipts. Attention will be given to likely growth, expansion, or reduction in numbers and special needs and desires. There will be maximum concern throughout for the true economy of accomplishing the largest results with what is available.

While the church school budget is preferably a part of the total congregational one, we must also consider a school's own budget. Again, every effort will be made to employ democratic procedures as fully as possible in developing it. The work may be headed by a special committee or an executive committee, though preferably in collaboration with the church school committee of the congregation or under its church council. The designated persons will meet well before the deadline and plan the financial transactions in a general way. They will know by experience and through records the usual receipts and expenditures. At the appropriate time the various superintendents will submit the estimates their groups have worked out for the forthcoming year. The committee will then make an equitable distribution in relation to contributions and needs.

Allocations

The purposes to which funds are allocated vary widely. The following are typical budget items:

Congregational Support: a share in the central treasury; a contribution to the church for such expenses as heat, light, and pastoral leadership.

Curricular Supplies: (beyond regular literature) paper, pencils, scissors, constructional or art supplies; films and recordings.

Ecumenical Relations: contributions to community and regional councils; needs among community churches.

Equipment and Furnishings: see Chapter XIII.

Family Program: literature; family night expenses.

Fellowship Activity: cost of social and recreational events; equipment, includes kitchen needs.

Leadership Improvement: funds for leaders to attend meetings and classes; expenses for visiting leaders; literature.

Music: hymnals and similar supplies, paid leadership if any; piano tuning.

Organization and Administration: postage and stationery; record and mimeograph supplies.

Promotion of the School: expenses of membership committees; publicity programs; literature to distribute.

Publications: Bibles; pupil and teacher guides; library resources.

Service Enterprises: special causes of the whole school such as support of missions and missionaries; funds for beneficent work by groups in the school.

Special Occasions: Christmas, Easter, Family Week, Promotion Day, and others.

SECURING FUNDS

With those three types of aims in mind—educational and religious as well as financial—what means can be used best to assure the essential support? There must be a program to accompany the system.

The church school executive will need to develop the school's practices in giving and spending; it is largely an educational task. He will disseminate information since no one will long or should give money to enterprises about whose finances he knows nothing. The unitary treasury plan provides that needs will be considered; the school that has an independent treasury system can likewise consider requirements. Stewardship lesson materials and other literature should find their way into the school and practical discussions of immediate situations are proper in all groups.

Closely related is the practice of letting everybody know where the money is going. In a certain kindergarten department the superintendent went from pupil to pupil, holding out her hand to receive the offering, and saying, "Now, give me your money this morning." That is how not to do it! Frequent reports on expenditures are the proper alternative. A further program suggestion is to make the most direct contact possible between givers and receivers. It was done in a school whose pupils sent their gift to an Asian mission and received letters from children who were helped by it.

By such educational procedures we develop the natural eagerness to give. That attitude is the ideal one to cultivate although there can be no harm in going beyond it to develop a sense of responsibility to do one's share. Groups can be led to measure up to reasonable expectations as long as the spontaneity of Christian giving is not lost.

EXPENDING FUNDS

Both the provision of adequate funds and the educational purpose require careful attention to proper expenditure.

Procedure

Under a unitary system there will be essentially one set of books, one bank account, one bookkeeper, and one treasurer. Under independent treasury systems there may be various modifications down to a multiplicity of personnel and records. In all cases proper books for all transactions should be provided, kept, and regularly audited.

In particular there will be a specific procedure for placing the funds in the treasury and disbursing them. All receipts and all expenditures should be handled by at least two people, both keeping records. If a teacher, secretary, group treasurer, or superintendent counts the money he will make one record. When it is turned over to the general treasurer, he will count the money again and give a receipt as a second record to the one from whom he received it. He should also make proper reports to the superintendent of the school and the church school committee or the church council at designated times. Under typical circumstances, the money should be deposited in the bank promptly.

Expenditures are properly made by the treasurer only upon order by the superintendent or other designated officers of a group. Particular care should be exercised to channel all funds to the cause for which they were given unless those who gave them have an opportunity to consider the change.

THE TREASURER

The duties of a church school treasurer—perhaps shared with a financial secretary, must have become clear although they may be modified to some degree for divisional, departmental, and class or agency treasurers; also special conditions may pertain in local conditions.

Job Analysis

Generally, a treasurer's job analysis will include:

1. Understanding the educational and religious aims as well as the financial aim of the school.
2. Being the chief official, with the superintendent, in securing funds for the school.
3. Helping to devise a financial system and seeing that it operates.
4. Co-operating to foster the financial program of stewardship education in general and to disseminate information concerning the local church school's giving.
5. Furnishing the records necessary to the committee that builds the budget and being a chief adviser of that committee.
6. Counting scrupulously all moneys, banking, depositing, or forwarding them to congregational treasurer, and accounting for them upon the records provided by the school.
7. Purchasing efficiently.
8. Providing that all bills will be paid promptly.
9. Issuing checks, on proper orders only, and exercising care that the budget is being followed at all times.
10. Making periodic reports to any workers who have use for them. This will include an annual report for audit. Statistics on trends of giving in the school are particularly important.

In all considerations of the treasurer's work, the function of educator deserves underscoring.

Educating for Giving

A financial officer's efficiency is not measured alone by the accuracy of his bookkeeping, but more fundamentally by his outlook and practice as an educator. That does not necessarily call for frequent speeches on finances. It means that he understands and helps others to understand that the church school is a place where people are to learn giving by giving. Furthermore, they will give and thus learn to give as they increasingly apprehend Christian teaching and share in the service the church is rendering.

Stewardship education, it will be seen, is not something to be tacked on as another fragment in the time schedule of the school. It is inherent in the whole school's organization and administration as well as its more formal curriculum. It is properly a component of the various units of activity tied in with all instruction, worship, fellowship, and service.

Such an approach is essential to the adequate financing of Christian education, indeed, of all the church. Besides, a Christian approach to the economic order and practice in it will scarcely be fostered elsewhere unless there are experiences of its operations in the church, including the church school.

CHAPTER XV

GATHERING AND USING DATA:
EVALUATING

One of a church school executive's less obtrusive duties, but a highly important one, usually accomplished with the aid of secretaries and treasurers, is to secure and utilize instructive data on significant matters. It includes activities that range from the simple keeping of minutes to participating in an extended piece of research. The immediate purpose in many of these activities is evaluation. Yet their ultimate value is in the improvement of the school. Data-gathering is expected to result directly in better learning and teaching or indirectly to that end through better organization, administration, and supervision. Whatever is undertaken in the area this chapter treats has not been completed until there is action in accord with the facts discovered.

EVALUATION

The core of the procedure with data is evaluating. We aim to see how well or poorly we are doing. *Carefully defined for us, evaluation is a process of gathering evidence systematically and analyzing it objectively for valid judgments about a church school.* We shall later locate the possible areas for evaluation in structure, process, and product.

Costly work of the type is regularly a phase of the public school enterprise. Educators want to eliminate as far as possible any ignorance or guess work about their outcomes. Norms are established so that workers can know what is to be expected; instruments and techniques of measurement are developed to indicate the extent and definiteness of achievement.

Evaluation belongs even more surely in Christian education where we have so much to do within such limited circumstances of time, personnel, and other factors. Yet very little, proportionately, had been done until recent times.

Needs for Evaluative Procedures

Christian educators have broad objectives in general toward which we wish our people to be moving in the curriculum. We have particular objectives for the several components of the church school. There are still more specific objectives to be reached through separate units and the various group sessions. We need to know whether people are reaching these as rapidly and permanently as possible.

Individuals are expected to have a mastery of certain facts of the Bible, for a simple instance. We can test knowledge. Yet our concern should go far beyond this. How well do our pupils comprehend what they have by way of facts? It is possible to know by comprehension tests. But we want our pupils to develop certain attitudes; these are among our objectives, too. While it is not as easy to measure attitude as it is to measure knowledge or comprehension, it can be done to a degree. Action patterns are the most important objectives of all and we can also measure these.

In summation we are concerned about total personality growth. While the teacher can be alert to usual evidences, and this is important, it is possible, we see, to proceed in more valid ways. Only when a church school executive has guided his staff—pupils too—in evaluating by those means can he act intelligently to preserve and intensify what is worthy and make alterations where weakness is discovered.

Possibilities and Methodology for Evaluation

Many types of evaluation are possible in those three areas of church school work: structure; process; product. Regarding structure we can deal with physical facilities, personnel—its organization and its management—also with the community situation. As for process, the curriculum and what pupils and leaders are doing in it can be examined. Product evaluation concerns pupils and their change as to understandings, attitudes, and action patterns.

There is a basic design for any sound evaluative study:

1. State the objective clearly. If it is essentially a problem-solving process, precisely what is the problem to be solved?
2. Determine the basic instrument; choose the particular devices.
3. Gather unbiased data at relevant points, the data that will answer the questions being asked.
4. Analyze the data for relevant findings in the light of accepted criteria for the use of such material.
5. Interpret the findings and formulate conclusions that relate to the purpose of the study.
6. Plan for change, undertake it, and complete it.

The devices to be used are numerous; just a few can be listed to suggest what is in mind: interview; direct observation; pilot enterprise; questionnaire; sociological analysis; tests.

We shall soon consider four different ways to study our structures, processes, and products evaluatively: researching, surveying, record-keeping, and measuring. However, our topic is the using of data as well as gathering it; fact-finding itself is not enough. So we must go on to deal with the interpretation of our data in terms of the findings of our techniques. Something must also be said about the proper way of reporting the results of our evaluation process. Throughout, we are concerned with, and shall finally conclude with, the all-important subject of action for improvement.

SECURING DATA

Among the four means for gathering data no solid lines of differentiation can be drawn; in a way all are researching. Yet each deserves special consideration. Research usually is a more extensive and scientific enterprise; survey is often less formal. Typical records are largely informal statistical data, evaluative when carefully interpreted. Measurement is largely in terms of "tests" and "measures," the familiar devices of the classroom. The first three—researching, surveying, and record-keeping— are somewhat more closely related to administrative affairs; measuring applies more directly to learning and teaching.

Researching

The current reconstruction of Christian educational theory and practice has resulted to no small degree from scientific fact-finding. In its related fields of general education, psychology, and sociology, for example, work has been done on individual differences, the nature and growth of personality, the learning process, and group process. In sociology we have learned to make analyses of sociological conditions. We are indebted to the industrial and military worlds for studies of leadership.

Christian education itself has begun to do similar work. Now the National Council of Churches has its department of research and so do several denominations. Universities have fostered researches in our field and foundations have provided funds for it. Even local church school leaders undertake elementary enterprises in research, if one may stretch the term so far, in order to solve problems in their schools.

Research starts with a problem, which it defines clearly. Sometimes the hypothesis or possible answer is established. Then the data concerning the problem or its various parts are sought. This may involve experimentation, trying things out one way and then another until the most satisfactory technique is found. Out of the data, and the findings built upon them, a solution to the problem emerges. After it has been verified it takes its place in the accepted body of theory or among the established methods of procedure.

Most of the recent research had been undertaken for curriculum designing and writing. A denomination may have studied its schools and their leadership before any writing was done. For example, one denomination discovered that its median school is in a congregation of approximately four hundred baptized members; less than half are members of the Sunday church school and the average school has a staff of about twenty workers. The median time spent by teachers in lesson preparation was from two to two and a half hours. Such knowledge provided fundamental guidelines for curriculum design.

Some denominations also selected a broad variety of school situations in which to try experimental issues of prospective publications; then final materials were written in the light of the evaluative reports. Churches are continuing this curriculum evaluation research for revising literature. The local church school participants have meantime discovered data as they worked and learned techniques for researching that more schools could helpfully undertake.

Surveying

Surveys are undertaken to locate prospective workers for the school, discover the preferred site for a new building, get the facts on population trends, show needs for new equipment or program. A typical form in which many churches engage is the census of a community in order to discover prospects for membership.

One of the most useful forms of survey is a congregational self-study. In one case a mimeographed announcement defined the enterprise: "The congregational self-survey is a means of taking inventory of the congregation's resources, studying its current program, discovering its strong and weak points, laying a factual basis for a long-term comprehensive program of improvement."

Since the building of a comprehensive, long-term program was in view, this survey was shaped toward such specific results as these:

1. List of types of persons to whom the congregation ministers and an outline of the main features in that ministry.
2. Statement of general aims for the total program and specific aims for the organizations and activities.
3. A program of evangelism with a challenging standard of membership and a definite plan for maintaining it.

4. A comprehensive educational program for children, youth, and adults.
5. A plan for unified and effective administration.
6. A plan and policy defining community and extra-parish relations for maintaining and enlarging church plant and equipment, for adequate financing.
7. A program of leadership development to undergird the operation.

Two years later the pastor summarized the "tangible results": ". . . (1) adoption of a long-range, comprehensive program for the congregation; (2) unification of objectives and activities of various age groups; and (3) practical education of current group of workers on the church and its present-day program."

There are unique advantages in these self-studies made by local leaders without professional services or with only minimal guidance. Possible resistance to the study and its results may be disarmed; studies by others may seem to threaten the security of members or encroach upon their authority. On the other hand, if the personnel can participate in an analysis—even personal self-analysis—for solution of problems in which they are interested, the reaction is more likely to be positive, the attitude more constructive and ultimate improvement more certain. Most important, self-surveying is educational in itself.

Record-keeping

Though records can easily become dead data, they can be living aids in the hands of intelligent users. A pastor recognized this when he wrote his recipe for a better school: "Install throughout the whole school the finest and most thorough record system you can find." As a general purpose records can preserve information about the pupils and the school that will provide measures of success or failure and disclose faults or virtues. Specifically, they can be used to stimulate attendance or giving, guide in organizing the staff and planning the curriculum, be a key to budgetary matters. They are essential in planning the promotion of pupils and can contribute to more effective teaching.

The records to be kept will depend, in part, on the size of the school and its means in money and staff, more practically, on the use to be made of them. Possibilities are listed below, no school will use them all; several can be combined on one card or in one book.

Attendance records measure the school's success to a considerable degree. They often include data on punctuality, offering, and church attendance. Absentee lists can be compiled from them for use by persons with absentee responsibilities; these may include space for a follow-up report.

Achievement records indicate the progress of pupils and furnish information for promotion. They may mention participation in class activities, attitudes, enterprises completed, conduct, even grades.

Business records can indicate the financial achievements, status, and needs of the school. They will include books and reports of treasurers, checkbooks, and files of canceled checks, order books, cash and budget accounts. There will also be minute books and files of correspondence.

Class records, a small book being the most familiar type, will include names, addresses, birthdays, and similar data on each pupil. They may take the place of other attendance or absentee records. They should also tell the story of the class' work.

Curriculum records preserve an account of the program for future reference as to pupil sequences for subsequent programs. They may list the units undertaken with copies of procedures and evaluations.

Enrollment records can indicate name, address, telephone number, birthday, parents' names and church affiliations, school grade or occupation, other church schools attended, service interests, and experience. They guide workers in the placement of pupils and may furnish lists of family prospects. Withdrawal and removal entries may disclose some of the school's more obvious failures.

Leader records are needed for the executive's guidance especially in a larger church. They will provide personal data on general and religious education and leadership experience.

Permanent records can combine several other types. Started when the pupil establishes his membership, they will follow him through the school with significant data on promotions, curricular program, and special services rendered the school.

Personality records can guide in the planning of pupil programs. They may report tests or rating charts and show experiences in vocational and recreational interests. They are sometimes kept as case histories.

Prospect records may be secured from a community census or gathered by the pastor, other workers, or pupils.

Records for parents may mention attendance, attitude, achievement, and punctuality. Research shows that, intelligently used, especially in elementary and junior high age groups, they may improve attendance, study, conduct, church relations, and parental interest.

Whatever records are kept, they should be in a form that makes them easily intelligible, economical of time, permanent, and up to date. They should be placed where the information will be readily accessible to those who will use them most frequently.

Measuring

This fourth type of data-gathering pertains more fully than others to problems of teaching. Teachers—perhaps also students—who have clear-cut objectives will wish to know how closely they are being attained. A teacher has undertaken a class; how is he succeeding with the persons involved? As for the pupil, are his substantial concerns being met? An executive, too, has developed an organization; how well is it meeting the needs of pupils and teachers? He is fostering a program; is it effective toward its pupil objectives? Basically for all, are persons moving forward at a maximum rate into increasingly higher experiences of abundant life; are they in actuality, for example, "using the Bible fruitfully"? Further, those questions are asked not as mere inquiries for facts. They are related to the deeper issues. What shall be done now, next, and better?

Where is the pupil now? Repeatedly it has been said that Christian education focuses its attention on persons, finding them where they are and working forward with them for their Christian growth. Not so long ago one primary question was asked in this regard: What does the pupil know already? Now we are interested in the pupil's total situation and his whole round of behavior. What are his home, school, work, play, health, and community conditions? What are his thoughts, attitudes, opinions, feelings, conflicts, and tensions as well as his information? Most important, in what kind of conduct does he typically engage? Tests, scales, and other measures have been devised to reveal those facts.

Where can the pupil go? What is possible for this pupil? Some things are impossible, therefore unwise to attempt; pupils have been discouraged because too much was expected of them. Others' potentialities have been wasted because they were viewed on too low a level of expectation. Some knowledge of capacity is important. Church schools which follow public school grading have indirectly made an adjustment to pupil intelligence but other factors are at least as important in religious development. Many of those, such as social attitudes, personal opinions, feelings, and interests can be measured by standardized tests. Thus, pupil capacity in the light of a whole complex of other factors that deserve attention for diagnosis can be revealed by proper measuring. To be sure, no one thinks that Christian capacity can be measured quite like an IQ. Yet obvious limitations do not invalidate the basic worth of the measurement technique and instruments.

Where should the pupil go? Christian education begins with the pupil's needs and proceeds on the basis of his interests. Perhaps the pupil is lamentably uninformed or misinformed, has bad attitudes, is guilty of regular misconduct. Perhaps on the other hand he has already started on a promising development in Christian leadership. He may be in need of simple readjustment or require relief from serious conflict; he may be in a state of high readiness to yield his life to the challenges of Christian commitment. Instruments are available to disclose such facts and point the way toward well-chosen goals.

How can we help the pupil arrive best? This is the ultimate question. Appraisal through measuring is not for itself alone. In medical practice, the nurse does not take the temperature merely out of curiosity; the purpose is diagnosis for better treatment. Similarly educational measurement is for guidance. What is to be done about the school itself: organization; administrative procedures; equipment and its use of it; staff; finances? What is to be done about the program: where should it begin; what pupil activities shall be included and what teaching procedures shall be employed; what unit is to be undertaken next and when? Measurement will provide answers.

MEASURING THE SCHOOL AND ITS PROGRAM

There are two particular ways to answer with some exactness those questions posed above and others under discussion. The more fundamental way is to measure the conditions in the lives of the pupils as individuals and groups. That will be discussed next. The other way is to measure the school itself. Experience indicates that, everything else being equal, schools of a certain type will yield more adequate results than others. If the leader can make sure that his school approximates one considered "good," he is probably achieving his objectives reasonably.

Standards

Instruments called standards have been developed for the purpose of measuring church schools. *A standard is a printed statement of the qualities of an "ideal school" with provision for measuring the various features of an actual school in relation to the ideal.* While the function of a standard suggested by that definition is to disclose how closely a given school approximates the ideal, its most important service is to reveal what strengths and weaknesses a school possesses.

Standards have been available in several types. Some have been provided by denominational boards of Christian education. One denomination called its instrument a "Guide for Achievement." The International Council of Religious Education formerly published *The International Standard for the Sunday Church School* and current standards follow this pattern in a general way. It covered major items such as curriculum, leadership, organization and administration, housing and equipment. Nineteen subtopics included worship, training of workers, budget, the pupils and rooms. The instrument consisted of two pamphlets. One listed in question form the items to be considered; as an example under worship, "Do pupils have opportunity to assist in preparing and conducting the program?" The second pamphlet was a scoring chart in which, opposite the item just mentioned, there was space to score the school from 0 to 8. Additional values were assigned other items to a total of 500 units.

One denomination now provides a twenty-page *Survey Guide for Parish Education*. After a congregation has completed this self-study a regional worker will collaborate in planning next steps. There is also a hundred page *How to Evaluate Your Christian Education Program,* a carefully devised and field-tested guide for thorough study of a church school.[1]

The use of any such instrument can be described by the procedure in one school. Its board of religious education had reason to feel that the Sunday church school needed overhauling. There were differences of opinion about the precise improvements needed, so one member suggested that they apply the international standard. The school's total score was 315 points of the possible 500. That was an interesting finding but not the prime one. Certain points of weakness and of strength had been revealed:

> Only 36 percent of those attending are present at the beginning of the hour.
> The supply of Bibles is low.
> Need for an increase in trained prepared leadership is evident.
> The pupils are promoted annually.
> The average attendance . . . throughout the year is only 47 percent.
> The school has a regular workers' conference.

While the total score gave no occasion for discouragement, the negative findings challenged the workers to undertake improvements. That is a typical result of employing a standard; it stimulates people to action and at the same time shows people what to do. This school organized a junior department, procured new hymnals for older groups, studied worship techniques, and made an organized effort to increase attendance and punctuality.

Other Means

Additional means of measuring selected aspects of a school are available. There are *rating scales* on which a worker's effectiveness can be estimated by the superintendent or by other workers. Some are printed forms on which workers can check for themselves their personal qualities and attitudes, method of preparation, and management of pupils. *Supervisory schedules* list questions with which a supervisor can go into a session he is visiting. He secures answers to those questions while in the session and discusses them with the leader afterward. While the schedules are meant for use by an actual supervisor, they can be used also by groups or individuals for "self-supervision." Questions like these could appear on a schedule for supervising a worship service:

[1] D. Campbell Wyckoff, *How to Evaluate Your Christian Education Program* (Philadelphia: The Westminster Press, 1962).

Were the physical conditions arranged as suitably as possible?
Had all possible preparation been made?
Did the leader exemplify the necessary principles of appropriate leadership in worship?
Was the program fully adapted to the pupils and the occasion?
Did the pupils participate heartily?
Were the intended outcomes achieved with satisfaction?

Closely related, *observation guides* are similar schedules with which an executive or a visiting consultant can look into the organizational and administrative affairs and curricular practices.

MEASURING THE PUPILS

The most direct way to discover a school's effectiveness with a view to its improvement is to measure the progress of the pupils. Ideally, a program of such measuring would begin by getting data on the standing of the pupils at a starting point. Then, after a period of work, the pupil attainment would be measured again. There may also be a "control group" that proceeds in a different way so that the progress of two groups can be contrasted. Meantime, there could be diagnostic measuring to guide the procedure.

Because of the work and expense involved, very few schools have carried through a testing program like that but a considerable number have worked at it a bit. The least a leader can do is to observe carefully whether his pupils as individuals and as groups give evidence of growing in the direction of the chosen objectives. Yet many leaders can now go beyond that minimum by using various types of testing with, for example, the forms often included in new curricular materials.

Tests and Testing

Tests may be used in the older essay or question-and-answer form to measure pupil outcomes at the end of a course of study, a unit, or a session. In most cases, these serve best a diagnostic purpose, revealing the status of pupils for the informal guidance of teachers and pupils in further procedure.

"New type" or "objective" tests offer several advantages. They are accepted by most pupils as more interesting, being somewhat like a game. The answers are either right or wrong so that teacher opinion is eliminated. They can cover the ground more thoroughly and fairly, and so give a better picture of the pupil's learning. Usually they are easier to administer and, although harder to prepare, are easier to score. On the other hand, there are limitations in objective tests, as in all others. Chiefly, they often deal with fragments of knowledge only and we dare not depend upon this as a complete index to reality and depth of Christian growth.

Workers in general education, and the pupils and parents of modern public schools, have become familiar with "standardized tests" of capacity and achievement. Their use has spread to the field of Christian education. Means have been made available, from time to time, for us to measure many components singly or in batteries of tests:

Attitudes—such as fairmindedness or churchly interests.

Biblical comprehension—the pupil's understanding of biblical verses and passages.

Biblical knowledge—Old and New Testament history and literature, the life and teachings of Christ; the work of Paul.

Christian practices—for example, prayer.

Conduct—as expressed in honesty, trustworthiness, loyalty, or reverence.

Knowledge of the church—its history, work, and practices.

Moral knowledge, judgment, and discrimination—immediate ethical problems which confront people daily and others such as race relations or peace and war.

Personality—factors like sociability, confidence, dominance, self-control.

Psychological status—intelligence, reactions, emotional maturity, and others.

Religious ideas and beliefs—in the idea of God, work of Christ, personal immortality, or "other religions."

There has been some regression in production and use of these instruments in recent years. Yet, while admittedly it is impossible to measure accurately all of the factors which enter into complex religious experience, a fair sampling made by a judicious combination of the available items would furnish trustworthy guidance at apposite points.

Various devices are used in such tests: best answer, completion, matching question and answer, multiple choice, rating or ranking, scale of values, simple recall, true-false, and cross out series. They are widely employed now in curricular guides; also they can be utilized by persons who want to prepare their own tests. A few directions for those who construct tests follow: represent a fair sampling of the various elements of learning, not memory alone; do not include trivial items; use a range of questions to cover the abilities of the group—not too many difficult ones and not too many easy ones; guard against guessing; use no puzzle, trick, or catch questions; employ simple, clear language and direct sentence construction; provide for simplicity of use; make the instructions brief, clear, definite; insure rapidity and accuracy of scoring.

While the administration of standardized tests is relatively simple, special care must be exercised in the interpretation, the reporting, and especially the use of the results. Many of the tests can be interpreted by norms of measurement. For example, in using a biblical knowledge test, we may know the average score made by a thousand eighth grade pupils in widely distributed parts of the country. Thus it may be disclosed that the eighth grade boys of the school are below the norm and the girls above it. Consecrated wisdom is needed to report and use such a datum wisely, not detrimentally.

There are other reasons for caution. All standardized tests have been checked for *validity,* the adequacy of a test to measure what it claims to measure, and *reliability,* the degree to which a test can be depended upon for consistent scores. Yet tests are not magical; they measure only what they measure and that with no perfect accuracy. They are to be taken as indicators of general status and not as perfect pictures of any individual. Within the field of personality, especially its religious aspects where there is abounding complexity and subjectivity, we must not expect to get exact and complete data on it by any paper-and-pencil procedures. For any far-reaching conclusions breadth of testing at a variety of points is essential.

Other Means

Church school leaders can employ other techniques for measuring pupils; many come out of child study, social case and group work, or public school procedure.

There can be *case studies* of individual pupils with a careful descriptive analysis after the manner of a child-guidance clinic. The *records and reports* of the school have bearing here. Beneath their surfaces, a discerning leader will find many facts concerning pupil capacities, needs, relationships, interests, attitude, and conduct. Some schools have files of *observation records* prepared by visitors in the home or by teachers and other leaders. These can report, as examples: how the pupil gets along with parents and how his brothers and sisters treat him; how he spends free time; how he fits into "the pack"; what are the religious practices in the home. Teachers' *weekly reports* on the class sessions are furnished a supervisor in some schools.

There are many numerous forms of *questionnaire* study. A simple form by which a teacher can learn a great deal about a class quickly requires only paper and pencils for the pupils. They are asked to write answers to these questions: What three things (1) do you fear most; (2) do you hate most; (3) do you want most to have; (4) would you like best to do with a holiday; (5) do you want most to do as a life work? Another instrument of this type is the *interest finder*—a checklist of items on which young people, for example, can indicate the things they wish most to consider in a group study.

MEASURING AS LEARNING AND TEACHING TECHNIQUE

Measuring can be an integral part of the learning-teaching process itself. Indeed, until it has reached this level its major utility has not been realized.

Learning Technique

Through measuring, the pupil can be helped with the management of his learning activity. He, too, can discover where he should and can go and what help he needs to arrive at his objectives. Further, pupils learn in the process of being measured. A group discusses the examination they have just taken; searches for the answers to the questions they missed; is eager to see where they stand. They learn things concerning themselves and place themselves more properly in relation to others. They not only gather facts, they meet new ideas, develop attitudes, form purposes, start activities.

Teaching Technique

Teachers recognize the value of measurement as a learning technique when they follow up tests with discussion and other forms of study on the test results. We have already considered its worth to diagnose a class situation and discover next steps. To determine the new experience for which a class is ready and arouse interest in entering it, there is scarcely a superior way. A teacher may be thinking about launching a unit on the life and teachings of Jesus. What do the pupils know already? That is the place to start the unit. In general, what religious concepts and attitudes concerning God, man, sin, immortality, and the like do learners already have? It is difficult for a group to proceed unless those facts are known. Most important of all, how is the pupil acting already in Christian conduct, and why? Diagnosis with a view to discovery of readiness is essential; testing is needful.

Measuring relates to teaching technique at another important point. Live teachers are restless to be doing things better. They may want to try something new in subject or procedure. Measurement makes experiment with teaching procedure possible because it reveals the facts about objectives and their attainment. What is the relative effectiveness of one teaching method over another? Two groups of pupils with relatively similar capacity and advancement are selected. Each is tested at the beginning of the experiment. Then two different methods are used. Each group is tested at the end of the educational experience. Which method proved more effective? Similar experiments can be conducted with two types of materials. Teachers who are creative in their work have these valid means of arriving at conclusions about it and improving it.

UTILIZING DATA

The ultimate value of any data-gathering procedure, with the essential element of evaluation, is consummated in constructive utilization. Three steps will be necessary: interpreting, reporting, and acting.

Interpreting

What do the data mean? Interpretation turns raw facts into findings that lift up the significance of what we have discovered. We compare the actual picture with our standards and objectives. We reach judgments toward the solution of our problem. We have had it in mind that a plan of action will be based on the findings. What type of action do they suggest?

In the more careful and extended researches, interpretation may require us to deal somewhat scientifically with statistics. Attention will be given to central tendencies, comparisons, or contrasts and what they signify. In surveys, the discovery of strengths and weaknesses may be of primary importance. A community leadership census provides names, addresses, and related items to consider in their relevance for enlistment. The records we keep yield findings according to their particular type. In the case of measurement enterprises we find meanings most often about pupils and their learning.

We have engaged in a study of one type or another for one or more of a variety of purposes. Now the data point the finger to the solution of basic problems related to such questions as these:

As to structure:

1. How effective is our organizational structure?
2. What is the real quality of our staff and how can we improve it?
3. What is the truth about our equipment?
4. Is our church spending enough in money, energy, time, and talent for its educational work?

As to product:

1. What kind of program do we actually have?
2. What are we really achieving in terms of Christian pupil growth?
3. How can we accomplish better results in abundant Christian living?
4. Are we ministering to our actual community situation?

As to process:

1. What is the capacity and ability of our pupils?
2. What are pupils' needs and are we meeting them?
3. What are the individual differences with which we are dealing?
4. Am I, teacher or other leader, doing things in the best possible way?

Reporting

At some point in the data-gathering-and-utilizing process, the data and findings will be reported. The proper purpose of reports is to call attention to important facts so as to secure effective action on matters that need attention. For example, the simplest sort of reporting, reading the minutes of a previous meeting, is to refresh the minds of the group and start them in their new work on that foundation.

The manner of reports as well as function could profitably be studied more widely. Results will be determined in part by their nature. Many would be put in different form if the educational purpose were clearly in view. For example, that typical Sunday church school report of attendance, offerings, and the like, can be a dreary recital of numbers. Actually, however, these figures disclose vital facts: the school's retention or loss of pupils; the abilities of teachers to win, teach, and hold pupils; the effects of rooms and equipment; departmental efficiency or the opposite; curriculum adaptation; even character development and religious growth. Proper reports tell what the figures reveal. They will include not only data but also findings with a certain amount of interpretation. The particular content will be in accord with response desired from the persons to whom it is addressed.

The story should be told in more ways than one: by printed as well as oral announcement on bulletin board or poster; in graph or chart; by letter or bulletin. Always it should be intelligible, brief, clear, and concise, and it should include enough description to suggest the responses desired. Certain reports should get beyond the school itself and parents, congregation, and community. Some should go into the local papers, church bulletins, to the church council, and congregational meetings.

A critical point in reporting is to recognize people's possible resistance to findings of research or other study. They may even oppose scientific method as a way of discovering truth in the areas of religion. Perhaps they are themselves under evaluation and may fear adverse data that will embarrass them, but studies can be made to appear as opportunities instead of threats. A report will aim to interest the people in discovering new insights for doing a better job. As an important precaution, the emphasis should not be on the negative material but rather on the positive and constructive.

Acting

Ultimately there must be a plan of action in accord with what the data suggest. The findings have perhaps made it pointed; possibly a report will have outlined it. How, now, shall it be effected? The question should have been in view from the very first. This requires that knowledgeable, competent, and practical people have been in charge. For a considerable local church educational study, the entire congregation may have undertaken it through its church council that placed the matter in the hands of the committee on Christian education. Now it will enlist all interested persons as far as possible in planning the action and working it out.

If they have examined *structure* they will reconstruct where possible, perhaps step by step. If they have examined *process* they will take necessary steps to correct weakness while conserving strength. If they have examined *product* they will adopt any reasonable new measures to achieve people's obectives more fully.

The plan of action must be realistic; indeed, the whole enterprise must have kept its feet on the ground. An undertaking needs to be manageable in terms of time, money, and personnel and be practical in its processes. Then it must be managed carefully.

An early chapter (IV) has dealt with "taking hold to improve." Its seven steps will be applicable. Step 7, "completing the enterprise" will particularly pertain. The following quotation, from *The Dynamics of Group Change*,[2] has in view a summation of the process. The authors deal with seven phases of it. (For our purpose "client system" means congregation, church school, or class; "change agent" means pastor, other executive, or teacher.)

> Phase 1: The client system discovers the need for help, sometimes with stimulation by the change agent.
> Phase 2: The helping relationship is established and defined.
> Phase 3: The change problem is identified and clarified.
> Phase 4: Alternative possibilities for change are examined; change goals or intentions are established.
> Phase 5: Change efforts in the "reality situation" are attempted.
> Phase 6: Change is generalized and stabilized.
> Phase 7: The helping relationship ends or a different type of continuing relationship is defined.

[2]Lippitt, Watson and Westley, *The Dynamics of Group Change* (Harcourt, Brace and Company, 1958), p. 123.

CHAPTER XVI

MAINTAINING WIDER RELATIONSHIPS

Ours becomes increasingly an era in which isolation, even in church school work, is impossible, even if it were desirable. Our people need a six-continent attitude and practice. Indeed, the history of the Sunday school for a century and a half has been already a notable instance of co-operative endeavor—church-wide and world-wide.

WITH THE CONGREGATION

Happy relationships between a church school and its mother congregation do not exist everywhere. One pastor wrote a searching article in which he listed complaints that have been lodged against the Sunday church school. He quoted the charge that it is figuratively a wild branch drawing sap from the production of proper congregational fruit. He reported a belief that there is a widening gap between school and church, with people attending and serving the former and not the latter. He showed how some are thinking that a division of loyalty hinders spiritual awareness, religious realization, worshipful emotion, doctrinal conviction, moral purpose, and Christian action.

That coin has another side. Sunday church school leaders sometimes deplore the church's lack of support for the school. For instance, some churches have depended upon the school financially while it goes without needed equipment and supplies to make its program effective. Even the ugly word "jealously" has been used to describe the attitude of certain church leaders toward the growth of the school and the enthusiasm it engenders. "If," asks the Sunday church school proponent with a thinly veiled meaning, "the people come to the school and not to church, are we to blame?"

Proceeding so that the total church school is the entire congregation educating itself in one organizational form has been stated more than once as the proper relationship. Using a somewhat inappropriate but useful figure of speech, the church school is not to be either a sideshow of the circus or the whole show but one of the rings under the big tent. Chapter V showed how to accomplish that purpose structurally.

Congregation and school being not separate and distinct but basically identical as to their purpose, they ought to proceed in accord. An ideal for the entire complex of congregational life can be stated: united as to ends and co-operative as to function, with a minimum of separateness and maximum of reciprocity. A pastor testifies for this ideal: "The whole work of the church including services, school, prayer meeting, young people's groups, finances . . . should be brought under one program and administration to avoid overlapping, waste and division."

General Relations With the Congregation

The congregation can do many things for the church school in maintaining a reciprocal relationship. While, in general, it should provide for a unified educational organization and program, fully identified with the congregational organization and program, an early writer on the subject enumerated several prerequisites as pertinent today as they were a generation ago.[1] He said first the congregation must understand that its purpose is not to be ministered to but to be a servant of all. Next, said the writer, the congregation must view itself as a group of children as well as adults, whereas most people envisage the adult portion only. Another prerequisite is to think of the church as something more than a pulpit-centered institution; while preaching is always to be exalted, that is but one means through which the purpose of the church is achieved. A final suggestion is that the church should understand its educational task, a demand that requires both ministry and laity to be educated with respect to this phase of their total work.

CHURCH FOR SCHOOL

Given a congregation with the prerequisites suggested, what shall it do for its church school?

1. Organize itself to maintain a comprehensive educational program.
2. Hold itself responsible for the support and effective operation of the school.
3. Provide for adequate financing and equipping.
4. Furnish a strong leadership.
5. Provide for all the people, including the children, to share in all the church's work all the time. This calls for total adult membership in the educational program.

[1]Henry F. Cope, *Organizing the Church School* (New York: George H. Doran Company, 1923).

6. Exalt the educational work for what it truly is, a major enterprise of the church, the whole church.

SCHOOL FOR CHURCH

What can the church school do with its responsibility toward the church?

1. Educate the members of the congregation, not only for "initiation" into the fellowship but also for mission in and through it. A complete curriculum will include units on the church's history, work, doctrines, and programs.
2. Work at the development of competent leadership for all church work.
3. Help the congregation recruit members, especially among the pupils themselves or parents and other adult relatives.
4. Encourage attendance at congregational services of worship. There are laments, we have seen, that this objective has not been attained. The basic solution for the problem scarcely lies in the elimination of the church school and not wholly in various devices to exhort or draft its members into church attendance. We may need a certain merging of the school program with the worship services of the church.
5. Help the church with its financing. The ideal is a unitary budget for the entire congregation with all persons contributing to all expenses (see Chap. XIV). Certainly, also, through lessons on stewardship, financial as well as other, the school should build the giving spirit and habits of the congregation.

Relations with Other Educational Agencies

A church school agency, as so often observed, may best be structured as the unified and sole educational agency in a congregation though, we have often had to say, a typical congregation may have a half dozen agencies. Thus, while the church school leader will rejoice at every manifestation of interest in education and foster an ever-expanding program of educational opportunity for the constituency, he will not favor the multiplication of educational agencies. If a new agency is proposed, he will ask certain questions: Do we need a new organization for that? Can we not serve that objective within our present framework? He will be ready, too, for mergers of other agencies outside of the Sunday church school, or absorption within it of any agencies whose work that school can do as well or better by some modification of the program.

Relations with Other Congregational Works

We have noticed already that education interweaves with all the other five works of the church and the curriculum includes attention to all. It is concerned especially with education itself, but also evangelism, fellowship, social ministry, stewardship, and worship.

The church school's relationship with the congregation brings it into reciprocation especially in the field of evangelism. As the new movement for religious education developed in early years evangelism and education were unfortunately placed in opposition because certain leaders of the new movement conceived evangelism largely in terms of revivalism and this was not acceptable.

Happily, the trend now is to recognize the validity of evangelistic education as well as educational evangelism. For many people, therefore, evangelism is given a more narrow meaning that can be called evangelization. It refers to the efforts which the church and its workers make to secure personal confession of Jesus Christ as God and Savior and commitment to discipleships and apostlehood with him. It is more or less identical with winning church members. Viewing evangelism in that more narrow way, the educational movement will aim to help bring its personnel into the beginnings of church membership and promote their active continuance in it. Similarly the evangelistic forces will recognize the importance of nurture for "the evangelized."

WITH THE HOME

Sociological studies show regularly that the home is likely the most important agent of all in character development. If the church school's work is to be effective, it must be conducted in lively co-operation with the home; there must also be a home program for Christian nurture within the family circle and toward Christian family living.

A "Home-centered" Viewpoint

Does the church or the home have the primary responsibility for seeing that the children are religiously educated? Perhaps the home should be made the primary agency of Christian education while the church school serves only a complementary and supplementary function.

If we were to take that home-centered view of Christian education, we would turn our congregational effort less exclusively to the development of a church school program. Instead, our churches would first foster the program of Christian education in the home by providing literature, home visitation, parent conferences, and the like. Then we would use the church school agencies in a supplementary capacity to provide larger social experiences of Christianity, also in a complementary manner to reinforce the teaching of the home. They would simply enrich and underscore the all-week-long Christian development which is taking place in the family circle of younger and older fellow learners in Christ.

Interrelated Effort: Home and School

Lacking any such approach, what can the home do for the school and the school do for the home as partners in a common task?

1. Let the home bring, not send, the pupil regularly, on time, with the right attitude and properly prepared. For that preparation the home will have to provide time, place, equipment, and example. General preparation will involve conversation and reading about the church, its work, and all it stands for. Specific preparation will vary with the curricular program. One author suggests three curricular manuals: for teacher, for pupil, and for parents.

2. Let the home strive to understand the school's needs, procedures, and purposes—thoroughly enough to co-operate as intelligently as with public schools.

3. Let the parents visit the school, get acquainted with the workers and work, consult the leaders about the progress of their children.

4. Let the home plan to carry forward with the work of the school. Daily prayer and Bible reading with regular habits of helping and giving, for example, can be cultivated only with this assistance. The whole scope of Christian character and conduct, indeed, must be fostered at home.

5. Let the home express itself in the councils of the school to a degree that will keep the workers informed of its needs, problems, and desires.

6. Let the school's leaders recognize in its curriculum the paramount importance of the home. Units on it, discussions about conduct there, literature for it, and planning for family worship are suggestions.

7. Let the leaders visit the home to get acquainted with pupils, build a co-operative attitude, know the home conditions, and relate the program to it.

8. Let leaders report to the home regularly concerning attendance and the like, also concerning the progress of the pupils.

9. Let leaders inform the home concerning their objectives and plans in parent conferences and letters. Special programs on special days, promotion services, and exhibits are profitable opportunities. A parent-leader meeting at the beginning of each unit is recommended by one denomination.

10. Let the school provide for parents to study, in and through the school, the home religious education of their children. Letters and literature, classes, conferences, forums, reading circles, parent-child relationship and guidance meetings or courses are indicated. A denominational program is described in Chapter XVIII.

Many of these ten desirables may be accomplished through a lively parent-teachers' association with programs in which to share experiences and extend mutual help.

WITH THE PUBLIC SCHOOL

No church school leader can afford to overlook the place of the public school in the life of a typical young American and the confidence with which his parents usually regard it. There are boundless latent resources in a lively relationship between the two schools if leaders are alert and willing on both sides; the counseling of high school youth is one example.

While we are committed in the United States of America to a separation of church and state with regard to the organization of the two types of schools, we could profit immensely by recognizing the mutuality of some basic purposes. Public schools, like church schools, are working toward more abundant living on the part of the pupils. The former emphasize abundant living in the more material realm, the latter in the more specifically spiritual. Naturally there are many points where the two can co-operate. It should never be forgotten that a high proportion of public school leaders are church people.

The task of religiously educating the great populace in America will never be accomplished completely of course, until one of two things has been done. One possibility is to work out a much more adequate system of church schools paralleling and co-operating with the public schools, extending from cradle to grave, and reaching all the people of the country for an adequate amount of time each week. Now, too, we are thinking of a possible dual enrollment. Still another possibility, very much in the limelight at present, is to teach religion once more, directly or indirectly, in public schools. These possibilities are discussed in Chapter XIX. Promising beginnings have been made and the recent Supreme Court decision has opened the way for a re-examination of the whole approach. In any case, however, we have only scratched the surface of a mere corner of the field. The final issue awaits great educational and ecclesiastical statesmen to lead movements.

Meantime, the church school leader can lead his pupils toward the practice of Christian principles in the public schools. He can aim to co-operate with the public school in certain extra-curricular activities. He can relate his program to the progress of the pupil in the public school, for example, in history. It is important, too, for church school workers to attend some of the public school programs and see the children or youth at work there.

It is particularly useful for a religious teacher to know the other teacher. As a negative instance, a long-time high school superintendent lamented that not one church worker had ever darkened his doorway. "We work with the same pupils," he said with an obvious appeal. Sometimes these two can solve a problem mutually.

If civilization is a race between education and catastrophe, and we are to win the race, a chief point of effort will be right relationships between the church school and the public school, both working at the new possibilities on the horizon.

WITH DENOMINATIONAL AGENCIES

Every church school leader can be helped by thorough acquaintance with his denomination's program and full employment of it. This will require such activities as these: knowing the nature and extent of its total educational enterprise, also knowing its administrative, secretarial, and editorial personnel and the services available through its national headquarters; using, in general, its lesson books and hymnals, reading its magazines, consulting its secretaries and sending workers to its camps, conventions, workshops, and the like; giving appropriate support to its regional and local programs of promotion and training. Help, indeed, can flow in two directions: from the denomination and toward it.

A typical denomination is concerned with both higher education and the work of a local congregation. In the former it directs and supports the programs of colleges, seminaries, and training schools. In the latter it fosters Sunday, weekday, and vacation church schools, youth and adult work, leadership education, research, and other features. It has an executive secretary, associate secretaries who work in distinctive areas, field workers, editors, and writers. It produces quantities of high quality literature of many kinds and other resources for use by pupils and leaders. It makes every effort to help improve their equipment and their programs. It not only fosters a fully rounded and comprehensive leadership education program but also publishes a monthly periodical for local church workers.

WITH INTERDENOMINATIONAL AND INTERFAITH AGENCIES

With nearly two centuries of co-operative work behind us, it is fitting that leaders in church schools co-operate increasingly with interdenominational and interfaith agencies of Christian education. As one value, this co-operation is contributing to the breakdown of exclusivism. When the history of the ecumenical development in this era has been written, co-operative work in Christian education will be adjudged a major factor in bringing about the measure of unified action ultimately attained. In many areas of educational activity there has long been neither race nor clan. Sunday and other church school workers and pupils have been studying, worshiping, fellowshiping, and serving, also training, without consciousness of denominational barriers. This is wholesome.

Second, every church school worker is profoundly indebted, week by week, to co-operative endeavor and can profit still further as he participates in it. Such items as uniform lessons, the gradation of pupils, and the leadership education curriculum are interdenominational fruitage.

The best things we have in principles and methods have been freely shared by those who, of whatever origin, initiated and developed them. The major leaders in every denomination have been educated in the same schools through the same books, and in fraternal study with persons of many denominations. Now they work together in co-operative publication of lesson helps, journals and books, promotion of weekday and vacation schools, even sharing of interdenominational editors, secretaries, and directors.

Third, church school workers can profit from, and help through, several promotional agencies described below. All these are devoted to the improvement of the results attained by their constituents. They seek to elevate standards, foster better management and teaching, provide better materials, disseminate information, assist with problems.

American Sunday School Union

The American Sunday School Union, too little known, is the oldest interdenominational educational agency in the United States. Dating from 1817, it continues to cherish its chartered purpose: "to organize and maintain Sunday schools and to publish and circulate moral and religious literature." In addition to an extensive publication program, the Union supports approximately 150 missionaries (see Chap. I). These workers establish and conduct the usual types of church school but also summer camps, conferences, retreats, and workshops. More informally, they lead Bible study groups, do youth guidance and counseling, hold significant training institutes. This work is done especially in areas removed from the beaten path of ecclesiastical endeavor. The various ministries are especially for the destitute in rural regions north and south. Recently, though, an urban thrust has been added, especially where downtown city churches have withdrawn to the suburbs. The extent of the Union's service is indicated by the fact that it works in thirty-nine states and has three thousand Sunday schools, with an emphasis on Sunday afternoon work. Where schools are established it is understood they shall eventually grow into congregations with a denominational affiliation; meantime, too, there is collaboration with adjacent churches.

Religious Education Association

A Religious Education Association, founded in 1903 fosters, more particularly, the theoretical studies on religious education and operates on an interfaith level. Its members are individual leaders of education, religion, religious education, and welfare. Although Protestants have constituted its majority, there have always been Jewish and Roman Catholic members. The Association has a stated aim: "To inspire the religious forces of our country with the educational ideals; to inspire the educational forces with the religious ideals; to keep before the public the ideal of religious education in the sense of its need and value."

The association publishes a journal, *Religious Education,* regarded as a most influential professional journal for interested, thoughtful, religious, and secular educators. National conventions are held from time to time and there are regional conferences. Local chapters are conducted in some cities. At present the Association is engaging in an extensive national study of religious beliefs, practices, values, and concerns of American youth between the years of sixteen and twenty-one.

World Council of Christian Education and Sunday School Association

A World Council of Christian Education was once the World's Sunday School Association, formed at a world convention in Rome, 1907, although its work dates back to a first convention in London, July, 1889. At its peak it federated the co-operative Sunday school work of some fifty nations from the Argentine through the alphabet to Uruguay. Recovery after the disruption of World War II was marked by a world convention in Toronto, 1950. Since that time it has held further conventions and four world institutes, the most recent at Nairobi in 1967. These institutes have included from two hundred to three hundred representatives from fifty or more nations, meeting for approximately two weeks.

The head office with the major program staff is located in Geneva, Switzerland; there are also London and New York offices. The council is composed of regional bodies on all the major continents and it works through these bodies. They may be national, ecumenical Protestant councils of Christian education or units of national, provincial, or state councils of churches. Some are Sunday school associations. Its personnel are representatives from such bodies, with members at large and consultants or representatives from related agencies. They are engaged in four principal program activities: service to the field; research, study, and experimentation; leadership education; and curriculum development.

One of the council's most significant services of recent years has been in curriculum development. Materials have been produced for eighty countries and will be used in nearly 150 languages.

It has provided significant face-to-face contacts of Christian educators around the world. It publishes a broadly based quarterly journal, *World Christian Education.* It is therefore one of the most significant agencies for world Christian community. Currently there are discussions with the World Council of Churches and the World Student Christian Federation so that in due time a wholistic approach to Christian education can be expected.

World Council of Churches

The World Council of Churches is the outstanding organizational expression of the ecumenical movement and a continuing organ to express further the church's unity in all realms of life. It held its constituting assembly in Amsterdam, 1948, and now embraces some two hundred member churches in sixty countries, representing major Protestant and Orthodox groups. An early bulletin mentions activities that include: relief action on behalf of needy churches upholding the Christian standard of conduct toward friend and foe, organizing interchurch aid, looking toward rehabilitation of church life, co-ordinating services for refugees and displaced persons, enlisting youth in the Christian world community, building a world fellowship in Christ and men of good will, giving Christendom a united voice and a center of united action.

At present there is no unit of the council concerned specifically with Christian education on the parish level, especially there is nothing for children. Its concerns are to some extent with youth-serving agencies and especially higher Christian education including student movements and specifically theological education. The missionary emphasis is strong; this adds an educational dimension.

National Council of Churches of Christ in the U.S.A.
(Division of Christian Education)

The Division of Christian Education in the National Council of Churches (1950) is one of the council's four program divisions; there are also divisions of Christian Life and Mission, Overseas Ministries, and Christian Unity. The co-operative work of the educational division goes back to the early years of the nineteenth century. In particular it carries forward the work of the International Council of Religious Education established in 1922. This continuity is represented in the division's journal entitled *International Journal of Religious Education.*

In the triennium 1960-63, the Division of Christian Education numbered in its membership nearly fifty denominational Boards of Christian Education, and approximately forty state councils of churches. The division's outreach is larger than the membership of the council itself.

At the time of writing there have been significant beginnings of reorganization. The division's work is to be carried forward in four departments: Educational Development; Higher Education; Education for Mission; Ministry, Vocation, and Pastoral Services. A major focus of concern is in the local congregation, the family, and the community. Yet the Department of Higher Education concerns itself with the programs of more than 450 Protestant church related colleges and universities, but also the church's ministry to state and independent universities. Special mention should be made of the Division's Standard Bible Committee, translators and custodians of the Revised Standard Version of the Bible.

The wide variety of work done by the Division can be indicated in a partial listing of the "associated sections," autonomous units of interested persons who participate in an annual meeting: Administration and Leadership; Adult Work, Childrens' Work, Youth Work; Directors of Christian Education; Family Life; Missionary Education; Professors and Research; Publishers; State Executives and Weekday Religious Education. Nearly 2,500 persons hold membership in these sections. It should be understood that significant work along similar lines is done also by the state and local councils who constitute a part of the membership of the national council.

Operating somewhat parallel to the National Council of Churches is a National Association of Evangelicals. This is a Protestant interdenominational movement founded in 1942 to promote interchurch fellowship and co-operation on an "evangelical," versus an inclusive, theological basis. Its membership includes thirty-eight denominations and many individual churches and agencies with a combined membership numbering more than two million persons. Its affiliated commissions are agencies serving some ten million American Protestants.

WITH OTHER COMMUNITY AGENCIES

There are useful community agencies not specifically church-related whose services can be helpful and which are legitimate outlets for service. The church school leader can co-operate with them advantageously at certain points.

In the Christian Associations or Scout movements the leader will discover men and women with ideals much like his own. They, too, are seeking to achieve a better Christian life for the people of the community. It is often possible to work out certain mutual problems and common objectives in helpful co-operation with them.

Once the churches did most of the needful social work. Now government is taking it over—service clubs, too. The church can co-operate with the work of social agencies and there is always more to be done. The welfare services of the community, including recreational agencies, are certainly related to the interests of church school leaders. The school can co-operate with proper relief organizations and institutions; the Red Cross deserves appropriate consideration. More recently child-guidance clinics and social casework developments have provided new areas for co-operation. The list might be extended to include governmental agencies like the federal departments of health, education, welfare, agriculture, labor, and others, as well as United Nations.

Local libraries and moving picture theaters are powerful forces for weal or woe in the community. Almost any librarian will co-operate in purchasing and featuring religious books and magazines. Radio and television stations are important community agencies. Closely related, the local newspapers deserve much more consideration than they receive. A later chapter will deal further with these and similar agencies.

The community provides the setting for a church school and it is to be used as a learning laboratory for the members of the school. Yet it is also a place of need for Christian action even beyond co-operative relationships with agencies. Just the way people treat each other can make of the church school a witness for or against Christ.

EDUCATION FOR WORLD CHURCHMANSHIP

It seems proper to say here that wider relationships can properly become quite specific curricular objectives. In our international and ecumenical era, education for world churchmanship is, of necessity, a major concern for every educational leader. It is a proper component for the work of every age group and must permeate all phases of church school work whether on Sunday or weekday, at home and when working or playing. Perhaps the weekday opportunities are major ones, in confirmation classes particularly. Yet in an examination of more than fifty membership preparation manuals, the material devoted specifically to membership in the world-wide church averaged only about one paragraph per book.[2] While this general objective can be found in other curricular units and deserves treatment in specific ones, the most extraordinary settings for desirable results are probably in real-life, out-of-class missionary and ecumenical enterprises.

"Missionary Education"

The two phases of this world churchmanship emphasis are (1) educa-

[2]Ralph D. Heim, "Preparing Members for the Whole Church," *International Journal of Religious Education,* XXXVIII (1961), No. 3, pp. 20-21, 46. Published by the National Council of Churches of Christ in the U.S.A. Used with permission.

tion for the world mission of the church and (2) education for ecumenicity. "Missionary education" like "missions" has a new look. This is
closely related to current understanding of the meaning of the church as
mission and of its people as ministers; under this view every Christian
is properly a missionary. We have already viewed this subject briefly
(Chap. XII) where we observed that the subject is now written into our
curricular literature. Nonetheless, the church school's leader will need
to be alert lest it be neglected; he can also provide for special occasions
or enterprises where the outreach will be fostered more directly. Visits
by missionaries and other travelers from abroad, reports by travelers, trips
to unusual American outposts, wider use of audio-visuals, reading of books
provided in the church library—all these are a few ideas in addition to
the very important participation in such an enterprise as a youth work
camp.

Education for Ecumenicity

Our pupils young and old should see themselves as part not only of
a denomination but of all Protestantism, indeed, of all Christianity including the Orthodox and Catholic churches along with the younger churches
of other continents. Leaders can also wisely guide people to learning that
all religions, though varied in their aspects, are a part of the living experience of all the world's people everywhere and always.

Education for ecumenicity takes place best by experiences in ecumenical
situations and endeavors. There is particular need to bring this sort of
thing down to the congregational and personal levels. Such experiences,
too, can be fostered in the weekday agencies by means similar to those
mentioned above under missionary education. Still better is participation
in interdenominational schools such as vacation or weekday church school
work and youth or adult community councils.

None of this needs to discount loyalty to a denomination or a faith.
Ecumenicity is one thing, denominationalism is another. Let unity be
recognized while diversity is preserved. Meantime, let mutual understanding and appreciation be cultivated.

CHAPTER XVII

PROMOTING THE SCHOOL

Promotion refers to advancing the interest of a person, cause, or institution—here the church school, its people and those who should be its people. This work is properly an activity of every church school member; it is one whose leadership resides very much with the executive.

WHY?

Why build up the church school in every way; especially, why increase the membership?

One reason is the well-being of people in general. Our broad goals are in people, not figures or lines on a graph, and people are to be viewed in terms of spiritual nurture. It is estimated that only about one American in four is a member of a church school at present. The American scene, community by community, needs the ministry of more church schools —many—with more members in the existing ones. There is a new urgency in social developments within a secularizing, urbanizing, and technological world. More specifically, a basic reason for promotion has to do with personal religion—need for the gospel in individual lives.

A closely related reason is a concern for the church's welfare. It wins more persons through its church school than in any other way. It could scarcely survive by adult recruiting alone; the church school reaches the young. The church school also produces the bulk of the churches' leaders; it develops the inner attitudes of responsibility and the skills on which sound church work depends. Without its school the church has no typical means for that significant and needful ministry of nurture. We do not want to herd people into the church without the understanding, conviction, and commitment which the church school can develop. We do want to keep our people within the churches on a rising level, not a static one. There is a temptation to promote the church school for its own sake or for the sake of bigness. Only when we realize those real purposes clearly and keep them constantly before us can we hope to be successful with the necessary mechanics of promotion.

PUBLIC RELATIONS IN GENERAL

Every zealous church school leader rightly wishes to see his school thriving. That involves the enrollment of new pupils, but more. While the leader does want his school to be increasing constantly in numbers, he wants it also to be winning a place of larger esteem within the congregation and community.

Building Morale

A first requisite for promoting the school in this general way is to develop finer morale. Schools with spirit will be winsome. Some have a pathetic lack of it; a worker in a recent conference declared with heartfelt conviction, "Our Sunday school is dead." Other schools have a yeast working within the loaf to make it light and tasty. It is desirable to have what one pastor expresses as, "Enthusiasm!"

Good morale is a by-product of other good things. To have clear-cut educational and practical *objectives* is a first essential. If church members have only vague conceptions of the school's reason for being, how can they be expected to consider it important? If parents have only the general idea that it may be a good thing, why should they be careful about sending their children—or coming with them? If the children do not know why they are sent or brought, how can they be expected to participate freely? If leaders are not conscious of their goals, what hope is there for a vital program?

Having a valued, challenging *program* is another foundation stone for spirit. Suppose the instructional half-hour is a boresome period of droning over a tawdry lesson-book with an unprepared teacher. Suppose the worship service is a haphazard and half-hearted time of hymn-singing, lesson reading, and announcements in an uncongenial setting. Suppose there is no fellowship opportunity beyond the casual contacts before and after the school session. Suppose the school has no service enterprises except the dropping of coins in envelopes. The seeds of our enthusiasms are our appreciation of values received by ourselves or others. We can become enthusiastic over worship that is communion with God, instruction that answers problems, fellowship that satisfies strivings, and service that advances welfare.

An inspiring, not only competent, *leadership* is still another requisite for a spirited school. "Our school is dead," was not said of one whose workers were enthusiastic about their work. What the teacher says and does is not the only factor observed by pupils. There is also the teacher's manner. Pupils will give their loyalty to a school whose workers are grateful that God has called them to work on that church school staff.

Schools that have spirit have gone out of their way to cultivate *fellowship*. A man spoke recently of the barrenness of life he would suffer if he would need to withdraw from the church with all the friends and acquaintances he had made there. "I do not know," he said, "of a single friend I have who did not come to me directly or indirectly through the church." To satisfy the craving of a spirit for human as well as divine fellowship can build church school spirit.

As a final suggestion, *Christian motivation,* manifest in a school, constitutes a major attractiveness. Deadly, dull monotony can scarcely lurk in a true corner of the kingdom of God. A school that is charged with radiant faith, hope, and love will thrive. Conversely, as we have seen in connection with attendance goals, the use of artificial incentives in the form of prizes, awards, banners, and the like should be reduced to a minimum or eliminated. They may cater to interests that are selfish and antisocial. Modest recognition of good records and of eminent service is another matter. Beyond that, the motives of spiritual growth should be relied upon to promote the school. Artificial incentives may be only "escape mechanisms" for avoiding the hard work of providing a vital program.

Representing the School Favorably

If a church school is to have a favorable image, its constituency must be representing it favorably before the community. People will not esteem our school unless they see that we have that appreciative attitude ourselves. There is too much negative attitude abroad already. Some people are disillusioned about the effects of church school attendance, even question the church's influence. They expect wholesome effects, discernible within and without the church. What the church membership is and does speaks more loudly than what it can say. Yet spoken and published messages have their place; we need to marshal all we can.

Pupils can help by saying good things about the school. A boy of eight was talking things over with a friend who didn't like to go to Sunday school. He had a reason, as he said, "The kids are all too noisy, fight with each other all the time while the teacher is trying to tell a story." The eight-year-old evangelist replied, "The kids in my Sunday school don't do that. Why don't you come with me next week and I'll show you." His friend accepted the invitation, became a member of the class and later a member of the congregation. What parents say is important, too. They will discuss with other parents what their boys and girls have said and done. If they see that their children are truly growing in grace under the cultivation of capable workers with whom it is good to have them associated they will tell others.

The workers also can help by speaking well of the school. Yet there are some who go about their task with the reluctance of sheep to the shearers. Somebody has to do it and it is their duty, they suppose. They are like rotten apples in the barrel, spoiling all the fruit. The only worse ones are those who engage in outright, negative criticism publicly. Joyous service issues in winsome appeal and loyal support. Chief among those who can help by speaking well of the school, except to criticize it constructively in the proper company, are the pastor and other officers. They should be using every opening with the various church officials, parents, pupils, and outsiders to arouse enthusiasm for the program of which they are responsible heads.

Having Everybody at Work

It can be emphasized repeatedly that the good church school is not one where leaders only *give* to pupils and pupils only *get* from leaders. The proper outlook sees leaders and pupils co-operatively giving and receiving for themselves and others. So it was recommended earlier that workers be given a full part in determining the policies and program of the school, similarly that pupils should have as large a part as possible in the organization and administration. It is even more essential that everyone is fully involved in all the curricular activities: contributing to the progress of study and instruction; planning and conducting worship; engaging in service enterprises; carrying on fellowship activity. The church school that puts its people to work at engaging tasks has a full list of investors who want to promote its dividend earning power.

GIVING PUBLICITY

A church school will be promoted more specifically through its publicity program. Publicity, broadly, is mass education that aims to inform persons so as to enlist them for a cause, develop their loyalty to a movement, or move them to act in some desired way. This purpose is inherent in the basic purposes of Christian education. Thus advertising media and techniques for the church have a special characteristic; they will teach as they attempt to arouse the membership, arrest the attention of the community, and attract the prospect.

People must know about the church and its program and what they know about it must make them think well of it. A prominent worker in the church declares that people will support church causes generously if only they know the facts about them. This means that many persons have been lost to the church who might be working busily inside it if they had been kept loyal and enthusiastic by proper information. Ask the average church member such questions as the following and further need for publicity will appear: How many missionary fields does the church occupy? What is the enrollment of your church school? What is the outstanding project of your youth fellowship? What lessons are the church school pupils studying? What was the per capita contribution to the church last year? We need publicity that brings people information that will lead them to wish to participate with us.

These are a dozen leading forms which church school publicity can take:

Weekly calendar and monthly church bulletin.
Posters and bulletin boards, including the outside bulletin board.
Postcards and letters to parents and others.
Newspaper releases, articles, pictures, and advertisements.
Oral announcements from pulpit and platform; sermons and other public addresses.
Telephone calls.
Pastoral and other personal calling.
Church school brochures, folders, pamphlets, and yearbooks.
Films and filmstrips.
Radio spots.
A "house organ" for the educational staff.
Pageants, exhibits, and demonstrations.

Obviously a well considered plan and program is needed, not a hit-and-miss jumble of this and that. An annual calendar of publicity is recommended. This can have its feature for each month as well as its continuous appeal. In some enterprises several churches can co-operate.

The how of these forms of publicity is a field of study in itself. Fortunately an abundance of material is available for the church library. These resources will suggest such things as a committee in charge, young people as reporters, a budget, the use of denominational periodicals and other publications for ideas, mailing lists, duplicating machine or printing press, poster equipment, and a host of others.

Good publicity programs, like all other good programs, must follow certain well-considered principles. These are a few simpler ones: determine the audience to be addressed; select the information that will win; be positive but sincere; recognize the attitude of modern man and his condition in a badly mixed up world. More can be found in the recom-

mended books on advertising. Briefly, those who do publicity for a church
school can test their work by the following questions: Will it attract attention? Will it hold attention? Will it win goodwill? Will it secure the
precise response?

SECURING INCREASED ENROLLMENT

Some systematic plan for membership solicitation is needed. It should
be a program with both long-range and short-range steps. A continuing
effort is better than any high-pressure campaign although there can be
seasonal efforts.

Just as for increasing attendance and punctuality, ten suggestions are
made below. Throughout it is understood that this work is, essentially,
evangelization. Winning persons for Christianity is to be the basic idea,
not only winning members for the school; yet the two are intertwined.

1. *Have a definite goal.* For all church schools together, the ultimate
goal is no less than universal enrollment of all available candidates of any
age; for an individual school, it should be the enrollment of every available pupil within that congregation's sphere of influence. However, we
must be realistic. A school can adopt as its more immediate goal a certain
number or percentage within the realm of possibility, perhaps a 10 percent
increase this year. The persons to be involved in solicitation should also
set the goals.

2. *Provide for everyone.* Our prospective constituency includes the
youngest children as well as the oldest adults. For many schools this ideal
means an emphasis on enlistment at nursery and adult levels—the two
points at which the typical school can most often increase its enrollment.
Present population trends indicate that more than ever particular attention
must be given to the adult program. With the increasing mobility of population we need to think of temporary residents, young adults at school and
working away from home, young home makers. However, many mature
adults, backbone members of the church have not been won for church
school work.

3. *Make the school vital.* A school that wishes to increase its membership in a substantial and stable way will devise an adequate educational
program as the first step of all. A program that recommends itself to the
members who are participating in it is a necessary basis for enlisting others.
Too, when persons have been brought into a vital school, they will remain.
"Have an able corps of superintendents and teachers . . . ," one pastor
advises. Another says, "the teaching has to be good and effective and the
material worthwhile."

4. *Make the school accessible.* Certain church schools are badly located.

Some of these have provided bus service or arranged car pools. Applications to the police department for a traffic officer to protect young children at dangerous crossings may help. Still another and, in some situations, a better idea is to open a branch school.

5. *Discover the prospects.* A prospect roll on pages or cards with data about the prospect is essential; it should include records of attempts at enlistment and the results. Where can prospects be found? The primary sources are within the church family. Study the congregational roll, family by family. Study the church school roll, including the roster of vacation and weekday agencies, for names of parents, brothers, sisters, or other relatives. Go over other organizational rolls; persons not yet members of the church may enroll in the church school. Beyond the congregation, secure reports about new people moving into the community; public school workers can be specially alert here. Let everyone think about neighbors; classes can suggest names of friends. Consider former members who have lapsed. As a final suggestion, conduct a prospect survey or participate in a community one. "Develop a prospect roll" is one pastor's recommendation; that summarizes it except to add, don't let the roll languish.

6. *Go personally to win the prospect with a definite and a trained organization.* How do prospects become members? Since Jesus went up and down the Galilean roads, Christianity has been promoted by personal evangelization. Other means have value, but Christian advance of any type is mainly propagated from person to person. One pastor stated: "Let the question, 'Where do you go to Sunday school?' be on the lips of all members." Another put it well: "Educate pupils to bring every unattached neighbor to Sunday church school."

Yet, for full results, a definite organization is needed, preferably a standing committee on membership. Membership campaigns—periodic or occasional—may be useful as crests of effort but continuous work, with duly constituted persons definitely in charge will be best. This does not mean that a committee alone shall be concerned. The increase in a school's membership should be viewed by everyone as the entire school's missionary enterprise. The spirit and practice of lay evangelization should be constantly inculcated as a part of the educational work of the school. The membership committee has planned wisely when it has every member involved—pastor, director, superintendent, teachers, parents, and pupils, even children and youth.

Yet people are not born with the requisite knowledge and skill for this task. There should be precise instruction in ways to approach people, methods of asking them to become pupils, how to answer the objections sure to be raised by some prospects. Role-playing is an excellent procedure in preparing workers for visitation. Persons can take roles alternately in being the solicitor and the solicited. They should practice dealing with the typical objections: "We've just moved here; we want to shop around." "We're too busy already." "Sunday school is for kids." "I'm just not interested."

After a worker has received an assignment a personal visit is best although a personal letter or phone call should not be neglected if there is no other way. In making a call the individual plan is best—the teacher of a class calls upon a prospective member, possibly with a pupil of the class to be entered. Printed material on the school's program should be left in the home. One call should not be regarded as sufficient.

7. *Use publicity.* The publicity discussed should always, directly or indirectly, be pointed toward recruitment.

8. *Emphasize Christian fellowship.* There is no more agreeable way to get acquainted with people than to play in company with them. If we like the people with whom we play, we want to be associated with them in other activities. Many young people, particularly, are won for church school agencies by an invitation to a social event where they may make likeable acquaintances. But fellowship is a broader factor. Throughout the church program, whenever possible, we should have strangers and visitors present. The regular church school sessions can have fellowship value. One man remembers across sixty years the cheery greeting of the superintendent in a country crossroads Sunday school. Meanwhile, it is understood that the fellowship emphasis is not only to win and hold but chiefly to educate.

When a prospect appears at the church school door there should be someone to welcome him; it is best if the newcomer is brought by the person who solicited his attendance. What about "the new one in the class?" Nobody lasts long in a climate that is cold. New members should be built into the full life of the school as soon as possible. There should be services of recognition for the newly enrolled.

9. *Avoid contests.* A big city school held a long-range contest with a similar school in a distant state. The contest ended on a Sunday when all the members of various schools in neighboring churches, whatever their denomination, were invited to help roll up the biggest attendance of all. This school won the contest over its distant neighbor, but the entire session that Sunday was spent in taking a picture of the mob. It is a grave question whether any desirable permanent results accrued from such activity. Indeed it is more probable that people become discouraged, some of them disgusted, with memberships solicited in that manner. Contests may undermine the Christian attitudes we are presumed to be building.

10. *Educate all concerned persons.* Again it is desirable to educate everybody involved. There should be a continuous "know your church

program" for the members of a congregation. Half of this program, by the nature of things, would be about the church school. Some members may not know a church school at all; others know it only from childhood experiences of which some may have been unpleasant. Through regular lessons, announcements, special day programs, church bulletins, and sermons people can constantly be reminded of their obligation and their privilege to win someone for the educational program as well as to participate in it themselves. This is the ultimate means of accomplishing the goals set by the slogan proposed in one church: "Want them; find them; bring them; greet them; teach them."

A Denominational Effort

There are specific suggestions as well as encouragement in the report of a denomination's enlistment effort. Church school enrollment was declining. The educational staff determined that the underlying reason was a recession in missionary zeal. All other causes, they believed, would have been overcome if the churches had possessed sufficient "passion for souls."

An enlistment program was instituted. The objective was "to win others to the Sunday school that, through it, they would be won to Christ and the church." A specific goal for enrollment was set and a general attack was made along the following fronts:

1. Impressing pastors and other leaders with the importance of the church school "in reaching as well as in teaching."
2. Developing all facilities, denominational and local, to maintain increasing enrollment and attendance.
3. Encouraging and planning for pupils and workers to win others.
4. Appealing for greater home co-operation.
5. Helping leaders and pupils to use the best educational procedures, which would result in increased enrollment.
6. Urging church school workers to seek the re-enlistment of lapsed pupils.

As one specific method, "enlistment demonstrations" were held at strategic centers. Congregational workers were instructed in methods of visitation. Then they went into homes and secured written promises to attend church school. Final statistics indicated an average of nearly one promise in each home visited. A later check showed that approximately 50 percent of the persons who promised were in attendance after three months had passed.

An important constituent of this entire effort was an accompanying attempt to improve the schools and their work. The local workers were led to make a study and then adopt from one to five projects for improvement. At the conclusion of the enterprise the director believed that a by-product of it has perhaps proved its major contribution, namely, the knowledge that enrollment can be increased. He writes: "When I came I heard, 'nothing can be done.' Later, people began to say, 'you've shown us that something can be done.' Now, it seems, the whole church knows that fact and we've changed from pessimism to optimism. . . ."

Working at the Task Locally

Over the years our church schools have had their ups and downs of enrollment with many factors, favorable and unfavorable, involved. On a country-wide basis, the present trend is not sufficiently upward. While national and world statistics are hard to come by, each church school can compute its own record. If all of them were attending to this responsibility vigorously, the upward trend would accelerate.

There are internal causes for the weakness: insufficiency of leaders; pastoral lack of interest in Christian education; multiple church services; the "Sunday school is for kids" concept; inadequate facilities; inferior educational methods; a breakdown of home co-operation and perhaps most of all a reluctance to witness.

External causes also are adduced. Population trends is one. The burgeoning birthrate is receding somewhat. This is scarcely an excuse; the population in general is growing. There seems to be some decline in church membership; at best, the church growth is not notably greater than the population growth. This, too, is scarcely an adequate excuse.

Whatever may make it difficult, more people could be attending church school. Besides, here and there, a school reports almost phenomenal growth. Leaders of several such schools have been asked to report the secrets of their success. They write statements like these:

1. Our schools and churches must emphasize evangelism.
2. Our workers must catch enthusiasm and show Christian zeal.
3. A Consecrated special visitor will be effective.
4. Willingness to work and leadership education explain our growth.
5. Our growth (about 100 percent in one and one-half years) represents just plain, hard work.
6. Consecrated, faithful, and trained teachers are needed.
7. Our leadership personnel has a deeply Christian spirit in the matter of interesting others.
8. The feeling of responsibility on the part of teachers and officers will be radiated to the pupils.
9. We must have less absenteeism on the part of leaders.
10. The whole set-up of the school is pupil-centered rather than organization-centered.
11. We have more attractive rooms, better teachers, more visiting by teachers, more personal interest in the pupils as individuals.
12. This church builds its annual program and carries it out.

13. We put our members to work.
14. We render valuable assistance to the community in these times.
15. You do not win Christians through contests; you win them through Christ.

For the leader who asks, "How can I keep my school growing?" an excellent answer is: (1) engender enthusiasm that is contagious; (2) provide a program that wins; (3) render a service that is notable; (4) see that people know about it.

PART FIVE

EXPANDING THE SCHOOL'S
MINISTRY

CHAPTER XVIII

ENLARGING THE PROGRAM (I)
On Sundays; At Home; Within General Education

No executive leader of a church school will ever, likely, be able to say, "Enough, our educational program is complete." Instead, there will always be need for more as well as better Christian nurture. Certainly every evaluative measure of our work refutes any claim of present perfection.

MORE TIME!

Why this partial failure of our church school work? There is ample reason in the time factor alone. Let it be repeated: an average member of the church is having not more than one hour of formal Christian education each week. Compare this with the time spent in general education. An American child will attend public schools six hours a day, five days a week, for 36 weeks annually—more than a thousand hours, equaling twenty years of church school experience! Indeed, perhaps half of our future citizens and a much larger percentage of adults are not now under any formal religious education.

To be sure, Christian education goes beyond specific hours set aside in a school. Indirect influences on Christian personality may be as significant as the direct. There are informal ways of learning and today's leaders are alert to ways of utilizing ongoing general experience for Christian education purposes. Nevertheless, a staggering ideal confronts us: to reach our people with, let us say for a reasonable beginning, two hours of excellent, formal Christian education each week. Until that challenge is met more fully we may expect to live in a world of increasing ignorance, secularity, immorality, and irreligion.

Some church leaders who lament the lack of time for adequate educational results have condemned the public schools and similar agencies for taking it. Defendants can remark that the churches do not

make full use of the time available to them. They do provide for relatively little use of the hours after school and on Saturdays for nine
months of the year, also of three summer months. Strangely, too, they
use relatively little of the Sunday which is widely regarded as church
time. Three chapters on enlarging the church school program will survey what can be done; we begin with the possibilities on Sundays.

ON SUNDAYS

An executive's first effort will be to raise the efficiency of the present
Sunday church school sessions so that the time spent there will have a
maximum productiveness. Yet the need of more time for these sessions,
so that there can be deeper, broader, richer, and more varied types of
fully-rounded experience, will remain. If, too, still other sessions are
possible on Sunday, these need to be exploited. Thus, as a leader's second effort, he will strive to expand and extend the Sunday church school
session and otherwise fill Sunday with still more educational activity.
After that, a third effort will be the development of related work in
allied agencies, nearly all for weekday work. Together they constitute
an amazing number of enterprises that often escape the attention of
those who, when they view and appraise the educational work of the
church, too often think only of its Sunday church school.

Expanded and Extended Sunday Church School Sessions

An obvious way to secure additional time is to expand and/or extend
the Sunday morning program. Come to think of it, there is something
odd and wasteful about getting children up, dressed, and away to the
church for just an hour. Why should not the older people, too, plan
for more time there?

A simple possibility is to expand the session, if only to add a quarter
hour or more. An extended session schedules a second morning hour,
its activities correlated with those of the first hour. If necessary it can
be programmed so that some of the pupils may attend only the first.
Some churches have scheduled a total of three church school hours.

A plan which gives somewhat similar results is the combined preach-
ing-teaching service such as that described in Chapter V. The younger
children, at least, would have a two-hour Sunday church school program except for periodic visits in the adult services of worship. For older
persons there would be a full hour of study-and-instruction under the
educational staff and an hour of worship, with preaching, in charge of
the pastoral staff. Eliminating any duplication in repeated sessions of

worship gives additional minutes for the more specifically educational activities.

Two major problems confront those who wish to take such steps. First, what shall be done in an expanded or extended session? Where only a quarter or half hour has been added, a slight lengthening of the class, departmental, or grade-level periods will suffice. For a two-hour program or longer, the newer views and practices in education can be introduced more fully. These would include use of the more informal procedures; there can be more pupil participation, with units of creative activity; there is time for more leisurely discussion, to do handwork activities and, in general, to finish plans. Schools may find this the best place to introduce supplementary audile and visual materials for which there is not enough time in ordinary sessions.

Where an extended session of the school parallels the church services, we may have to think of a dual program. The first hour may be much like the present one. A second can be a special study unit or other group enterprise: making things for the sick and aged of the congregation; working out a service of worship for the following Sunday; discussing immediate problems of right living; studying the hymns of the church; doing units on the various forms of the church's work.

The second major problem, especially with an extended session is how to secure workers with the different competencies required and a willingness to give additional time, particularly if it keeps them out of "church services." Are church members to serve or to be served? Some will find that their most fruitful service is to do this needful educational work even if they must attend worship at other hours. Again, there can be a relay system in which certain workers serve for a term, then return after another term passes. A director of Christian education or equivalent worker can give continuous oversight and guidance to the program.

Formal Worship with Adults under Pastoral Leadership

There is a present trend toward "the family pew." Educational values are claimed for it. We do learn to worship by worshiping, even by participating as a spectator in part. There is much for even the small child to see, hear, and feel in an adult service of worship. However, we must ask several questions. As a serious one, can there be negative learnings? There are others. Where and how can the maximum values result from this hour of "the service" for the spiritual welfare of all concerned. For the young, can there be richer values within a program designed for their specific needs, such as an extended session?

Unquestionably the young should be introduced as early as helpful to all the dimensions of the total Sunday program. A time comes, too, when children and youth are to become regular attendants. As to when and how, opinions will differ as do practices within congregations or denominations. Among the practical issues are the size of the congregation, transportation problems, and the form of the building, as well as the tradition of the congregation. The view of baptism and the meaning of membership, too, will likely influence decisions. Always we need to keep asking, though, what is best for the child, the youth, the adult, the family with children, and for adults without children.

Here, in general principles only, we must think chiefly of educational values. What can be learned in the time used and how can it be learned best? Unquestionably the typical church service is gauged for adults—liturgy, where the form is liturgical, the music including the hymns, the sermon—all these have adult experience in view. We would not take preschool children into the adult class hours; shall we take them here? There can be occasions, perhaps monthly, when the total membership will be together. This will recognize the unity of the congregation and this is a worthy objective. At such times the service can be modified so that there is something for each age group at least on alternate Sundays.

When, then, shall regular attendance be expected? For the churches where there are confirmation classes or similar groups, the beginning of that work may well be the chosen time. Certainly it should be the latest time. "Membership" classes are leading to fuller understanding of doctrine and practice. They furnish a cumulative background that will obviate misunderstanding or wrong "learning." The pupil will be readying himself for "graduation" into his full church participation. His personal needs will be more adequately addressed by this worship hour when he has reached this stage. He will then be present with the community of those who are more nearly his peers than when he was a small child. His elders, too, will not need to be distracted from their full participation along with him. Meantime he will have had as much work as possible for his own age level needs.

Sunday Afternoon and Evening Sessions

Young people's groups of high school age, and of older youth, have been utilizing portions of Sunday afternoons and evenings as more time for further Christian education. More in line with present trends, various upper classes, grades, departments, or divisions of the church school will be having supplementary sessions at these times. The same groups with the same staffs if possible, or the same pupils in other groupings with other leaders, will work at a related aspect of their Sunday morning activity or at a correlated but different unit. In any case, there would be no separate agency, just an additional portion of the program with an emphasis on less formality and more pupil management but with competent adult advisement. This curriculum may stress worship, fellowship, and service while including the necessary study-and-instruction. It can properly include worship planned and conducted by the pupils themselves. There can be special fellowship events along with the fellowship that accompanies other forms of work. Service enterprises may predominate. Such ways of learning as dramatization, role-playing, surveys, trips, and workshops will be possible along with discussions that need not end with the bell.

Weekday Dimension of Sunday Work

According to older policy and practice, the weekdays preceding Sunday were times to get pupils ready for the Sunday session. They were to study their lessons and be able to recite. That general idea has not been fully discarded and in certain forms should not be, as we said earlier. Yet it was never very successful. At worst, it created a division of the class between the prepared and the unprepared so that teaching problems ensued.

More recently we recognize that Sunday is the first day of the week and as such, it is the day of beginnings for Christian living throughout the week. We shall have prepared for it, of course—as teacher, sometimes as a whole class or a committee or individual pupil. Yet we shall treat it mainly as a first of seven days in all of which we are to live under its impetus.

Yet there is work to be done in relation to Sunday sessions—before that day but especially after it. Reading, researching, planning, witnessing, rehearsing, thinking, practicing, talking about things, experimenting, fellowshiping, worshiping, serving—all these have their daily place in relation to learning and, above all, to living out the objectives of Christian education as we learn. Attending an isolated hour or even two on Sunday is a caricature of Christian educational work at its best. Properly, the "lesson" has only begun when the closing bell rings. Education is a seamless robe.

AT HOME

Homes are places where "more time" is available and it can be made richly productive in many directions by many means.

Need

We have seen in Chapter XVI how church and home must work together as hand in glove if there is to be more and better Christian nurture. While the school has a distinctive contribution to make to a member's Christian development, the lack of specific attention to the family itself dooms important Christian learning to only moderate effectiveness or less. The resulting demand upon the educational executive is dual. The first half of his responsibility is to foster a program of Christian education within the home circle. The family setting is the principal matrix in which we enact our Christian lives; only education right there will make this phase of a total life what it can be. A second half of executive responsibility is to provide church school education for that Christian family living—school work outside the home to help its members live as Christians in their homes. These two phases of effort, it must be noticed, can interact and be by-products of each other.

The efforts of both home and school will require a co-operative struggle against difficulties. The social order throws up immense barriers: disrupted and disruptive homes, mobile families, a superfluity of activities with overheated time schedules, parent and youth recreational problems, difficult working conditions, overwhelming temptations. Parents and children alike are placed in jeopardy. An almost unnoticed fact is that families are no longer isolated within four walls. For many youth, the entire community is their home and the elders have not yet found ways to Christianize a home that is constituted by school, playground, club, street corner, drugstore, theater, and all the rest.

Christian Nurture within the Family Circle

We shall soon be giving attention to the second phase for the church school leader's devotion, namely, church school education toward Christian family living. Yet that actual living, with its educational result, deserves first place though the two aspects cannot be separated fully. Parents being the first, they should also be the foremost teachers of religion—learners while they teach. Siblings, too, can be teachers and learners, for weal or woe.

Nowhere better than in the family circle can children learn the meaning of love and trust, hope and faith. What examples of stewardship of the world's resources, or waste thereof, are young people most likely to follow except the parents'? Where can the strongest beliefs be shaped, the highest aspirations be nurtured? In the family the warmth of Christian fellowship can be appreciated best. Here is a primary place for service and worship. This is a workshop to try out one's faith-life under guidance and succeed or fail within a sympathetic group. There can be daily guidance of thought, daily example in attitude and action. Relationship education is specially significant here.

Learning of those types will be by the doing, of which studying is only a part. Much of it will be informal—just what naturally takes place in the family's human relations: behavior in sorrow or joy, work and play, perplexity or exaltation, anger and love. There will be conversations, questions and answers, discussions, advice, controversy. In all these the Christian note can be sounded and above all acted out with sanity and fidelity for growth towards potentialities. There are also the more formal educational enterprises at home. Frequently mentioned are: home altar, devotional services, reading of books and Bible stories and story books, controlled radio and television programs, religious projects, religious music, table grace and bedtime prayers, use of the Bible in meeting life problems, devotional reading of the Bible, home supplementation and complementation of church school lesson material. Also in their homes, under parental guidance, the pupils will get ready for and carry to completion their church school learning experiences.

We shall consider the church school's part more fully soon. Briefly here, it can provide help for the above home activities with literature, studies, readings, and conferences as well as classes. Also parents and children should have opportunities to consider home issues under guidance in various classes while the home is serving as the school's major laboratory with all the family as fellow learners and teachers.

Church School Education toward Christian Family Living

While a major phase of the executive's endeavor can be his work at revitalizing the practice of Christian living in the home—just to get the idea underscored is of high value—the church school has its own specific role.

GENERAL PROGRAM

The school's more precise education toward Christian living in the family may begin when the nursery child learns to help others in the preschool division. It can go forward properly with each church school session for children whose home is recognized by teachers, parents, and himself as a special learning laboratory for his Christian faith living. Related teen-age studies can be moving forward until there are units on the meaning of Christian marriage. Young couples can be helped to plan for homes that will be Christian and be given first-aid in getting them started. After that will come preparation for their own parenthood and an unending study of Christian child rearing. Very early, children will need help concerning their relations with siblings and parents. This can continue in adulthood until we consider the family relations of and with the aging. Never to be forgotten, Christian family education is subject not only to study but it must be chiefly a learning by doing under guidance with consideration in groups. This is how people will learn "in depth" the real meaning of Christian concepts and practices: love, fatherhood, forgiveness, grace, sacrificial service, and much more.

A DENOMINATIONAL PROGRAM

Much of this work, but not all of it, can be clearly a factor in the typical church school curriculum where it can enter into almost any unit and type of curricular experience. One denomination provides for it also in special ways.[1]

Courses. Seven six-week courses in a *Christian Family Education Series* are of the essence in this church's family education program. Each is meant for parents of children of a particular age from birth through twelfth grade. A parents' manual and a teacher's guide are provided for each course; the materials can be used as a guided reading program. The aim is to help parents discover the ways in which their children are ready to grow as Christians, learn how to foster that growth in the informal climate of family living, and discover ways of helping their children meet in a Christian way the life situations they are encountering.

Family Nights. Although the family may come to church together on Sunday, it is often said that they too rarely have other opportunities to come to the church as a family. So the LCA curriculum provides for family nights. While these are designed to serve the usual church purposes, they are to be a special opportunity for religious experience that bears on home matters. They are to help build stronger bonds of Christian love and understanding among the members of the family; they are to create awareness of the values of leisure time activities shared by the family. Parents in particular are to discover and assume their Christian responsibilities for factors in the community—religious, social, political, and economic— which affect family life. Eating the evening meal together is one of the features. The major program emphases are: worship, fellowship, and a special feature that can include speakers, audio-visual presentations, panel discussions, and other procedures. Printed materials for family nights are made available.

Parent-Leader Meetings. Special meetings will be designed to meet some specific need in the general aim for leaders and parents to get better acquainted and to co-operate more fully in the program. Individual conferences between parents and the teachers of a particular child can be

[1]The Lutheran Church in America in its Parish Education Curriculum.

arranged. One continuing purpose is to help the parents know the objectives of the school and what their children are doing in its curriculum. Very important, a parent-leader meeting could show parents how they can help their children effectuate specific Christian learnings begun in the church school.

Christian Family Week. Observance of this annual event sponsored by the National Council of Churches is to be a part of this curricular program. The council itself suggests a theme but a congregation may develop its own emphasis. Special materials such as posters, handbills, devotional booklets, and suggestions are made available each year.

WITHIN GENERAL EDUCATION

Can the churches secure additional time for more effective Christian education by having some form of association with general education?

The Church and Public Schools

Early American religious education was conducted on weekdays in the general program along with reading, writing, arithmetic, and others. Recently it has been in danger of being rather meticulously excluded from the public schools of the United States, though it has never been officially eliminated by law. Some now hold that the departure from the early practice was unnecessary and undesirable, also that the return is possible and essential; others would prefer to build a permanent "wall of separation."

LEGAL PROVISIONS

Naturally, in a nation where pluralistic religious orientations are quite complex, these relationships between religious and general education have been troublesome. The controversy has gathered around the principles expressed as "freedom of religion" and "separation of church and state." The exact focus nowadays is often on the issue of public support for church-sponsored schools.

In solving the problem reference is always made to the First and Fourteenth Amendments of the American Constitution, particularly the First which reads in its pertinent part as follows: *"Congress shall make no law respecting an establishment of religion, or prohibiting the free exercise thereof...."*

Some students of the constitution have asserted that the principles of religious freedom and church-state separation to be adduced from it will forever exclude religious elements from public schools. Contrariwise, others conclude that those principles have assumed a negative meaning which was not the intent of those who evoked the principles. If the latter are right, the teaching of religion which is free from creedal emphasis and sectarian purpose can be compatible with the privileges the constitution was meant to safeguard.

What does "freedom of religion" mean? First, it clearly guarantees an individual's privilege to believe and to worship as he will, without dictation by government. Second, it supports the corporate privilege of developing any church body not obviously subversive of good citizenship. What does separation of church and state mean? Clearly that there shall be separate administrative control for each, church and state. Yet this principle certainly does not deny that, to a degree, the purposes of church and state are broadly similar. Thus church and state may be considered co-operative as to function with regard to the common welfare though they are to be separate as to administration.

Both principles taken together—freedom of religion and separation of church and state—doubtless require that a citizen shall not be forced to accept views of religion alien to his conscience. Also they demand that public funds shall not be used to foster a particular branch, denomination, or sect of religion. Yet, to the exact point, does either mean that religion must be excluded from the education of a child or that public funds cannot be used to foster religion in general?

Recent decades have been stirred by several Supreme Court rulings on that basic question. Their purport has been that sectarian religious exercises in schools cannot be financed by tax monies and cannot properly be held in school buildings; also schools must not be managed in any such way as to coerce students for either religion or nonreligion and particularly for or against any particular faith.

The point was made somewhat differently, but with the same meaning, by Mr. Justice Brennan in his concurring opinion on the Abington (Pennsylvania) school district case of June, 1963, when the court forbade the reading of selected verses of the Bible in the classroom and the praying of the Lord's Prayer in unison there. To quote Justice Brennan:

> What the framers meant to foreclose, and what our decisions under the Establishment Clause have forbidden, are those involvements of religious with secular institutions which (a) serve the essentially religious activities of religious institutions; (b) employ the organs of government for essentially religious purposes; or (c) use essentially religious means to serve governmental ends, where secular means would suffice.[2]

However, Mr. Justice Brennan's opinion includes additional statements that are pertinent. One makes clear the proper attitude of government as

[2]Supreme Court of the United States, *Opinions,* Nos. 142 and 119, October Term, 1962 (Washington, D. C.: U. S. Government Printing Office, 1963), p. 67.

neutral, not hostile: ". . . the first amendment commands not official hostility toward religion, but only strict neutrality in matters of religion. . . . The state must be steadfastly neutral in all matters of faith, and neither favor nor inhibit religion. . . ."[3] In harmony, there is specific reference to nondevotional use of the Bible in public schools; also, a general statement that study *about* the scriptures and *about* religion, presented objectively, is not to be discouraged: "Indeed, whether or not the Bible is involved, it would be impossible to teach meaningfully many subjects in the social sciences or the humanities without some mention of religion."[4]

This latest judgment of the court is more significant for what it allows than what it disallows. Attention has been focused, and rightly should be, on the possible freedom to do objective teaching of religion in public schools. This can be the most fruitful development of recent times, a breakthrough in the long controversy concerning this whole issue of church and state regarding religious education.

RELIGION IN THE GENERAL CURRICULUM

It seems that now we need not be fearful about attempts at both indirect and direct teaching of religion in public schools if they are done properly. Indirect teaching has been widely recognized as a legitimate endeavor in public schooling and has been given approval by the Supreme Court's decision. Administrators and teachers are always able to make quiet Christian witness within school relationships through their manner of living, speaking, counseling, and the like. Further, mention of the religious dimensions of art, literature, music, and branches of the social sciences, especially history, is widely acceptable in most communities if there is no effort to proselytize. Indeed, as the court has said, how can such material be omitted if the pupil is to be truly and fully educated in such subjects or realms?

Now, too, it seems that a long-range effort, carefully devised and wisely administered, could put religion back into the curriculum of public instruction. We may have to deal with an objection which could arise from the wide variety of parental opinion about religion. People may not want their children to meet variant forms and alien ideas. Yet teaching need not mean indoctrination in the distinctive convictions of any particular group. The new approaches in education and the new techniques are suited to such a demand. Also, cannot the basically religious versus the narrowly sectarian be distinguished in choosing the content for public instruction in religion? Subjects can be selected with this distinction in mind:

The history of Israel and of Christianity.

[3]*Ibid.*, pp. 68, 71.
[4]*Ibid.*, p. 72.

The influence of Judaism and Christianity upon government, art, litera-
ture, and music.
The English Bible and the story of its development by synagogue and
church.
Ethics and the ethical implications of Judaism and Christianity.
Men and women of the Bible and other outstanding religious contributors.
Masterpieces of biblical literature.
The other religions.

Very important, it can be understood that these will not be required but
elective courses.

There is already a large body of experience along such lines within
higher education. Professors in church colleges have long been teaching
groups as widely divergent as any that would be met in a typical public
school classroom. Increasingly too, as we have seen, state and municipal
colleges and universities are developing departments of religion where
Protestants of many hues, with Catholics and Jews, mingle in a fellowship
of study concerning the religious culture and enterprises of the race. It is
proposed only to extend such experience downward into secondary and
elementary levels of public education.

However, the churches should take great care that they do not abuse
their privileges. Teachers must be considerate of other people's faiths. We
do live in a religiously pluralistic culture, just as our culture represents a
wide range of political doctrine. We want a democratic state; we accept
the fact that there will be differences of opinion. Likewise religious diversity must be recognized with understanding and tolerance. There is a
Golden Rule.

The churches need now to be alert for a totality of responsibility that
may include such activities as these:

1. Seeking assiduously to serve the intent of the First Amendment without fear of others' faiths or favor for one's own. Developing throughout the church an objective attitude that promotes Christian fidelity
   but shuns bias. This will be fostering the ecumenical spirit in which
   both unity and diversity are understood and appreciated for their
   worth.
2. Striving to understand public school purposes, programs, and problems
   while refusing to be a party to any current wave of merely destructive
   negativism.
3. Showing positive interest in the schools by participating in their enterprises; serving on boards of education and otherwise helping to improve the school situation.
4. Encouraging young church members who have the requisite aptitudes
   to enter public school work.
5. Encouraging public school administrators and teachers to make Christian witness in appropriate ways.
6. Helping school workers to master the fundamentals of Old and New
   Testament data and church history; also to understand the principles

of Christian doctrine and ethics. (This may require special study groups in the church school program and necessary books made available in libraries. Perhaps the churches of the community should pool their resources. Certainly our colleges and universities should have such needs in mind and foster appropriate programs.)

7. Supporting all carefully considered local enterprises for objective teaching of religion in public schools.

Parochial Schools

What has been called the parochial school, sometimes the Christian day school or full-time weekday Christian school, has had a long history in this country and elsewhere. In former times here and in many other countries the churches made themselves responsible for education in general. Now typical church school work is provided largely in addition to and separate from general education in America; the same pattern is developing in many new nations and even in Europe. Yet some effort to combine religious with general education in a full school week continues both here and abroad.

STATUS

In this church-sponsored system of general education the Roman Catholic churches hold the lead. Catholics are reported to have as many as approximately 10,000 elementary schools and 2,500 secondary schools. There is mention of nearly 8,000,000 students under instruction in their schools of all types. However, it should be added that about half of the Catholic school population is under public education. Also, we read that Catholics are yielding their prerogative here or there and are training leaders for a church school program after the Protestant pattern. Already, they have Sunday church schools in numerous parishes.

Statistics on Protestant parochial schools are given in Taylor,[5] as of the end of the 50's and there has likely been some increase since that time. The numbers are as follows: elementary schools about 3,000 with more than 250,000 pupils; secondary schools about 600 with an enrollment in excess of 75,000. It will be seen that the average Protestant parochial school is small. The greatest number of them are maintained by Lutheran bodies, notably by the Lutheran Church, Missouri Synod. Seventh Day Adventists come next, followed by the Christian Reformed group and Protestant Episcopalians. There are also Jewish day schools enrolling roughly 50,000 pupils in what is reported to be a growing movement. An indeterminate number of schools with similar purposes are "independent,"

[5]Raymond S. Moore, "Protestant Full-Time Weekday Schools," in *Religious Education: A Comprehensive Survey*, ed. Marvin J. Taylor (New York: Abingdon Press, 1960), p. 242.

operated sometimes by a group of parents entirely free from church administration. The presupposition for all these efforts is that no education is complete unless its religious phase is incorporated sufficiently.

EVALUATION

Benefits such as the following are claimed for the parochial school:

1. It can produce a more satisfactory result than the typical church school's fractional and optional program; children can be indoctrinated in the fundamentals of Christianity more adequately and educated more fully for total Christian living.
2. Children are given an opportunity to grow under church guidance; this can correct the secularistic environment and program of public education.
3. A well-balanced union of religious and general education will help solve basic problems in private and public life; we need this counter-agent for such evils as juvenile delinquency and adult irresponsibility.
4. Education for Christian living is properly an enterprise for parents, educators, and the whole church working closely together.
5. Children can learn better in situations that do not resemble mass production.
6. Parochial schools can be a means of evangelism.

There is at least an equal number of objections to the parochial school plan. In addition, doubt has been cast upon the policy by recent researches into some of the claims made for the superiority of these schools. As usual, the potential is not always translated into reality.

1. There are such financial and other limitations that the product may not be up to the level of public school results. It is difficult to secure enough competent teachers; the cost of physical facilities is prohibitive in many cases; at best, parents are forced to support parallel school systems.
2. This is segregation of a type; pupils may not be adjusted to the broader demands of life in a democracy.
3. Parochial type schools, if multiplied broadly, would be a threat to public school education. Innumerable school systems in the United States could be divisive to the point of serious detriment for church as well as national life.
4. There is danger that, even in such schools, the Bible and other religious topics will be treated only as subjects, not genuinely integrated into the total program of the school and life of the pupils.
5. The resulting church could be isolated from the mainstreams of cultural developments. Religious bigotry and prejudice may be intensified while children are denied their ecumenical contacts.
6. The churches that engage in general education may be diverted from their more specific tasks.

There is nothing in the foreseeable future to encourage belief that this type of school will flourish. It should be repeated that Catholics are re-examining their practice and that there are strong indications of a movement toward our system of church school work parallel to public general education. They may eventually give up their elementary and secondary schools as most Protestants have.

Possibly, though, there are special circumstances where a parochial school is needed. When public schools fail to maintain high educational and moral standards or to provide adequate opportunities for all pupils, a congregation may be justified in establishing a school. Normally, the church should work for the correction of anything undesirable in the public school system and it has a duty to foster what it considers to be good. The state is the social institution best equipped to insure the opportunity for an adequate education for all its citizens. It seems best for Christians to support fully the twofold system of education that is indigenous to America: (a) the public system and (b) the parallel church school system. Both need our maximum and united force to strengthen them.

As one exception, considerable successful work is being done on one level. Excellent Christian nursery or kindergarten programs are maintained by some local churches. These can be especially useful, even needful, where there are no public facilities of this sort. They have even stimulated the public sector to establish such work in some localities. Meantime, parents have been helped and the pupils have profited.

Dual Enrollment

A new concept called "shared time" or "dual enrollment," has appeared within this debate over public education and church education. Under this plan pupils will be enrolled in two schools—one a public school and the other a church-controlled school. The programs will be conducted partially in each. Pupils will share their school time between the public school which provides general education in a religiously neutral context and a church supported school with a specific religious emphasis. This policy recognizes that the child, as commonly assumed, is under the control of his parents who must see that he is educated; they may decide what that education shall be—within limits—and choose the agency to provide that education. Parents who want their children to have classes in which religious values are specifically significant will provide schools for the purpose under church auspices. The same children will attend the public school for their other classes.

A modest instance, yet a significant one because it has continued for many years in Hartford, Connecticut, is frequently cited; there are other such situations. In Hartford, the parochial school pupils attend public school for industrial arts (seventh and eighth grade boys) and home economics (seventh and eighth grade girls). As another instance, seventh and eighth grade students in the Detroit area have been studying mathematics, science, physical education, music, arts, shop, and home economics at a public school; their other subjects are completed in a Catholic school.

Some have hoped that serious practical difficulties already existing and greater ones in prospect—if, for example, the Catholic school population expands beyond the ability of the church to cope with it—can be ameliorated in this manner. Protestants, too, who are dissatisfied with some features of the public school situation may be pleased by this possibility. Perhaps the tension over the whole church-state issue in education would abate somewhat under this solution. However, reports over the experiments with dual enrollment are conflicting; the reactions to the plan are varied. Undoubtedly the implications for both church and state are far-reaching. The experiment should continue as the issue is studied carefully and debated fully. We may discover that dual enrollment subjects pupils to pressures from two types of school programs instead of only one and that it includes the weaknesses of both types.

There is still reason to believe that the typical church school program raised to a higher level, and coupled with the new vision of religious work of an objective nature in the public school, will be the most desirable program for all Americans.

Institutions of Higher Christian Education

The churches' efforts at higher Christian education date back to the time when this education was provided largely by the church. Beginning centuries ago this condition prevailed in the United States to roughly the middle of the nineteenth century.

CHURCH-RELATED COLLEGES AND UNIVERSITIES

At the present time Protestants have in the neighborhood of 500 colleges and universities; Catholics have at least half as many. These schools typically feature church control and financing, with an ecclesiastical emphasis in governing boards, administration, and faculty. They have also an overall concern for religion in the curricular program, enforce requirements for religious courses especially in Bible and, often, require chapel attendance. Common, too, are special religious observances and a religious factor may be evident in extracurricular activities.

With the burgeoning college age population the church-related higher institutions are thriving, but they feel the competition of state institutions that draw away students and they experience the pinch of financial need as they aim to keep their academic standards high. However, church-state controversy has remained largely on the level of elementary and secondary schooling. Christian higher schools suffer less public resistance despite governmental low cost loans for buildings, provisions for scholarships, and awards of research projects. Fundamentally, their religious work is not compelled by the state; it is elective and voluntary at least in the sense that parents and students have selected the schools.

As an overall evaluation, the schools justify their existence as servants of human welfare and merit denominational support when they are different from other schools but not narrowly so. They give witness to the educational and cultural interest of their churches. They can foster the ecumenical ideal when they favor broadly religious interests and treat understandingly the members of a variegated student body. They may be viewed as educational arms of their respective churches to help meet educational needs. Many have the virtue of smallness and offer that particular value at a time when massive student bodies are common. Under current crowded conditions in major colleges and universities some of these schools accept those who would otherwise lose their higher educational opportunities and they are often well equipped to help these young people render a maximum service to the social order. Much of their religious value, however, will depend upon their type of government, their personnel, and their curriculum.

CHURCH PROFESSIONAL SCHOOLS

The churches have still another level of educational work in training schools of many types and in their theological seminaries. These schools see themselves as centers of intellectual culture for the church while their major purpose is to develop church leadership on the professional level. At one time this leadership was exclusively pastoral; now the schools are providing for many types of specialized ministries such as educational staffing. They are also giving attention to continuing education for their graduates. A recent development is their service for what has been called, unfortunately, "lay theology." In general, the concept recognizes a ministry of all the "people of God." In particular, lay people with strong interests in religious study on a higher level attend classes provided by the staff of a college, seminary, or similar school.

A local church school executive will encourage students of his constituency to use the facilities of the higher institutions described above for their further Christian growth. He will also find places on his staff in which he can use the graduates of these schools to enhance the effectiveness of his church school's program. He will not fail to recruit for pastoral and other church leadership to attend the professional schools. He will follow with helpful interest all his people engaged in higher educational work.

CHAPTER XIX

ENLARGING THE PROGRAM (II)
VACATION AND WEEKDAY SCHOOLS
YOUTH AND ADULT GROUPS
(includes Confirmation Classes)

To provide more time—basically more effectual Christian educational opportunities—church school leaders can foster, we have seen, a larger program on Sunday, a home program and work within general education. Yet churches have developed numerous additional agencies, chiefly weekday ones although some overlap Sunday. Incidentally, weekdays have historically been the favored time for Christian education.

Two agencies have become, with the Sunday church school, a typical triad in many churches: the vacation church school and the weekday church school. These are usually conducted for children but youth and adult members have been reached through them. Further expansion, especially of weekday school work, offers an unusual opportunity.

VACATION CHURCH SCHOOLS

Vacation church schools are likely the most popular of all our educational agencies. Pupils and parents alike are enthusiastic about them when they are conducted in their proper style. The vacation church school movement is international in scope. In America we are approaching the time when ten millions of pupils will be attending each summer. A high percentage of churches conduct them; one church body found that 86 percent of its congregations include this agency in their total educational programs.

A vacation church school is a short term, concentrated effort during the summer months when public schools are not in session. Originating about the turn of the century, it was first called "The Vacation Bible School." The new name came as the general idea of a total church school gained recognition. At first the emphasis was specifically on Bible work.

Now the program is comprehensive, with features additional to the Bible emphasis although the Book continues to have a significant place. While the general objectives are the typical ones, these schools are meant to provide for enrichment beyond the central curriculum in the Sunday church school.

In earlier days a typical school would be conducted for five weeks. Now, unfortunately, the usual materials are published for only a two-week period although they can be expanded for three weeks. The commonly assigned reason for the reduction is shortage of qualified leadership for a longer term. A daily schedule is usually two and a half or three hours on a weekday morning, five days a week, starting soon after public schools close. Yet there is wide variation in scheduling. Successful experiments are reported with all-summer schools and with evening schools for the whole family.

Possibilities

Vacation church schools have unique possibilities. From the first, a major potential of vacation time was to be recognized: this is to be a more free and joyous type of Christian education appropriate to the season. This approach provides the ideal learning-teaching situation more nearly than other agencies. Here is an opportunity to luxuriate a bit in unusual themes and procedures. We have a block of at least two weeks with pupils meeting on successive days for several hours. These longer and consecutive daily sessions allow for continuing work with sustained effort. It is possible to conduct units that are more creative. There is time for activities that require more than one period to complete or cannot be spread easily over sessions a week apart. Because the schools are held in the summer time, they provide for an unusual variety of educational experiences; as an example, pupils can get around to unusual places on trips. Besides, everyday clothes and weekday time allow for activities not always suitable for Sunday. Usually, too, the out-of-doors can be a resource so that this kind of schooling offers some of the values of camping.

Very often children of the community will drop in, whether they belong to a particular church or not, and may remain in the church school membership. Many such pupils need this conservation of their time particularly if they live under crowded city conditions. The church can provide them with a place of quiet and fellowship where they will have worthwhile work instead of getting into trouble. The summer vacation is often a social, psychological, and moral problem for parents and pupils; the vacation church school can help. In the early days of vacation church schools there was frequent mention of idle churches serving idle children.

New leaders, as well as new pupils, are recruited for other church school agencies after vacation school closes. Besides, this work can be a laboratory for the development of creative leadership. Some who have worked in a stereotyped way in a Sunday church school find the new and informal ways of vacation church school comfortable and desirable. Pupils, too, have been initiated into more creative procedures.

Program

The program of a vacation church school includes the usual activities of study-and-instruction, worship, fellowship, and service within units of work in the typical learning areas: Bible, music, church, doctrine, Christian conduct. However, these schools have always stressed the more active enterprises: dramatics, creative writing, rhythmics, choral reading, and such things are common. Handwork, including various forms of crafts, has been featured from early days. Much emphasis is placed on recreation and learning through play. Service enterprises are favorites. The schools have special programs, most often a closing service planned by the pupils for their parents and other guests.

Curricular materials usually include a guide for the teacher, perhaps a reading book or workbook for the pupil, portions of activity material which are to be manufactured in handwork. Major denominations publish their own materials correlated with their other church school materials. Often the materials are made available in a cycle. One church body has adopted this sequence: first year, ten commandments; second year, Apostles' Creed; third year, Lord's Prayer. Another uses units centered around, respectively: God, Jesus Christ, the Church, and the Bible. The National Council of Churches fosters a series of co-operative texts especially for use in interdenominational schools. Their themes are widely varied so that almost any need can be met.

Organization and Administration

Many local churches conduct their own schools; others join neighboring churches in a community school. Each type has its advantages. In an individual church's school, the curriculum is more easily related to the rest of the church school program. More and better leaders can sometimes be secured from a community effort because of a larger pool from which to draw. In addition it is good for the pupils to work with friends from other churches; here is education for ecumenicity.

As in other educational agencies the quality of a vacation church school is determined largely by its leadership. Workers need to be recruited early so that they can get thoroughly familiar with the purposes, procedures, and materials. Denominations usually offer help through literature and conferences. Many councils of churches or denominational boards send teams into their areas to train prospective leaders through workshops for leaders of leaders or for all the workers.

Because a vacation church school should be managed as one unit in a total educational program, the committee on Christian education should be itself responsible for the administration, leadership, and general oversight. The budget is properly a part of the educational budget of the church. Pupils are usually grouped according to public school grades. Preschool children ought not be included unless churches have ample, skilled leadership and appropriate physical facilities.

WEEKDAY CHURCH SCHOOL WORK

The weekday church school is another major branch of the church school tree. These schools are of many kinds but two general types are community schools and congregational ones. The former may be denominational or interdenominational, sponsored by several or all the churches in the community; the latter type is sponsored by a single church. In many ways this is the preferable kind. When a congregation establishes its own school it can determine what shall be taught and how. Further, the pupils and staff can be built into their own church background. On the other hand there are values in the co-operative work that provides further education for ecumenicity. Sometimes, too, the broadly representative administrative body can accomplish more in community relations, especially with public school authorities.

Time

A major issue in weekday school work is the time to meet. There are three possibilities. Some schools, chiefly the congregational ones, are on *free time*. They meet after the public school day has closed—in the afternoon or evening, at night, or on Saturday. The sessions may last one hour, two, or more. There is no involvement at all with public education.

Two other types of weekday work are done in collaboration with public education. Under *dismissed time* all pupils of a given public school are excused from that school for some to attend church school classes while others are free. The dismissed period may be the first or last in the morning or afternoon. Details of dismissed time church school sessions will differ in the various churches of the community, or be decided by the churches in co-operation. A third type of weekday school, the one of which most people think, is conducted on *released time*.

Released Time Schools

In a released time school the children, by written request from their parents, are excused from public school at scheduled hours to attend classes in nearby churches or in other facilities provided by the churches. Pupils who do not attend weekday church school remain in their public school classrooms. Different grades may be released at different times of the day or on different days of the week. This makes it possible to use fewer teachers, sometimes professionally trained ones whose vocation is full time teaching of this sort.

HISTORY AND STATUS

Weekday church schools of the released time type are usually dated from 1914 when William Wirt, superintendent of the schools of Gary, Indiana, began to experiment with the plan. Statistics on the development are difficult to gather but several hundreds of systems have been established and they exist in most of the states. They have had their ups and downs. One difficulty is getting responsible and effective leaders; another is cost. Sometimes there has been a problem of housing or transporting the pupils.

The chief difficulties have been legal. That American principle of separation of church and state has often been interpreted stringently. A series of related legal cases in the 1940's, notably one which had been initiated by Mrs. McCollum in Champaign, Illinois, were carried to the United States Supreme Court. According to the decisions it is entirely proper for schools to release pupils, on the request of parents, to attend weekday church school sessions under the sponsorship of their churches. Such work, however, cannot be done in public school buildings and cannot make use of the public school system or its funds in any other way.

Continuity and support depend heavily upon the standards maintained in the schools. Public school boards have a right to expect high standards if they allow the plan to operate and there are systems where excellent work is being done. Many public school leaders are strong supporters of the weekday church school and welcome its contributions; others are less enthusiastic. The dissidents may belong to certain religious or antireligious groups who oppose it; often though, the opposition is based on the unsatisfactory quality of work. Even in favorable quarters, there has been some disenchantment. Both church and public educators have to lament such factors as limited time, substandard work and lack of wholehearted church support where such support is needed.

Weekday church schools of any type are usually closely graded and regularly follow a carefully planned curriculum with materials somewhat comparable to those used by the pupils in their public school classes. Quite opposite to the freer spirit in the program of the vacation church school the weekday church school is often more formal and school-like than either it or the Sunday church school. Study and instruction are stressed.

ORGANIZATION AND ADMINISTRATION

A local church weekday school will be under the general management of the congregation's church school committee. Released time programs are necessarily developed with express approval of the public school and most, if not all, the congregations in a community are required to support the program if permission is to be granted. Sometimes the work is done denominationally, but usually by interdenominational co-operation through ministerial associations or city councils of churches.

The key to any effective weekday church school, too, is leadership. It is best when professionally trained teachers for whom weekday church school teaching is a vocation are employed. Good work can be done when the staff is volunteer but with supervision, perhaps paid. Many local councils provide training opportunities if the work is done on a lay basis; these may include special conferences and workshops, retreats and in-service institutes as well as courses. Even so, supervision is essential to maintain a desirable quality of program.

For a released time school the budget should include supervisory and teaching costs, materials, transportation if required, and other necessary items, the budget being approved by the participating churches and underwritten by the congregations. Somewhat similar provisions should be made by congregations for the free time school.

Evaluation

Distinctive values claimed for weekday church schools, especially released time ones, include the following:

1. They provide an evangelistic opportunity. A considerable percentage of the pupils in these classes are without any other church connection at the beginning of the school year.
2. This is an opportunity for pupils to share religious experience across interdenominational lines. It should increase respect for the beliefs and values of others and lead pupils to accept the differences while evaluating them.
3. In excellent schools parents, pupils, ministers, and others testify to the amount of work that pupils accomplish.
4. These schools enable the church to include Christian teaching within the pupils' work week and have it closely related to his public learning-teaching program. They can give public school work a religious interpretation.

5. They reach a pupil in the group with which he associates during the five school days. Boys and girls can experience the strength that comes to each other as school friends receive the same Christian teaching.

Obviously such values depend upon the seriousness with which the schools are conducted. Only where the churches are willing to provide adequate and competent staff under a sufficient budget to do a quality of work reasonably comparable to that of the public school can their maintenance be justified.

YOUTH AND ADULT GROUPS

Work with youth and adults, far beyond Sunday church school classes alone, is both possible and important. The groups are thriving where there is an adequate program with wise leadership. Yet the typical provision for youth is inadequate and the country-wide program for adults is spotty, though improving. There are areas in the United States and Canada where, for at least a century, there have been strong adult Bible classes; in some areas there is even additional work. Elsewhere the program for adults is almost nil. Youth work has had more vigorous promotion with correspondingly greater response but there is still a long way to go.

The need for continuous Christian education is as insistent as for any form of education. Yet the church is far behind the general educational programs for youth and adults. Youth do drop out of public schools alarmingly but the church parallel is no less than catastrophic. At present the typical youth group includes only a fraction of the potential number in any given church. Soon, it is estimated, there will be twenty-five million teen-agers in the United States. What percentage will be in our churches? There is, to use a hackneyed phrase, an explosion of adult education throughout the world. It is said that more than ten million persons beyond the age of twenty-one are pursuing substantial programs of self-education in America. How many of these are in our church school work and, comparatively, how vigorous is the program?

Youth Work

A major activity of any church school leader can be his service for youth. There are the irreligious and unreached ones who constitute a challenge to an evangelistic ministry which may reach them through educational channels. Others are caught in the conditions of which we hear so much: delinquency, early marriage, unemployment for the unskilled and uneducated; dropping out of school. There is equal need among the many more who are idealistic, dedicated, and capable. Too often they have been kept on relatively infantile levels in the church school until they are lost to it if not to the church. They need work in which they can stretch their minds and cultivate their highest talents for the kingdom of God. Urgent, too, is occupational guidance that will turn some of them into church or closely related vocations. The fact that such needs are being recognized is evidenced by the employment of a growing number of "directors of youth work." However, there is little more than a beginning at what needs to be done.

FELLOWSHIPS

Educational work for youth, beyond the Sunday church school program, has been carried on largely by special youth agencies. These may be dated from the inauguration of Christian Endeavor societies, interdenominational in character, beginning in 1881. There followed a long era of denominational leagues, such as the Methodists' Epworth League; these are still maintained in a few denominations. Sometimes they are treated as "auxiliaries" or "arms" of the church program; they should be merged into the mainstream of the total church enterprise.

Most denominations, beginning in the 1940's, have accomplished this goal and now have youth fellowships. A fellowship may engage in a systematic curricular program of Sunday, vacation, and weekday church school sessions as well as other typical Sunday meetings of youth. The same groups may have a wide variety of special weekday enterprises. This kind of program reduces the tendency to graduate out of Sunday church school while it enlarges the total opportunity. Ideally there will be three groups: junior high, senior high, and post-high school.

PURPOSE

Objectives need serious attention throughout all youth work. Many psychologists believe that adolescence is characterized chiefly by the young person's dual striving for identity and for independence. This gives us our purpose: to help them (1) realize a true identity within their Christian relations to God and to man, and (2) gain an authentic independence by a Christian sense of responsibility rather than a pseudo-independence through rebellion—self-realization under Christian guidance.

If the church is being viewed as the continuous ministry of Jesus Christ, a church school leader's vision for his youth work could well be "the youth ministry of this church." This would mean that the young people themselves, to the limit of their capacity, are participating in the church's ministry. Not merely being served by adults, they are, in collaboration with adults and one another, sharing meaningfully in their own nurture through living churchmanship. This program would put the accent on opportunities to build oneself into the full life of a church along with maturing experiences in the world-wide thrust of its mission.

PROGRAM

The new youth program, consequently, would be perhaps threefold. It would permit youth to participate in that ongoing life of the congregation as responsible members of the total community of faith; it would also provide for an intimate special group of their own age mates to increase their discipleship and apostlehood. At appropriate times, that total youth group would become several small groups or cells to pursue some chosen enterprise. Finally, they could still participate in the big three—Sunday, weekday, and vacation schools, along with the home program.

A major problem with youth in the churches after confirmation or similar acceptance into a complete membership is to find some way of letting them have, indeed, the fullest possible participation in church enterprise. Service projects need particular attention. These can be within the congregation itself, within the home, family, or community. Particularly important opportunities at this point may be found in city or other youth councils where the youth have guidance for interdenominational activity. Extensions beyond the local community program elicit vital interest of youth; many volunteer service projects are possible: caravaning, tours, seminars, and work camps. Youth, and they must be commended, have made financial contributions to youth projects on a world-wide mission basis. They can help personally to build the one world, the ecumenical world, in which they will live.

Worship observances, too, are a significant phase of youth work. Best worship for youth in their special agencies would be informal. It should be conducted on the age group level and be in charge of the young people themselves except with advisement. No one has ever fully experienced the total meaning of worship who has not helped to plan and conduct it. There is a rich treasury of resources to make worship varied and meaningful though these are insufficiently known and used.

Social fellowship is to so great a degree the life of youth. Possibly the future development of increased leisure—although many youngsters have a superfluity of it now—will demand even more attention to this factor. Here, too, resources are available for new and more wholesome types. Finally, there are surpassingly rich and rewarding possibilities for typical study-and-instruction. Even more emphasis can be put on this phase of a total program. But churches must catch up with the development of youth; there is more intellectual maturity under current conditions than we have realized and provided for. Churches must also strive to match the procedures and materials to which youth are accustomed.

APPROACH

A key consideration in work with any youth group is the manner of approach. Youth cannot be expected to work in procedures of a bygone age. They require an opportunity to work with their own minds, mouths, feelings, feet, and hands without too much intervention by adults. Adult counselors and advisors are properly resource persons and as such are needed. Yet the young people themselves should be in charge of their programs to the fullest extent possible, even with some allowance for learning by the mistakes they make.

As for the leader himself, he is not to be a dominating teacher. Ours is not the day of "you sit still and listen to what I have to say; let me do the talking." Among the specific methods to be used, there can be a limited amount of telling, along with question and answer and similar procedures which characterized an older day. However, there must be more of the new and dynamic type: report and research, display, class trip, service project, discussion, panel, forum, buzz group, musical and dramatic event, worship service, recreational affair. In all of these the youth themselves will be allowed as much self-determination and self-management as possible.

The ideal for a youth group "at its best" has been admirably described:

> Sometimes it can truly be said that in the youth group, the authentic Christian life was being lived in experience, that the koinonia existed, that evangelistic outreach and social action concerns were pursued, that honest questions of faith and belief were discussed, that challenges to vocation and mission were present, that high discipleship was evident. In short, this youth group even now expresses the high hopes of good churmanship. . . .[1]

Adult Work

We cannot have a strong program for children and youth in the midst of an untutored and nonparticipating adulthood. Besides, there are the adults' own needs for continuing Christian education; growth in grace must be a lifelong process, and it can be fostered from beginning to end. For such reasons the churches are pushing their adult agencies, beginning with the Sunday church school but spilling over into the weekday.

PROGRAMS

We have had several special agencies, notably women's missionary societies and men's brotherhoods, but none reached anything like the potential constituencies. Some have been reconstituted as more compre-

[1] Henry N. Tani, "Youth Groups," in *The Westminster Dictionary of Christian Education*, ed. Kendig Brubaker Cully (Philadelphia: Westminster Press, 1963), p. 741.

hensive organizations; for example, there are denominational and local women's and men's groups. Increasingly such agencies are becoming involved in the total mission of the church with all those six works of education, evangelism, fellowship, merciful ministry, stewardship, and worship. By these means the educational possibilities for adults have been expanded though certainly not exhausted. Adults still need specific church schooling.

For adults as for everybody else, education is most effective at the point of individual need. Adult needs are widely varied. As one point of differentiation, their time schedules are complex. Interests change and diversify as persons grow older. In a wide span of ages and comprehensive accumulation of experience known as adulthood the variety of concerns will naturally be marked. Differences and similarities of academic level and vocational background cannot be ignored. All such factors make flexibility and variety of educational opportunity essential as to topic, agency, procedure, and schedule.

Churches are providing for this extreme diversification as to time and place. Groups meet when they can and wherever it is convenient—home, office, shop, school, church, camp, retreat center, or elsewhere. A course may last over a weekend or over a year. The group may be permanent or not. Specific age may have nothing particularly to do with it; interest will determine the objectives and structure more largely. The work continues in the typical agencies but there is movement toward free-floating small groups that are self-initiated and self-liquidating.

APPROACH

The former procedures in adult groups had become too stereotyped.

In many classes the adult had been only a spectator who heard (?) a lecture. Now, in adult work too, we recognize that learning requires involvement. Although there is a time to listen, too much of what may be listening is only that. A dissertation by the teacher may result in no growth or less than growth, just a further settling back. Provisions for adults now, as for youth, favor self-determination for the educational work and self-management of it under competent help if, where, and when needed. Elective courses, cell groups, short-term courses, high-level camping, conference and retreat experiences are recommended.

While the denominations provide basic materials in their new curricular programs they are stressing the provision of elective guides. A group can find guidance in denominational and interdenominational resource materials for the widest varieties of concern. Indeed a group may not need typical printed matter; it may originate its topic, plan its units, locate or develop its own materials. It may lead itself with its own personnel.

A notable development on the adult level is the counterpart of the justly famed lay academies in Europe. A typical lay academy, or its substitute, is a program held at some stated center where, for example, a group of doctors, lawyers, teachers, or other professionals will gather perhaps in large numbers for a considerable period of time to think about and discuss their religious profession in relation to their vocation. Another interesting development recently is a program of "lay theology" classes conducted in connection with a Christian college or theological seminary (see Chap. XVIII).

EDUCATIONAL MINISTRY TO AND BY OLDER ADULTS

Increasing numbers of senior citizens are joining the ranks daily as candidates for our programs. Chronological age is a poor measure of capability to grow through Christian education, also to make a contribution to Christian education. To make later years helpful, satisfying, and meaningful, we dare not wait for crises in health and welfare. Starting early, education for aging, about aging, and through aging should be prominent concerns. Later, programs of study-and-instruction, worship, fellowship, and service can be expanded instead of contracted as too often happens. The aging have spiritual problems, also time and willingness to work with them if churches provide the facilities in groups, books, and leaders. Moreover we are thinking now not only about service to older adults but also about the reservoir of skill, experience, and time that can be tapped for a variety of voluntary services to others. We can conserve, develop, and utilize the talents of these people while providing a ministry to the persons themselves.

A NEW DAY

In the new curriculum designs of the denominations, adults are offered new means for continuing maturity in their Christian faith-living. The United Church of Christ will emphasize the values of smaller groups in an informal adult curriculum. This denomination's "auxiliary" men's brotherhoods and women's guilds are being replaced by a "ministry of lay work and lay life." The purpose is to co-ordinate all adult study and work of the congregation. In the American Baptist Convention adult classes are urged to use discussion rather than lecture with the teachers serving only as moderator and resource person. The lecture method is to be used only for the sharing and summarizing of pertinent information. In the Lutheran Church of America's curriculum there are to be new dimensions in Bible study. The Sunday church school will provide basic educational experience in all areas of faith and life. Some of these courses are fundamental surveys but these are supplemented by a wide variety of elective courses which will provide for special interest groups. The church's encounter with communism and the rise of the ecumenical movement are examples of current developments for which study provisions are made. Yet the new curriculums include weekday programs of adult study. Provision has been made for (1) short-term study courses of six to ten sessions; (2) weekend workshops, conferences, and retreats; (3) a guided reading program; (4) informal fellowship and study groups.

CONFIRMATION, COMMUNICANTS', MEMBERSHIP OR PASTOR'S CLASSES

An ancient form of Christian education, now increasingly emphasized, is that phase of a total program, usually a weekday enterprise, which is often called catechetical instruction—better, confirmation class work—or equivalent. With a bit of imagination it can be said that Jesus was the first catechist, his disciples the first pupils. For a few centuries after Christ the early church provided a catechumenate largely for adults; following the Reformation chief attention was given to such work with the young.

The Current Situation

In churches having Calvinistic or Lutheran backgrounds confirmation class work has been a tradition from the beginning and confirmation is often a requisite for "complete membership." Typically it is a pastoral teaching responsibility, largely for high school youths but also for adults. The practice is world-wide; it gets one common designation from the use of a catechism as a major resource with confirmation as its conclusion.

DEFINITION

Attitudes and procedures are quite varied because of differences among the churches. The meaning and manner of evangelism, the understanding of the sacraments and the customs as to their use, the relation of confirmation to baptism—these and other issues have important bearings. A spate of related problems is being freshly studied: the desirable age for confirmation, the meaning of the rite, its relation to fully active church membership especially admission to holy communion, its relation to baptism and conversion, the amount of study desirable and what should be included in it, basic standards to be enforced, relations with a total educational program.

Charles U. Harris in Cully has given us this definition of confirmation: *"Thus we understand confirmation today as providing the person who had been baptized as an infant with the opportunity to make, under the guidance of the Holy Spirit, the conscious response of repentance and faith, of renunciation and obedience."*[2] A pupil's work, leading up to this rite, will properly be an intensified period of Christian experience that is meant to be specially efficacious in growth for his present and future church membership. Its basic standard of effectiveness would be the assurance that the confirmand has grown in his appropriation of the saving grace of God in Jesus Christ. He should have become unquestionably a disciple and an apostle. The content of the work can include whatever is possible of doctrine and morals, worship, the scriptures, church history, and church work. Much of this can be included in careful use of a catechism but would involve use of many other materials.

TRENDS

Often the class sessions have been largely exercises in memorizing a catechism. There are significant trends in current practice:

1. More time given to it—at least a year but not uncommonly two or three years.
2. Employment of newer educational goals and procedures. The effort is not so much to secure quotation of the verbiage as to provide realistic experiences in units of learning.
3. Recognition of individual needs of pupils; the work is meant to be relevant.
4. Concern for doctrine but also for broader interests that include a more complete set of objectives for the whole pupil's full round of Christian relationships.
5. Conducted, in some churches, as a component in the whole program of a complete church school. For example, the confirmation classes may be part of the parish weekday church school's curriculum.

Resource materials are getting serious attention also. New aids for the work are appearing within the flurry of revised curricular materials for other phases of educational work. These do not exclude the catechism but they usually include much more and employ the ancient book as only one of many resources. These are not necessarily outmoded by the approach described below. They can be adopted texts while that general procedure is kept in mind.

A Developmental Approach

The basic debates about theory and procedure center in the usual question of traditional or developmental education; shall it stress general

[2]Charles U. Harris, "The Anglican Understanding of Confirmation," in *Confirmation: History, Doctrine and Practice*, ed. Kendig Brubaker Cully (Greenwich, Connecticut: The Seabury Press, 1962), p. 30.

indoctrination or personal learning with growth at major points of need? Increasingly the answer is in the developmental direction. As usual, textbooks, including catechisms, will be used adaptably as resource materials, not followed to the letter.

The following outline describes the developmental possibility that is in some cases an actuality:

1. Have your aim(s) clearly in mind. Understand that you are guiding a unit of pupil activity that has in view the confirmation experience and subsequent fuller membership of Christian persons in the church.
2. Know your pupils from friendly, previous contacts. Have some estimate of their present status as to faith and conduct, also their capabilities for growth.
3. Hold an opening session in an informal setting where you and the pupils discover the most urgent, substantial concern of the majority at some point relevant to the general purpose.
4. Start working at that particular concern, whatever it is.
5. In working at the first concern you will discover the next to be undertaken—and so forth.
6. Strive always to keep your status as helper while the pupils themselves work for their growth as individuals and group.
7. As pupils and teacher, use various procedures and various resources of catechism, other books, audile and visual aids, and the like.
8. Sometimes the group may be divided to pursue particular concerns as individuals and small groups—the findings to be shared with the whole class.
9. There may be a time when you will ask the pupils to come along with you into some study which had not occurred to them as being important. As they trust and follow, you will lead them into additional values.
10. You know the catechism or other guides and the areas for consideration. You can do a certain amount of steering into them, also putting things into necessary sequences so that the essentials, at least the major concerns of the pupils, will have been covered. If certain items important to you have not been treated, you probably could not have secured much learning even if you had "dragged in" those things.
11. Do not miss any opportunity to integrate the pupils into complete membership which includes Christian action as well as belief—a totality of knowledge, attitudes, and action patterns.
12. As for memorization, it is "a desirable way of enriching the life of the pupil when it is done on the basis of the learner's appreciation and sense of utility."

Adult Program

Adult confirmation or other means of inducting the newly evangelized into the church membership presents unusual difficulties. Class work requires willingness on the part of the candidates and a meeting time possible for the pastor as well as the people. In many churches very little attention is given to this and only a declaration of faith is required. There are pastors, however, who have managed a program extending over a considerable period of time; not a small number would insist upon at least a half dozen sessions. The subjects of those sessions will vary according to the individuals' concerns and the emphases a pastor chooses. If the pastor is able to gather the people into such a class there are advantages in their having been in their new-found fellowship, reflecting together about these matters of their divine and human relationships. However, in many cases, it will be necessary to have the instruction on a completely individual basis. This is not entirely to be lamented because people's obvious needs can receive more specific attention.

CHAPTER XX

ENLARGING THE PROGRAM (III)
CAMPS: MASS AGENCIES
UNUSUAL MINISTRIES

Still other means are available to provide more time for a more adequate program of Christian education.

CAMPS, CONFERENCES, AND RETREATS

Campsites, which may be also conference and retreat centers, have added a new wing to typical church school plants.

Camping

The camping idea is as old as human life. The Judaeo-Christian story begins, in a way, with Abraham's encampments. An organized camping movement for Christian education is usually ascribed to the first quarter of this century. A dramatic expansion with tens of millions now invested in property has occurred in the decades since that time. The idea of providing Christian education in camps now encompasses the globe.

All the varieties of camping could scarcely be listed. Camps are conducted for families or for children, youth, and adults alone. They have been held for boys or girls singly although the value of coeducational camping is being explored. Along with the typical resident camping there are day camps with children going home at night.

Special interest groups use camps for art, drama, and music enterprises. There are leadership development camps on many levels. Youth travel all over the world for work camping. These create communities of understanding through shared labor for reclamation, rehabilitation, and construction across racial, cultural, and religious boundaries after the manner of the Peace Corps. Some camp equipment is being winterized so that a wide variety of events can be scheduled across the entire calendar.

ORGANIZATION AND ADMINISTRATION

Camps are typically organized according to age group programs, the property being used successively for one or two weeks by first one age group and then another. The basic administrative staff may remain the same throughout; teachers and counselors will change from period to period so as to fit best for each of the age groups or major purposes.

"Small group" camping is an important trend now. It refers to a program for perhaps a dozen boys and girls with two leaders, preferably a man and a woman. The plan is to provide an opportunity for each individual to find his place in a unit which includes his peers on a coeducational basis. The members eat together, work together, worship together, study together, serve together and, it may be, suffer together. Thus each small group in the camp is responsible for planning and conducting its own life although it needs to co-ordinate with the other groups.

Procedures attempt to bring about maximum conditions for Christian learning and teaching in relation to day by day living situations. There are frank discussions—perhaps in the evening—about the things that have happened to individuals and the social relationships that have developed during the day; the emphasis is on matters related to spiritual development of individuals. A significant result is to be an increase of responsibility for one's own actions and for others in the total group context.

To facilitate this small group experience in Christian living, buildings are often now scattered widely over a larger area, radiating from a central administrative structure. An effective operation demands unusual leadership. Careful selection, preparation, training, guidance, and supervision of leadership are needed for all camp enterprises but especially here.

PROGRAMS

Possibly because camping has grown so fast, the churches are only now developing adequate philosophies of Christian education through church camping. Too often the program has been a somewhat hectic combination of religious schooling with an emphasis on recreation after the manner of a recreational camp. At its best it should be a guided experience of living out-of-doors in a corner of a Christian community, somewhat isolated and specialized, and there learning to live in Christian ways for the return into typical life situations.

Churches are trying to actualize the unique values for Christian growth that camping, with a fuller and freer life on an unhurried schedule, with nature as a resource, can afford. Camping programs offer a variety of activities especially suited to informal life in the open: exploration, trips, campfires, cabin devotions, dramatics, music, fun events, games, and swimming. Leadership education is a motif in many camping programs; the church looks to the time when these young people with these special opportunities will become leaders in educational and other work at home.

Good camping programs stress full group participation on the part of the campers. Leaders strive to allow an individual his freedom to take responsibility for himself on his own initiative while they seek to develop his responsibility within and for group life. Relationship to "nature and nature's God" is the unique thing—highly significant in our urbanizing age. Yet still greater effort must be made to prepare those who take groups into the out-of-doors so that they can help their wards better to interpret whatever happens in the light of religious values.

Conferences and Retreats

Conferences and retreats are often held at campsites; college and seminary campuses too are increasingly used. Special sites, purchased particularly for retreats, are becoming common.

There is likely no such thing as a typical conference. However, we may think of a weekend or week in which a group, relatively small, meets for concentrated consideration of some issue. Closely related, we have a wide variety of programs such as conventions, institutions, workshops, seminars, and laboratories that partake of the conference idea and are often held at similar sites. New curricular designs provide for more of these.

Retreats are often places and programs that emphasize withdrawal from ordinary circumstances in order to cultivate the Christian inner spirit. For such a purpose there is high value in the out-of-door setting with its isolation from the typical stresses of living. Programs may emphasize an opportunity for solitude but also for association with a select company of likeminded persons. The term retreat is also applied to a planning enterprise, where, for example, a church school staff or youth leadership group will spend a weekend at a center where they may think through their program for the coming year with its objectives and procedures.

The Future

Use of the out-of-doors for the program of Christian education will likely proceed with an increasing degree of acceleration. The church has only begun to discover the educational use of a natural setting in the full sense of the word and on a wide scale. This is especially important in learning to appreciate the creative activity of God and our place within it. Families, children, youth groups, men's groups, and women's groups will make more use of the summer for such purposes. The shortened work week, also the hot and crowded city in summertime, along with the wholesome desire of many people to get their feet on the ground, are factors that will impel further development. Groups will increasingly find experiences here that will add another dimension to their lives.

Local Church School Relationships

Because all these and related agencies are extraordinary new opportunities for effective Christian education, the wise church school leader will foster attendance and himself seek to participate. In addition he needs to recognize what has happened to the members of his constituency who have attended. Too often the return to a stereotyped program after an exalted experience in camp has had a disillusioning effect on the church school member. In particular, high school youth who have been fired with enthusiasm for service may find no outlet in the home church. Those who have glimpsed new ways of procedure at camp find the old ways of the home church unattractive. Maturity of personality gained at a camp conference or retreat can regress unless the person who had attended one of these uplifting experiences can continue his growth from the level attained.

Leaders who plan camping experiences, conferences, or retreat programs, need to give them the most careful attention. Good experiences do not merely happen; poorly planned ones can turn into harm. The success of these ventures like all other educational ones, depends so very much on the quality of leadership, and adequate leadership is not easy to find. The churches, let it be repeated, have a primary task in the development of such leadership.

MASS AGENCIES FOR CHRISTIAN EDUCATION

Among the resources for Christian education our learners and our leaders including parents can employ, several may be termed mass agencies. These include resources provided on the air, through the arts, and by the press. Again it will be seen that while some of these are ancient agencies, others are extraordinary inventions of this century. All demand attention under current conditions; they will likely become even more significant.

We shall think about them chiefly as they reach people broadly addressed, touching a casual, changing throng here and there, now and then. Usually they are not employed by particular groups "gathered" in a school, classroom, or family circle. Yet they may be utilized there in one way or another; they may be drawn into, for example, a Sunday church school program.

Despite any evanescent character, these mediums shape people's thought patterns, have potential to change attitudes or revise value systems, and may impel conduct. As they affect basic reactions they are either a threat to Christian nurture, or an opportunity for it. While their motivation is often commercial, this is not the whole truth. Intentionally or not they have moral and religious significance; sometimes it is intentional. If they are not directly used, at least they dare not be ignored.

Resources on the Air

Radio and television have become vast purveyors of fact and fancy; some of it can be helpful when properly ministered. This possibility has not been adequately exploited by the churches. Such resources can enter the lives of Christians and non-Christians for good but not necessarily "just naturally." Guidance is needed. Commercial broadcasts and telecasts are now an awesome aspect of our peoples' culture; we must determine whether they are used productively or not.

The great networks, while so much they offer is trivial or worse, have programs that can be made profitable: reportage of historical events, serious drama, music, discussion, panel, and documentary. Now, too, the country is being blanketed with "educational television." The churches, through their national bodies and state or national councils, also in other and sometimes irregular ways, are reaching the millions with their own broadcasts and telecasts. These purvey religious news, devotional and church worship services, children's programs, evangelistic appeals, lessons —even Sunday school lessons by air and university courses, special events of musical, dramatic, and informational character. The hundreds of local, low wattage radio stations and an increasing number of local television units provide for canned or live programs in religion.

What can be accomplished toward our Christian objectives by all this medley? For one thing, there can be an undreamed of "horizontal spread of the gospel." Second, no small contribution can be an introduction to "one world." Third, we meet our brothers, Christian and otherwise, far and near.

What can be done specifically to put this tremendous asset really to work for Christian education? The enterprise is so vast, and the research as yet is so unconvincing, that we scarcely know the precise answers but we can begin to dig in.

Christian educators can first of all be aware of need to get in on the act with an everlasting alertness about objectives to be served. The least that can be expected of a church school leader is knowledge of the extent to which the air is affecting vocabularies, interests, value judgments, customs, and modes of living. We cannot know our people unless we recognize the forceful contacts being made by these communication mediums.

Perhaps we have paid too much attention to efforts at production and not enough to the consumption end of things. Yet production should not be neglected. Our greatest educational opportunity is in the local production where children, youth, adults, or congregational and community groups provide programs, for example, of drama and music. The radio ministry can be overshadowed by the spectacular appeal of television. We still need radio and should use it, particularly on local stations. Television requires technique and cost beyond ecclesiastical resources except in limited quantities. Besides the churches are only learning the what and how. In any production, quality of substance and finish in the production are requisite. The air is too full already of what is cheap in both dimensions.

Most directly, church school leaders can foster the hearing and seeing of what is best. The air can be one of the resources used in classroom and at home if people are guided by bulletins or other announcements for the best to see and hear during the week. As another service, the church school can provide situations in which people can think together about what they have heard or seen and finally act out in real life the good impulses that may have been generated. A principal lack with regard to both radio and television is involvement. When a listener has only heard and the viewer has only seen, education may or may not have taken place. The church can sometimes supply the involvement.

The Arts

The arts are not ordinarily classified as mass mediums of communication but in no small sense, and increasingly, they are. They are not only becoming more broadly available to the masses but their mass appeal is growing. More and more of our church people participate in production as well as consumption.

We shall mention five particular arts: architecture, especially the great churches; literature, especially drama and meaning mostly in the theater; the motion picture as it appears on the public screen; music, in the churches but especially in concert halls; pictures as a general title for what is graphic in painting, sculpture, and symbols, as used in the churches but especially as shown in galleries.

The arts have been long in the service of the church. They allow persons to speak and hear the message of the church in another way and they allow educators through this medium to help guide, stimulate, and empower our people as they live and grow as Christians. The church school leader can foster their use in the two ways that may be called consumption and production. He will foster use of the arts outside the local program and provide for interpretation of them. He will help to provide items for use in the local program itself and see that they are wisely employed. He can encourage creative production that will favor learning through artistic expression and through the preparation required for that expression. In turn these items can be useful for the education of those who view them as well as those who participate in their rendition.

Architecture. The architecture of the church with its accompaniments of decor, altars, paraments, vestments, vessels, and the more utilitarian articles with their frequent use of symbols, offers high teaching values often overlooked unless educational exercises give attention to them. Religion has been built into our ecclesiastical structures and their equipment. We need to help people become aware of it and let it serve them. The great cathedrals and basilicas or historic structures and contemporary experiments, seen actually or in pictures, have a role to play.

Literature. Literature, especially drama, has long served the church school program directly. Our pupils can go far beyond pageantry and puppetry or informal dramatization and role-playing though these can be significant educational agents. The many possibilities include the reading and writing of literary drama, viewing and discussing stage productions, planning and producing plays in the local church and community.

Here, though, we are thinking chiefly of the more indirect services. Much of what appears on the stage is negative. Disregarding the worst, there is a current treatment of the hopelessness of the sin-tossed and unbelieving. The subject cannot be left there; this emphasis needs turning into a positive meaning. However, now and then there are plays with a positive religious significance. Numerous dramatic works have, for example, biblical references as their themes; they often are working out basic problems of dogmatic or ethical problems. At the least, the church can be a sort of stage on which people can give attention to current dramas in one way or another.

Concerning literature other than drama, our people need help to choose and use what is worthy while they shun the wasteful or worse. The church school can help them to develop standards, also to hear or read what can be adjuncts for educational experience. Contemporary novels have been a center around which groups have held interesting study groups. Creative writing, even on a very amateur basis—biography, fiction, or poetry are examples—is a fruitful exercise that can advance Christian growth towards maturity for those interested.

Motion Pictures. We have not been utilizing fully the motion picture resources of specifically religious nature available for our purposes. Indeed, we have fallen far behind general education in both production and usage. Here, however, we are thinking mainly still about the relation of the public theater and its films as resources for our purposes. There is so much froth and worse. Nevertheless, again we can think about the possibilities of guiding our people to what is good—of which there is some—and helping them see anything good in what may be available, even while we strive to counteract any deleterious influences. Class studies and special discussion groups are indicated.

Music. Religious music and education concerning it are a major phase of a total educational program. More of this emphasis is built into our newer curricular literature where there are related units of many types. Always, too, provision is made for an abundance of music in worship. We are blessed by the new equipment in records and tapes.

There is room for still more emphasis on music as an educational resource and it need not be necessarily music that is specifically religious. Happily, music, religiously oriented or not, is an increasing part of our culture and our young people are being brought up to appreciate and participate in it. Production, preparation, rendition, or appreciation alone in the church or in the home, by air and by recordings as well as personal performance, can advance our Christian educational purposes.

Choirs have special value. The church school leader can foster those groups of adults, youth, or children whose first responsibility is to lead the congregation or its parts in corporate worship. The interest can include public school choirs, community choirs, college choirs, who render the larger and greater musical compositions such as oratorios. There can be informal music groups for listening to recordings and for related study.

All great music has power for spiritual uplift. Too often attention is given to music for music's sake, for sentiment, or for outward effect, not for growth. We can lead toward such appreciation for it while we are interested primarily in its value for knowledge, feeling, and action.

Pictures. Pictures and related forms of art such as sculpture, also long used in religious education, have possibilities not always realized for their fullest value. Coloring within the lines of an outline or the back of a leaflet is scarcely the acme! Trips to galleries to see the great or less great masterpieces can be richly rewarding. Churches and homes can provide copies of these silent teachers; books of great art that is beautifully reproduced can be available in church or home library. Public school experience can be laid tribute.

Newer curricular literature is using choice artistry. This is not meant merely to make books attractive; it is to be studied and appreciated for its meaningful influence. Recent emphases and practices around the world are enabling leaders to see the significance of created pictures, especially those produced by children. These are revealing beyond measure as to what children are gaining from other forms of learning. Even little children show unexpected insight into what religion means to them and what human relationships ought to be. Such results need to be further cultivated toward a harvest in Christian education.

The Press

In listing and evaluating agencies for Christian education the extremely significant place of Christian publication is often overlooked. Not to be forgotten, the Bible itself—best seller of all—is a product of the religious press. There are scores of denominational and interdenominational houses. The tons of literature their presses grind out annually find numerous readers but not nearly enough. A perusal of the seasonal catalogs distributed by the publishing houses and religious bookstores, of which there are hundreds, will convey some idea of the volume as well as variety of Christian publications: theology, history, biography, fiction, poetry, devotional helps, and others. There are also the weekly, monthly, and quarterly periodicals besides pamphlets and tracts of almost every description.

On material specifically for Christian education the production reaches the volume of trainloads. Publication of curricular materials particularly has assumed mammoth proportions in the recent revisions of curricula. Publishing houses have outdone themselves to produce books instead of quarterly pamphlets. Many of these are of the highest quality according to all standards, for instance with regard to the art work. The literature for church school leadership is notable. If we are to have the better results that we need, the church school executive will see that all such books and periodicals are provided and that they get used by the individuals who need them.

In general, too many Americans are not reading, although the reading habit is growing. Also, what people read has increasing significance as people become more and more highly educated. The printed page has advantages over the oral message. It is permanent, it may be read again and again, revitalized with each reading. The printed page safeguards the content whereas oral messages are often misquoted. Printing encourages a private perusal. Finally, the reader becomes involved, he does not merely sit while his teacher is working.

There is a negative side of the coin. Much that the general press produces is not wholesome. Daily newspapers may have psychological coloration; cartoons may be loaded with propaganda; outstanding magazines may be of high quality but the newsstands are laden with things that are profoundly questionable. It is particularly difficult to find good literature in current fiction. When so much that appears in print is detrimental, the church school leader needs to help all his people be wary; a particular responsibility is to help youth shun what is bad.

On the other side of the coin there is good journalism in both books and periodicals. The constructive use of the good will be the emphasis throughout. We do have wholesome fiction and nonfiction books, instructive weekly and monthly periodicals. All these can be a significant resource for Christian education programs. Many will not be read unless arrangements can be made to have them readily available and publicized.

While people need guidance with regard to all their reading, we need to make special provision for them to read in the field of religion more broadly and deeply. The particular attention of the church school leader can be given to the great volume of publications by the religious presses and the religious publications by the responsible, commercial publishers. The vast number of religious books covers almost any conceivable theme; more and more of them are coming in less expensive paperback editions and deserve wide usage. A church library can be well stocked and the leader can promote its use. He can help the denominational journals, now improved in quality, to get more comprehensive circulation.

UNUSUAL MINISTRIES

Church schools that are serious about enlarging their programs may find their richest opportunities in new ministries for persons and groups that are still waiting for someone to serve them. Each school should review its entire constituency, both on its rolls and in its community. How many neglected or forgotten persons and groups are there? Where is there something to do, or more to do, for them? Where can they be served in the present or possible program, or what special provision can be made to carry the program to them?

The Aging and the Aged

In an average congregation more than 10 percent of the people are over sixty-five; it is expected that there will be twenty millions of these persons in 1975. Some have been lifelong members of the church and are still active in it. Many are unevangelized; church school attention might be a route into the church. All are subject to emotional problems that go with retirement, loss of income, changing relations with family, meaning of life, what to do with time.

The best services that can be rendered any older adults will be those which enable them to remain as long and fully as possible within the fellowship of the regular church school work. The more active can have special classes in Sunday church school or they may be candidates for weekday work. There can be informal, special interest groups at the church or in homes; some may have been waiting for an opportunity to make advanced studies in religion. But some are "shut-ins" or "shut-outs," confined to homes or institutions; congregations should have home departments to minister to these types. Still other aging and aged will live in residential centers where church school classes can be set up. The fellowship phase can be a prime factor in a program. We have already noticed that no small number of this group are available for useful services in the church and especially to their own type.

The Culturally Different

No church member is to be considered basically better than another; yet there are genuine differences. Economic background is significant; so is origin, rural or urban. Some of the church school population will be more sophisticated than others; there may be profound differences in schooling. Some congregations have a heavy proportion of professional people while others include many unskilled or skilled laborers.

While the mingling of these varied types in a church school can be wholesome, special attention must be paid to the several segments. It is important that teachers recognize the differences and make sure that each can learn for himself in accord with his need and capacity while he helps others learn about his experiences and points of view. There can be elective courses for specialization in particular needs. The school can, in some cases, house a special ministry for a particular type. At the same time there can be a rich sharing of heritages in study; fellowship and worship across the lines can be enriching; service enterprises can use varied talents.

The Gifted and the Retarded

In a typical church school membership a considerable number are "exceptional," either gifted or retarded persons.

Out of a hundred pupils several will have potentialities that justify calling them gifted. There are variations in gifts: intellectual ability, creative thinking, scientific outlook, social leadership, mechanical skills, artistic talent. Some have been termed "blotter" or "problem-solver" or "creative" types. There must be a degree of different planning and procedure for each to realize his full potentiality.

In a way these persons are extremely fortunate yet they do have special needs. Because they learn faster, understand more, and have wider interests, they may be rejected by their peers and this can be particularly distressing to, for example, the adolescent. They raise religious questions two or three years earlier than others of their age and the questions may be more profound. So they may find the typical church school work dull and unchallenging; they often become an embarrassment to their teachers. They may obstruct ongoing work.

The church school should remember that when their needs are met these persons can make a greater contribution as disciples and apostles than other people. Further, the school must recognize their problems lest it harm them. History records too many brilliant men and women who lacked a sense of responsibility to the common good and had little use for the church.

There are three general ways of helping: special groupings for the gifted, scholastic acceleration, enrichment in the regular classes. Larger schools can have teachers of brighter sections. The gifted can be advanced a grade or two but not too rapidly lest they become socially maladjusted. It is better to supplement their work on their own grade level and give them leadership opportunities. Some materials may be omitted and others supplanted or substituted. They can make special use of the library, do creative tasks in which their special talents can be employed; they can make more use of the community resources for the common good. In some cases pupils with special talents can help with the normal groups.

Estimates of the number of retarded persons in the United States vary but there are a few millions. A distinction needs to be made between the merely slow learner and the more severe cases with mental deficiency. Too often, the seriously retarded have been kept behind closed doors but a new day has begun; a number of congregations or groups of congregations are pioneering for these unfortunates.

All the retarded need to understand themselves, to understand others, and find their places in life. All have the usual needs to be accepted, to be loved, to belong, to have some sense of accomplishment and recognition. The church school faces four problems: (1) to secure an acceptance of the group in the regular school when possible; (2) to find sympathetic and competent leadership; (3) to have materials and procedures that fit; (4) to have proper places of meeting for those who will be served better in this way. To help meet those problems, experimental situations are becoming available for observation and books are appearing. This is a particular ministry for which interdenominational work can be specially serviceable. Churches need to remember that the families of these people also have special needs.

The Physically Handicapped

This heading includes a wide variety of persons: the blind or partially seeing; the crippled in braces or wheelchair; the deaf or hard of hearing; the neurologically impaired such as the palsied; the defective in speech. All these have needs—personal, emotional, educational, vocational, and spiritual. Some handicapped persons must be homebound; examples are spastic children or older persons who are also infirm. The church school program must be taken to them. Others have handicaps so severe that they need to be in institutions or special schools; the church school should follow them. Some can be kept in the church school; this is best.

It is hard to recognize the limitations that some of these handicaps place upon individuals. Normal people are inclined to forget the disability and expect the disabled to be like everybody else. Each must be treated as a unique individual. The emphasis should always be on what the person can do and not on what he cannot do. We can remember that the blind are alive to music and the deaf are alive to art while both are alive to fellowship. Our programs can be pitched in these areas. Many handicapped can make extraordinary contributions to the persons who are well. Fellowship can be mutually helpful.

The Physically and Mentally Ill

From its beginning the church has been concerned about the physically ill. Almost every congregation has its members who are ready to do calling, send flowers, cards, letters, and gifts or otherwise let the fellowship with the sick be expressed. If persons are homebound or hospitalized for any length of time the church school may go to them with its program; it should try to reach the unchurched ones also.

Not so much has been done about the emotionally disturbed and mentally disordered. Many are in serious condition; a vast group is wandering in the no man's land between happiness and frustration, success and failure; many are so anxious as to see little meaning or purpose in life.

We have learned, above all, that these unfortunates should not be isolated from the community unless necessary. They need the acceptance that is a basic ministry of the church. Particular attention should be given to their rehabilitation within church school group life. The church itself should be a mental hygiene station; well directed community participation, church membership, and church school involvement can be beneficial.

The Poor and the Affluent

We live in a society that, however much we lament it, has many classes. There are certain advantages in this condition when understanding reaches across the barriers; yet class structure creates problems which the church school can be expected to surmount.

A common classification is on the basis of economic status. The church has always been concerned about the dispossessed; it has accepted a responsibility to feed the hungry and clothe the naked. An enormous volume of social welfare has grown largely out of the church's concerns. Yet Christian education has not always accompanied the welfare programs.

Much of the church's attention rightly goes to the relief of economic need. Yet with a low social status, deprived of educational and vocational opportunities, the poverty-stricken have psychological, emotional, and spiritual needs that cry for church school attention. Luxury, too, may be a cross. People on the gold coasts have problems; we are inclined wrongly to think of them as self-sufficient. Church school objectives need also to deal with the general affluence of our society. As its best approach the church school's members can be spontaneous neighbors who care for both poor and affluent, and invite them into the mainstream of church and church school life.

The Racially and Ethnically Different

Church bodies have long been examining conditions and developing approaches to specific problems in the field of race. Recent history indicates how far from solution the problems are. Church schools can be significant factors in building a genuine, basic fellowship of understanding.

There are other minority groups. The church has given particular attention to migrant laborers, often Spanish-speaking people. Worship services have been provided; vacation church schools and church school classes on Sunday can be organized. A child care center is a possibility, or a make-up school for children who are educationally delayed. There has been mention of traveling libraries, story hours, teen-age clubs, downtown welcome and rest centers. The ultimate effort is to integrate all minority groups into the life and work of established churches.

The Socially Handicapped, Crippled, and Underprivileged

A typical school has done almost nothing for a broad spectrum of persons who grievously need more direct contacts with Christian persons, including normal group relationship in the church school. It has even tended to shun them.

The Alcoholic. It is estimated that uncontrolled drinking affects one out of ten people. Their individual plight is tragic; so is the effect they have upon their families. Alcoholics Anonymous offers help; advances are being made in medicine and counseling. These people need acceptance, more understanding of the nature of their difficulty, something done to lead them to a new sense of dignity and respect. A church school program should include some type of fellowship for the victims; preventively there can be serious study, on the part of youth in particular, lest they be drawn into the group.

The Delinquent; the Imprisoned and Released. Several hundreds of thousands of people appear before the courts each year, a large percentage very young. Some are on probation. There are also vast numbers in correctional institutions; these will need help when they return to society and begin the difficult job of rehabilitation. What have the churches done? What can they do—for the potentially as well as the actually in trouble? Wherever possible, a big brother or sister who cares, provides literature, helps with some of the terrible, practical issues will render an important service.

The Problemed Family. Thousands of divorces are granted yearly, each with its own story of defeat, humiliation, loss, and despair. This says nothing of the innumerable homes broken by desertion or separation and the thousands of couples continuing to live together though no real appreciation or understanding exists. The home which should provide life's greatest satisfactions is for them and their children an area of contention and strife. Both preventive study and remedial procedures are needed. Church schools should view some of these situations as the result of their program failure and plan anew their Christian home curriculum.

Vocational Groups

The typical church school will include a variety of persons, vocationally speaking, although some communities may be highly specialized. In each case the church school program must take the facts into account. On the one hand we can let the people share their advantages; on the other hand we can approach them in varied ways so as to fit a particular outlook while broadening it. Especially, we must help all to be at home within the circle of our ministry.

Much has been done already for academic communities. Students on campuses have been given chapels and campus ministers; special workers and work in local churches have been provided. Here are people who will increasingly dominate the world's development. Our high purpose is that they develop religiously, as well as in other ways, for future leadership. To this end, students and their faculties must be enabled to participate in a vital, relevant, and intellectually respectable Christian educational movement.

The military has gone far to provide a ministry for our armed forces through chaplaincies to serve on the field and on the bases, not only for the men but also for their families. Permanent bases may have what are rather typical church schools. There is a unified Protestant Sunday School Curriculum for Armed Forces. A strong leadership program is administered by the military itself. It is important for the home church and church school to keep in touch with these presently absent members.

We are progressively seeking to go to people where they work—in atomic energy centers, the financial district of Wall Street, the garment district of New York. Chaplains are provided for some of the great industrial complexes. They or volunteer workers can minister during noon hours, for example.

In relation to all such vocational and similar groups it is extremely important to listen to what the people are saying. We may be trying to answer questions they are not asking.

Varieties of Religious Experience

There has been long, in the history of the church, a tendency to enforce conformity to a type of religious experience. It should be understood, however, that "no two are alike" and we should be glad for a degree of variety. We are accustomed to speaking about the conservative and the liberal; should there be a little more elbow room for each? Certainly it is not necessary to found a new church for each new idea; in fact, most ideas are not new, they are just deviations. We should expect, therefore, to have the progressive and the opposite, even in some cases the radical or eccentric, in biblical outlook, doctrinal or ethical belief. Our procedure can aim to let each make his contribution and let each learn what he can.

Almost surely these issues concerning unusual forms of educational ministry will become increasingly significant in our era of drastic change, multiplication of knowledge, religious ecumenicity, and universal human relationships. It is our calling to make room for all to come as disciples and allow all to share as apostles while we lead them toward Christian maturity in every possible way.

INDEX

INDEX

Absentees, 135

Activity: definition, x, 24; *see also* Curricular activities

Administration: correct general principles, 65; definition, 63, 64; of pupils, 130; of staff, 93

Adult work, 327, 329

Aging and the aged, the, 343

Altar, 196

American Sunday School Union, 10, 281

Arts: as resources, 339; devotional, in worship, 190

Attendance, securing regular, 134

Audile and visual equipment and materials, 210, 234

Audiovisual coordinators, 101

Awards, 137, 289

Bible: functional approach, 152; in curriculum, 152; in early schools, 8, 11; in general education, 311; potentialities in usage, 153; *see also* Scripture, Objectives

Budgeting: allocations, 254; procedure, 253; *see also* Financing, Funds

Buildings: standards, 237; types, 236; use, 239; *see also* Physical facilities

Camping, 334, 335

Catechetical schools, 6

Catechism, 7, 8, 11, 331

Catechumenate, 6

Choirs, 100, 341

Christian education: before the Reformation, 5; before the Sunday church school, 4; definitions, 38; in early America, 7; mass agencies for, 337; modern movement in, 13; *see also* Developmental, History, Sunday church school, Education

Christian specifics: emphasizing, 19

Chronology, 12

Church: as school, 15; defined, 15; every, an individual, 221

Church council, 78

Church professional schools, 316; *see also* Higher Christian education

Church school: current characteristics, 17, 20; definition, 17; inner city, 226; integrated, 84; keeping the school a, 65; large, 221; one-room, 141, 243; present status, 14; promise of, 22; released time, 322; rural, 222; small, 221; suburban, 224; *see also* Unified

Church school committee, 79
Classes, organized, 143
Committees, 104
Communication, 114
Community agencies, relationships with, 284
Conferences, 336
Confirmation, communicants', membership or pastor's classes: adult program, 332; current situation, 330; definition, 330; developmental approach, 331
Congregation, relationships with, 274
Constitutional amendments, 308
Content: procedure with, 30; purpose with, 30; results of, 30; using as resource, 29
Contests, 137, 139, 294
Contracts and covenants, 53, 112
Cooperative Curriculum Project 50
Creative emphasis, 19
Creative experience, 31
Culturally different, the, 344
Curricular activities, 155
Curricular series: Lutheran Church in America, 149; Seabury, 148; United Church of Canada, 149; see Lessons
Curriculum: as life's activities under guidance, 151; basic theory, 150; Bible in, 152; definition, 146; examples, 148; from old to new, 220; in terms of life's experiences, 150; physical facilities for, 234; recent developments, 147; the new, 147; theology in, 154; see also Fellowship, Instruction, Program, Service, Study, Worship

Data: acting on, 272; interpreting, 271; reporting, 271; securing, 260; utilizing, 270; see also Measuring, Records, Researching, Surveying
Decision-making, 114
Denominational agencies, relationships with, 280
Determination: by pupil, 55, 143; by worker, 113
Developmental education: as creative experience in living, 28; Christian education as, 42; definition, 19, 24, 28, 33; limitations, 35
Directing: fellowship, 198; service, 203; study and instruction, 181; units, 214; worship, 186
Director of Christian education: duties, 82; relationships, 83
Discipline, 139, 141
Distraction, freedom from, in worship, 196
Drama, as resource, 340
Drop-outs, 136
Dual enrollment, 314

Ecumenicity, education for, 286
Education: activity definition, 25; theories and philosophies of, 23; senses of definition, 26; traditional, 24, 27; typical definitions, 25; see also Developmental
Educational organization, integration of, 77, 86
Educational work: nature and place, 15
Enrollment: securing increased, 292
Equipment: securing new, 243; see also Physical facilities

Evaluation: definition, 258; methodology, 259
Evangelization, 41, 277

Family: nights, 307; pew, 91, 302;
  week, 308; see also Home
Fellowship: directing, 198; educational aim, 200; guiding events,
  202; meaning, 199; need, 200;
  program, 200
Films and recordings, 210, 234;
  see also Audile and visual
Financing: motivation, 249; principles, 246; purposes, 247; systems, 249; see also Budgeting,
  Funds, Stewardship, Treasury
First and Second Series leadership
  courses, 121
Funds: control, 247; expending,
  255; securing, 255; see also Budgeting, Financing
Furnishings and supplies: standards, 241; types of furnishings,
  239; types of supplies, 241; use,
  242; see also Physical facilities
Future: of buildings, 232, 236; of
  camp, 336; of church school, 22;
  of parochial school, 314; of
  structure, 63

Gifted, the, 344
Giving, education for, 248, 257
Group: and maintenance, 176;
  and task, 175; and welfare, 176;
  what is a, 174; see also Groups
Group dynamics, defined, 59, 177
Grouping pupils: bases, 131; practice, 130; purposes, 130; sizes of
  groups, 132; see also Organization
Group life institutes, 121

Group process: teachers in, 179;
  see also Group and Groups
Groups: and leaders, 58; focus on
  persons in, 18; forces and roles,
  61, 177; how act, 177; how learn
  effectively, 178; sessions, 208;
  see also Group, Grouping
  pupils
Growth, 146, 153, 186, 188, 192,
  194, 200, 203
Guidance, teaching in terms of,
  171

Higher Christian education: as
  agencies, 315; for leadership
  development, 120
History, 3; see also Chronology
Holy Spirit: in education, 41;
  serving under, 20; see also Sanctification.
Home, Christian education at: a
  denominational program, 307;
  need, 305; toward Christian
  family living, 306; within the
  family circle, 305; see also
  Family
Home, relationships with, 277
Home study and correspondence
  courses, 120
Hymns: in worship, 192; standards for, 192; studying, 193

Instruction: large group, 209;
  place, 183
Interdenominational and interfaith agencies, relationships
  with, 280
International Uniform Lesson
  Series, 11, 160

Jesus Christ: as Savior and Lord,
  40; as teacher, 5; ultimacy of, 40

Jewish Education, 4
Job analyses, 93
Junior church, 91

Kindergarten, 314

Laboratory schools, 120
Leader: being a, 58; definition, x; and group, 58; what does, 60; what is, 58
Leader relations, control within, 113
Leadership: correct general principles, 65; development, 123; general activities, 61; types, 61; variables in practice, 61, 177
Leadership development: group agencies, 119; in general curriculum, 119; local church agencies, 122; means, 118; motivation, 128; needs, 118; standard, a, 129
Learning: laws of, 169; theory of, 168
Learning activity: description, 166; phases in program, 146; steps in, 168; time elements, 167
Legal provisions, 308
Lessons: elective, 162; graded, 161; International Uniform, 11, 160
Librarians, 100
Library, 100, 159
Literature, as resource, 340
Liturgy, 190
Location, adaptation to, 222
Luther, Martin, 7
Lutheran Church in America, Parish Education Curriculum, 149, 307

Management: correct general

principles for, 65; essential virtues in, 67
Manual of procedure, 64, 93, 111, 115
Materials: criteria for selecting, 162; handling, 164; in program, 159; installing new, 163; selecting, 159
Measuring: as learning and teaching technique, 269; the pupil, 267; the school and program, 265; values, 263
Meetings, 213, 208
Membership committee, 88, 293
Methods (see ways of teaching)
Ministries, unusual, 343
Missionary education, 209, 285
Morale, building, 288
Motion pictures, as resource, 341
Motivation: Christian, for promoting, 289; for financing, 249; for leadership development, 128
Music: as resource, 341; in worship, 191
Music leaders, 100; see also Choirs

National Council of Churches of Christ in the USA, 283
New curriculum: examples, 148; trends, 147

Objectives: activity statement, 51; age group, 51; criteria for, 55; defined, 43; denominational, 50; determining, 46; for agencies, 53; for units and sessions, 54; functions, 44; in local church school, 52; in public education, 48; interdenominational, 49; need for, 43; organizational, 46; personal, 46; statements of, 48; teaching in terms of, 170; types, 45

Offering, in worship, 193
Organization: correct general principles, 65; defined, 63, 64; integrating, 77; pupils, 84; purposes, 66; school, 84; staff, 85; standards for, 75; unifying, 86

Parent-teacher association, 278
Parochial schools: early, 8; evaluation, 313; prognosis, 314; status, 312
Pastor: in education, 79; relationship with director, 81
Personnel, overhead, 78
Personnel committee, 107
Physical facilities: basic needs, 234; current trends, 233; for curriculum, 234; future, 232; major considerations, 231; purpose, 230; rendering more effective, 242; see also Buildings, Equipment, Furnishings and supplies
Physically and mentally ill, the, 346
Physically handicapped, the, 346
Pictures: as resource, 341
Poor and the affluent, the, 346
Prayer, 193
Press, the, as resource, 342
Program: building a total, 157; for particular schools, 158; providing a, 146; see also Curriculum, Materials
Promotion of pupils: need, 132; special cases, 134; standards for, 133
Public relations, 287-290
Public schools, church and: legal provisions, 308; religion in general curriculum, 310

Public schools, relationships with, 278
Punctuality, 138
Pupils: administering, 130; determination, 55, 143; guiding activities, 166, 186; in integrated school, 84; in unified school, 87; knowing, 144; organization of, 85; see grouping

Racially and ethnically different, the, 347
Radio, 241, 338
Raikes, Robert, 2, 8
Recordings (see Films)
Records and record-keeping, 262
Reformation, the: and education, 6; Christian education before, 5
Relationships: with congregation, 274; with denominational agencies, 280; with home, 277; with interdenominational and interfaith agencies, 280; with other community agencies, 284; with public school, 278
Religion, freedom of, 309
Religions: definition, 37; in general curriculum, 310
Religious education: definition, 37; pre- and non-Christian, 3; within general education, 308
Religious Education Association, 281
Researching, 260
Retarded, the, 344
Retreats, 336
Role playing, 293
Roman Catholic education, 7, 312

Sanctification, Christian education as, 41

Scientific method and normal procedure, 20

Scripture in worship, 194; *see* Bible

Seabury series, 148

Secretaries, 98

Service: criteria for enterprises, 206; in church and church school, 204; directing, 203; education in, 204; meaning and place, 203; program of, 205; standards for enterprises, 207

Services, special day, 210, 211, 212

Size of school: adaptation to, 221

Social ministry: engaging in, 205

Socially handicapped, the, 347

Staff: in integrated school, 85; in unified school, 87; job analyses, 93; organization, 85; providing members, 107; qualifications of, 104; selecting members, 104; *see also* Workers

Staff and line functioning, 114

Standards: building, 237; fellowship events, 201; furnishings and supplies, 241; hymns, 192; leadership development, 129; measuring school, 265; organization, 75; personal, 73; promotion, 133; service enterprises, 207

Stewardship, 210, 249

Study, 181

Summer assembly, camp, school, 119

Sunday afternoon and evening sessions, 303

Sunday church school: allies, 11; American developments, 10; beginnings, 8; evaluation, 21; expanded and extended sessions, 301; in present program, 21

Superintendents: activity, 96; age groups, 95; agency, 97; associate, 97; general, 93

Supervised study, 183

Supervision: correct general principles, 65; definition, 63; technique, 126

Supervisors, 103, 126

Supplies (*see* Furnishings and supplies)

Supreme Court, 309, 322

Surveying, 261

Teacher: instructing, 184; job analysis, 103

Teaching: descriptions of, 170; incidental, 213; and principles, 171; programmed, 172; *see also* Ways of teaching

Teaching-preaching service, 90

Television, 241, 338

Terminology, 23

Tests and testing, 267

Theology: lay, 316, 329; and objectives, 46; place in curriculum, 154

Time schedules, 164

Transition and concern, international, 14

Treasurers: and education, 99; job analysis, 256

Treasury: independent, 252; unitary congregational, 250

Unified church school: nature, 87; organization, 85; program, 89; relationship to common services, 90

United Church of Canada: curriculum, 149

Units: defined, 156; example, 219; meaning, 214; stages in mangement, 216; supervising, 216
Ushers, 102

Vacation church schools: defined, 318; organization and administration, 320; origin, 12; possibilities, 319; program, 320; *see also* History
Vocational groups, 348

Ways of teaching: in group process, 180; listing, 172; team, 173
Weekday church school work: evaluation, 323; history and status, 322; organization and administration, 323; origin, 12; time, 321; types, 321; *see also* Church schools
Weekday dimension of Sunday work, 304
Workers: appointing, 110; enlisting, 109; inducting, 111; reassigning and dismissing, 113; retaining, 112; sources of, 108; *see also* Staff
Workers' conference, 124

Works of the church: education in, 16, 203; listed, 16; relationships with other, 276; the six, 16
Workshops, 120
World churchmanship, education for, 285
World Council of Christian Education, 282
World Council of Churches, 283
World Institutes, 14, 282
Worship: definition, 187; directing, 186; preparation for, 210; time for, 189; total program, 188; *see also* Family, Junior church, Worship services
Worship center, 241; *see also* Altar
Worship services: approach, 197; common, relation of church school to, 90; conducting, 195; elements, 190; formal, 302; leadership, 197; order of elements, 195; physical setting, 195; preparation for, 219; planning, 189; selecting elements, 194; *see also* Worship

Youth fellowships, 325
Youth work, 324

Type, 10 on 11 and 9 on 9 Granjon
Display, Lydian and Vogue

LEADING
A CHURCH SCHOOL

by RALPH D. HEIM

Leaders and those preparing to be leaders in church schools will find in this book the resources, information and guidelines to equip them for their task. Without becoming unnecessarily technical the author develops theories underlying the educational task in their relation to practical issues and problems. Principles governing the organization of the church school are set forth together with their application in the area of administration and supervision. Teachers are given guidance enabling them to see their role in relation to their total task as well as to the pupils who are to learn and grow in living the Christian faith.

Using his experience as an educator who has a detailed acquaintance with Christian education in churches not only in North America but also in European and Asian countries, the author develops his thought in the context of present churchwide and worldwide perspectives. .